THE
GOLFER'S
SOURCEBOOK

by Cliff Schrock

A ROXBURY PARK BOOK

LOWELL HOUSE

LOS ANGELES

CONTEMPORARY BOOKS

CHICAGO

Publisher: Jack Artenstein
Editor in Chief, Roxbury Park Books: Michael Artenstein
Director of Publishing Services: Rena Copperman
Managing Editor: Lindsey Hay
Designer: S. Pomeroy
Illustrations: Elmer Wexler
Index: Michelle Graye

Schrock, Cliff, 1959
        The golfer's sourcebook / by Cliff Schrock.
            p.   cm.
        "A Roxbury Park book."
        Includes bibliographical references (p.) and index.
        ISBN 1-56565-908-2
        1. Golf.   I. Title.
GV965.S3155 1998
796.352--dc21   98-14774
                                                      CIP

Manufactured in the United States of America
10 9 8 7 6 5 4 3 2 1

CONTENTS

ACKNOWLEDGEMENTS

Completing the text for this book was basically a one-person operation, but there is still plenty of thanks to go around to some worthy individuals. I'd like to recognize the following people: Nancy Crossman, who did a fine job as my agent, liaison, and cohort throughout this entire process. My Lowell House connections: Editor Michael Artenstein—we worked well together although we were three thousand miles apart; and managing editor and all-around organizer of every little detail, Lindsey Hay. Don Wade, who made the initial suggestion to Nancy that I would be a worthy author of this book. Elmer "Red" Wexler, one of the best golf artists ever and a fine illustrator, period. Byrute Johnson, Sue Sawyer, and Margaret Farnsworth, who made small contributions in research and production that collectively were a big help. Mom and Dad Schrock—Shirley and Donald—for all of their support. And to my wife, Mary, and daughter, Joelle, who were dragged through this whole affair with me, not by choice, but who hung in there spiritually with me and supported me through many late days and long weekends. Thanks for your love.
—C.S.

PREFACE

Golf has the remarkable ability to fit into society no matter the era or the social changes that are occurring. The game has been a well-received recreational pursuit throughout its history. It had a mysterious inception, and its hold on the heart and mind of the player can be equally mystical. This has been true despite sweeping changes during the last half of this century in income levels, time constraints, and providing every golfer equal playing privileges.

Golf is a timeless game in more than one sense of the term. Even in today's hectic world, golf reminds us of its rich history in which players have always treasured the time they invested in a round. A day at the golf course was an event and still is. Although the magical four-hour round is ballyhooed as the ultimate playing time, there's something to like about a game that doesn't have a time limit. Within reason, players dictate their time allotment on the course and in pre- and post-round social events in the clubhouse.

Golfers have always been highly protective of their golf time and with good reason. They usually have invested a lot in equipment, lessons, and other costs to play. With all they've put into becoming a player, golfers have felt it's within their right to devote large amounts of time not only to play golf, but to read about, watch, and talk about it.

The golf bug affects people in different ways. For some it can be a quick sting that instantly lures them like a potion. But in keeping with the thought that golf is a game of a lifetime, for some it takes a lot longer to fall in love with its charms. Golf waits us out until we have the wherewithal and frame of mind to give it a try. Golf, if you don't mind it being spoken of as a person, knows that once we give it a chance, we become devoted and advance its traditions decade after decade to other generations.

Yes, it makes perfectly good sense to think of golf as a romancer who wants to win our hearts and embrace us, never letting go through good and bad times.

Am I exaggerating? Not really, as any golfer will tell you. Golf has a strong effect on people who take an interest in it and show patience in letting it get under their skin. The reward is many rounds of pleasure and moments that leave an indelible mark.

I can speak as one subtly smitten and eventually taken in for good. I was a relatively easy catch, as I imagine most of you were. The majority of golfers, if they were to examine their relationship with golf, would admit they didn't take long to fall under golf's spell.

I feel blessed that golf wooed me at the young age of 12. My first physical contact with the game was watching my oldest brother, Jeff, chip balls in our backyard, using what appeared to be miniature tennis balls that were the size of golf balls.

Shortly after that backyard experience came my first invitation to play on a golf course. A neighborhood friend had me join him and two others to play at the Illinois State University course in Normal, Illinois, the town adjacent to my hometown of Bloomington. Knowing now what I do about the learning process golf newcomers should go through, there was no way I should have gone on that first round before becoming consistent in advancing the ball. But I played that first round without knowing much of anything and it showed. I think I must have hit into every pine tree on the course on my way to shooting a 150.

Probably I shouldn't have played that round until I'd practiced and learned the fundamentals. It's a surprise that, after shooting so poorly, I ever came back, but thankfully things worked out well. I gradually improved by playing more and I began reading about golf as much as I could. I started following the PGA Tour and picked out everyone's hero, Arnold Palmer, to be mine, too, although in the early 1970s he was on the back nine of his tour career.

As any golfer can tell you, when you're hooked by golf, you end up doing strange things that you wouldn't do otherwise. You'll stand up at the oddest times at work or home and practice your swing, or pretend to be gripping a club while watching

TV. Growing up, I cut a circular area of our backyard grass as short as I could and put a cup in the ground to serve as a miniature green. Then I plotted out three "holes" I played around our house using plastic balls.

During one of my early years as a golfer in the 1970s, I decided to send Arnie a birthday letter, in which I told him how much fun I was having as a golfer and bragged a little on my improvement. One of my greatest treasures is a letter he sent back, thanking me for the birthday wishes and complimenting me on my play. If I needed any more convincing about becoming a golfer, Arnold Palmer's gesture took care of it!

I've had my share of sad moments. I can recall during my high school years playing a round by myself one day at the course I grew up on, Highland Park. It had been a lousy round and I was really in the dumps by the 13th tee. On that par 5, I hit a tee shot so far to the right that it was two holes over. At the same moment, I saw a friend from school hitting a nice shot off the hole he was playing. I just stood there in anguish, tears flowing down my face, flustered at my feeble effort.

Golf will do that to you, but if it affects you the way it did me that day, it just shows how much you care about it. As each year went by, I set out to do things that kept adding to the depth of my golfing fun, and they're the kinds of things you should strive to accomplish, too: I started a golf library; played 54 holes in one day; began reading golf periodicals; tinkered with club repair; collected golf items; went on golf vacations; attended tour events, and got around to different golf courses to see a variety of design styles. I've kept track of the number I've played or seen ever since.

I made it a goal to get to as many major championships as I could, and through my position at *Golf Digest*, I got to make a golfer's ultimate trip, seeing a British Open at the Old Course at St. Andrews. And the day after John Daly won in 1995, I got to play that hallowed links.

All golfers learn to celebrate important milestones. I don't recall where I got my first birdie, but once I made it I started keeping track of all of them. I'm up to 425 and counting in 25 years of playing. And on my office wall at *Golf Digest* is a certificate, from *Golf Digest*, congratulating me on making a double eagle, which is a 2 on a par 5. I've never made a hole-in-one, but most people will tell you a double eagle is harder to achieve.

Golfers are always searching for improvement, as I try to do. To work toward that, starting in 1984 I kept track of my rounds statistically, which is something I suggest every player do to learn their weak areas.

Why tell you about all of my peculiarities? The answer is simple: To illustrate the extent to which someone will go to show his love for golf. And I, by no means, have been as fanatical as others I know. It's up to each golfer to give what she wants to the game in time and energy. For you newcomers, a word of caution: Be sure to give golf plenty of time. You must show staying power and determination; golf cannot be learned in a day, a week, or a month. It takes all the patience you can muster.

A good way to look at golf is to say, What do I expect golf to be in my life? If it's to be physically demanding, then focus your mind and condition your body to be as good as possible. If it's for social activity, then it only requires bare-bones input. If it's to have a game to play in retirement, then get fit enough to play it regularly and play it with the mind-set that it's just a sport to keep your mind and body active. Golf can be whatever you want it to be. Make the choice and put a plan together to have golf fit into your lifestyle and within your expectations. Always keep in mind that there can be great pleasure in simply experiencing the game.

My hope is that this book helps beginning golfers know the game a lot better than I did before playing that first round of golf, so you can enjoy the moment better and be able to improve at a faster rate than I did. And for you veteran players, there's plenty of information here that will supplement your knowledge and improve your golfing experience.

Within this book are the tools any golfer can use to increase their love of golf, from beginning as a new player to those players constantly searching to take a few strokes off their handicap.

Here's to your future golfing success.

Cliff Schrock
Stratford, Connecticut
December 7, 1997

 Chapter 1

THE LURE OF GOLF—
A HISTORY LESSON

Considering how, where, and when golf began compared with where the sport stands now, a strong case could be made that golf has had the most phenomenal growth and development of any other sport. Golf had no formal start-up, no inventor who could pinpoint the precise moment inspiration for the sport struck him. Golf fell into place and evolved into the pastime enjoyed by millions of players around the world because of good fortune and luck.

To truly appreciate the great advancements made in golf, today's players would need to be eyewitnesses to the first form of golf played, by most accounts, more than 500 years ago. From shepherds and farmers playing on their unkempt pastures, we now have multimillionaire professionals jetting around the globe in their own planes competing for an unlimited supply of prize money.

But whether it's the elite of the game playing for big money or a farmer paying an $8 fee to play a nine-hole public course next to his farm, golfers smitten by the bug play for one main reason: the challenge of the game combined with a beautiful outdoor setting and a social atmosphere. That scenario can't be matched by any other sport.

There are essentially three "lures of golf." Together they make an unbeatable combination.

First is the beauty of seeing a well-played shot. Although the nongolfer may not notice it, the sight of a ball in flight heading toward a target—the putting green—and landing within a few feet of the hole stirs the heart. And there is beauty in watching the well-timed, effortless, yet forceful swing that produced it. A coordinated swing is golf's equivalent to the gracefulness of a baseball outfielder, quickness of a basketball guard, or agility of a football running back. The constant search for the perfect swing can be the primary source of golfing pleasure.

The second lure is the playing field. The dimensions of other fields of play in basketball, football, and baseball remain relatively the same in whatever stadiums the games are played, but golf courses have been and continue to be ever-evolving and changing. Like fingerprints, there are no two courses exactly alike. Even courses in the same vicinity can have different looks. This architectural variety keeps a golfer's interest in the game alive wherever he plays. And, of course, the beauty of the good earth and the chance to be outdoors in a peaceful setting don't have an equal in the sports world.

Champion golfer Nick Faldo demonstrates the beauty of a well-played shot.

The third lure of golf has to do with our human nature and the desire for social interaction. Golf is the one sport in which its participants intermingle while playing. Golfers can discuss life's events, business affairs, news of the day, even commiserate over each other's poor play. This is impossible to do racing up and down the basketball court. In golf, there is the overwhelming sense of oneness with nature, playing companions, and one's own self.

Those three lures have always been present since golf began. But there's still more "evidence" of golf's allure.

It is the one game of significance that the player can compete in alone, all by himself, relying on no one else. Doing so puts the golfer in the basic scenario: herself, the course, and whatever weather conditions are prevalent that day. To play alone can certainly put the golfer in the ultimate "man versus nature" setting, where he has a oneness with his surroundings.

Golf also provides an opportunity to erase the day's anxieties. Golfers have used the course for years as an escape from the tensions that affect them in their jobs and other activities. Golf affords them a chance to reflect on life's events with renewed vigor.

And golf is, after all, the game of a lifetime. It can be played from childhood to old age without the worry of looking foolish regarding quality of play. Other sports may be more vigorous, but golf is a walking game that doesn't require great strength to play well.

All these factors have been a part of golf's popularity for decades. Every player discovers them and treasures them as a regular part of their golfing lives.

> "A workman is no better than his tools, and it is a poor golfer who blames his, providing he has good equipment. Of course, if his clubs are outmoded, he then has fair grounds to blame his tools."
>
> SAM SNEAD

HOW THINGS GOT STARTED

If no one can take credit for creating this great sport, what was the spark of inspiration that got it going?

The answer is as misty as the famous Scottish weather. There may not be unequivocal evidence of a solitary inventor, but there are details that indicate golf is a mix of many different creators, and that Scotland was the primary place where today's game first took its form.

But let's look at some of the other options theorists have put forth. When historians look for details about the game's origins, they look for an activity that had a target of a hole in the ground, was played with a mix of different clubs, and had the player competing alone without teammate support.

A study from the early 1990s came out in support of a Far Eastern game called *chiuwan* that European traders brought to their homeland in the Middle Ages. This game was played before the year A.D. 1000. A Chinese professor said that he found the game recorded in A.D. 943, and explained "chiu" means hitting and "wan" means ball. The research showed the game was played until the fifteenth century, but by starting in the first millenium it was 400 years ahead of the first Scottish references.

The Dutch played two games that had the ring of golf—*kolf* and *colf*, words that mean club. *Kolf* details indicate it was more like hockey than golf. Players used a thick-shafted club that resembled a hockey stick to hit a heavy rubber-type ball toward targets within the confines of an enclosed courtyard.

Colf was played in the 1200s, according to the earliest records, with similarities to golf insofar as it was played on a big field. It was a popular game that by the end of the fourteenth century had made its mark among the Dutch, who named large areas of land "municipal courses," a common golf phrase today. The first recorded *colf* match was played in 1297, many decades before the first written reference to golf in Scotland.

The *colf*-golf tie-in makes wonderful sense, but there are other theories as well about when golf or a form of it was first played.

Roman soldiers played *paganica*, a game with a leather ball filled with feathers and a curbed club. A similar game called *cambuca* was played in Britain during the time of King Edward III in the 1300s. Illustrations of *cambuca* players do indeed show a game resembling golf, but the club has a hockey stick appearance.

The French had a game called *jeu de mail* (pall mall) that had similarities to golf since it was played in an open field with a target about a half mile from the starting point. Another game in France and Belgium, *chole*, was also played on an open field with a target, but it involved teams advancing a ball toward a selected target as each team tried to prevent the other from getting there, which, again, sounds a lot like today's hockey.

And there's always the chance that a form of golf was being played in another region of the world while these other games were going on. After all, how simple of a thought is it to think that someone could have strolled along a field with a stick in hand and took a swing at a rock to see if he could strike a target with it. That's the primitive form of golf, but chances are someone would have uncovered evidence of other games by now.

All these games have one thing in common: similarities to golf. And because nations traded goods with each other, it makes sense that discussions about games and pastimes would develop. Countries learned about each other's games and shared the pleasure of each other's company. All these games, in some way, may have contributed to the development of what was played in Scotland, for it is there that the game of golf we know today, historians acknowledge, was played, thrived, and developed. Scotland can rightfully claim that it is the ancestral home to golf, but perhaps not the origin of it.

The Scottish terrain was ideally suited for golf. The first courses were the gentle rolling fields along the seashore. One can envision Scottish shepherds walking in their fields, staffs in

The Old Course at St. Andrews: the classic example of how Scottish terrain is the perfect setting for golf.

hand, hitting a stone with it and seeing the stone tumble into a rabbit hole. That is the romantic, quaint notion of how things started, but no one will ever know. It was, however, within that setting that golf in Scotland began.

Scotland Initiates a Global Game

Golf was definitely played in Scotland in the 1400s. The game was called golf due to the *kolf* and *colf* terms because there was no word in the Scottish dialect of that type until it was referred to in written records in reference to the game. Golf must have been popular since the first written reference to golf in Scotland was an admonishment.

It appears golf was interfering with Scottish archery practice, so in an act of the Scottish Parliament in 1457, James II banned golf, saying, in Old World language, "that fute-ball and golfe be utterly cryed downe, and not used." If the king felt the need to make an official proclamation, it's an indication that golf must have been established and proliferating among the citizens. Golf's first growth spurt was under way.

It is not known at what point golf's present-day format developed. It must have occurred over the course of many decades as nuances were discovered. The course setup (discussed in Chapter 2) took a few hundred years to evolve.

The direction golf went after the decree of 1457 is less a mystery than its first few years in Scotland. There were other decrees in 1471 and 1491 that ruled against playing golf, including a fine for those who broke the rule. Despite the laws, there were many rule breakers who could not abandon their favorite game. About 1500, when Scotland and England signed a peace treaty, Scottish king James IV himself took up the game and the anti-golf laws were eased. Records show the king asked his treasurer for nine shillings to purchase balls and clubs. Golfing royalty had begun, and today it continues unabated with such players as U.S. President Bill Clinton.

The House of Stuart was golf's first royal family of note. Records show James V was a golfer, as was his daughter, Mary Queen of Scots. She made the unfortunate mistake of playing golf a few days after the suspected murder of her husband, Lord Darnley. The seemingly uncaring widow was brought to trial in part due to her ungrieving ways. It was definitely a bogey of major proportions.

Her son, James VI, was probably the game's first big promoter. He had his own clubmaker, William Mayne, and when James took the English throne and was recrowned as James I in 1603, he was so dismayed at the amount of balls imported from Holland that he placed a large tariff on them and began to build up the domestic market. James' arrival in England was also that country's introduction to golf. James encouraged his sons, Charles and Henry, to play golf. After Charles became king in 1625, he was on the golf course when news reached him of the Irish rebellion.

When the Stuarts faded from power, it only meant the lessening of royal prominence within the game. There remained the general populace to continue golf's growth, although their devotion to the game was the cause of some consternation by the authorities. Laws were issued against playing golf on the Sabbath or a fine had to be paid. (Sounds remarkably similar to the struggle churches have today with their golfing members!) In the end, a compromise was struck that allowed golfers to play on Sunday as long as they had attended a church service. An order that was released by Charles I in 1633 read, "This our blessed father's declaration to see that no man doe trouble or molest any of our loyall and dutifull people in or for their lawful recreations, having first done their duetie to God."

The game in the 1600s was still very much unorganized, and golfers weren't particularly concerned about rules or their form. But as golf entered the 1700s, it took on a shape recognizable to today's game. Clubs soon sprouted up, which

During the 1700s and 1800s, golf's dress code eschewed comfort for formal, cumbersome clothing.

were organizations of players as collective groups, most of which were attached to their own course. The Honourable Company of Edinburgh Golfers in 1744 and the Society of St. Andrews Golfers in 1754 were two of the most prominent then and now. (St. Andrews renamed its club The Royal and Ancient Golf Club of St. Andrews in 1834.) The Edinburgh group, in fact, agreed upon a Code of Rules—thirteen articles—that were the first set of rules ever organized (see Chapter 8).

As the eighteenth century came to an end, there were just ten golf clubs. That number steadily grew in the 1800s, including outside the confines of Scotland, with the Calcutta Club in India in 1829.

England had been briefly exposed to golf by James I in the early 1600s, but the game wasn't seriously played there until the 1850s on the north coast of Devon. In 1864 the Royal North Devon Club was formed, and its course, Westward Ho!, is the oldest seaside course in the world outside Scotland. France was the site of the first course on the European continent with the Pau Golf Club in 1856.

The caliber of play at the time was not outstanding, partially due to the courses being unkempt and the greens not well cared for. A score of 100 wasn't broken until 1767 when James Durham won the Silver Club at Muirfield with a 94. But over time, as knowledge about the swing, strategy, course conditions, and other factors increased, all phases of the game improved and the word spread about the enjoyment of golf.

The number of golf clubs in the United Kingdom grew from seven in 1800 to 34 in 1870, 387 in 1890, 2,330 in 1900, and 4,135 in 1910.

As the number of clubs and courses increased, the social side of golf became more significant. It was not unusual for players to retreat to the nearby tavern or pub for a drink—or four—to rehash their play. They were already dressed in what was required golfing clothes for the period, as stated by the Burgess Golfing Society code: "a dress coat, colour of dark claret, with black velvet collar, lined in the skirts with white silk or satin, primrose dress vest."

Often the affair included dinner and arrangements for the following week's matches. The banter was a continuation of what had gone on during actual play. All of this is similar to the interaction among today's players, who exchange barbs and insults on the course and then settle any wagers at the infamous 19th hole.

In 1860, the competitive fires of the Scottish clubs merged to establish an Open Championship, in which the winner would receive a leather belt. This start to the British Open preceded the game's global spread into other parts of Europe, America, and distant places such as China, Australia, and Japan in the late 1800s.

America Embraces Scotland's Game

Golf didn't just hop across the Atlantic to America during the period its popularity increased in Scotland and England in the late 1800s. Although it is commonly thought that golf came over at that time as if it were an imported piece of merchandise, golf was introduced in the United States much earlier.

A form of the game, in fact, resembling a hockey-like game called shinny and hurley, was played by approximately sixty Native American and Mexican groups when European settlers arrived in North America. Another game, *tokka*, was played by hitting a braided leather ball with a crooked stick. And there are some accounts that Scots demonstrated golf to the people of the American Southwest, using a hardened calfskin ball stuffed with fur. It was struck from a stationary position to holes marked by flagsticks.

The Dutch game of *colf* was played in present-day Albany, New York, in 1659. In an old court document there, three defendants were charged with playing the ice-hockey-type game on a day of prayer, but there's nothing to suggest they were found guilty.

The first mention of golf in the American colonies was seen in the house inventory of a deceased Scottish merchant, Andrew Johnston, in 1759. His estate, and others from 1798 to 1806, listed golf clubs and balls. Another golf reference was made in an April 21, 1779, advertisement in the Rivington Royal Gazette in New York. The paper often advertised sporting goods, and it's clear the reference here is to golf equipment: "To the golf players: The season for this pleasant and healthy exercise now advancing, gentlemen may be furnished with excellent clubs and the veritable Caledonian balls, by enquiring at the printer's."

The next reference to golf in America is from the Carolinas in the late 1700s. As had happened with Scottish merchants who spread the game around Europe, the same occurred during trips back and forth from Scotland to the United States, particularly the Charleston, South Carolina, and Savannah, Georgia, areas. The South Carolina Golf Club was founded on September 29, 1786, in Charleston, and another club began in Savannah in 1796.

In Charleston, golfers played on Harleston's Green located in town, but the "course" was set up in crude fashion. Players hit to a hole, but there was no flag-pole, teeing area, putting surface, or designated number of holes. Before play began, participants drew to be "finders." If picked, rather than participating in the game they had to find the hole and identify it in some way for the others.

Since clubs such as at St. Andrews and Edinburgh had been established in Scotland by this time, the Charleston and Savannah clubs used them as models for conducting their business. No actual club records remain, but newspaper and almanac notices mention numerous meetings and play dates for the clubs.

It is believed these two clubs faded out about 1811, since newspaper accounts end at that time. What was the reason? Probably a variety of factors. First, the game didn't hold the interest of the general populace and didn't become a major part of society. Second, there wasn't a strong enough communication network to spread the word. And third, it would appear the intent of these clubs was more social than athletic because no scores were kept in competition. Getting together for meetings and parties seemed to be the focus, while playing was secondary. The golf bug had not fully bitten. Harleston's Green was eventually taken over by new housing, just the opposite of what usually happens today at golf community developments where courses and houses go up together.

After those clubs died off, golf was quietly absent in the United States, although influential figures—such as Charles Blair Macdonald in Chicago in 1875—probably hit balls in vacant fields. There is record of infrequent play in Iowa, Nebraska, and Florida, where short, four-hole courses were laid out.

Golf wasn't truly revived in North America for more than sixty years, this time in the northeastern section of the continent. First was the Royal Montreal Golf Club in 1875. Clubs in New York and Massachusetts followed in the 1880s. Other Canadian clubs were founded in Toronto, Quebec, and Ottawa.

Numerous courses that attempted to take hold at this time didn't survive, such as Oakhurst Links in West Virginia in 1884. Golf was described there as "grown men following a big marble over the hills." Imagine how difficult it would have been at that time without today's sophisticated communications network to expand a new sport across the United States from the British Isles. Trying to get golf clubs past U.S. customs officials was in itself a tricky situation. Courses had to be built, players recruited, and rules taught. Often, news of golf had to be passed by word of mouth. Poor play also stopped interest from spreading.

The first true golf club in the United States was probably the Foxburg Golf Club, in Foxburg, Pennsylvania, founded as a result of John Mickle Fox' trip to Scotland, where he learned the game. The club is still in existence and is the oldest golf course in continuous use in the United States (since 1887).

John G. Reid, the often-titled "father of American golf," was a Scotsman ironworks executive who had obtained some clubs and balls from Scotland. Reid had three holes put together in a field near his home in New York. In early 1888 he demonstrated the game to some friends, who liked it enough to form the St. Andrews' Golf Club in Yonkers, New York, on November 14, 1888. The first mixed foursome played a round on March 30, 1889. Reid and his "Apple Tree Gang" (an apple tree was a makeshift "clubhouse") are named with the Foxburg Club and the Dorset Field Club in Vermont (1886) as the first golf clubs in the United States. However, Foxburg and Dorset don't have the club records from that time as evidence.

The St. Andrews' Golf Club had a strong influence on the game and marked the point at which golf became firmly rooted in the United States. Other courses quickly followed, such as Merion near Philadelphia; Chicago Golf Club, the first eighteen-hole layout in the United States, in 1894, and Van Cortlandt Park, the first public course, in Riverdale, New York, in 1895. Shinnecock Hills in Southampton, New York, was the first professionally designed links, by Willie Dunn, another Scottish native.

By some estimates there were at least 1,000 courses in the United States in 1900, many associated with golf clubs. Numerous clubs joined with the U.S. Golf Association (USGA), which was formed in 1894 and immediately held its first U.S. Amateur and U.S. Open the following year.

American golf clubs differed somewhat from the clubs in Great Britain. In England, the upper class lived in their country homes and joined clubs in the city; the reverse was true in the United States. People wanted to escape the strain of city life and get to the fresh air and open spaces of the country.

In the early 1900s, the country club became a meeting place to do business and organize gatherings in the lounge after play.

It didn't take long for the exclusivity of the country club to be apparent. The clubs had servants and exclusive sports events. At the turn of the century, a reporter wrote, "Golf is a sport restricted to the richer classes of the country." It's a label the sport has both cultivated and dreaded at the same time. In the 1990s, club membership is still a status symbol.

Most of the new American courses were located in the Northeast, but by 1900 there were twenty courses in California, and wealthy aristocrats had found winter havens from their northern clubs at resorts in Florida, Georgia, and South Carolina. The beauty of playing amid beaches, hills, and woodlands in warm, sunny weather while the home area was blanketed in snow is still the main attraction for resort business today.

More than any other country, Scotland had a substantial role in the growth of American golf. Scottish players were hired as instructors and course designers, often helping to direct workers building courses. They would bounce around from giving lessons to serving as greenkeepers to selling balls and clubs. American clubs

The hilly and treed aspects of Muirfield Village in Ohio are a distinct contrast to the flat and barren courses of Scotland.

continued to use their Scottish counterparts as basic models for their operation. Dozens of Scots came to the United States to be a part of what amounted to a gold rush because the American golfers were more likely to spend extravagantly compared with the Scottish.

One Scottish element that couldn't be copied very well was course design. America didn't have the linksland that Scotland had, so when courses were built in the United States artificial hazards had to be created, such as lakes, bunkers, and strategically placed trees.

Another difference was the way the game was played. In Scotland, players used their natural instinct to judge distances and gauge the effect of wind. In America, the game became a science where golfers needed exact yardages and flagstick locations on each green. Golf wasn't just an activity; it became an organized sport with numerous tournaments.

The quality of American golf took a while to develop. Foreign players typically had the upper hand, but those who worked at country clubs weren't treated much better than in their homeland. Some of the Scottish pros were glorified caddies or clubmakers who were criticized for drinking too much. Although prized for their knowledge, professionals were kept away from the rest of the club in separate shops. Still, many a Scotsman felt comfortable enough in his new home to remain permanently in the States.

At the time, amateur players were seen as more industrious than professionals and earned a reputation as harder workers. The positions of both have switched nearly a century later. The professional receives great adulation and is treated superbly, while the amateur has to work hard to be able to afford competitive golf. He has less time to practice his game.

The great English writer Bernard Darwin commented on how the professional now has the upper hand in playing a better game than the amateur. "Generally the professional will excel the amateur as he does in other walks of life, just because he is a professional and the game is his means of livelihood. That is the great and abiding distinction between the two classes."

There was significant apathy toward golf by the general masses prior to the 1920s in the United States. But things changed rapidly in the Roaring Twenties as golf's popularity spread from an exclusive upper-class sport to include about three million players. Playing in a regular weekend group with a wager on the line became a ritual as much or more than attending church. The golfer considered his foray onto the golf course as a great adventure to experience and a challenge to be met.

When America's Francis Ouimet, an amateur, beat Britishers Harry Vardon and Ted Ray in the 1913 U.S. Open playoff, a boom in American golf expertise was jump-started. During the next twenty years, Walter Hagen and Bobby Jones captured the fancy of American spectators, who increased gate receipts immensely. The pros played for more money, although they still needed to hold down club jobs, play exhibitions, and sign endorsement deals to stay ahead financially. The number of courses in the United States grew to 5,586 by 1930. And international golf received a big boost when the Walker Cup for amateurs and the Ryder Cup for professionals began during the 1920s.

Golf did not grow in the 1930s as well as it did in the '20s, but important advancements were made. When the great amateur champion Jones retired in 1930, some luster left the game as a worthwhile endeavor, but the Depression and the advent of World War II also affected golf in a negative way. By 1946 around one-third of the country clubs in the United States had folded. There were 4,800 courses then, down from 5,727 in 1934; 2,000 of them were municipal or privately owned, daily-fee courses. The professional tour became firmly established under promoter and tournament director Fred Corcoran, and excellent strides in equipment and balls were made. Steel-shafted clubs replaced hickory as a new era of equipment modifications emerged.

> "Good golf is easier to play—and far more pleasant—than bad golf."
>
> BABE ZAHARIAS

The bold, charismatic play of Arnold Palmer brought new golfers to the game in the 1960s during the birth of TV golf.

When America came out of World War II, three shotmakers charged out of the blocks—Ben Hogan, Sam Snead, and Byron Nelson, although the latter was nearing retirement from competition. Those three golfers raised the level of playing precision, and set up the golf world for a major boom. Their modern swings were a marked improvement over the flat swings Scottish pros had taught earlier in the century, a swing more useful in the wind of a Scottish links.

During the 1950s, President Dwight Eisenhower's passion for golf and his many visits to Augusta National gave golf a huge amount of publicity. Country clubs, which were not expensive to join then, became the social center for golfers. A lot of drinking and dancing went on as the marriage of the country club and the golfer's social calendar was extremely strong.

In the middle of the decade, charismatic Arnold Palmer began his professional career. When television began beaming golf regularly into the nation's homes in the 1960s, the double effect of Palmer and TV gave the game a boom of immense proportions. The number of players in the United States doubled from 4.4 million in 1960 to 9.7 million in 1970. The number of television hours in 1956 was five and a half—for the entire year. Today, one tour event is shown for that long during a weekend. (Palmer himself was instrumental in getting The Golf Channel (TGC), an all-golf network, up and running in the '90s. In 1997, there were 1,058 hours of televised golf, a major increase from 519 in 1991. TGC accounted for 300 hours in 1995.)

Palmer appealed to everyone, and through his bold style and ability to play to the gallery, the public saw golf in a new, exciting light. The 1960s also saw the infusion of celebrity players in prominent roles. Actors, sports heroes, and other stars were known to play golf, but tour events soon carried the names of well-known figures who brought others of their type to the tournament in a professional-amateur format. Bob Hope, Bing Crosby (starting in the 1940s), Jackie Gleason, Glen Campbell, Dean Martin, Danny Thomas, Andy Williams, Ed McMahon, and Sammy Davis Jr. were some of the celebrities associated with the tour who helped make golf glamorous. And where there was glitter, there was an overwhelming number of commercial sponsors who not only helped the tour grow but golf in general with their charity contributions.

Golf at the grass-roots level was mightily affected as high schools and colleges began or enhanced golf programs to give young players a better chance of learning and improving. Many young people were motivated by the PGA Tour, which took off from offering forty-one events and $1.34 million in prize money in 1960 to forty-five events and $75.2 million in 1997. (One of the sporting world's biggest phenomenons was the start-up and success of the Senior PGA Tour, which began as a nostalgia-type tour of two events in 1980 and $250,000 in prize money and by 1997 had forty-four events with purses of $40.8 million.)

Golf's growth in the 1970s slowed due to rising costs for green fees and other expenses, the increasing problem of slow play, and golf course access. The number of golfers went up modestly from 11.2 million in 1970 to 14.6 million in 1979. The economic expansion in the 1980s, however, resulted in a jump from 15.1 million players in 1980 to 23.4 million in 1988, with an increase in rounds played during that time from 358 million to 487 million.

THE CONDITION OF GOLF TODAY

As the year 2000 approaches, golf is an absolutely global game, played in some of the most isolated locales on earth. It is estimated that there are 50.7 million golfers in the world, most of them (nearly 25 million) in the United States.

Golf's health is a mixed bag. In the most recent National Golf Foundation (NGF) figures, two main growth indicators have been holding steady for six years in the United States. There were 24.7 million golfers through 1996, a minimal decrease from 24.8 million in 1992. And the number of rounds played has actually fallen more, to 477.4 million in 1996 from 505.4 million in 1992. Golf analysts believe, however, that a 16-percent increase in senior golfers since 1991 bodes well for golf economics because of their buying power. The youth and women's markets are also expected to be strong financially.

The younger generation appears to find golf becoming "cooler" as a sport, which could ensure economic growth for the golf business. Research in 1997 with consumers ages 20 to 29 showed that golf ranked first among sports they say are getting "cooler," ahead of mountain biking, snowboarding, and women's professional basketball. It can be deduced from this research that golf is becoming more upscale and is liked for its individualism among the young.

Although participation numbers have declined, golf consumer spending has nearly doubled since 1986, from $7.8 billion to $15.1 billion, an indication golfers haven't lost a desire to remain in the game and invest in it. One place they'll look more and more for golf products and news is the Internet, which forecasters predict will generate $5 billion in overall sales revenue by the year 2000.

Tiger Woods' impact on the golf world in the 1990s has been the most significant since Arnold Palmer's.

Another key indicator is that the 18-to-29 age group has been the leading source of the two million beginners that come into the game each year. As golf moves ahead during the next five to ten years, this group will be crucial to watch, especially in observing how it reacts to Tiger Woods, whose talent, ethnically mixed background, and youth (born in 1975) have already helped him reach legendary status.

In a report issued in August 1997 by the Associated Press, it was estimated that the Woods influence had brought in $653.5 million in new money during his first year as a professional. That accounts for increases in ticket sales, TV ratings, interest in golf, and products he endorses. It was skyrocketing TV ratings due to Woods that helped the PGA Tour arrange a television package of enormous proportion. During 1997, 29.3 million people watched the four men's major championships on TV, a 51-percent increase over 1996. Weekend television ratings as a whole on the three major tours—the PGA, the Senior PGA, and the LPGA—were up 16.6 percent. When the PGA Tour negotiated a new four-year deal with the TV networks beginning in 1999, it was worth $650 million, double the $325 million contract due to expire in 1998.

The TV revenue bonanza means the PGA Tour will be thriving as the new millennium arrives. The average tournament purse in the year 2000 will be more than $3 million, nearly double the $1.7 million of 1997. By 2002, it will be $3.5 million and a total prize purse of $158.5 million, more than twice the $75.2 million of 1997.

But getting back to the real world of golf—nonprofessionals—many courses have tried to speed up the pace of play, but five- to six-hour rounds (around four is the norm) are common occurrences. The amount of time it takes to play will have to decrease to prevent borderline golfers from going to a different activity.

In 1997 it was revealed by the NGF that 40 percent of all rounds played in the United States are just nine holes instead of the standard eighteen. The less time a golfer spends at the course could likely mean less money spent on golf products.

New construction of golf courses, an important barometer of the game's health, showed vigor in 1996 with 442 courses opened, just shy of the record 468 in 1995. Another 850 courses were under construction with 808 planned. The number of new course openings has grown from just more than 100 in the early 1980s to the recent strong construction. Most of the new courses (88 percent) are in the public category and have green fees at or below the average fee for their market.

Socially, the private club is not what it once was. Instead of spending huge chunks of time at the club playing golf, having drinks and dinner, many clubs resemble sport clubs. Golfers play a game, have a diet soda drink and light lunch, and head home.

As for golf course conditioning, the hard fairways and sparse rough of the 1950s are long gone. Plush, thick, heavily watered ribbons of fairway, along with manicured bunkers and greens, are seen as the hallmark of a great course. These features are expected and often demanded by players, especially at private clubs and upscale public courses.

A major trend in 1997 was a great amount of industry talk about building nine-hole courses, pitch-and-putt layouts, and facilities for juniors. Although traditionalists don't believe these courses are "real golf," most golf leaders realize that for golf to be affordable and accessible to more players of all ages, sex, and race, these shorter courses could be the crucial contributor to a major growth spurt.

INCLUSION, GOLF'S BIGGEST CHALLENGE

With the professional segment and course construction in excellent shape, and other key areas showing stability, what could hold golf back from continued growth? It comes down to two areas.

The first is affordability. No matter what it costs, golf consumers seem to have little problem purchasing hard goods, the expensive pieces of equipment, apparel, and accessories that make up a golfer's arsenal. The doubling of consumer spending since 1986 is evidence of that.

A key cost figure is green fees. The average green fee for a weekend round, including a cart, was $56 in early 1997. Fees range from just $5 to $10 at municipal courses in the rural Midwest to the approximately $300 at famed Pebble Beach in California. There has been no problem in getting people to pay for a round of golf at a shrine such as Pebble Beach, but the low-end cost must stay within reasonable reach for the majority of players to stay involved. Golf has come a long way in trying to be more affordable for more people and thus shake the label that it's a game for the wealthy.

The second, more visible area is inclusion. As you've seen, golf's history has had many years of elitism, particularly in the first half of golf's growth in the United States. At American country clubs especially, women's groups and minorities have historically been outcasts, either totally excluded from membership or made to feel like second-class citizens.

Women have recently gone to court to fight for more rights, all in the name of equality. They desire equal access to the course for tee times, equal access to parts of the clubhouse such as the grill room, and equal privileges for membership costs. And the battle has turned into more of a victory than defeat. Various states have enacted laws that make it illegal to discriminate against any group. Although progress has been made, don't expect this issue to fade away for many years.

The cause of African-Americans and other minority groups has a long history. Faced with years of discrimination, the participation of blacks in professional golf tournaments was approved by the PGA of America in January 1952.

But their cause received unprecedented attention beginning in 1990. That's when Hall Thompson, the founder and owner of Shoal Creek, the course selected for the 1990 PGA Championship by the PGA of America, drew attention to the club's discriminatory policy against blacks and minorities. But it wasn't just Shoal Creek that had such regulations. It was a widespread problem. But there was an unspoken rule that people remained silent about these unfair practices. It simply wasn't talked about.

Up to that point, a great many private clubs, either by club bylaws or unwritten rules, refused to allow minority members. The policies were common knowledge, but there had been no movement against them. Prior to the 1990 PGA, Thompson had said Shoal Creek didn't admit African-Americans and wouldn't have anyone pressure them into doing so. It proved to be the watershed moment for which minority groups were waiting.

There was a pronounced and immediate reaction from protest groups, as well as, most importantly, the lead organizations in the golf industry. Sponsors threatened to withdraw television support from the event and pickets were threatened. To quiet the storm, Shoal Creek admitted a black member, local businessperson Louis Willie. The event went on, but the governing bodies reacted swiftly with new polices. The PGA Tour, the LPGA Tour, the USGA and the PGA of America all established antidiscriminatory policies for clubs hosting their events. The clubs couldn't hold one of their events if it discriminated by race, sex, religion, or national origin. Some affected clubs continued their policies and decided against holding an event, but the majority complied.

Some results included: Minority groups were allowed in previously closed clubs; minority intern programs were set up on tour and within the industry; corporations added minorities to high-level positions; the PGA of America sought to more actively recruit minorities for its club professional program; and the USGA added a black to its executive committee. Audits and surveys were conducted to see exactly where and how many minorities were involved in the game. Even Augusta National Golf Club, the Southern home of the fabled Masters, admitted a black member.

The golf world seemed to wake up to the fact it had been a closed shop for decades, although it had been more of a U.S. problem than anywhere else. Because golf has traditionally been slow to make changes, the battle for minority rights will, like the case of women, be an ongoing effort for years.

The monumental presence of Tiger Woods will be a major part of that effort. With a heritage that ranges from African-American to Asian to Native American, Woods, with an awesome dimension to his golf game, is the most important minority player in the game's history. He has the double appeal to the young as well as diversity in his background.

After joining the PGA Tour in August 1996, he created his own foundation to promote the game and began a series of teaching clinics to bring golf to minority groups. A year later in August 1997, he believed his efforts were paying off. "I have definitely seen an increase in minority participation in the sport. And that's great to see people coming into a sport in which, traditionally, they hadn't either had the chance or never thought golf was cool enough to play, never took it seriously. You're going to see, ten, fifteen years from now, a lot of people playing golf, all different backgrounds, not necessarily the old traditional country club kids anymore. I think people are starting to see that golf is becoming a core sport in America. It's becoming cool enough to play."

 Chapter 2

THE COURSE—BEING IN TOUCH WITH THE LAND

One of the most comforting benefits for any golf devotee is that golf puts the player in touch with the land. Athletic events are most enjoyable when they can be held outside. Being outdoors is what makes most people feel alive and vibrant. Golf is the sport that most effectively brings the participants in contact with nature.

The golf course itself can develop a personality; not in a literal sense, of course, but it can be friendly or harsh, kind or penal. Golfers can even become so close and acquainted with a golf course that they give certain elements of the course names, such as a few of the famous bunkers like Hell's Half Acre at Pine Valley, The Principal's Nose at the Old Course at St. Andrews, and the Church Pews at Oakmont Country Club. Holes have names, such as The Road Hole at St. Andrews; names have been given to a series of holes, such as Amen Corner at Augusta National, and to an entire course, such as Riviera Country Club as Hogan's Alley.

This close affinity to the playing field has been a golf feature since the first golfers played on what, for them, served as "golf courses." In comparison with the courses of today, the early golf ancestors had closer contact with the good earth than modern players.

It is difficult for today's golfers to think of a time when there weren't courses as we know them in present form. But this must be understood so modern golfers can appreciate what they have to play on. The image that the word "course" brings to mind must be overcome in order to understand the way it was for the first players. *Course* gives the impression of something that has shape, form, and a logical direction and routing to it. There's also the sense that *course* refers to something with boundaries or is confined to a certain area.

Those are all correct impressions of the kind of golf course played today. But the first golfers played not so much on a golf course as much as golf *land*. Very little was done to lay out a course or routing. There was a starting point and an ending point on what passed for "holes." The holes could change from one day to the next: in direction, length and the number in a certain area. And the land used for golf was the fields and pastures in the countryside. The land was unkempt and raw, as much unmanaged then as today's courses are manicured. The guidelines for play were certainly as changeable as the landscape.

The popularity of golf and the search to find ideal playing fields led players to the linksland by the sea, specifically on the eastern coast of Scotland for the very first courses. The sandy soil, ideal for wonderful water drainage and growing grass, also had pockets of gorse, whin and heather, types of tall grass. Linksland wasn't of much use for farmers; it "linked" the "land" and townspeople to the ocean, bordering the beaches on one side and the farmable land on the other. But the links was the home to rabbits, nesting place for birds and a grazing area for sheep. Undulations of various shapes and slopes were caused by the receding sea and whipping wind, and sheep and burrowing animals caused bunkers in great abundance. It was on this type of land that the first actual courses, the designs that today's courses resemble, came to be laid out.

The links provided their own hazards, some of which had to be artificially designed in the United States. There were the tall grass and bunkers, streams, and the ever-present wind off the sea. A links course didn't require a lot of creativity to plan the hole routings, which were just five-hole layouts in many cases at first. Links designs have a natural flow. There was and is no need to move a great amount of earth. Green sites seemed to always fall nicely upon raised areas of ground. Golfers began a course at one point, played along the coast to a certain stopping point—perhaps stopped by the town or a natural obstacle—then went back the other way. This process is a characteristic of a true links course, with nine holes going out, and nine coming in.

Many of the great Scottish courses, such as St. Andrews, were built on this type of land. There is some evidence that links courses were first played as long

Links courses in Scotland "link" the land and local people to the ocean. The course grass is cut short but the surrounding vegetation retains its raw look.

ago as the early 1600s. But they really had their birth in the mid-1700s when groups of golfers created clubs. Then the 1800s was the big boom period in course construction in the area around Scotland. Most of the clubs had their own links course, usually named for the nearest town. Because the links was most likely public land, some links became the recreational focal point for the town, which is the case at St. Andrews still today. Golf was the primary activity on the links, but the land was used as a park and picnic area during some parts of the week. When the links was used by golfers and nongolfers at the same time, the scene was a mix of flying golf balls with dogs, horses and people roaming around.

Hidden bunkers, creeks, tall grass and bushes served as the hazards and obstacles golfers contended with. Even the simple undulations in the ground were trouble enough. Links ground is firm and compact; when the ball hits the ground it runs a great deal, but the tricky rolls and bounces send balls in unpredictable directions. A drive that looks like it will stay in the fairway can run off into high grass or a pot bunker.

Trees were non-existent, but the wind created an all-around challenge compliments of Mother Nature. There was very little definition between the greens and tees. On the early links, the hole was just that, a hole, perhaps created by a rabbit. To play the next hole, golfers took a small amount of sand from the hole and used it to tee up the ball for the next shot, standing just one club-length away from the hole. The holes gradually got bigger and bigger, and they varied in size. When hole liners and flags were used at a later time, the tee was moved further away, but the teeing area was an offshoot of the green. This can be seen quite vividly at St. Andrews, where many tees are connected to the previous green by a plateau walkway.

The number of holes varied from a few to the 22 at St. Andrews, depending on the space available and the length of the holes. How the tradition of building courses with 18 holes began can be traced to St. Andrews in 1764. In that year, William St. Clair "handled" St. Andrews' 22 holes in 121 strokes. Afterward it was decided to eliminate two holes, but since two holes shared a fairway and green, it reduced the number from 22 to 18. St. Clair's adjusted score with four fewer holes would have been 99. Because of the shaggy course conditions of the time, a score around 100 for 18 holes was considered quite good.

The more whimsical explanation for 18-hole courses is the tale told about an 1858 decision at St. Andrews to standardize the number of holes. Since a committee couldn't come to a mutual number, an oldtimer came forward and said that to him the ideal number should be 18. He based that on the fact that it took that long for him to consume a fifth of whiskey, which he said was needed to fortify himself against the rain, wind and cold. Whether true or not, it is accurate that the early players loved to consume their spirits, but not necessarily for their ability to keep a golfer warm against the cold and wind.

As golf grew more popular in Scotland, Ireland and England, courses were designed inland, routed through treed areas and constructed with more thought and detail. This design practice started in the late 1890s, as the great British golf writer Bernard Darwin wrote: "It was discovered that the waste country of heather and bracken, sand and fir trees would make such courses as had not been dreamed of. Seaside golf was still the real thing in excelsis but there was a lesser but still real thing inland and sand was no longer the exclusive boast of links as opposed to courses."

Concentrating on inland golf courses was also the direction architecture went in the United States when designers started laying out courses with more frequency around 1900. From 1900 until the late 1930s, the U.S. had its classical period when some of the most revered and respected courses were built, coinciding with

America lacks typical links land, but classic courses such as Baltusrol in New Jersey show how designers utilize water hazards, bunkers, and trees.

the added distance of the new Haskell ball. Many of these designs have withstood the test of time, and their traditional look and playability are still challenges for the modern player, even with his better ability and equipment, than golfers 50 to 100 years ago.

In the early 1900s, U.S. course builders employed the design services of Scots who had come over to thrive in a land that had recently discovered the sport and had great promise in its infancy to grow it. America had few genuine links sites, which must have constant wind to make ordinary shots difficult, plus natural grass, dunes, gorse, subtle contours and sandy soil. U.S. builders had to create many of these hazards, especially water and sand bunkers, and rely heavily on tree growth to overcome whatever the land lacked in natural trouble spots. A great amount of earth was moved to form special shapes and details that framed golf holes amid the trees.

With the rise of inland golf, designers became more creative and artistic in their work, taking the time to study and learn from previous great holes. It was the birth of the method course architects use today of borrowing and refining ideas from previous designs. From Darwin again: "With the rise of inland golf there came an immense upward step in the art of designing courses. With the 20th century, the golf architect came into being."

The early architects had to rely on horse power to move earth around, sometimes shaping slopes and curves by hand. Later, after World War II, tractors and large earth movers made the work more efficient and the designs more elaborate, allowing architects to reshape the ground to match their theories of design. The strides made in mowing and maintenance machines have allowed designers great leeway in using materials such as railroad ties and in implementing unusual and severe dips and plateaus.

One of the greatest advances in course design and maintenance is the automatic watering system, which grew in popularity from the 1950s on. Teaching and playing great Paul Runyan said, "I think the improvement in the watering system might be the single most important point where golf course design and maintenance is concerned." Prior to the automatic method, tees and greens were watered by using long hoses linked to random water spickets. Grass growth was very spotty. But automatic watering allowed consistent growth of the tees, fairways, greens and first portion of rough.

Crisscross mowing on fairways and greens is part of the extreme manicuring American golfers are accustomed to and often demand at their golf courses.

During the years of hose spraying, the ball rolled forever on the hard, dry ground. But the softer ground due to the newer method changed the way course architects designed holes and altered player strategy because of reduced roll. The location of trouble spots and the bend in doglegs had to be re-assessed.

Much of what course architects do today is for course definition and allowing players to see the shape and direction of a hole. This is especially a hallmark of American design; links courses in the United Kingdom don't have hole definition for the most part. The game is played with much more stress put on having a feel for the shape and roll of the land, sensing the direction of a hole.

Another difference between American and British courses is maintenance. Links courses are primarily left to thrive or wither at the whim of the weather, although some of the more noted links courses have installed watering systems. The grass height is usually left on the shaggy side, and if the course coloring is of a brownish hue, no one worries that the course is in need of some help.

American courses are as manicured and well kept so as to lay down a pillow and blanket and sleep on them. Green is the color of choice as course superintendents do all they can to make sure the grass looks as healthy as possible, and thick, too. The grass is cut for the ultimate playability standards: fairways at ⅜ths or 7/16ths of an inch, rough at 1⅝ths to 2 inches, and greens at 5/32nds. The push for Softspikes at hundreds of courses is designed to alleviate grass damage and ensure beauty.

The push for plush has resulted in large doses of chemicals, pesticides and fertilizers being applied to the course, putting course builders, designers and golfers, in general, in direct conflict with environmentalists, who more often than not clash with course owners on the effects a course will have on a piece of land. Golf courses, say their opponents, ruin the environment, disrupt wildlife, waste water resources, destroy wetlands, and send pollutants into neighboring water supplies. Local residents have also provided zoning opposition to a course project, forcing the developer to exert more time, money and energy to put together plans that would convince the locals that the community and course can co-exist in harmony.

To get approval to build golf courses, owners must pay millions in permit fees, which can take many years to process, and include numerous studies and plans, even down to describing any historical or archaeological sites that may need protecting, preservation or removal. Once the course is built, the cost for these permits is often passed to the golfer in the form of high green fees.

Each side in the battle for future course development holds firm to its beliefs, making the search for new golf sites one of the biggest stumbling blocks the game faces if it is to grow in the coming years.

On the positive side, the U.S. Golf Association has spent $14 million on environmental research in the last 10 years, and the USGA's Green Section has conducted or funded 110 studies on the environment and golf since 1983. There has been a decrease in the amount of chemicals and water courses have needed to maintain the green look. More effluent (treated waste water) is used on courses than in previous years. The Golf Course Superintendents Association of America does more than 60 seminars a year on the environment to better inform its members. Thousands of acres of natural wildlife habitat have been protected or restored at golf sites to support birds and animals.

Also of key importance is the improved dialogue that has occurred between environmental groups and their golf counterparts. An important event to breaking the ice was the January 1995 Golf and the Environment Conference at Pebble Beach, California, backed primarily by the National Wildlife Federation and Golf Digest magazine. Eighty persons representing the major environmental and golf groups met. The groups sent 120 persons to a second meeting in 1996, at which time they ratified a set of environmental principles for the location of and building of new courses in the United States.

Part of their principles was this set of guidelines that tells golfers how to make golf more environmentally friendly.

1. Recognize that golf courses are managed land areas that should complement the natural environment.
2. Respect designated environmentally sensitive areas within the course.
3. Accept the natural limitations and variations of turfgrass plants growing under conditions that protect resources (e.g., brown patches, thinning, loss of color).
4. Support golf-course management decisions that protect or enhance the environment and encourage the development of environmental conservation planning.
5. Support maintenance practices that protect wildlife and natural habitat.

6. Encourage maintenance practices that promote the long-range health of the turf and support sound environmental objectives. Such practices include aerification, reduced fertilization, limited play on sensitive turf areas, reduced watering, etc.

7. Commit to long-range conservation efforts on the golf course and at home.

8. Educate others about the benefits of environmentally responsible golf-course management.

9. Support research and education that expands the public's understanding of the relationship between golf and the environment.

10. Take pride in our environmentally responsible courses.

The course layouts of the 1990s have continued to push the boundaries of course design with an "anything goes," spare-no-expense mentality in many cases. There's virtually no site that an architect can't transform into a course or incorporate into a residential golf community, one of the more popular construction combinations in the golf business, where a golf course intertwines with the homes

Golf is played in some of the world's most exotic locations. In Hawaii, golfers can call upon the god of lava, Moki, to return errant shots to the fairway.

of a new community or subdivision. New upscale public courses are also a big trend, but their affect has been more evident in the amenities and treatment offered in the clubhouse and on the course than in the course layout itself.

LEARNING YOUR WAY AROUND THE COURSE

No matter whether the course has the traditional, classic look of a Winged Foot or the contemporary appeal of one of the PGA Tour's Tournament Players Courses, a golfer can be inspired by the beauty of a golf course. The majestic surroundings of Mother Nature and the design of the course can combine to stir a player's senses and raise his or her playing level.

It's amazing how often a golfer can complete a round of golf and remark about a course that "it felt so natural to play here." Some pieces of land just look like the good Lord intended for it to be a golf course because of its natural appearance. Architects often remark that when they see property they will work on to design a course, their task is a simple one of cutting away the trees and growth that will unveil the 18-hole routing hidden there.

Each golf course, no matter it's status or condition, is a distinctive collection of holes with unique qualities and features. Unlike a basketball court or football field, a golf course is special to itself. Bernard Darwin said, "Golf differs from almost every other game in that every piece of land on which it is played has its own characteristics and scenery and flavor. It is no flat, bare expanse, but is made up of miniature hills and valleys, each with a personality of its own."

Golfers experience variety in wherever they go, at all parts of the world. Cultures and customs differ from one country and region to the next.

In Hawaii, for instance, golfers are encouraged to call upon the name of Moki, the god of lava. When a ball is headed toward the lava rocks, the player shouts, "Moki, help me!" in the hopes that the lava god will kick the ball back into play. Of course, Moki doesn't help everyone.

In Nigeria, golfers don't hit toward greens, but "browns." The putting surface there is a concrete saucer 50 feet in diameter filled with oiled sand. Caddies smooth the surface each time a player putts.

But perhaps the most unusual ruling occurs in many parts of Africa, where golfers get a free drop if their ball comes to rest in footprints made by a hippopotamus.

As modern players have improved, course architects have devised unique—and controversial—ways to thwart them, such as the famous island green 17th at the TPC Stadium Course in Florida.

Regardless of course location, the basic structure and components of a golf course are the same for every layout. Most golf courses have 18 holes taking up approximately 130 acres; some courses have just nine holes. A hole can't be called a hole unless it has a starting point, known as the tee, and a finishing point, called the putting green. In-between is the area that connects the two ends, called the fairway and rough. The fairway is the closely-cut grass that is the ideal path to the hole. The rough is the taller grass that usually causes beginners and poorer players to post a high score on a hole.

Holes fall into three yardage ranges, which help designate their par score. (Par is the score an expert player would be expected to shoot on the hole during pleasant weather conditions. It is the number of strokes it takes to reach the green, plus two putts. So on a par 5, the player should reach the green in three shots and take two more strokes.)

Hole pars can be either 3, 4, 5 and, occasionally, 6. Par 3s are the shortest holes on the course, with a distance not greater than 250 yards for men and 210 for women. The next longest holes are par 4s, which take two shots to reach the green.

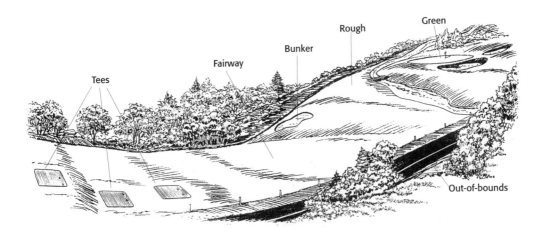

A typical golf hole: Play begins on the tee, which can be set up at different lengths, and continues to the putting green. Golfers "hope" to play along the fairway, but wayward shots may lead them to sand bunkers, out-of-bounds, water hazards, and tree trouble. This hole would play as a par 4, meaning the typical player should take two shots to get to the green and hole out in two putts.

They can be 470 yards or less for men and 400 or less for women. And par 5s are the longest holes on the course, usually more than 500 yards for men and 400 yards for women. It takes three shots for the average player to reach a par 5.

An 18-hole course usually has a par score ranging from 70 to 72 for men, and up to 74 or 75 for women. This score is the total of all par scores for the 18 holes added together. Other courses that also provide a wonderful challenge are par-3, or executive courses, and pitch-and-putt courses. These courses are often just nine holes in length, and quite short, but very challenging at the same time because the greens are usually smaller than on a regulation course. Construction of these courses is being seen by the golf industry as a key to sparking more interest among new players and easing overcrowded regular courses.

After playing from the tee to hit the first shot on a hole, a golfer must avoid the trouble spots that architects strategically place to entrap wayward shots. These include the rough, the grass that is taller than fairway turf, and which runs down the side of the fairway to catch shots that have gone too far left or right. Sand bunkers are placed in the landing areas of the fairway and around the green. A bunker can also be grass filled. Trees are seen on most courses lining a golf hole on each side. Water, in the form of creeks, rivers, ponds and lakes, are alongside or across the fairway. When water runs parallel to the intended route to the hole, it's a lateral water hazard and is indicated by red stakes or lines. If the water is between the player and the hole, it's a regular water hazard and is shown by yellow stakes or lines. And out-of-bounds can lurk dangerously close to the sides of the fairways; OB areas are usually caused by the presence of housing developments, roads or waste areas of sand, grass, marsh and trees. OB is ground from which play is not allowed; it's usually indicated by white stakes.

A GOLF COURSE IS THE PLACE TO BE

There's one last image to have of the golf course, and it requires your full imagination. Picture the course as an extension of your own backyard or as ground connected to your place of residence. And imagine a "Home Sweet Home" sign next to the first tee.

The golf course should feel like home to you the more you play the game. It's comfortable and friendly. It's a place to go to enjoy the outdoors, clear the mind of any distractions and focus on one thing: the pleasure of a place that can be uplifting and help ease the tensions of a difficult day.

Golf builds character in a person. An individual can learn more about him or herself from playing golf than any other game. When a golfer plays the golf course, he or she embarks on 18 or nine short adventures or trips. Each hole is a challenge to conquer. Each hole is a checkpoint for how strong a golfer's fortitude is for that day and how in tune they are with their golf swing. It's a unique challenge that is new and different each time the golfer walks to the first tee.

 Chapter 3

GETTING EQUIPPED

Course design, swing instruction, and equipment have been the three areas with the greatest effect on golf and its practitioners since the game's inception. It is difficult to pick which of the three has been most influential, but it is for certain that if golf hadn't advanced beyond hickory-shafted clubs or the feathery ball to the present age of high-tech design, what an archaic game it would be. It has always been true that, in any era, top-notch golf could not be played without the latest and best materials.

The painstaking refinement of equipment into the current collection of innovative products is one of the greatest stories in golf history. With equipment sales worth $2.35 billion in 1997 alone, there is a lot of pressure on manufacturers to develop products that will catch the fancy of the golfing public and become huge money-making hits for years to come. One obvious example from the '90s is the Big Bertha line of drivers and woods from the Callaway Company. A product such as Big Bertha is rare because there are few new ideas left to

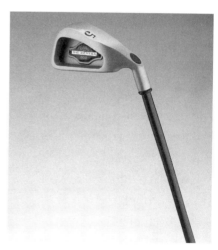

The Big Bertha line of clubs from Callaway is among those leading the equipment market competition.

The scope of equipment shows has expanded as product development has created great market competition.

develop. Most innovations today have to do with new materials, which make clubs lighter and clubfaces harder for increased distance.

The race to capture the fancy of the buying public is no more evident than in the growth of the two big merchandise shows of the year, each open to PGA of America golf shop professionals, retailers, and distributors of golf products, and, of course, manufacturers over a three-day period. The show held in January in Orlando, Florida, has been around since 1954, when a group of golf merchandisers set up a tent in a Dunedin, Florida, parking lot and peddled their wares to a small group of club professionals. The show moved to Orlando in 1985, and since then has grown so vastly that 950,000 square feet of exhibit space is used to showcase items for nearly 50,000 buyers from seventy countries.

Also making a big expansion is the show in September at Las Vegas, Nevada. Originally designed as the West Coast Show for California buyers, the renamed PGA International Golf Show has grown from 350,000 square feet of space in 1994 to 750,000 in 1997. Nearly 1,100 exhibitors displayed products and more than 20,000 buyers attended. The size of the two shows has increased the buying options but also made those options tougher to decide upon, as the choices for equipment, apparel, balls, and nearly every accessory imaginable has branched out into dozens of lines.

Modern equipment is sleek, colorful, and highly functional, as far removed from the implements of long ago as imaginable. The ball, too, has undergone substantial changes, internal and external, to make it durable and adaptable to the type of shot trajectory the golfer has or desires to have. Taken together, the ongoing process of tweaking the performance of both clubs and balls has taken the limits of playing ability to new heights the golfers of olden times couldn't have fathomed, unless they had a Jules Verne-type vision of the future.

CLUBS: THE TOOLS OF THE TRADE

From the very beginning, golf clubs have consisted of a grip, shaft, and clubhead. But, oh, how the materials and performance of the club have changed, particularly in the last 300 years!

Improvements in club design have taken place in two main areas—the shape of the clubhead and the performance of the shaft, both improved greatly due to newer materials that designers discovered are more functional. Many of the club improvements have been made with the poorer player in mind, so that mis-hit shots aren't affected as much and the ball won't be as likely to fly into trouble.

When the first clubs were made, there probably wasn't much, if any, thought put into making the game easier for the player through equipment enhancement. The club maker simply realized the player needed something to hit the ball with and came up with a basic piece of equipment to do that. The first club makers made golf equipment as a side job since the sport was barely in the mainstream. Club makers made military gear, such as clubs and bows. Golf simply added to their income.

The first reference to the manufacture of clubs specifically meant for golf was around 1500 for King James IV. The gradual increase in the number of golfers created a slow increase in club makers. Once demand was up, there were more craftsmen who devoted their total attention to golf clubs and balls. Those early clubs didn't even have grips; the shaft was wider at the grip end, but later sheepskin was wrapped around the shaft for better gripping.

Probably the oldest known clubs still in existence were found quite by accident in 1889. Six long-nosed, wooden "play" clubs and two irons were pulled from a closed-off cupboard during renovations to a house in the east-central coastal town of Hull, England. The clubs were from the mid-1700s, since a newspaper dated 1741 was found with the clubs. But some historians believe the clubs could be up to 100 years older than that. One of the irons, called square toe, is one of two still around and the other iron, a spur toe model, is one of five still in existence. The clubs have been in the possession of the Royal Troon Golf Club since 1915 and have an estimated worth of up to $5 million.

The great clubmakers of the wooden-shaft era came into being in the mid-1700s, with names such as Forgan, Dunn, and Park. During this feathery ball era, club makers constructed all-wood clubs with leather-type grips, or grips made of cloth or satin. The golfer used about five wooden clubs and a special club called the rut iron to get the ball out of sunken lies. Other irons weren't used at that time because they would have damaged the feathery ball.

Hazel and ash wood were used up until 1825 in Scotland, then hickory from the United States was introduced as the wood of choice because of its toughness and resiliency. The shafts were thinner than the earlier clubs, and the clubheads were thin and elongated blocks of wood, flat on one side for striking the ball. Around 1860, American hickory was used exclusively as shaft material. Clubheads were made shorter and wider beginning around 1850 when the gutta-percha ball came into use. This ball, harder than the feathery, banged up clubfaces and damaged them to the point of uselessness. Besides changing the dimension of the clubhead and switching to more durable beech wood, club makers also put material such as leather on the clubface to cushion the blow and prevent damage.

Hickory-shafted clubs were in the bags of nearly every golfer from the 1820s until approximately 1925. During this time, clubmaking became a major employment opportunity for local economies. In some cases club shops had forty to fifty workers and found a market for their clubs outside the immediate area. Clubmakers also started the trend of creative advertising, publicizing their wares in ways that caught the public's fancy, even though research into club specifications was unscientific.

Britain was the world's clubmaking leader during this period, exporting clubs to America in the late 1800s when golf took hold here. When Spalding began producing clubs in 1894 in the United States, creating a method of mass-producing products, American companies started growing in stature. MacGregor had its origin around 1900, and Hillerich & Bradsby in 1916.

The tubular-steel shaft was devised in the 1920s. It worked more effectively than hickory, which did have problems with breakage and had to be kept out of rain or extreme heat. Either condition caused the hickory to warp. When players were done for the day, they set their clubs upright to avoid warping. It wasn't uncommon for players to trim the shaft a little with a knife to make it torque properly on the downswing. If the clubs got wet, they would shrink upon drying and not fit into the hosel as snug. But the problem could be fixed by letting the shaft soak in water for a half-hour and swell up again. It's plain to see that golfers had to not only know how to play golf, but had to be handymen as well.

Prior to steel-shafted clubs, clubs were known by certain names, such as cleek, brassie, and mid-iron. Over time, numbers replaced the names for both woods and irons. For each type of club, the lowest number indicates the clubs that hit the ball the longest and lowest and have the longest shafts. The highest numbers, on the other hand, are those clubs that hit the ball the shortest and highest and have the shortest shafts.

Initially, the steel shaft was not a great alternative to hickory. Steel was too heavy and didn't heft well in a player's hands, facts that hickory companies and traditionalists emphasized in trying to hang on to their treasured wood. Steel didn't provide a golfer the touch and response of hickory, but eventually it was constructed with walls thin enough that it didn't feel overly heavy. Steel was stronger than hickory and more reliable. And steel could be made in greater quantity more quickly than hickory, which, when broken, took a long time to replace.

Billy Burke was the first person to win a professional major championship with steel shafts, in the 1931 U.S. Open. After that, the steel-shafted club became the starting point from which club designers made their refinements. Production techniques and machinery improvements helped grow the industry, the affects of which we still feel today. The shaft still comes in steel, but graphite and titanium are still very prominent today while aluminum was one type that didn't catch on.

Wooden-headed clubs (the preferred wood type is persimmon) are made less and less these days, replaced by metal woods beginning in the late '70s. The metal market, once exclusively the funny-looking club you'd see at the local driving range, has turned the golf industry on its ear and could be said to have started the high-tech phase club companies are in today. It's also a high-cash phase, with drivers easily selling at $500 to $1,000 and sets of irons at $1,500. Those prices used to be the top end of the market only 10 to 15 years ago.

Metal woods themselves have been modified into oversized clubs, turning the oversized metal driver into a must-have club because there is more mass behind the ball and more forgiveness when shots are mis-hit.

Irons are, amazingly, still iron-headed, but their size and shape, too, have been tinkered with during the last 20 years. They come in large size and regular; they've been made hollow like a metal wood and given "reflex" clubfaces, and they've been made light as a feather and given different groove designs of U and V shapes. Inserts have been added for lightness and better contact, and perimeter weighting has been a godsend for the high handicapper along with oversized drivers. Copper and nickel have been utilized, along with ceramics, manganese bronze, beryllium copper and beryllium nickel. The traditional stainless steel approach has expanded greatly.

The metal with the most marketing sizzle today is titanium, or just "ti", which is a light, hard metal used in airplane hulls. It's now the metal of choice for drivers and fairway woods and it's threatening to take over the iron market altogether. There's no telling what its limits might be in the market. It had been utilized in some testing in the 1980s as a shaft material, but its cost and the fact that graphite and steel were going strong kept it from breaking in. Then in 1992 the material returned, this time in metal woods.

Titanium costs three times the price of making a steel clubhead, but it is admired for its improvement over steel in hardness, lightness (it's 40 percent lighter than steel) and strength-to-weight ratio. It suddenly was a perfect find for use in the oversized driver market, and despite its extreme cost, it has been a phenomenal seller. Titanium was introduced in iron clubs in the mid-1990s, either as a clubface insert or all-titanium head.

Consumers have grown wiser, too, since the mid-1900s when they put a lot of stock in what professionals played. A pro's endorsement of a certain type of club had a strong influence on the golfing public's buying choices. Today, though, with so much information about the performance of equipment available, golfers realize that specific equipment is at their disposal for their specific swing needs. Technology has opened their eyes to selective shopping.

BALLS: THE SEARCH FOR DISTANCE

The similarities between the golf balls of today and long ago begin and end with one simple fact: they are round. The materials are different on the inside and outside, and the manufacturing process is different, too.

Ball makers have worked just as feverishly in an attempt to perfect the ball as clubmakers have endeavored to create the perfect club, but their efforts aren't as noticeable because internal upgrades can't be seen; they can only be felt during play.

The balls used in the games that were forerunners to our present-day golf were often leather on the outside and tightly stuffed fur or feathers sewn shut on the inside. Some games had wooden balls. It is possible that the early Scots used the most circular pebbles or rocks they could find.

Golf balls in the 1500s and 1600s were brought to Scotland from Holland until the Scots were able to make balls of equal or better quality. The ball that historians place first in the progression of ball development is the feathery, which was the most popular ball until around 1850. The outside was made of cow and bull's hide pieces stitched together, with a small hole left for the ballmaker to stuff a top-hat sized portion of boiled goose feathers. He would continue stuffing to make the fit as tight as possible; the outside leather contracted when it dried and the inside feathers expanded, forming a surprisingly hard sphere. The process was not speedy: It took all day for a good ball maker to put together four to six balls, which was the main reason the balls were rather expensive—at one point three times the cost of a single club—and were not easy to keep in ready supply.

Besides the fact the ball didn't provide a great deal of distance for most players (one golfer was said to have hit a drive that measured 361 yards, however), the feathery was not all that durable. It could split open like a popped kernel of corn, especially in wet conditions. So because it was best for use in dry weather, it was not convenient to scheduling a game when a person's activities didn't correlate with weather conditions.

The next ball development was the gutta-percha, or guttie, in 1848. Gutta-percha is a tough plastic substance that resembles rubber and is made from tree sap. When heated in a mold, it formed a hard ball that stood up to usage much

The feathery was the precursor to today's modern golf balls.

better than the feathery. But there were two drawbacks. First, the ball was perfectly smooth, unlike the feathery, which had raised seams and stitches that gave a good trajectory to the ball. New gutties didn't get airborne as well, but, probably to the golfers' surprise, they flew better the more they were nicked up. Eventually, ballmakers made new molds that created indentations in the gutties from the start, and presto, golf balls had their first dimples. The second problem was that the guttie was causing havoc with the durability of the club, which, as discussed earlier, was the main reason clubs went from elongated pieces of wood ideal for hitting the feathery to shorter but wider pieces that weren't torn up by the stronger, more durable ball.

Most golfers and clubmakers embraced the switch to the guttie, but one holdout was St. Andrews' Allan Robertson, one of the most influential golf figures in the 1800s and an expert clubmaker. He did not endorse the guttie until much later, and, ironically, became one of Scotland's greatest players using it. Robertson stubbornly believed that nothing could improve upon what was already in use. Perhaps he feared he wouldn't continue to have the success against other players by using the guttie that he'd had with the feathery. Quite likely he felt that the cheaper gutta-percha ball would ruin his profit margins. Robertson resisted the newer ball so much that he gave caddies money to bring him any gutties they found so he could burn them. In the end, he relented and used the newer ball until his death in 1858.

The influential Alan Robertson resisted the gutta-percha ball at first but later relented.

In the 1870s, there was some experimentation with putting ground-up material such as metal and cork within the guttie, and one inventor even wrapped thin pieces of rubber around a small core of gutta-percha then put that core within another layer of gutta-percha, which was a forerunner to today's ball construction.

Around 1900, this type of ball became extremely popular and made the guttie obsolete just as the guttie had done to the feathery. Inventor Coburn Haskell of America wrapped thin rubber windings around a core ball, then encased it in gutta-percha. When expert players embraced the ball, the Haskell ball was a success, advertised as "an ideal combination of speed-flight and durability." Sandy Herd was one of the first players to use it in Britain and won the 1902 British Open with it.

Working off that basic construction, designers came up with the two types of balls we're familiar with today. The first is the three-piece, wound inner-core ball. Internally the ball has a liquid core encased in thin rubber, and rubber windings wrapped around the core. The outer layer is balata. The ball is extremely popular with better players who say they feel it better on the clubface, and that it is very workable for shaping shots. The balata cover is not a hard substance, so it can cut on mis-hit shots, but as that's not a problem of expert players, they use this ball more often than the other type.

The second design is a two-piece ball with a solid core wrapped with *Surlyn*, a much harder and cut-resistant material. This type of ball is known for going greater distances than the three piece, and along with its durability, it is a favorite of poorer players who need as much yardage as possible and who don't want to worry about ball damage.

These two types of balls have been adjusted and refined over the years in an attempt to make them attractive for all golfers, but the rule of thumb still is that good players use three-piece balls and poor players the two piece.

Types of balls: two-piece balls, and three-piece with liquid-and hard-core centers.

The primary design philosophy today that drives the ball market is customization. Companies tailor various ball lines to suit the skill levels of all players, from expert to novice, so that, as one company puts it, golfers "will optimize their individual games resulting in increased enjoyment round after round." They do this by tweaking the ball's design and construction here and there, making the wound core heavier or the core of a two-piece ball bigger or softer or winding the rubber-tension bands tighter on a three-piece ball.

In the mid-1990s, twists on the two- and three-piece balls were introduced. A modified version of the two-piece ball—the multilayer ball—came out that had the regular solid core but an additional layer under the cover. The design was intended for better players who wanted extra spin. A hybrid of the three-piece ball was the—surprise!—four-piece ball that also had two covers mainly for added durability. In 1997, one ball company even came out with what it called the world's first four-piece ball that has four distinct sections, two inner cores and two layers.

When a new ball design comes out, it is ballyhooed in advertisements for having different playing properties for different golfers. New materials, such as tungsten and titanium, get even bigger headlines to help the ball find a niche in the market. But sometimes what is new isn't really new at all. When titanium came out in a ball, not many consumers knew that a dioxide of titanium has been used in golf balls as a whitener since the 1930s.

Dimple designs haven't been ignored, either, over the years, although it's the internal construction that's more crucial. Ball companies have competed to have the highest number, the lowest number, and the most aerodynamic shapes, including octagon, teardrop, cone, and a combination of big and small circles. Balls need dimples to gain lift, because the rough surface counteracts the negative pressure exerted by the air. If the ball was completely smooth, a professional couldn't hit it more than 125 yards.

Balls have come a long way from the feathery, when a ball didn't have a lot of fancy marketing jargon attached to it. Now ball descriptions such as "a large solid core, covered with an elastic mantle layer with a soft urethane outer shell" are part of the choices, all for the cause of more distance, feel, and durability. If it sounds confusing, it's just one example of how diverse the ballmakers have become in trying to find a corner of the market. Professional golfer Lee Janzen described the situation best when he said: "Each ball out here has its own great characteristic. It's really up to the individual player as to what he's looking for in a ball. Someone who hits a low ball wants a ball with a lot of spin while somebody who hits it very high doesn't want a ball that spins a lot. Most balls have certain little things that make each of them different from the next."

Selecting the ball that is best for you is a matter of choice, trial and error, and seeing which one feels best for your type of swing for the type of clubs you use and the type of course conditions you play in most of the time.

PUTTERS: GOLF'S GREAT EQUALIZER

There are five basic stylings to putter shapes. The first is the blade, one of the most classic putters around and used by Ben Crenshaw, one of the finest putters of all time. The blade has a shaft attached to the hosel; the putterface appears, from a front view, to be shaped like the curved end of a table knife, with a protrusion out the back. This putter is best for golfers

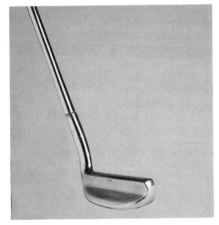

The blade putter is best for golfers who stroke, not jab, their putts.

who like to stroke the putt rather than strike it with a quick jab. The blade isn't very forgiving on mis-hits, so it's not for you if you have trouble hitting the sweet spot.

The second is the mallet, which has the appearance of a flattened metal wood driver-head that's square on one side. It provides a solid feel due to a lot of weight behind the face. The mallet, used by good putters such as Nick Price and Billy Casper, is harder to align the ball correctly than most putters, but the solid feel at impact should provide weak putters with a lot of confidence.

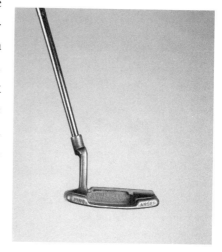

The Ping Anser: a classic example of a heel-and-toe balanced putter.

The third is the heel-and-toe balanced putter, favored by Tom Watson and Seve Ballesteros. The heel and toe is quite likely the most popular model today and the most successful putter design of the past thirty to forty years, made famous by the Karsten Company. The clubhead has a fairly wide bottom sole, but the "secret" is a cavity behind the middle portion of the head. Clubhead weight is greatest at the heel and toe so that if the ball is struck off center there is less twisting of the club-head and the ball's roll isn't as far off line. The heel and toe sits on the ground nicely and is easy to line up. The shaft and hosel connection is offset so the hands can be ahead of the ball at impact to keep the putter-face square.

The fourth is the center-shafted putter, most often seen in the Bulls Eye line and played by Tom Kite. The center-shafted model is the simplest looking putter of the bunch (and it's the most popular model you'll see at a miniature golf place, with red and green handles to boot). The shaft enters the club-head just short of the center of the blade, which is the thinnest of any putter model. The putter's sweet spot is nearly right at the point

The Bulls Eye putter is ideal for those who strike the sweet spot consistently.

The Schenectady was an early mallet-type putter.

where the shaft attaches to the head, so there is a solid feel when the ball is struck perfectly. The center-shafted model is a little like the blade in that mis-hit putts don't end up too well, so it's a great putter for the better player who strokes the ball consistently well. You will likely see this putter made in a soft-brass material for better feel.

The fifth putter is the long-handled, or broomhandle, variety, seen more frequently on the Senior PGA Tour, by a few regular tour players, and anyone else who struggles with the short putter because of bad putting or the yips, the condition whereby the golfer has nervous twitches with his hands and arms while putting. The long putter has an extra-long shaft, between four to five feet (even longer than the driver), which is meant to separate the hands and eliminate the yips. The long putter usually has a heel-and-toe style putterhead, and a fairly heavy head so the putter swings like a pendulum. To use it, a golfer stands more upright than normal, placing the butt end of the grip against the sternum, which is used as a fulcrum or anchoring point. The left hand goes on the grip at top and the right hand about halfway down the shaft. The putter is stroked like a pendulum, going straight back and through. This putter helps a golfer line up correctly since he stands tall and has his eyes directly or nearly over the ball. Because of the erect stance, the long putter puts less stress on the back than conventional putters.

When picking a putter make sure to scan every type. A player you like on tour may be using a mallet putter, but it might not be the right one for your game. Get a putter that looks good set up to the ball and is the best at helping your aim. To do the latter, most putters are made with a hash mark or directional line on the top of the putterhead.

If the putter looks good to you visually, make sure it feels right in your hands and isn't too light or heavy. (Most good players use a heavy putter rather than light for a better, solid feel.) Stroke putts with it and make sure the feel of the ball striking the putterface matches the visual image you have.

Most putters don't have perfectly straight clubfaces. There are usually a few degrees of loft, just enough to get the ball rolling with little ground resistance.

While it is important to experiment with different putters, don't make it a search for the Holy Grail. Too much messing around can make you more confused than you were at the start. Putting is a what-feels-right process and very individual. There's a putter out there with your name on it, in plain view. And it doesn't have to cost you a couple hundred dollars. There are economically priced models that will get the job done just as well as the luxury models.

SPECIAL WEAPONS FOR SPECIAL JOBS

Your golf set has the basic configuration if it has a driver, 3-wood, 4-wood, plus the 3-iron through pitching wedge and sand wedge. When you add a putter, you've reached thirteen of the fourteen-club limit allowed by the rules.

That leaves one more club to add in, and it certainly is an important choice. You could add a 2-iron or a 1-iron for precise driving on narrow holes. You could add another wedge—a lob wedge—for shots around the greens. Or you could add a club that is specially designed to alleviate a gap in your game, whatever that might be. This latter group of clubs is known as specialty or utility clubs. Their sole purpose is to help your game under certain weather or course conditions, or simply make you a more complete player, as a 1- or 2-iron might do.

Special Clubs to Choose

The rules say you can have no more than fourteen clubs, but golfers should have sixteen to twenty clubs they select from depending upon their need for each round. Here are some of the special clubs from which to pick:

The trouble wood   Here is one of the more well-used utility clubs around because of its ability to help poor players escape from high grass. Trouble woods usually have the loft of a 4- or 5-wood, but their special feature is a set of rails or concave sole that have less drag out of tall grass and a low center of gravity for solid contact. The rails, in particular, help the clubhead be less affected by grass. The clubhead doesn't lose as much speed or is misdirected. The trouble wood is ideal for any golfer who wants a club that gets the ball out of rough and advances it decently down the fairway.

The chipper   Here's another well-known club, but it often doesn't get the respect it deserves. The chipper has a clubhead about the size of a putter but the face has the loft of a 6- or 7-iron. Since most low-handicap players think of the chipper as below their talent ability, having one in the bag could set up a player for ridicule. But critics overlook the fact that the chipper is quite effective as a club for shots around the fringe, little chip shots that need to run low like a putt. Since it doesn't get the ball up very high, the chipper can't be used as a pitching club or from high grass, but as a club to hit off the fringe it can't be beat. It takes a short, putting-stroke-type swing.

The 1-iron   Also known as a driving iron, the 1-iron looks almost impossible to hit for the high handicapper. And, actually, it's not a club that poor players or anyone who doesn't have a fast swing speed should use. But medium to low handicappers could find success with it. Because there is little loft, the 1-iron is difficult to get airborne. It's almost exclusively a club for hitting off a tee when fairways are narrow. If hit correctly, the ball bores through the air like a line drive and gives the player adequate roll. And the shot doesn't curve much because few people can hit it hard enough to cause any spin, so it's pretty much a straight shooter. If your course is flat and dry, the 1-iron is useful. Don't put it in the bag if the course is hilly and often wet.

The lob wedge   This is one of the utility clubs that's made a big impact in recent years. It's also been called the trouble wedge or the gap wedge. It's a gap wedge because its loft—60 degrees or more—helps fill in a hole for the clubs needed to hit shots of 40 yards or less. Some golfers have found that having a regular pitching wedge with its 50-degree loft wasn't enough. The lob wedge gets the ball up quicker and higher, and makes the ball stop faster. It's a great club at courses with elevated greens, bunkers that are up close to the greens, and/or hard greens. Although it sounds like a club best utilized by high handicappers, it's hard for them to use it because the swing must be precise and they're better off using a regular short iron to make sure they get the ball on the green. But because the lob wedge can be swung with a full swing from 40 yards or closer, the player who gets in plenty of practice with it will reap great benefits.

The high-lofted fairway wood   It's not well known, but iron clubs have a corresponding partner club on the wood side. For instance, the 1-, 2-, 3-, 4-, and 5-irons could be replaced by the 3-, 4-, 5-, 7-, and 9-woods, respectively. The advantage of going the wood route is that the woods have lower centers of gravity, meaning they get under the ball better and get the ball up in the air better than irons. The ball lands softer and the wood cuts through higher grass better, all good advantages for the poor player. The woods are only worth going to, however, if you can't hit the irons very well. Senior and women players might find it worth going to the wood clubs no matter what. One disadvantage is that the wood clubs are poor ones to use in the wind.

> "Learn the fundamentals thoroughly at the start, a far simpler procedure than trying to eliminate habitual errors later."
>
> BABE ZAHARIAS

The heavy, high-lofted putter   Today's putters have around 5 degrees of loft, not much but just right for quick, manicured greens. If you play courses with shaggy greens that are slow and bumpy, or even on Bermuda greens, a putter with about 11 degrees of loft would be a good alternative. The extra loft gets the ball up in the air enough that it can roll on the taller grass and not be affected as much. Heavy putters also help on bumpy greens because they make the ball move on line with more punch than what a lighter putter would do.

The 2-wood   This club was known as the brassie back in the wooden-shaft days, and during much of the 1900s it's been a forgotten club as the driver was used almost exclusively off the tee. The 2-wood has 12 to 14 degrees of loft, a few degrees more than the usual driver. The extra loft helps the ball get up, which gives the high handicapper more confidence. Because the ball travels nearly the same distance as a driver, the 2-wood is useful for players who want a little more directional control off the tee, such as on narrow golf courses. The club can even be used off the fairway if the ball is sitting up.

MAKING SENSE OF THE OPTIONS

With nearly 400 iron lines to choose from and another 400 putter options available to the buyer, how can anyone make sense of the market? It's not impossible, as the buyers of 13 million irons, 6.5 million woods, and 2 million putters a year worth $3.6 billion can attest. The average golf club buyer gets a new set of irons every four years, a new wood every ten months, and a new putter every two years. How you make a decision comes down to four sources of information: books, magazines, and manufacturer literature; friends and fellow golfers who are astute about the latest market developments; a club expert located at a golf shop or off-course store; and feedback from your own club testing.

When conducting a search for the right clubs, make sure you gather details from more than one source. First, ask friends you know who have the necessary smarts and tell them where you stand as a golfer. A beginner doesn't need the best and most high-tech stuff available until she has played a few years and become capable of playing a good game. A nice, well-built set that will stand up under play for a few years will do.

Before getting really good equipment, you could still make one more move up to a medium-quality set until you're a middle handicapper or better, which would be up to a 15 or 18 handicap.

After a friend has given you an opinion on what kind of equipment to get, look through an equipment book and study advertisements. Be careful, however, with company claims and ad gimmicks. Some equipment makers get a little loose with promising too much and you won't know you got the wrong product until it's too late.

Once you feel fairly informed, make a visit to a local golf shop at the public course and also to an off-course discount store. See what they have to say about what you're looking for and make notes of how it checks out with what you've already been told and read. Be careful of places that too easily agree with what you say and don't take a solid interest in your situation. It's a good sign they're too anxious to make a sale and don't really have your best interests in mind.

In doing your research work, it will be helpful to know a few terms you're likely to come across. Here are the important ones:

Lie angle   Take a club and set it on a tabletop in front of you as it would be soled if you were in the address position. With the sole flat on the table, notice the angle of the shaft. Lie angle is the direction the shaft comes out of the clubhead. This angle is not the same in every set of clubs in the golf shop. Some clubs have upright angles, some are flat and others are in the middle range.

The correct lie angle for you is the one that has the club sitting squarely on the sole as you stand in the address position. If the toe of the club is raised off the ground, then the angle is too upright and the ball will fly left of the target. If the heel is raised, then the angle is too flat and the ball flies right of the target.

The lie angle has a great effect on accuracy if it's not correct, even if you make a textbook swing. A correct lie angle allows the clubface to make square contact; the wrong lie angle tilts the face approaching impact. If your divots dig in unevenly, it could indicate a lie angle problem. Also, you can do a test at home if you're not sure the lie angle is correct. Just take a 2-foot-square piece of plywood or old countertop and lay it on the grass. Put a strip of black electrical tape on the bottom of your 5-iron. Now make a swing so that the bottom of the club strikes along the wood, just as the club would hit the grass if you were swinging at a ball. Then look at the bottom of the club. If the tape has been nicked toward the toe, the angle is too flat; if toward the heel, the angle is too upright; and if in the center, the lie angle is fine.

Incorrect lie angle is no big deal when you're trying out a set. Either find a set that has the type of club you seek, or have the seller alter the set before you take it home. If you have an existing set that needs fixing, it's not financially smart to do it yourself because a loft-and-lie machine costs several hundred dollars. A professional club repairperson can make the adjustments for you at a much lesser cost. He'll bend the clubhead at the hosel; some clubs, however, depending on the metal hardness, may not be fixable.

Although there are not many things considered standard in the equipment business today, here are the standard lie specifications.

MEN'S			
Club	Flat	Standard	Upright
1-wood	53	55	57
3-wood	54	56	58
5-wood	55	57	59
7-wood	56	58	60
1-iron	54	56	58

MEN'S			
Club	Flat	Standard	Upright
2-iron	55	57	59
3-iron	56	58	60
4-iron	57	59	61
5-iron	58	60	62
6-iron	59	61	63
7-iron	60	62	64
8-iron	61	63	65
9-iron	62	64	66
PW	62	64	66
SW	62	64	66
LW	62	64	66

WOMEN'S			
Club	Flat	Standard	Upright
1-wood	51	53	55
3-wood	52	54	56
5-wood	53	55	57
7-wood	54	56	58
2-iron	53	55	57
3-iron	54	56	58
4-iron	55	57	59
5-iron	56	58	60
6-iron	57	59	61
7-iron	58	60	62
8-iron	59	61	63

WOMEN'S			
Club	Flat	Standard	Upright
9-iron	60	62	64
PW	60	62	64
SW	60	62	64
LW	60	62	64

Loft   The loft of a clubface is the amount, in degrees, that the face is angled backward from the leading edge or sole to the top edge. Loft controls the trajectory and height a ball travels after impact. Golf is certainly challenging enough without the golfer limiting himself to the number of clubs he plays. If there were only one loft for a golf club, there would be only one type of ball flight. If it were a low flight, it would be fine for making the ball go long distances. But it would be horrendous in playing shots from close to the green.

Loft lets the golfer use a variety of clubs to hit the ball the proper distance yet give it the right amount of height to make it land softly and stay on the green. For instance, a 100-yard shot requires a short-iron club and a 200-yard shot a long-iron club.

The clubs with the greatest loft are the short irons, meaning they hit the ball the highest and shortest. The least-lofted clubs are the long irons and woods, which make the ball go the lowest and farthest. The less loft in a club, the more the ball will roll.

The primary concern for average golfers is not that they have certain lofts in their clubs, but that they know how far they hit the ball with each club. There is no use comparing how far an amateur hits his 5-iron, for instance, with the 5-iron of a professional since the pro has most likely put stronger lofts in his bag.

In essence, his 5-iron may play more like a 6- or 7-iron. Using normal lofts, a pro would hit a 5-iron much farther than an amateur anyway, so it's best for the weaker player to play his own game and not compare how lacking he might be in terms of distance.

What were standard lofts of the last thirty to forty years have been tampered with by club companies as part of their marketing and design efforts. For instance, you might see a 6-iron today at 32 degrees of loft instead of the standard 36. When this happens, the club has been made "strong" so that it hits the ball longer than a normal 6-iron. If the loft went the other way, which is highly unlikely, the club would be "weak."

The following are standard lofts, in degrees, but not necessarily lofts followed by every manufacturer today.

LOFTS		
Club	Men's	Women's
1-wood	11	12
2-wood	13	14
3-wood	16	17
4-wood	19	20
5-wood	22	23
6-wood	25	26
7-wood	28	29
1-iron	17	--
2-iron	20	21
3-iron	24	25
4-iron	28	29
5-iron	32	33
6-iron	36	37
7-iron	40	41
8-iron	44	45
9-iron	48	49
PW	52	53
SW	56	57
LW	60	61

Length The length of a club isn't measured from the end of the grip to the toe of the clubhead but rather the length of the shaft from grip end to the sole. And like loft and lie, the standard measurements that were once written in stone for length have been changed in recent years.

As an example, take a men's driver. In a standard set off the rack, driver length was 43 inches. Today, since it is well known by club companies that extra length means more distance, the standard has become 45 inches for most companies. They've been able to add length because newer materials like titanium have made the clubhead lighter, thus the extra weight can go in the shaft. Likewise, a woman's driver had a standard length of 42 inches, but many professional women golfers have also gone to drivers of 45 inches.

Most golfers can get by with clubs manufactured to standard specs. A golfer's height is not the major factor in how long his clubs should be. Arm length should be, measuring how far the hands are from the ground. A short player with long arms could use the same length in her clubs as a taller person with short arms.

If your clubs are the wrong length, it's a major swing concern. If the clubs are too short, you'll bend over too much and swing too upright. Long clubs cause a flat swing and make it difficult to make square contact at impact.

Here are the standard lengths for men's and women's clubs in inches. You might find that clubs you're planning to buy today are a quarter-inch longer throughout the set.

LENGTHS		
Club	Men's	Women's
1-wood	43	42
2-wood	42.5	41.5
3-wood	42	41
4-wood	41.5	40.5
5-wood	41	40
6-wood	40.5	39.5
7-wood	40	39
1-iron	39.5	–
2-iron	39	38

LENGTHS		
Club	Men's	Women's
3-iron	38.5	37.5
4-iron	38	37
5-iron	37.5	36.5
6-iron	37	36
7-iron	36.5	35.5
8-iron	36	35
9-iron	35.5	34.5
PW	35.5	34.5
SW	35.5	34.5
LW	35.5	34.5

Matched set If you examined the set makeup in most golfers' bags, you'd see a hodgepodge of different styles. Excluding the putter, you'd see a driver from one company, a fairway wood from another, and probably a lob wedge or two from still another. The irons would be from yet a different company.

However, this could still be a matched set, the reason being the golfer feels each club is compatible with the other. What makes a matched set is the consistency in grip size, a half-inch or so height progression from one club to the next, similar shafts, similar swing weights, and lie angles that are properly soled for each club.

When clubs are matched within a set, there is no need to adjust body posture for each club. As the clubs get shorter, your body gets closer to the ball and your swing is more upright. The taller the club, the further you stand away from the ball and the flatter the swing.

Grooves These are the markings on the clubface, seen as a series of hash marks, punch dots, and, of course, the familiar long, horizontal groove that is the traditional marking on iron clubfaces today and has been the standard for most of the 1900s.

The groove basically serves one purpose: It allows the clubface to grab onto the ball at impact and send it forward, and if the ball is struck perfectly well, it helps apply backspin to the ball to make it stop closer to the hole. The USGA, which governs the making of equipment, specifies that grooves can have a maximum depth of .020 inches, a maximum width of .035 inches and .075 inches of space between each groove. The groove itself can have a V shape or a U shape, and manufacturers sometimes make products that give the player a choice between the two.

The U groove is preferred by golfers who want to put a lot of backspin on the ball, or for use only in short irons because those clubs are used for shots of 100 yards or less around greens when stopping power is necessary. V grooves are better for longer clubs because, in most cases, it's not necessary to stop the ball as quickly.

One of the biggest equipment controversies in golf history took place in the 1980s when the Karsten Manufacturing Company pioneered work in the U-groove area with its Ping Eye2 brand of irons. The first Ping Eye2 design with U grooves was refined because the edges were too sharp and damaged the ball. But when the edges were rounded, the USGA ruled the clubs were illegal because the grooves were too close together and the players using them would have an unfair advantage in backspin control.

The disagreement was settled after many years of debate among Karsten, the USGA, the PGA Tour and the

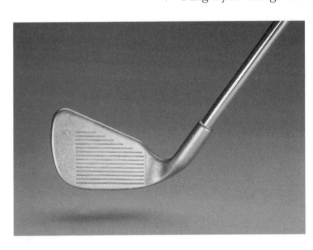

The grooves of the Ping Eye2 irons created one of the biggest equipment disputes in golf history.

Royal and Ancient Golf Club. Karsten redesigned the irons, but it was agreed the previously made clubs could still be used.

Some companies believe that grooves don't make a great deal of difference on clean hits. Where everyone agrees grooves play an important role is when moisture, grass, dirt, and sand get in the way. There is such a strong force at impact that when any of these objects get in the way they are smashed, but their presence on the clubface takes away the amount of backspin on the ball. The smashed material finds an escape within the groove canals, and the groove is partly able to get its job done. Since the U-shaped groove has more space for this debris to go than the V shaped, it is usually thought of as the type of groove to use if you want to have a lot of backspin.

Because grooves get filled up during play, golfers are smart to make sure their grooves are free of any residue for each shot; if the grooves are clogged, the clubface, in essence, is smooth and doesn't have gripping power over the ball, an especially troublesome problem with the short irons. A sharp tee, small wire brush or another type of groove cleaner should be available to the golfer to get the clubface in proper shape. Another groove maintenance concern golfers should monitor is that grooves, after a couple of seasons of heavy play, can become less effective by the edges wearing down. Some companies offer services that regroove the clubs and put them back in good working order.

One of the bigger developments in groove markings in the mid-1990s is the look of metal woods. Clubmakers have eliminated grooves altogether in some cases, made others shallower and thinner, and for others arranged a series of dots and dashes in Morse-code style. Besides causing an aesthetically good-looking change to occur, the groove designs, companies say, help playability.

Previous metal-wood groove designs spun the ball at approximately 3,700 revolutions per minute at impact, which helped the ball become airborne quickly, but it also dropped quickly from the apex of its flight. The newer type grooves lowered the RPM rate to 2,800 and even 2,200 for woods without any grooves at all. This gives the ball better trajectory and more roll after landing. Of course, some club experts downplay the effect of grooves in this type of design on a metal wood and say the spin rate is primarily affected by the center of gravity and the amount of loft on a clubface, not the grooves. The companies making these groove changes admit that part of their reason for changing groove patterns is to attract attention in the golf shop and make their product stand out more.

Swing weight   This term, specified in figures such as C-8 and D-4, isn't easily explained and is probably an overemphasized measure. As described by club repair expert Ralph Maltby, swing weight is "the measurement of a golf club's weight distribution about a fulcrum point which is established at a specified distance from the grip end of the club." That doesn't completely clear up the mystery, but the process of determining swing weight is done by a scale at a clubmaker's shop, so you don't need to know how to find the reading.

What swing weight means to you is that its range of numbers specify how heavy a club feels in the clubhead as you hold it at the grip end. Think of it as a golf club's weight distribution. A rating of C-4 and C-6 is a good swing weight for women, not too light or too heavy. For men, something around D-0 or D-2 is fine, particularly in irons, but none of these numbers is set in stone. Don't be confused about one thing: Swing weight is not a club's overall weight, which is usually 13 ounces for a wood to 16 ounces for an iron.

Shafts   From the wood of the pre-1930s to the steel, graphite, and titanium of today, the shaft material used has always been what the clubmakers of the day felt was best and most useful. Today we know the shaft does a variety of things during the swing, and that's the reason the shaft is the source of a lot of confusion when buyers search the club market. As the club is swung, the shaft bends from side to side and from front to back, and there are torque and vibration factors, too. There are weak shafts, stiff shafts, medium shafts, and extra stiff shafts.

The purpose of the shaft is twofold: It is like a lightning rod as it carries the energy and force of the swing down to the ball at impact, and it also sends back to the golfer the feel of how the clubface and ball came together at impact. It must do this on a consistent basis for every golf shot, not only with one club but also with every full-swing club, so that the feel of hitting your 3-iron is the same as hitting the 8-iron. This consistent feel throughout the set is what makes it a matched set because elements of the set such as shaft material and swing weight are the same for each club. The golfer learns one swing to use with a variety of clubs, rather than learning to swing differently with each club.

During the backswing and start of the downswing, the movement of the club-head and its weight store energy in the shaft and make the shaft bend. Ideally, the shaft should be just still enough that when contact is made with the ball, the shaft has recovered and is relatively straight. This ensures that the energy has been released at the proper time and that the club-face is square to the ball for straight shots. A shaft that is not at the correct stiffness can cause off-line shots and doesn't allow the proper release of power.

To help the golfer hit the ball different distances, not only do the lofts of the clubhead have to be different but the lengths of the shafts also have to be different in a corresponding fashion. The longest shafts are attached to the lightest and/or smallest heads. The shortest shafts are attached to the heaviest clubheads. In this way the feel of each club can more closely resemble each other. One of the ways shaftmakers accomplish this is by making the shafts stiffer as the clubhead weight increases.

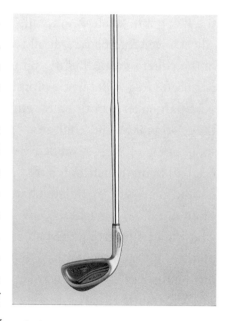

The hump shaft is intended to provide control and stability.

Shafts are labeled according to their flexibility, or simply flex, and the amount of flex a golfer uses is closely tied to how fast she swings the club. The extra stiff shaft (X) is for strong golfers who swing the club with a lot of speed; the extra stiffness prevents excessive bending. A stiff shaft (S) is best for the next speed, the regular shaft (R or T) for most amateurs who don't have a lot of swing speed, flexible (A) is useful for older players, and the most flexible designation is L for a women's shaft. Manufacturers deviate from those flexes to some extent to refine the feel of a club, but keep them as their primary groups. Through the weight of the shaft, the shaft diameter, and the thickness of the shaft wall, the shaftmaker can control how flexible the shaft will be.

The shaft is matched to a player in taking into account three shaft characteristics: flexibility, flex distribution, and weight. As mentioned, flexibility indicates how much the shaft will bend during the swing. Manufacturers measure flex using a flex board. The grip end of the shaft is clamped in a horizontal position, a seven-pound weight is hung from the tip, and the deflection is measured in inches. The flex distribution, or flex point, is the point on the shaft where the greatest bending takes place. A close look at a shaft will show steps or positions on the shaft where the shaft decreases in diameter. The arrangement of these steps dictates the flex point. Shaft weight falls into 3-, 4-, and 5-ounce categories. It is generally believed that players should use a shaft as light as possible that fits the tempo of the golfer's swing. Lightweight shafts do allow for faster swing speeds, but are not useful to a golfer who swings slowly.

Shaftmakers continually refine shaft construction so that, like the golf ball, they can build shafts that are conducive to the golfer's ability and desired shot style. Some of these modifications include shafts with a high flex point to send the ball flying lower and more controlled with better backspin, for use by low-handicap players; extralight shafts to increase clubhead speed and thus achieve more distance; a low flex point shaft for middle handicappers or poorer players who want help getting the ball airborne; a middle flex point shaft for use by any player wanting a regular ball flight; and a light shaft with middle flex point for hitting the ball at a regular trajectory and using a faster clubhead speed.

Whether the shaft is made of a high-alloy steel, graphite, titanium, or some other composite, golfers must consider the shaft's amount of bending, resistance to twisting, weight, and toughness. If a shaft twists during the downswing, an off-center hit will only serve to increase the amount of twist and the wildness of the shot.

In the 1990s, shaftmakers looked to the shape of the shaft as their next frontier. The Bubble Shaft was the first creation. The grip looked to have normal width, but just under the grip was a bulge that then narrowed down as usual to the hosel. The maker had taken 10 percent of the weight at the grip end and moved it to the middle of the shaft. That weight transfer was designed to let the golfer swing the club faster without swinging any harder. And increased club speed means more distance.

Other shaft innovations include the "hump shaft," which has a hump located near the hosel, a design the manufacturer says gives the golfer more stability and control. That's also what is helpful about the "fat shaft," which is just what it sounds like. It's a wider shaft that

The bubble shaft opened the door to other deviations from the traditional shaft shape.

prevents the clubhead from twisting at impact. There's also been a "flare shaft" and a "rifle shaft" for more stability and less vibration at impact.

Another recent shaft trend has been devices within the shaft that eliminate or reduce the vibration caused at impact. The devices don't make your swing any better in the sense of returning the clubface squarely to the ball, but shaft-makers point toward the extra feel the device provides.

Torque   This is the imperceptible twisting the clubhead and shaft do prior to impact. Clubs are designed with special features to limit the amount of torque so the clubface is less likely to be misaligned at impact.

Shaft frequency   This is the rate at which a shaft vibrates when the butt end is put in a clamp and the tip is bent down and released. The vibrations are measured in cycles per minute. The more CPMs there are, the stiffer the shaft.

Swing speed   Swing speed is the speed of the club at impact, not just the speed of the swing from start to finish. Good players have swing speeds of 90 miles per hour or more. Professionals surpass 100 MPH.

CUSTOM CLUBS: THE PERSONAL TOUCH

Chances are you can find a set of clubs at a golf shop or discount store that will fit your game and physical shape. But you should be aware of the growing number of companies that offer some kind of custom club fitting service and trained personnel who can fit you for the proper loft, shaft, offset, grips, lie, and club length for your game. It's the perfect joining of golfer and club.

The custom process is not just done for woods and irons, either. Putters are also being personalized with special systems put together by putter companies.

The great thing about custom clubs is that you're paying for clubs that you know fit your style and game. There's less chance of a bad fit. Different clubhead designs are made for different handicaps.

It's always hard to know whether it's you or the clubs that cause the ball to fly all over the place. However, if an instructor believes your swing is in good shape, then it's time to customize your clubs. They're not the right ones for you. You can tell, for instance, the clubs are a bad match if you're always hitting the ball off the heel. That's a sign the shafts are probably too long. If you're always off the toe, the shafts are too short. Or if you have a favorite club like a 5- or 7-iron that you always hit well, and you struggle with the others, you should have your clubs checked and matched with the club you hit well. There's a chance the other clubs aren't jiving with the favorite club.

The time-honored source for the best custom clubs, of course, is a local clubmaker or club repairperson. You schedule an appointment with a club maker just as you would with a golf teacher for a lesson. (Contacting the Professional Clubmakers Society in Louisville, Kentucky, at (502) 241-2816 or 1-800-548-6094, can help you locate a good clubmaker.)

To start, a clubmaker measures a player's hand strength and size and the distance from the ground to the golfer's hand at address and while standing straight. The next step is telling the clubmaker your shot shape, goals, physical limitations, and other player profile details. The clubmaker then measures the player's existing clubs to see how much they've been affecting the player.

The process continues with dynamic fitting in which the club maker observes the golfer hit balls and checks for swing speed and uses other instruments to determine the effectivenes of the player's swing. That's followed by impact tests to see where the player is striking the ball on the clubface and on the sole to determine the correct lie angle.

The final step is trying demo clubs the clubmaker has on hand with different shafts, sizes, and clubheads. Finally, the player is told if the present set needs to be modified, a completely new set is needed, the set needs to be rebuilt, or the present set is fine but the golfer needs more work on his swing. The last option provides great relief, indeed.

WHERE TO SHOP

For hundreds of years, the one place to buy golf equipment was the golf shop located at a golf club or course. The clubmaker, professional, or instructor was in charge of managing the shop, being sure to order all the necessary supplies and keeping inventory full. In the very early years, the clubmaker and ballmaker were on site, making the equipment and putting it on display for purchase or specific orders.

As clubmakers became a rarer breed in the late 1800s and early 1900s, the golf professional was still in charge of the golf shop, bringing in products from the big manufacturers. This was the setup at both public and private courses.

Golfers knew that if they needed anything for their game, be it balls, clubs, tees, or bags, they could find it at the golf course.

For a faithful group of golfers today, the on-course golf shop is still the place to go. For them, the course golf shop is the traditional equipment source and they won't entertain thoughts of going elsewhere. Loyalty is even stronger at private country clubs, where the clientele believe their golf shop is a special privilege of their membership dues and they're not about to lose it. So they are willing to pay for merchandise there that isn't close to being competitively priced with other golf stores. But golf buying is all relative, and equipment manufacturers know that golfers will pay for anything that they can afford. A $1,000 driver is not a huge price to pay at a private club, whereas a public course golfer would probably prefer to do a lot of bargain shopping.

Since the 1960s, one of the economical, alternative locations has grown in popularity and leaped past the on-course golf shops as the equipment source. Discount, off-course stores have taken over, most notably Nevada Bob's, Las Vegas Discount, and Edwin Watts Golf Shops. These stores are located in shopping malls and main drags away from the course. They also offer their products through detailed, catalog-style advertisements in major publications, listing toll-free numbers for ordering by phone. As of 1997, 60 percent of all golf merchandise was bought at discount retailers, as was 85 percent of all hard goods, such as clubs and balls.

Even though determining where to shop has caused turmoil with golfers who want to support the place they play the game, they know that because of financial concerns they have to utilize the lower prices at off-course stores. The public golfer doesn't have much choice but to see how much he can save at the discount store. Actually, the battle between loyalty to golf shops and low prices did cause a good change in the way golf shops do business, forcing them to spruce up their decor, plan better displays, compete on pricing, improve customer service, and pay attention to trends in the industry. Off-course outlets, too, have had to change. Known early on for untrained workers who knew little about golf, discount stores now work to ensure their employees have the latest information in product news, are smart about the business, and can properly fit and talk to a customer about clubs. The stores also upgraded their facilities for golfers to test equipment on-site rather than buying without having hit a ball.

Some manufacturers entered the fray, declining to sell to the discount stores and working only with green-grass shops. In the early days of the dispute, the off-course stores had their products sent to nearby golf courses for pickup before fulfilling orders. A ruling in 1977 said companies were violating the law with this practice and from that point the shipping and fulfilling of orders was more open. In the past five to ten years, harmony has existed among on- and off-course outlets and the manufacturers after many years of battling for consumer dollars. Green-grass professionals and off-course retailers are working together on inventories and buying so they can coexist and make money. Manufacturers are working with both sides in supplying product, although the on-course shop still has the edge when it comes to apparel lines, getting the newest and most exclusive.

The Edwin Watts stores, headquartered in Fort Walton Beach, Florida, and numbering more than thirty-five, is the major player in off-course business today, with more golf retail square footage than any other outfit in golf. A typical store not only has plenty of clubs, balls, bags, apparel, and other accessories but also clubfitters, a teaching area that can be used for testing clubs, a putting area to try putters, and an entertainment area.

Some of the newer discount chains are Grand Central, Golf Day, Golfsmith, Pro Golf Discount, Back Nine Golf, and Golf USA. About the change in the off-course store market, Editor Ken Cohen of *Golf Retailer* wrote: "It used to be an off-course store was a Nevada Bob's, Edwin Watts, or a mom-and-pop repair shop. Today's off-course stores include sporting goods superstores, department stores, golf superstores, and mail-order catalogs. They're getting bigger, better, and more comprehensive. Large hitting areas, putting greens, apparel sections, even snack areas are now part of many new off-course stores."

Whether purchasing from a discount store or an on-course golf shop, the customer should make sure of a few things in getting equipment. Specifically, ask a salesperson to be waited on by the best clubfitter in the shop. There's no sense in entrusting your money to someone who is unsure of him or herself. Get that person's opinion about the kind of clubs and balls you should use. Make sure to give them a little bit of your playing history and details about the kinds of clubs you may be using presently. When they tell you the kind of clubs you should get, question them again by asking how the clubs will benefit you and why this set is the best for you.

Establish pretty early how much you're willing to spend on clubs so you're on the same wavelength and don't get led down the wrong path. A beginning golfer should not get talked into buying a full, expensive set. The best way to start is with clubs that get the ball in the air—clubs with plenty of loft. That would mean a set with the 5-iron to short irons and the 3-, 4-, and 5-woods.

Don't overlook the possibility of getting a used set of clubs at first. Remember, you're just learning the game. It makes perfect sense to beat up a set of old clubs while you practice rather than get a top-of-the-line set that won't last very long.

A note about buying balls for the first-time player: Don't put your money into the expensive stuff yet. Make your first ball purchase be X'd-out balls (factory blemished) or balls reclaimed from water hazards (water balls). You'll pump a lot of money down the drain if you buy the good stuff but haven't yet learned to keep the ball in play.

When you do get ready to invest in better quality balls, ask yourself if you want a distance ball or one that offers you feel and improved spin for control. You can get low-, medium-, or high-spin balls. Low spin provides extra distance and curves less, the high spin is for good players who want to work the ball and make it stop quickly.

> "It is not solely the capacity to make great shots that makes champions, but the essential quality of making very few bad shots."
>
> TOMMY ARMOUR

THINGS TO DO AFTER YOUR CLUB PURCHASE

Presumably you tested your new clubs at the golf shop to make sure you're a compatible couple. But there are still some things to do after the purchase to help make the clubs feel comfortable and familiar to you sooner rather than later.

First, make sure you get plenty of practice with the sand wedge from the bunkers. The new chrome reacts differently than chrome that's been scuffed up a little. Hit a few dozen bunker shots and you'll have it broken in right.

Second, find out as soon as possible how far you hit each club. If you've switched to a new set, you're not likely to be hitting the ball the same distances. If you can, hit balls at an open field and walk off the yardages as best you can or go to a driving range that has legitimate yardage markers. You can also walk off yardages during your first round with the clubs.

And third, because clubs are built better these days, don't always expect the same club to perform the same purpose for you. For instance, you might be able to use a new 3-wood from a lie for which you always went straight to your old utility wood before.

TRICKS OF THE TRADE

It's not unusual that the right set of clubs is just sitting on the shelf waiting for you. "Standard" clubs are the most-stocked clubs in a golf store, and they're standard for a reason: Most players have the same needs, although some are different in size and shape.

There are many subtle changes or tricks of the trade that can positively affect the way clubs work for you. Here are a selected few:

Forged Versus Investment Cast

Forged irons, made by hand in a time-consuming process, were the irons of choice for most of the 1900s. Craftspersons actually hammered and shaped the steel into beautiful iron heads. The best response came from hitting the ball in the center, the precise sweet spot. Investment cast clubs came along in the 1960s, opening a major avenue for the poorer player. The club is produced with a cavity in the back, which allows for weighting to go around the back perimeter of the clubhead, known as perimeter weighting. That weight distribution means that balls hit off-center aren't affected as much as they would be with cast clubs. The investment-cast club has been tagged a game improvement club, and it's an accurate label. Poor players would be smart to use the investment-cast irons to enjoy the game more. Better players who hit the center of the face more often than not are the best candidates for forged irons.

Grip Size

The correct grip for you is one that, when the left hand is wrapped around the butt end, the middle fingers don't hit into the thumb pad too deeply. Going too big or too small may be of help, however. A large grip doesn't allow for regular wrist action, so it would help a person fighting a hook. A slicer could benefit from a thinner grip. A club repairperson ought to be able to help increase or reduce your present grip sizes.

Shaft Flex

Too many players give themselves extra credit for their capabilities and use shafts that are too stiff. Stiff shafts are for players with fast swing speeds or who can hit the ball 220 to 240 yards. Beyond that, the player should use extra stiff. Most golfers would benefit from a regular shaft, which is best for 175- to 220-yard hitters.

Shaft Length

This has been a prominent club adjustment in recent years as golfers have found increasing the shaft length increases the swing arc, and the wider the arc the more distance the ball travels. The trade-off is less accuracy and an increased chance for mis-hits.

Persimmon Driver Versus Metal

The beautiful persimmon driver is in such short demand that it is nearly absent from company offerings, having started a slow decline in the late 1980s. Metal woods are still the best club for poor players because they reduce the effects of off-center hits. But the extra spin a wooden wood puts on the ball can be a key in controlling ball flight and helping the golfer hit fades and draws. Consider the persimmon when you get to a low- or middle-handicap level. The persimmon driver might also be attractive for its much lower cost than a high-tech metal driver.

Is Titanium Worth the Cost?

It isn't if you always hit the ball on the center of the clubface. But if you're inaccurate, then titanium is a confidence booster because your mis-hits won't be as far short or off-line as they could be. Titanium's lightness and hardness lets companies make bigger clubheads, thereby increasing both the sweet spot and the margin for error. Titanium shafts are also lighter and contribute to the added inches in length and less overall weight. A longer club with the same or less weight of an older driver can result in increased distance because of greater swing speed.

How Long Should my Driver Be?

As each year goes by, advances in equipment technology make it necessary to consider a move to high-tech clubs, in particular the driver. The standard 43-inch driver of not too many years ago has been replaced by 45- and 46-inch versions. These extra inches increase the length of the swing radius. And when you increase the length of the swing lever—the swing arc—you increase the distance the ball travels. The longer club can be swung faster than a shorter club, but only if it is, at impact, rotating around your swing axis at the same rate. Common thinking nowadays says that 45 inches is a good limit because anything beyond that becomes too hard to control.

What's the Best Sand Wedge?

The sand wedge is one of the few clubs you can adapt to the kind of terrain you play. Make sure you get one with 53 to 56 degrees of loft. Then notice how much bounce the club has. Bounce is the distance between the leading edge of the club and the lowest point on the sole. If you look at a profile of your sand wedge and compare it with the pitching wedge, you'll see what bounce looks like. Bounce prevents the sand wedge from digging into the sand, as the pitching wedge would, rather than sliding under the ball as desired. If the sand at your course is soft, use a wedge with more bounce, or if it's hard, use less. Also, a wide flange (width of the sole) is best for soft sand, a narrow flange for hard. And use a dull leading edge for soft sand and sharper edge for hard. For comparison purposes, 12 to 15 degrees of bounce is considered a lot.

THE VERSATILE GOLF BAG

Consider the bag as a mobile locker and medicine chest all in one. It's not just a holder to transport your clubs around the course. In addition to packing a couple of pairs of gloves and ten to twelve balls, the well-stocked bag includes many or all of these items: lip balm and sunblock, adhesive bandages for cuts and medical tape to wrap blisters, insect repellent, ball-mark repair tool, headache relief, ball marker, a pencil or pen to mark your ball, tissue, a copy of the Rules of Golf, a hat for sun protection, and rain gear.

Some of the features to look for in a bag are lightweight polyester or similar material, three or four separate compartments to put the clubs in different groups (such as the woods and putter in their own), an automatic kickstand to prevent a lot of bending over, double straps to distribute the weight evenly on both shoulders to ease back strain, and large zippered pockets. To more fully protect clubshafts, some bags come with a fourteen-hole organizer, either of plastic or foam, that can also be purchased separately.

DOING THE OLD SOFT SHOE

The status of shoe development in the mid- to late-1990s has been one of the most closely watched areas in the golf industry. In attempting to make putting greens smoother, and thereby make it more likely that a golfer's putting will improve, the traditional metal spike is being slowly phased out.

The spiked golf shoe hasn't been around that long as far as golf equipment is concerned. Up until the late 1800s, golfers wore whatever shoe they normally had on. But as anyone knows who has tried to swing in their street shoes, nonspiked shoes don't provide any traction. Some players stuck tacks through their shoes or boots to alleviate the problem, and then in 1891, the first studded golf shoe was put on the market. Kits were offered that turned regular shoes into spiked shoes.

Golfers didn't take to the studded shoes until World War I, continuing to adapt their own shoes with nails and tacks. Spiked shoes were very much standard equipment by the 1920s, and then removable spikes were created after World War II.

The switchover from metal spikes to alternative spikes has been a two-step process.

First, more shoe manufacturers are making their primary shoe lines with alternative spikes rather than making them the option and the metal spike the normal offering. The alternative spike, first seen with the Softspike brand in 1992, is basically an all-plastic, miniature cleat with smaller nubs that are not as likely to raze the surface of the putting green with spike marks as the metal spike. Although the metal spike itself is blamed for spike marks, the type of grass on the greens (bent is worse than Bermuda grass, for example), the type of soil, the type of terrain, and the number of rounds also contribute to spike marks.

Most companies, golfers, and course personnel agree that Softspike-type spikes leave the greens smoother. The plastic spikes also make shoes lighter and more comfortable. And with less wear and tear on the greens, maintenance costs have been positively affected.

The Softspike mood is so strong that not only have shoe companies increased their line of alternative spike shoes, but around 2,000 of the 14,000 golf courses in the United States have approved policies banning the use of metal spikes and that number is increasing. If you go to an alternative-spike course, most will change your spikes for free to comply with the rule.

A set of alternative spikes should last fifteen to thirty rounds, depending on your swing, how much you walk or ride, and how much you walk on hard surfaces such as concrete, wood, or asphalt.

The alternative spike has made inroads with professional players, who, because of their place in the spotlight, help set the marketing pace in many products. Most players on the Senior PGA Tour have used or are using Softspikes. On the regular PGA Tour in 1997, approximately thirty players were using alternative spikes on

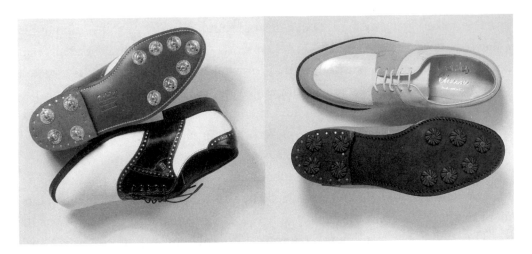

The traditional metal-spiked shoe (left) is giving way to alternative, nonmetal spikes that are said to cause less damage to the putting greens.

any given week, and the number was somewhat higher on the LPGA Tour.

The one big knock against nonmetal spikes is that they cause some players to slip during their swing or in wet conditions. As the newer spikes have become more popular, though, that concern hasn't been raised as often, making it likely that the number of Softspike devotees will continue rising. Companies are also offering metal spikes that are shorter than previous metals, 8 millimeters to 6 millimeters, because the latter does less damage but still gives the stability for which golfers ask.

Other shoe developments are similar to what has happened in the making of bags. Shoes are lighter weight, provide better support for the arch, have more cushioning effect, and are waterproof. Look for shoes that are constructed so that the sole and upper material are seamless or have some kind of sealing system to keep out moisture.

Shoe prices are nearing the $100 mark, but a good pair can be found in the $40 to $90 range. You're better off going as high as you can afford and taking good care of the shoes rather than buying cheaply because you'll have to buy shoes more often when buying the cheaper pairs. And since you're on your feet so much playing golf, it's best to invest in shoes that keep you comfortable and provide good support.

In getting a golf shoe, follow the same pattern as you would for a street shoe. Make sure you have the exact size of your foot. If you haven't sized your foot in a dozen years, see if there's been a change. The proper fit is a shoe that has about a thumbnail's width of space between the big toe and the tip of the shoe. Don't get tight fitting shoes and expect them to expand, because even though the leather will loosen, your feet will tend to swell as a round is played.

Be sure the width gives you plenty of side-to-side support but isn't so tight that the edges of your feet protrude over the sole edges. Cushion, of course, should be a main shoe feature. And the buyer should have an open mind as well. You may have used traditional welted shoes in the past, but be open to buying a comfort shoe or an athletic type that has a tennis shoe appearance. Unless you are trying to maintain a traditional image, you may find the best comfort in the more modern style. The athletic style is also less expensive and lighter than the traditional style.

After buying a pair of shoes, take the time to prepare them for use.

1. Apply a waterguard product to the sole and uppers.
2. Remove the spikes and drop oil into the spike wells to prevent rusting.
3. Invest in a good pair of wooden shoe trees to keep the leather from shrinking after use.
4. Use a shoehorn to slip into the shoes so the backs aren't weakened from bending.
5. Clean grime and grass off the shoes after use so course chemicals don't damage the leather.
6. Don't leave the shoes stored in the trunk; heat causes the leather to crack over time.
7. Be sure to polish the shoes as needed. Once dirt has settled into the leather, no amount of polish can totally hide the smudge.
8. Synthetic leather shoes can always be cleaned with water and dish detergent. Diluting a product like Spic & Span is also useful.
9. If the shoes do get wet, stuff crumpled paper in the shoes so the paper absorbs the moisture. Don't put the shoes near heat to dry, because it causes premature cracking in the leather.

New shoes are notorious for being hard on the heel and Achilles tendon area during the break-in time. Some shoes have extra padding in this area, but that eventually wears out. If you can handle it, it's probably better to do without padding as the shoe will fit the heel better once its broken in.

If you get bad results with whatever pair of shoes you get, remember to gripe about them to the seller and/or the manufacturer. Most shoes come with guarantees of solid performance and durability.

HOW TO GET A GLOVE THAT FITS

The fabled cabretta leather has had a long history as the material of choice in glove designs, but there is an ever-increasing amount of newer synthetic materials, too. Whatever kind you get, be sure it has good tackiness to it and doesn't feel glossy or slippery.

To put on a glove, always make sure the fingers have been completely inserted before pulling on the rest of the glove. The thumb should go in last, then gently pull the rest of the glove over your palm and the back of the hand. Do this slowly to avoid ripping. Make a fist and pull the Velcro or other strap closure over about three-quarters across and fasten it.

A well-fitting glove should allow you to stretch your fingers comfortably without straining the glove, but there shouldn't be any loose leather at the ends. The glove should be comfortably against the bottom of your finger notches. And the palm of the glove should react like a drum top when your fingers are extended.

Gloves come in small, medium, large, and extra large sizes, and in narrow and regular widths. Be sure to get a good fit because anything loose won't allow you to have the best feel for the club grip. After use, flatten the glove and put it back in the original wrapping so it dries properly if wet. Crumpled gloves tend to dry out and crack more quickly.

Glove options today even allow the most fair-weather golfer a chance to stay out in rainy and/or cold conditions. Grip control is the No. 1 swing problem at that time, and slippery grips and numb fingers take away confidence and make your swing a guessing game.

New all-weather gloves help golfers retain swing control. In wet conditions, synthetic, water-repellent models help grip the club, but when it's really wet, the latest "wet gloves" have proven effective. Made out of a special cotton weave, these gloves work best the wetter it is. The cotton fibers expand to keep control of the club. And the gloves are thin enough that the golfer can feel the grip.

In the cold, protection has improved from hand warmers and bulky mittens, although those methods still help. Thick, winter-type gloves of the past didn't allow for much freedom of movement, but thin, grip-sensitive gloves for cold weather have warmed to the task. They have regular leather in the palms and fingers, but the rest of the glove is made of a special insulating material that works well in ranges of cool to cold weather.

GETTING THE RIGHT GRIPS

Clubs off the store shelf have either leather or rubber grips. Which one is better is a matter of personal preference and could depend greatly on a person's hands. If the hands get oily or sweaty quickly, simple leather or rubber won't help. A combination all-weather type grip, such as a half-chord and half-rubber, would help.

If there isn't a problem with extra moisture, then the type of grip is a matter of comfort and what feels right.

TAKING CARE OF THE INVESTMENT

Proper care of every piece of equipment you have is simple common sense. Like any expensive investment, the products will serve you for many hours of enjoyment if well maintained.

Golf clubs should be wiped clean and the grooves wiped down as often as possible. Shaft protectors inside the bag prevent nicks that would require the club to be reshafted. Headcovers, for both woods and irons, also prevent damage to the clubfaces and leave the clubheads looking as new as possible. Grip life can be extended by washing the grips in soap and water a couple of times a year.

When equipment gets wet, remember to dry, dry, and dry! You'll prevent rust, warping, shrinkage, and soiling.

If you need a club repaired or fixed, look for a qualified repairperson in the phone book or your local course, or send the club back to the company. You could also save money in the long run by doing minor fixes yourself. To learn about this part of the business, look for two of the best club repair and making books ever written: *Golf Club Design, Fitting, Alteration & Repair,* by Ralph Maltby (first edition in 1974 but reprinted often, by Ralph Maltby Enterprises, Newark, Ohio), and *The Modern Guide to Golf Clubmaking,* by Tom Wishon (Dynacraft Golf Products, Newark, Ohio, 1987). They may be at a bookstore or at the local library.

"It is true that a player can bring his score down to what is considered good golf without instruction, but he never will be able fully to enjoy the game until he has developed a certain amount of consistency. The beginner should never go near a golf course until he has some idea as to how the ball should be hit."

SAM SNEAD

 Chapter 4

ON THE COURSE

The game of golf seems so simple: a player, the course, a set of clubs, and a ball. There are no referees running around with whistles, no timeouts, no 300-pound tackles charging toward you, no managers to tell you when to be bold or play it safe. Sure, you have to watch for out-of-bounds areas, and you do incur penalties, but golf is the natural game of sports. In this ecologically minded age when everything is natural this and that, golf truly is a game played as naturally as possible.

The out-of-bounds next to the fairway could be the Pacific coast at Pebble Beach, California, or a farmer's field in the Midwest. As for the penalties, lo and behold, it is the golfer's responsibility to recognize when rules are broken and to call them on himself. If you violate the Rules of Golf, you must make the honest decision to penalize yourself and suffer the consequences. Golf also has a lot of do-it-yourself aspects. Those golfers who play the game in its basic form—carrying their own clubs and walking—do a lot of things for themselves. For those people who are independent and like to make their own playing decisions, golf is the perfect sport.

Because it is the golfer alone who is responsible for how well she plays and enjoys the game, golf, from its beginning has been a sport of honesty and fair play— a "game for gentlemen" is one traditional way of saying it. Golf is a character builder.

Honest and accurate scorekeeping is rewarded with a satisfied feeling of having played by the rules so that the golfer has dealt evenhandedly with himself and fellow players. Having fun and reporting a fair score are two important goals to have when playing golf. Dishonesty, even if it's known only to the offending player, is a cold, empty feeling. There is no true satisfaction in knowing that something was achieved through dubious means. And when a golfer develops a reputation for playing on the sly, she quickly finds she's the last person with whom anyone wants to play.

In Chapter 2 you learned about how the golf course is set up and where the action occurs, beginning on the tee and finishing on the putting green. This chapter describes the specific actions of playing the game.

PLAYING IN GROUPS

Golf is played in groups of players who move around the course after receiving an assigned time or the go-ahead to begin play. Most courses don't allow more than four players per group. Golfers can play as a single, twosome, or threesome, but they should expect golf shop personnel and first tee "starter" to join groups together to make a full group of four players. This is a good method to keep play from slowing down with too many groups of just one or two players, and it contributes to the social atmosphere so important in a fun golf game.

Before heading out to the course, a new player should make sure he's done two very important things: learned how to advance the ball consistently down the fairway and studied the basic rules and course etiquette as well as possible. (Chapter 5 describes many of these codes of etiquette.) Both areas help golfers enjoy the game, fit in better with experienced players, and not hold up play. It's an embarrassment to be on the course before a golfer has learned swing basics and courtesies of the sport. It wouldn't be right to drive a car on the highway before receiving the proper training. Likewise, golfers shouldn't drive a ball around the course without learning the basics, too.

Assuming you've taken care of the two guidelines above, you're ready to head out to the course to experience the fun of golf firsthand. Selecting which course to play is the first part of the adventure. You may have a close group of friends that always plays at the same course at the same time, or you and other golfing friends may be the adventuresome types who play as many new courses as possible.

Any way you do it, the preparation to play the round, scheduling it to fit in with other activities, and touching base with the players before getting to the course all add to the experience of playing the game.

Courses come in the public, resort, and private varieties. The first two are open for all players; the private course is for members only and their guests. At a private club, groups usually tee off on a first-come, first-served basis. At public courses, however, golfers are often encouraged to phone ahead for a tee time. These times occur at eight- to ten-minute intervals and can start as early as 6 A.M. or 7 A.M. and finish in mid-afternoon. Some courses tack on a small charge for reserving a time. Reserved times can take up every single slot during an hour, or a course might skip every other time, alternating between reserved groups and nonreserved ones.

Depending on where a golfer lives, arranging a tee time can either be as easy as ordering a pizza or tougher than getting through to an insurance claims adjuster. Areas with a high concentration of golfers and a low number of courses are a golfer's nightmare. It can be nearly impossible to reserve a time. Some courses have sophisticated phone systems or an equitable method for taking personal tee-time requests and there's never a problem; the tee-time policy is fair and equal for all. At courses that still haven't joined the new technology, golfers seeking a tee time are often told they must come and put their bag in line or use a ball rack. Players tee off according to when their bag or ball reach the front of the line. This latter method can be extremely frustrating, even for a veteran player. Some courses are plagued by the "buddy system," in which the starter lets his old friends and pals go ahead of golfers who have waited longer.

Golfers trying to get on overcrowded courses that have poor tee-time practices have few options. They either have to work with the system, join an affordable semi-private or private course, or join together with other angry golfers and work for change with the club management. Course access and affordability are two areas that are most affecting the growth of golf. Whenever tee-time systems are changed for the better, it means a main obstacle to enjoying golf has been eliminated. A golfer's worry changes from, "How am I going to get on a golf course?" to "How well am I going to play today?"

How to dress for golf depends on a few factors: where you're playing, who with, and the weather. Playing at a private club means there's probably a dress code. One type of code might be golf shirts (no T-shirts or collarless shirts), knee-length shorts, dress pants (not even dress jeans), skirts, and appropriate evening attire if there's dinner after golf. Playing with an important group of players is another reason to follow a tasteful clothing code.

On the other hand, public-course golfers, in general, are free to wear whatever they like, although some of the upscale public courses have high dress standards. But public-course dress codes are so loose at some courses that cutoff jeans are okay and men can go shirtless on the course. The bottom line is the golfer should make the effort to call ahead and coordinate clothing with the course's rules. And if there's ever any doubt, put on the best clothes possible. It never hurts to dress nice since it gives nongolfers a favorable impression of the game.

After arranging for a tee time and putting a group of players together, it's time to get to the course. It wasn't too long ago that a common site at public golf courses was seeing golfers park in the course lot, change their shoes next to their opened car trunk, leave their clubs just outside the golf shop door, and then get their instructions from the cashier inside on how long before they can tee off. That scenario is still played out at a host of public courses, but another type of public course has emerged. It's the upscale course, with a beautifully landscaped drive, attendants ready to grab a golfer's bag at the curb, valet parking, hole-location sheets, a separate starter's shack from the golf shop, and other amenities previously unavailable to the public golfer. These courses charge a pretty price for such luxuries that once were exclusively seen at private clubs, but the market has made upscale public golf possible. And course owners feel justified in charging high green fees if they have a quality golf course to back it up. If there isn't a well-maintained and well-designed golf course, no amount of coddling could convince a golfer to play there.

Upon arriving at the course, golfers must check in at the golf shop in the clubhouse to pay a green fee, settle any other costs such as buying balls or renting a pull cart, and find out what they need to do to get started on the first hole. Keep in mind that a tee time means the time one of the players in a group should be hitting his ball, not the time to show up at the tee. Golfers should get to the tee a few minutes early to be ready at the correct time. (For further details about getting to and onto a golf course, see Business Golf under Chapter 13.)

While in the golf shop, players should grab a scorecard. The card fits into a pocket and lists the holes, yardages, and pars, and may have diagrams of the course and the holes individually, spaces to record the scores for each group member, the handicap number to each hole, and space to keep track of how the scorekeeper stands in any competitive matches or bets.

By deciding how early a golfer arrives at the course, she establishes whether she wants to warm up for the round or begin play cold, which is an obvious disadvantage. However she prepares, play begins on the first tee, with two rare exceptions. First, groups may be allowed to start on the tenth tee if a group can fit in without delaying groups coming off the ninth green. Second, a "shotgun tournament" format begins with groups going out to assigned holes and beginning play at the same time. There is usually one group per hole, but two groups on a par 5. The starting signal used to be the sound of a shotgun blast, but nowadays it is more likely to be a siren or a specified starting time. Play concludes with the groups finishing, at nearly the same time, on the hole prior to their starting point.

THE ORDER OF PLAY

Figuring out the order of play within a group—who has the "honor" to play first, then second, third, and fourth—is done in the following ways.

On the first tee, it is decided by lot, such as

- The players standing in a circle and one player flipping a tee to see who it points to when it lands. That player goes first and others follow in clockwise order.
- Going from highest to lowest handicaps, or lowest to highest so the better player can guide the other players around.
- Making a coin flip.
- Teeing off according to the set of tees being played, golfers from the back tees (longest) hitting first.
- Odd or even number on the ball (a player guesses if the other players have an odd- or even-numbered golf ball).
- By how the names are listed on the scorecard if it's a tournament and a committee made the pairings.

During the actual playing of a hole, both on the fairway and the putting green, play continues with the person farthest from the hole hitting first. If players appear to be an identical distance, the golfer ready to play should go first. On the green, in tournament competition, a referee may actually measure who is farthest away.

In casual play, golfers will learn that a variety of measures can be applied to help speed up play, such as tapping in a short putt if it doesn't need lining up and is not in another player's line of play, or playing a shot from the fairway and then helping a group member find a lost ball. Match play is the only time a golfer can be asked to play a shot over if he has hit out of turn.

The results of the hole just played decide the order of play on every tee except the first. If a birdie, par, and two bogeys were recorded, the birdie shooter has the honor. If two players have the lowest score, the order between them reverts back to the order on the previous hole. If the golfers in a group are using more than one set of tees, as might happen with a group of men and women players, the same procedure for play should be used for each set of players. And in a two-person team event, the team that wins a hole plays first on the next hole, and the partners can hit in any order they desire.

There are two ways the tee, or teeing ground, is the starting place for the hole to be played. First, players tee off from a designated area indicated by two tee markers, which are set apart in various widths. The markers define an imaginary rectangular area two club-lengths in depth. The golfer doesn't have to be inside the tee area, but the player's ball does. Otherwise he must add two strokes to his score and replay the shot from within the area.

Second, the tee, more than any other place on the golf course except the clubhouse, is the place where camaraderie among group members can let loose. Conversations take place about the previous and upcoming holes, the condition of the course, or maybe something completely nongolf-related, such as personal or business life. It is these opportunities to interact with fellow golfers that make the game the best combination of sport and the social spirit.

OBJECT OF THE GAME

Unlike the swing, the playing of the game is relatively simple. The object is to advance the ball from the tee to the putting green and get the ball into the hole in the fewest number of strokes possible using a set of iron- and wooden-headed clubs. The player has the ultimate responsibility for keeping track of his score on the hole, and having it recorded by the person keeping the scorecard. Every stroke taken by the golfer has to be counted, even penalty strokes, to come to the final score for a hole.

What's the definition of a stroke? Does a swing and miss (also known as a whiff) count as one? A miss *does* qualify as a stroke because it meets the definition of a stroke: the forward movement of the club with the intent to hit the ball and move it. That's it, plain and simple. If you meant to hit the ball—and here's where honesty comes in again—no matter what the result is, it's still a stroke. However, you can halt the downswing before the clubhead reaches the ball and it is not considered a stroke.

Golf courses use an assortment of tees set up at various distances from the green. The tees are usually color coded with the tee listings on the scorecard, especially at upscale courses. The variety of tees gives golfers an option of how difficult they want to make the course. Obviously, a set of tees that makes the golf course play more than 7,000 yards will be more difficult for a beginning player than a set at 6,000 yards.

It's a simple concept, but one golfers often overlook: The course should be played at a length that matches a golfer's playing ability. For some reason, golfers like to make it difficult on themselves and play from a longer set. This is probably a reaction to the high price they may have paid at one of the finer courses, and to get their money's worth they've decided they're going to see the entire course.

But don't let ego or skewed thinking get in the way of common sense. Be good to yourself as a beginner and play the course from a reasonable length. Make it a goal to improve so that you can move up to the next length as soon as possible. You'll enjoy the game more if you don't put yourself through a more difficult learning process than you have to.

Older public courses may not have sets of tees using a color code, but instead have three tee lengths: back, middle, and front. This traditional setup is done so very good players can use the back tees; average players the middle; and juniors, seniors, women, and beginners the front. It's that kind of mentality—playing from tees that suit your ability—that you should use when playing modern courses that have up to seven or eight sets of tees.

In addition to playing from the correct set of tees, players need to observe one other guideline linked to a course's setting amid nature. Golfers should play the course as they find it, with no alterations to the placement of tee markers, hole location, hazard, or out-of-bounds areas. Golfers simply play the course as it was set up for play that day. And with the exception of having to make a drop or perform a rules procedure, the ball cannot be touched once the golfer has teed off. Golfers can touch the ball to tee it up, and can even move it around on the teeing ground with the club to find a good lie as long as the ball stays within the teeing ground boundaries. But once the tee shot has been struck, the ball can't be touched again until reaching the putting green.

The ball is played as it lies in the fairway and rough, even if it means hitting the ball from an old divot or tall rough (see Winter Rules in Chapter 8). That includes not altering the ground conditions around the ball by pressing down grass or vegetation with the club or foot. There are a few legal situations, according to the Rules of Golf, when you can touch the ball. Such times are when your ball

- Comes to rest in casual water or ground under repair. (Rule 25 allows the golfer to lift and drop the ball at the nearest point of relief.)
- Comes to rest in a water hazard. (The player may retrieve the ball or drop another when it cannot be played from the water. There is a penalty stroke.)
- Comes to rest so that you may take relief from an obstruction.

As you play the round, scoring is kept on a scorecard by a member of the group. Each player, monitoring her play by the Rules of Golf (a copy of which she should tuck away in her golf bag), and showing courtesy to fellow players, reports her score at the completion of a hole. The scores for each hole are totalled to constitute the total score for the round (either nine or eighteen holes). In competition, for a stroke play tournament, the player or team with the least number of strokes for the duration of the tournament is the winner. In match play, the player or team with the lowest score on a hole wins that hole; the side that wins the most holes wins the match.

Your success on the course will ultimately be determined in two ways. First, you may be the kind of player who plays golf for the sheer enjoyment of being outdoors and getting a chance to walk around the course. In that case, you'll find pleasure in occasionally striking a great iron shot or rolling in a long putt. Score will not matter to you, the experience of playing will.

Second, you may be analytical and want to measure how well you're doing by score. In that case, you will be interested in seeing how your score measures up against par, whether you can be a bogey player, a par shooter, or a par breaker. The golfer's object is to shoot par or better. The term par refers to the score a good player would be expected to shoot on a hole. It takes into account the number of strokes needed to reach the green, plus two putts. Most holes are par 3s (the shortest holes), 4s, or 5s (the longest), with a rare par 6. It should take one shot to reach the green on a par 3, two shots for a par 4 and three shots for a par 5. The eighteen holes on a course usually add up to a par of 70 to 72 for men and up to 74 for women. If a golfer finishes a round with all pars, it's called an even-par round.

A score of one-over par on a hole is a bogey, one under a birdie. Two over is a double bogey, three over a triple bogey and so on. Two under is an eagle, and three under a double eagle.

No matter whether you are casual or analytical, you will come across opportunities to play under different formats other than just meeting your regular group for a round of stroke play. Here are some additional ways to help you enjoy the competitive aspect of golf.

- *Match play*   Some would say this is golf at its ultimate best. An individual or team plays against another individual or team. Hole score is much more important than total score for nine or 18. The side with the lowest score on a hole wins the hole. If a hole is tied, it is halved and neither side wins it, and the score is not carried over to the next hole. The match is over when one side leads by more holes than there are number of holes remaining. For example, winning 3 and 2 means the winning side was three holes up with just two holes left to go. The losing side didn't have enough holes left to make up the difference.
- *Medal play (or stroke play)*   This is the way most people play golf, counting all their strokes. Medal play is a common format in tournament competition, too. It can be either a team or individual game and last nine, 18, 36, 54, 72, or more holes. The simple goal to win: have the fewest strokes taken. Medal play can be completed by counting gross (actual) scores or using handicap (net) strokes.
- *Best ball*   This is a team game that has three possible formats. The lowest score of the team is used, with either no handicap or handicap included, and winners are computed either at stroke play or medal play. The three possibilities: using the best ball of two players, the best ball of four players, or the best two balls of four players.
- *Scramble (captain's choice)*   A fun four-player team game that lets poor players mix in well with better players. All players hit off the tee, then select the best tee ball for their second shot. All players hit a ball

from within a couple feet of the chosen ball and select the best shot to play next. This continues until the ball is holed. The scramble is an enjoyable game that often results in low scores and a lot of strategy to form teams and decide the order of play on a team.

- *Alternate shot*   A similar game to a scramble, but this time with two players. Both golfers play from the tee and then select the best of the tee shots for the second shot, which is played by the partner whose ball wasn't picked. The players alternate shots until the ball is holed.

- *One-club event*   Great for the off-season, this format has the players selecting just one club to use for the entire round, even for putting. Most players pick a middle iron, such as a 5- or 6-iron. A one-club event is wonderful for teaching a golfer how to use imagination and creativity to play different shots.

- *Skins*   The skins format has become popular since the made-for-television shows first appeared in 1983. A skin is one betting unit. A person wins a skin by having the lowest score on a hole; either gross or net scores could be used. If a hole is tied, the amount of money is carried over to the next hole and added to that hole amount.

Most of these golf events are played on a handicap or net score basis, which is the actual score minus handicap (see handicaps in Chapter 7). A handicap is the number of strokes you need subtracted from your actual score to reach a course's USGA course rating, which varies from course to course. Golfers use handicaps to form competitive games with players of various skill levels. In addition to a regular USGA handicap, you may have heard of handicap systems such as Soley, Callaway, Peoria, and Scheerer. These are all variations of making a competitive event equitable for all playing abilities, and are usually only seen at special one- or two-day tournaments. For casual betting games, using a USGA handicap is sufficient.

The best method for pairing partners in a foursome is to match the handicaps as evenly as possible. For instance, in a match with 5, 12, 15, and 30 handicappers, the 5 and 30 would pair together against the 12 and 15.

KEEPING THINGS INTERESTING

Some golfers need a game going on while they're golfing to make the day more fun and enjoyable. Here is a collection of games that can accomplish that goal. The competitive nature of these games can help golfers stay focused on their game and thereby sharpen their skills.

Nassau

This is probably the most well-known, and easiest, betting game in golf, played in match-play style. The sides—one versus one, two against two, etc.—usually play for three points, one each for the front and back nines and one for the entire round. The sides agree on a money value for each point, such as $2 or $5. If a side wins the front nine, the back nine, and the entire match, and the bet was $2, the total amount won would be $6. In a match of two against two, each winning player would get $6 and the most a losing player would have to pay would be $6. A "press" can be employed in the match, meaning if one side ever falls into a 2-down deficit, it can press on the next hole to double the bet. The press is in effect for the rest of the holes on that nine. The side in the lead doesn't have to accept the press, but it's customary to do so.

> "To some, golf is work; to others, it is only play. It has been said that golf should always be fun, yet the fascination of the game lies in the fact that it goes beyond merely having fun. Golf is uniquely appealing because it offers a challenge found in virtually no other game. Golf defies you to master it. It wants you to be a slave to it, and the game has succeeded in enslaving many of us."
>
> BOB TOSKI
> AND JIM FLICK

Junk

This isn't the name of a game, but the word many golfers use to describe the little side games that can be played during a Nassau match. In addition to the regular Nassau bet, players compete for extra side bets, each of which could be worth the same money unit as the Nassau bet, but it's usually a little less. The junk games include barkies (making a par after hitting a tree on the hole), sandies (saving par from a greenside bunker), greenies (hitting closest to the pin on a par 3 and making par or birdie), an Arnie (making par without ever being on the fairway), and a Watson (chipping in, no matter what score). There are other traditional contests, such as fewest putts, most fairways and greens hit in regulation, and longest drive, that can enhance any competition.

Three Clubs and a Putter

A pleasant variation on the one-club event, this game for a foursome has players picking out three clubs to use and a putter. Those are the only clubs they can use for nine or eighteen holes, and each player is allowed to pick whichever set of three clubs and a putter they want.

Bingle-Bangle-Bungle

This popular format has three points up for grabs on each hole. Each point is worth a certain monetary value, such as a dime, quarter, or 50 cents. The golfer who hits the ball on the green first gets a point, the player closest to the hole after everyone gets on the green gets a point, and the person who holes out first gets the third point (golfers must putt in proper order, furthest out first).

Needless to say, the point for being the first on the green is not given when the hole is reachable in one shot. When the round is done, the points leader earns money from the other players. Each player subtracts his or her points from the leader's points, then pays that amount. If the winner had twenty points, and another player ten, the second player would pay ten times the agreed-upon point value.

Wolf

This is a quick-thinking game for three or four players. A player is designated as the wolf on each tee on a rotating basis. The wolf hits first, then selects a partner from the other players. He does this by picking a player immediately after seeing the result of all the drives. The wolf plays alone if he doesn't pick anyone, or a rule can be applied that the last player to tee off must be the partner if no one is selected. The partners team in a best-ball format. If there's a single wolf, the bet doubles. Handicaps can be used. If there is a tie, the bets don't carry over to the next hole.

Low ball, High ball

This variation on a nassau match is for a foursome, with two players playing against the other two, using handicaps. Two points are handed out on each hole. One point is given for the low net score on the hole but one point is taken away for having the high score. Another format for this type of game is giving one point for the low net score and another point for having the lowest combined team score.

Blind Partners

In an 18-hole stroke-play event, players form foursomes with whoever they want to. After the last group has teed off, partners are joined together in a blind draw so no one knows who their partner is while playing. The results are tabulated under a best-ball format, using handicaps.

Mixed Foursome

One of the few events that joins the opposite sexes together, a mixed foursome has two sets of male-female partners. One of the partners hits drives on odd-numbered holes and the other on even-numbered holes. After the drive, the players take turns hitting the ball until it's holed out. When handicaps are used, the team handicap is half of their combined handicaps.

Alibi Golf

Players get to re-hit the same number of shots equal to the player's handicap during the round. But just one shot can be replayed per hole.

Blind Holes

In an eighteen-hole, stroke-play match, nine holes are picked at random by the committee in charge after all players have teed off. Those nine make up the holes that count toward the final score. Players use half their handicap for net score results.

Points

Instead of using score as the determining factor, points are awarded on each hole and added together at the end. Three points are given for birdie, two for par, and one for bogey. Full handicap can be used. The player with the most points is the winner.

Replay

An opponent can make the other player replay four shots over the course of eighteen holes, even the best shots.

Round Robin

In a match with foursomes, partners are changed every six holes so that a player ends up having three six-hole matches. The usual format is best ball with full handicap.

Throw Out

Using full handicaps under a stroke-play format, a player can throw out his three worst scores for his final total.

Win, Place, Show

In a match with foursomes using their full handicaps, points are awarded for how well a player scored within his group on each hole. Three points are given for having the low score, two points for the second lowest, and one point for the third lowest. The player with the most points wins at the end of the round.

For more information on games and how to conduct tournaments, look for these two excellent sources. *Planning and Conducting Competitive Golf Events* is available from the National Golf Foundation in Jupiter, Florida, for $35 by phoning (561) 744-6006. *Golfgames: The Side Games We Play and Wager,* was written by Rich Ussak and is available from Contemporary Books (Chicago, 1993).

There are dozens of other popular ways to play the game other than the many listed above, but that doesn't mean you need to come up with something different just to get out and play a round. Find your own way to enjoy the sport and let its pleasures be your passion.

 Chapter 5

ETIQUETTE AND STRATEGY— WHAT IT TAKES TO BECOME A GOLFER

There's a moment or period of time for anyone learning golf in which they are transformed from someone who *plays* golf to someone who can be called a golfer. Until that moment, if a golf novice is asked whether she plays golf, the response is most often, "I'm learning to play," or "I've just started." It's never a definite, "I'm a golfer."

It's the same in many sports. In baseball there are athletes who play baseball and professional-level ones who are ballplayers. It's a status-symbol sort of thing.

"Becoming a golfer" should be the ambition of everyone who plays the game, but it takes time. When you feel comfortable enough to call yourself a golfer, it means you feel you've adequately learned swing mechanics, etiquette, traditions, and shot strategy. You know the lingo and procedures that were once quite unnatural to you. You no longer are just a golf beginner. You're a *golfer* and you feel comfortable in conversation with other golfers.

This magical blossoming as part of the golfing fraternity occurs at different times for everyone. It could finally be triggered during a particularly enjoyable weekend of golf, or after a unique shot, or following a post-round get-together with others at the 19th hole.

When it happens, it's quite satisfying and increases the golfer's desire to expand their knowledge even further into all areas of golf, not just the swing and its procedures.

Anyone who is called a "golfer" knows a lot about golf verbiage. Until a beginner commits many phrases and words to memory, the words used by experienced golfers might as well be a foreign language.

There are two parts to what makes a new golfer feel comfortable as a beginner: First, becoming the best they can be at swinging the club, and second, understanding etiquette, procedures, and rules. (This chapter and Chapter 8 on rules take care of the second part.)

Playing well and learning how to talk golf lingo are the best ways to feel at ease in the company of better players and anyone who has played golf for a long time. It helps the new player fit in and feel a part of the brotherhood of players.

ETIQUETTE

Proper conduct on the golf course centers on what is courteous and respectful of others. Golf etiquette can be broken down in the following sections. Observing these Golden Rules of Golf will make any golfer a friend to the game and a compatible playing partner.

General Dos and Don'ts

After golfers have finished playing, they should have left the course in as good—or better—shape as it was when they began playing. They do this by fixing divot holes and ball marks, raking traps, and picking up trash. Consider yourself one of the caretakers of the golf course.

Bringing a cellular phone or beeper to the golf course may be fine if you are a person who must be notified during an extreme emergency, such as a doctor, but for everyone else there is no need to have those devices on the course. The course is supposed to be a place to get away from interruptions, not continue them. And consider what a nuisance it is to have a phone or beeper go off at the wrong time. They can bother your playing partners and reflect negatively that you didn't have the courtesy to help them play in peace and quiet. Some courses don't allow phones and beepers, and they are definitely discouraged when watching a professional golf tournament in person.

Remain still and silent while another player is hitting a shot. Be careful to stand out of the golfer's peripheral vision or view. Make sure your shadow doesn't fall upon the ball or on the putting line on the green.

Golfers commonly leave a club or headcover laying around and forget to pick it up. If you see someone else's equipment, pick it up and check with everyone in your group. If no one claims it, take it along as someone in the group in front of you will probably come back and ask about it. If no one does, turn it into the golf shop. If you're in a tournament, give the club to an official; never stick it in your bag because it could put you over the fourteen-club limit.

There's nothing wrong with taking a practice swing before an actual shot, but don't turn each shot into a private practice session. Only take one practice swing, unless you have to hit a chip or pitch and need to develop a feel for the shot. Avoid taking a divot on a practice shot—but replace it if you do—and don't do anything to slow the game. The goal during a practice swing is to develop feel and tempo, which are maintained for the actual shot. Never swing the club, either for a practice or actual shot, unless you know no one is standing near you. Don't assume other players know what you're planning or doing. The club should never be swung toward someone because it could send debris their way or the club could slip from your hands.

Don't play to a green if the ball can reach the green and players are still on it. Let the players move off to the next tee before playing. Likewise, don't hit a shot off the tee until the group in front has moved at least 20 yards out of range of the longest hitter in your group. But be realistic in your abilities. If a group is still on the green, and you know you can't reach them with your next shot from the fairway, go ahead and play and don't wait for them to clear the green.

An act of cheating is an intentional attempt to fool someone else. On a golf course, it can take several forms: mismarking the ball, moving the ball into a better lie, not reporting the correct score, dropping another ball when an original is lost, and, of course, disregarding any Rule of Golf. In casual golf, it's not terribly difficult to cheat because there aren't any rules officials to worry about. It's up to each golfer's integrity to resist the temptation to cheat. Most people who cheat know exactly what they're doing and that it's wrong. If you catch someone cheating, one option is to avoid a confrontation and vow never to play with them again. In casual play, cheating doesn't affect other golfers, and it doesn't give the cheater an accurate score. In tournaments, however, it's a different matter. The advantage to telling someone about cheating is that, if they didn't know about it, you can help correct an embarrassing situation. If they did know about it, you've served notice not to do it again. Emphasize that golf is a game of integrity and honesty and should be carried on that way, and in no way does anyone gain from cheating.

Golf is a game governed by a specific set of rules. Those rules cannot be waived or set aside by the players without a penalty being applied.

New players should schedule their golf at times when the course is the least crowded. They will enjoy their round more if they don't feel pressured and rushed by better players. When are the best times to play? A phone call to someone working in the golf shop will lead to the answer.

It's been written in this book that the ball is supposed to be played down, as it came to rest. An exception to that takes effect if you are a new player. Beginners should feel free to tee their ball for each shot to build confidence until that point in time when they feel comfortable hitting off the ground.

If you're playing with better players, don't apologize or feel the need to tip someone off that you're a new or poor player. Everyone has to get started some time, and if the other person(s) doesn't realize that they should give a newcomer some slack, then they're not displaying good sportsmanship. Don't belittle yourself, and don't overdo compliments to a better golfer. And be sure you know what you're doing so you don't have to ask a lot of questions about procedures.

If you've taken eight or nine shots and still haven't holed out, just pick up the ball and continue to the next hole. Don't linger or make the round drag out just for the sake of holing out for a 10. Be sure to keep up with the other players so you aren't labeled a slowpoke.

Give a shout of "Fore!" if your ball appears likely to strike someone or land in the area of other golfers. Yell as soon as possible to give the players a chance to react. If your ball goes onto the fairway of another hole, the players on that hole have the right of way to proceed. Wait until they've gone through before you play the next shot. If your ball finishes on the wrong green, let the players on that hole finish and then drop the ball within two club-lengths of the green, no closer to the hole you are playing, and hit away.

If you're the person on the other end of the "Fore!" shout, turn your back to the direction the ball is coming and cover your head with your arms. Don't face the warning cry because you're likely to get struck in the front. If you're going to be hit, it's less painful if the ball strikes the legs or back.

Avoid talking while another player is hitting, unless you whisper so your voice can't be heard. If the group is in the middle of a conversation, put it on hold during the time players are hitting.

Unless you're good friends with the person, don't pass along swing tips that weren't requested. If you feel you just have to say something, wait until the end of the round. Most golfers can't handle advice during the round as they'll try to work on their game and play the round at the same time.

Stay level-headed if you're the person keeping the scorecard. Keep it up-to-date so you can give other players a current and correct tally of where things stand.

Make sure a shot finishes well before saying something nice about it or commenting on how great a shot it was. Some shots that look good in flight end up in trouble by the time they come to a stop, and it's an embarrassment to hand out a compliment for a shot that goes into trouble.

On the Tee: Be Ready to Play

The goal on the tee is to be ready to hit when it's your turn, but also waiting for the right moment to take it. If you're not the golfer with the honor, don't put your tee in the ground while the previous player is in the process of playing their shot. Wait for them to finish their swing and move away.

Each player should announce their ball brand and number on the first tee so it can be known whether any players are using duplicate models. Put a distinguishing mark on the ball (a series of dots, your name, etc.) so you can further ensure you'll know which ball is yours.

If you hit a ball out-of-bounds off the tee, don't automatically hit another one. Wait for the other players in the group to hit and then play your next shot. This lets others play in the proper sequence and gives you a chance to regroup.

On the Fairway and Rough: Stay Alert for Order of Play

Golfers must keep track of where each player is within their group during the course of playing a hole. That starts on the tee by watching the flight of each ball. As group members reach their balls in the rough, fairway, or wherever it might be for their second shots, each player should look around at the others to ascertain who is farthest away, next farthest, and so forth until each player knows when they'll play their shot. The golfer farthest from the hole plays first and that routine continues all the way to the green, even for chip and pitch shots.

Avoid walking ahead of a person in your group or standing so you're in their line of sight. There's nothing wrong with moving ahead to your next shot, but don't be disruptive. Try to do it in the least noticeable way possible.

When playing from a bunker anywhere on the course, enter it from behind and avoid stepping on bunker edges, which can be fragile and broken easily and cause you to lose your balance. It is okay to walk into the bunker with a rake, but don't use it to scrape or test the consistency of the sand. Just place it on the sand to the side so it won't stop the ball if you fail to get out of the bunker.

After playing from a bunker, be sure to rake it. Smooth the sand so it is as perfectly level as possible, being sure to get the area where the ball was struck and your feet were situated. Exit from the bunker along the same path you came into it, smoothing the sand as you leave. When done, lay the rake on the outside of the bunker (unless it came from the golf cart). Try to rake other uneven spots when you are done hitting from the sand, but not before.

On the green: Watch your step

There are two overwhelming concerns on the putting green: Avoid walking on the putting line a player's ball will take to the hole and keep track of whose turn it is. The footprint cast by your shoe—especially on soft greens—can affect the roll of the ball. So be aware of where each ball is and avoid walking on those putting lines.

After everyone is on the green, make sure you know the order of putts; the person farthest away putts first and the closest golfer putts last. Do everything you can to prepare for your putt and then play without delay when you're due up.

The putting green has the shortest grass on the course, so be sure to pick up your feet when walking to avoid scuff marks. And don't run on the green—unless you just won the club championship.

Be accurate in marking and re-marking the ball. A dull, small coin is the best marker and it should be slid directly behind the ball, which is picked straight up. The ball is re-marked in reverse order.

If a player's ball marker is on the putting line your ball will take and could affect the ball's roll, ask the player to move the marker out of the way to the side. This is done by finding an object in the distance, such as a tree trunk or boulder, in the direction the coin is to be moved. The putterhead is put alongside the coin extending toward the object and the coin moved to the other end of the putterhead. The coin usually only needs to be moved once or twice. The coin has to be moved back to its original position before that player can continue putting.

Spike marks—those pointed bits of grass brought up by spikes on shoes—cannot be tapped down while playing the hole, but they can and should be fixed after putting out.

When a player needs to have the flag tended because of a lengthy putt, it's the role of the player whose ball is closest to the hole to tend it.

To tend the flag, stand on the side of the hole that the ball will break toward and about a foot behind the hole. Grab the flag itself and hold it still as you grasp the pole. Before the player putts, pull the pole out and reinsert it to make sure it's not stuck. Remain still while the player putts, letting the other arm hang by your side. When the ball is about five feet away, pull the pin straight up and step back out of the way.

Any player or caddie can remove the flag when all players have reached the green and no one indicates he needs the flag tended. The flag should be lifted straight up to avoid damaging the edges of the hole, and should be placed, not thrown, well enough away from the hole or on the fringe so that it won't affect anyone's putting line or be in the way if a ball goes off-line. The flag should be replaced by the first person to hole out, being sure to put it straight in and unwrapping the flag so the next group can observe it for wind direction.

After holing out, golfers should not lean on their putter as they retrieve the ball because this causes an indentation in the green within a few feet of the hole.

Don't leave the green and head for the next tee immediately after you've holed out if others are still putting. Wait by the side of the green until everyone is finished. If you're trying to get your group to move faster, say something like, "We've got to pick up the pace." By rushing off by yourself, the only thing you'll accomplish is upsetting your playing partners.

If you want to try a putt over again after missing it, wait until the entire group is done and try it once more, but only if it won't hold up players in the next group.

PULL AND RIDING CARTS: EASING THE LOAD

For those golfers who like to lighten their load, pull and riding carts are available for rent at most golf courses. Both can also be purchased for outright ownership.

Pull carts help golfers remain true to the game's walking heritage while easing the load on their backs. Riding carts should be used only by those golfers who need them for medical reasons, but unfortunately, they're unavoidable because they're mandatory at many facilities, primarily in the United States. Whether you use a pull or riding cart, they must not be taken over wet spots, ground under repair, or placed near tees and greens. Most courses rope off an area within 50 yards of the green, directing drivers to go around the green. Cart riders should always observe all directional signs.

Riding carts are sometimes limited to paved cart paths only, which is a major time consumer in that it forces golfers to go back and forth from their cart to the ball, sometimes having to walk to the far side of the fairway and back. A more user-friendly rule is the 90-degree rule, which says the carts must stay on the path until the cart is level with the ball, then the driver can cut over at a 90-degree angle, play the shot, and return to the path.

Riding carts are not toys, but many people, especially young golfers who shouldn't be in a golf cart in the first place, think they should be driven like go-karts. A golf cart should not hold more than two players and their clubs, unless there's a special apparatus on the back for more sets of clubs. Probably the best uses for a golf cart from a walker's perspective, besides helping golfers who need one for a medical reason, is that they can be used to drive ahead and check out blind shots, and they come in handy to drive back a hole or two and retrieve a lost club or item from the group.

> "Swing-wise, the best club to start with to create or improve a swing is the wedge, the heaviest club in the bag. Its weight enables you to feel the clubhead more, so for your own sake always start with the wedge when you warm up."
>
> MICKEY WRIGHT

There is a sticker, required by law, within each golf cart that describes other rules for using it. Carts should never be ridden along the side of a hill; always go up and down slopes to avoid flipping it over. Avoid making sudden turns, as it could throw out a passenger. Always tell the other rider which way you'll turn so they can be prepared. Use the brake quite often going downhill. Don't have feet or arms dangling out of the riding compartment. Always drive the cart from the driver's side, not the passenger's. And don't move the cart while players in your or an adjacent group are playing. The sound of rattling clubs or a gas engine will distract their play.

If you aren't happy about being paired with a person who likes to walk and leaves you driving them around like a chauffeur, set the ground rules early in the round. Tell them you'll split the riding and walking duties, perhaps switching from one hole to the next, so you both get some exercise. If there continues to be a problem, take matters into your own hands and walk off to your ball with a few clubs in hand as he's getting set to play his shot.

Carts can slow up play if the two players in the cart hit in opposite directions. In that case, both players shouldn't go to each other's shot and watch the other play. One player should be dropped off at or near his ball with a few clubs while the other goes to his. When both players have hit their shots, they can join up to move down the hole.

COURSE CARE: GET IN THE HABIT

Of the many reasons for poor course condition, one of the most frustrating is the golfer herself. Too many players take the attitude that it's not their responsibility to help take care of the course. They feel they've paid their green fee and earned the right to ignore maintenance rules. It only takes a handful of players with no regard for course property to make things ragged for everyone else. The little things that keep courses looking nice and playable only take a few seconds and help prevent days of mending by Mother Nature. Golfers should pay attention to and abide by all signs posted by the course personnel on course care. Here are three areas that anyone who considers himself to be a friend of the game should observe:

Ball Marks

When the ball lands on the green, many times it makes an indentation in the grass. If this ball mark is not repaired, the grass dies, a small hole is created and it takes many days for the hole to fill in with new growth. These marks are only a half-inch deep, but an old ball mark causes a putt to deflect if the ball rolls over it. A tee or a special ball-mark tool can be used to lift around the edges of the mark and push the turf toward the center, then the turf is tapped down with the putter bottom.

Divots

The pieces of grass and dirt that are torn from the ground when a golf shot is played are called divots. (The word divot is from an old Scottish dialect and means "a loose piece of turf.") Sometimes they're thin and sometimes thick, although the size is not a sure sign of how well the shot was struck. (The direction of the divot can tell a lot about how the shot was struck and which direction it went.) Divot holes, if left unfilled, mar what is a beautiful green expanse of grass, kind of like a case of course acne. After creating a divot, golfers should replace them immediately afterward and step on them. This is the only way the grass roots have a chance to grow back so it won't take weeks for grass to cover up the divot hole. When playing on courses with Bermuda grass, such as in Florida, the grass divots cannot be replaced because Bermuda grows more side to side than vertical. In that instance, golfers should pay more attention to the hole than the divot. Most Bermuda-grass courses provide a small bucket of sand and fertilizer to fill in the hole and help the grass rejuvenate quickly.

Bags and Carts

Greens and tees are for shoes only. All bags, pull carts and riding carts should be kept clear of the green and tee surfaces and the fringe around the green.

PACE OF PLAY: QUICK AND COURTEOUS

Playing without delay should be the goal of every golfer, no matter whether playing in competition or just getting away from a job and a hectic lifestyle. If each golfer had her own golf course, she could play as slow or as quick as she wanted. But golfers must share the course with dozens of other players, so it's up to each one to do their part in keeping the round moving.

Slow play gives the game a bad reputation and image. No golfer can have the game all to himself, so by playing quickly it helps present golf in a positive light for future players. Playing quickly doesn't mean running around the course. It means not wasting those moments during a round that could be used for advancing the ball with either shot planning or swinging the club. No one has a right to make the game last any longer than it has to. So to those players who are indignant that they are expected to play without delay, remember that you aren't the only golfer out there. Be courteous and aware of all golfers' rights.

A common goal is to play a round of eighteen holes in four hours or four hours and fifteen minutes. That's not a Rule of Golf, but it's the consensus time that seems to be ideal. Some courses that strictly enforce pace-of-play guidelines post times they expect groups to take to reach certain parts around the course. They may stamp the time a group teed off on their ticket and later time them at those checkpoints to see if they're keeping correct pace. But groups can avoid trouble if they make it an aim to stay in contact with the group just before them, never letting them get more than half a hole in front.

If a group can't keep up with the one in front of it, and it's being pressured by the group behind it, it should let that group play through. This is a procedure that lets faster players get in front of slower ones, but in no way should it be taken as an insult to the slower players. No one is penalized for letting others play through. In fact, it's something to cheer.

It's up to the slower group to recognize it should let a group go by. Unfortunately, there are too many times when slow players let pride get in the way and the group behind them has to practically beg to go through. (Faster players should resist the temptation to "force" slow players to let them play through by hitting shots into the slower group. This only causes arguments rather than solves the problem.)

A par 3 is a good hole for one group to pass another. The transfer can be done on the tee if the two groups meet there, or if the slower group is on the green, it can get the attention of the other group and wave the players to hit. The slower players stand to the side as the shots are played. When everyone has hit, the slow group has the option of finishing the hole while the other players approach the green, or it can remain to the side while the faster golfers play out. As the faster players go through, they should be sure to tell the slower players to "have a great round and thanks for letting us through."

There hasn't been a scientific study done on the benefits of playing quickly, but even if you play fast and score badly, you're better off than playing slow and scoring poorly. There's no sense in dragging out the misery of a bad day at the course. Expert players often cite the benefits of playing quickly rather than slowly.

Even one of the most easygoing professionals in the history of golf couldn't stand a slow pace of play. Said the late Julius Boros: "It hurts my game to play slowly, and I believe that applies to many others. I learned to play fast when I started out and that became my normal pace, regardless of the situation. Playing fast becomes just a matter of pattern. Anyone can play fast if he wants to. He doesn't have to make a production out of every shot."

A common expression is "miss 'em quick," meaning when you play a shot, play it without delay. Don't horse around. Get up to the ball, make your club selection, get set over the ball when it's your turn to play, and hit it. Overthinking a shot gets people into a lot of trouble because they end up unsure about what to hit and how to play the shot. Most amateurs, especially high handicappers, hit the same poor shot whether they took thirty seconds or three minutes to play.

How quickly a person plays is often related to their personality. A quick thinker and mover plays quickly, but a deliberate person is likely to be the same on the course. But anyone can play quickly if they put their mind to it. It begins before they even get to the first tee by deciding to play the set of tees that are at the best length for their abilities and skill. Here are some other tips on playing efficiently:

Since novice golfers hit so many off-line shots, one of the best things they can do is follow the flight of the ball all the way to the end. Don't turn away at the sight of a bad shot. Save your moaning for when the ball has come to a stop. Keep an eye on where the ball finishes, marking the position with a landmark in the area, such as a bush, tree, or other item. Then you can go straight to the ball and save time by not searching. And it wouldn't hurt to keep an eye on the balls of everyone in the group so you can help someone if they didn't stay with the shot.

Save in-depth conversations with playing partners for the tee and during delays in play. Between shots walk briskly to the ball.

As you near your ball, look for any yardage indicators in the fairway, such as sprinklerheads. Then walk off from the marker to your ball so you don't have to retrace your steps. Most of the time the yardage total is to the middle of the green. Some courses use a 150-yard marker on one or both sides of the fairway; the marker could be a small bush, a pole, a boulder, or a course emblem. Another way to indicate yardage is stone tablets in the fairway. They usually occur at 50-yard increments, starting at 100. It's common that the 100-yard marker is red, 150 is white, and 200 is blue. No matter the kind of marker, the yardage is to the middle of the green.

Be sure to make a preshot routine a part of each shot you hit, and make it last no more than a half minute. Make the routine consistent so it becomes second nature to you.

When it's not your turn to hit, plan your shot and pull the club to use so when you're up you can step right up to the ball and fire away.

Don't get too bogged down in waiting for the person farthest from the hole to play. If they're having trouble getting set to hit, and you're all set to go, ask if you can go ahead and play. In most instances you'll be told to hit. But don't play without asking first. Otherwise it can be distracting to have a couple of players hit at the same time. The key to playing shots prior to reaching the green is to pay more attention to your own game rather than watching the other players play their shots. Always be ready to play your ball.

After reaching the putting green, always place your golf bag or position the golf cart on the side of the green that leads to the next tee. This gets you off the green and out of the way the quickest.

If you have reached the green, and someone has just chipped up and their ball is on your putting line, you can mark the ball for them and move it out of the way as long as they give you permission.

What happens if the person farthest from the hole is on the putting green but there is a ball on the fringe closer to the hole? The person on the green should still play first even though not everyone is on the green. But in casual golf, it doesn't really matter who plays first as long as someone knows they will be going first and an order of play has been decided.

Don't forget some procedures from the Rules of Golf when it comes to pace of play. First, you only have five minutes to look for a lost ball once you reach the area where you think the ball is sitting. Another ball has to be put in play if the original isn't found by then. Second, be sure to hit a provisional ball if you believe a ball has gone out-of-bounds or is lost. This prevents you from having to make the trek back to the tee or previous hitting area if you can't find the original ball.

Even though in most instances it's the person farthest from the hole who plays first, when on the putting green, players should putt out if they've hit a putt that finishes within tap-in range.

It's not necessary to mark a tap-in putt and come back to it later. Be sure to avoid stepping in anyone's putting line.

Not only should you develop a consistent preshot routine for full shots, but there should be one for putts, too. Try to read as much as you can about your putting line before it's your turn, then finish your "read" when you're due to play.

Get a line on the putt, step up to the side of the ball, take a practice stroke or two, step up to the ball with your proper stance, align the putterface, take one or two looks at the hole to make sure the putter is lined up correctly, then make the stroke.

Avoid overanalyzing any shot; it will most likely result in poor confidence in the shot you decide to play.

Don't keep track of the scorecard while standing on the green or anywhere that it slows up the next group of players from playing their shots. Mark the card on the way to or on the next tee.

It is against the rules to give people swing advice during the round. It is also a cause for slow play. Save any comments about helping a golfer until the round is finished, then help the player during a practice session.

KEEPING THINGS SAFE

A golf course is basically a safe place, but there are a few reasons to be concerned about safety. Injury, of course, is always a possibility, and could occur in a number of ways, from slipping down a slope to hitting a root during the swing to getting whopped by someone who made an unexpected swing.

Correct riding-cart operation, as noted earlier, is a must to maintain safety.

Weather is another concern, particularly lightning. When lightning is visible, no matter how distant, the only course of action is getting off the course and into the clubhouse. Don't be concerned about finishing the round. If the skies clear up, you'll be allowed to go right back to where you left off.

There are few places to hide during a lightning storm, so try to find shelter in a building. The places not to go include next to isolated trees, fairways, tees and greens, golf carts, and near ponds and lakes. Don't hold up an umbrella or golf club. If you do get caught in the open, bend down on your knees and tuck your head.

STRATEGY

It's not enough to learn how to *hit* the ball; the best golfers learn how to *play* their ball, too. What's the difference? Hitting the ball means building a swing that is consistent, repeatable and efficient. Playing the ball means the ability to "strategize" your way around a golf course, being able to take in all the variable factors such as weather, the course, and your feel for the swing that day, and not letting them overly affect your final score. As Mickey Wright has said, "A beautiful swing isn't enough. You have to learn how to play golf, to learn that strategy at times can be more effective than the swing."

Strategy is most often thought of, in golf terms, as the planning a golfer puts into playing a hole, where to place the ball off the tee, where to play to when hitting to a green, and so on. But strategy can also mean a host of other outside elements, such as selecting the fourteen clubs to be used during the round or whether to learn the swing left-handed or right-handed.

This section covers a host of these factors.

Preshot Routine

Prior to each shot, it's important to follow a regular pattern known as a preshot routine, to get into the correct posture, alignment, and aim. As with anything that needs aiming, it's best to stand behind the ball and line it up with the intended target. In golf, imagine a line extending from the ball to the target and pick a spot a few feet in front of the ball along that line. Keep that spot in mind as you step to the side of the ball. Place the clubhead down first behind the ball so the clubface is lined up with the spot as you step into the stance with the right foot. If the clubface is square to the spot, you can have confidence it's in proper alignment with the target. Next, put your other foot into the correct position so both toes are parallel to the target line. Make sure your knees, hips, and shoulders are parallel with the target line, too. This puts you in a square position and is a routine that should be followed for every shot.

Leftie or Rightie?

At one time, it was a simple decision to decide which side of the ball to play from. Right-handed people played right-handed and left-handers played as southpaws. But one line of thinking, not totally endorsed by all teachers, is that people should play the opposite of the hand with which they are most dominant. Because the lead arm in the swing (the left for right-handed players) is so important during the downswing, the case has been made that right-handers should play left-handed so their stronger right arm can lead the downswing, and vice versa for a leftie. Backing this argument are players such as Walter Hagen, Bobby Jones, and Johnny Miller, who were left-handed but played as righties. Phil Mickelson is a right-hander who plays left-handed. Another key to going leftie is that the quality of equipment for left-handers has improved. About 10 percent of the golf population is left-handed—3 million golfers—so it's not a lonely group. It's not a bad idea to experiment from both sides and then stick with the one that feels natural.

Which Set of Tees to Use?

Too many golfers feel they need to play all of the golf course, at the risk of playing miserable golf from a set of tees too long for them to handle. A good rule of thumb is to stick with the medium, regular tees if you are a double-digit handicapper or more, and don't try the longer tees unless you're a 9 or less.

Club Distance

You can't make concise club selection if you don't know how far you hit all your clubs. Write down your precise distances for each club during a practice session or as you play shots during a round, then commit them to memory. You'll discover that there's around a 10-yard increment between clubs. You should especially pay attention to driver distance. By knowing how far you hit your tee shot, you are better able to decide how to play shots off the tee. And don't be fooled by remembering distances of thirty years ago or going by a career shot you hit once. Be realistic in your yardages.

Bunker Play

Unless you've become very proficient with a sand wedge, there should never be a question with what to do with a sand shot. Simply get the ball on the green with one shot, no matter how close you can get it to the hole. Getting cute with a shot, if you don't have the talent, will surely mean you won't escape from the bunker. Keep in mind that the higher you need the ball to fly the more loft you need in the clubface. Although you can't carry a dozen sand wedges to satisfy all situations, you can increase a sand wedge's loft by opening the clubface. As the length of your bunker shot increases, the clubface should be gradually closed so that for the longest shots it is square to the target.

Long Par 3

If you have to hit a wood into a long par 3 and lack the confidence to hit it straight, play a shorter club to land the ball within 50 yards of the hole so you have a chance to get up and down for par. You are better off taking a chance for par than knocking a tee shot out-of-bounds.

Flat Lies

Make your best attempt to hit shots that leave you with flat lies for the next shot, even if it means not hitting the ball as far. For instance, if you plan on laying up on a hole, do it so you can have a flat lie and a longer shot rather than a funny sidehill lie that's closer.

Trouble Spots

Always play away from the trouble areas around a course. That's common sense, and easier said than done, but it should be of primary importance. Don't flirt with trouble areas unless the odds are better than 50-50 in your favor and/or you're using a club with which you feel very comfortable. If a mis-hit shot will put you in a worse spot than you presently are, it's not worth the chance. Lee Trevino's advice is, "You must concentrate on the shot at hand but always think one shot ahead. Look over the shot you are about to play and then figure out where you would like it to be if you could carry it out there and place it for your average distance."

Club Selection

The components of good club selection are knowing your yardage, the lie of the ball, where you want the ball to go, the direction the wind is blowing, and your ball flight tendency.

Aiming to Greens

There really is no reason for beginners or high handicappers to hit their ball at the flag. Aim to the center of the green on all approach shots and you'll hit more greens than you miss. Professionals use this thinking more than anyone realizes. Keep your aiming thoughts simple. Also, if you have to favor one side over another, make sure a mis-hit shot will end up on the side of the green that allows the longest chip with the most green to work with. In other words, miss on the open side so the next shot is a long chip to an open green rather than a short chip over trouble. A good drill is to envision playing your course without flags, because it forces you to always play to the center of the green. Whatever you do in aiming your shot, see and envision success in your shot before you hit it. Ask yourself where is the ideal place to hit the ball, and where is the worst place. If the two spots are close together, aim for the safest area where making par is a realistic chance. Observe what the late teacher Tommy Armour said, "Play the shot you've got the greatest chance of playing well, and play the shot that makes the next shot easy. Every golfer scores better when he learns his capabilities."

Tee-Shot Tips

There are a few things to keep in mind when deciding where to tee up the ball. First, look for a level spot where both you and the ball will be on a flat area. Second, observe where the trouble is on the hole and tee the ball on the same side as the trouble so you can aim the shot away from the problem area. If water and trees are on the right, set up on the right and aim away toward the middle and left. Third, note the shape of the hole and set up to give yourself the straightest shot to take the shortest route to the green. For a dogleg right, tee the ball on the left to make the drive a straight shot. Fourth, if you hook or slice the ball consistently, allow for the curvature and you'll enjoy a better round. Aiming for the middle, as if you were hitting a straight ball, will frustrate you all round long as you see the ball sail off into the rough or woods. And fifth, use the location of the flag to determine where you hit the tee shot. If you know the flag is on the right, play your drive to the left of the fairway so you'll come in from a good angle.

Water

Having to play a shot over water intimidates golfers probably more than any other shot. Why? Most likely because hitting a ball in the water is a sure penalty, unless the ball barely makes it in. Golfers know that with sand or trees, there's a chance to hit an escape shot. Water doesn't allow that. For this reason, new players should only try to clear water when the distance to carry is not a concern and the player is using a club in which she has confidence. There's nothing wrong with laying up short of the water as a beginning player. It keeps down the frustration level and the cost for new balls as well.

Warm Up

Hitting balls and practicing a few putts for thirty to forty-five minutes before a round of golf is a great idea, but not always practical when most golfers have a hard enough time getting to the course on schedule. If time is running a little short to make your tee time, try this approach. Swing a couple of irons and do a few stretches to loosen up. If you're allowed to chip on the practice green, hit a few shots with your sand wedge, pitching wedge, and 7- and 8-irons to get the feel of having the clubface strike the ball. But do so from close range to the green for safety's sake. Next, swing your driver five to ten times with an imaginary ball, each time pretending that you're actually hitting off the first tee. Finally, hit a few putts, mixing in a couple of long ones with medium-range putts and three- to five-footers.

Pitching Clubs

The short irons are designed for specific purposes and distances. Wedges are for pitch shots over trees, bunkers, water or for wide-open holes in front. The putter, 7-iron, and 8-iron are good clubs from the fringe. There are so many short-game options that it's worth anyone's efforts to practice as many as possible. The more a golfer practices and plays, the better she'll be at judging the length of backswing needed to hit the ball a certain height and distance. When faced with a short shot, examine the turf condition. The more the ball sits up on the grass, the easier the shot will be. If the ball is in thick, tall grass, it will have a greater amount of roll than one sitting cleanly. The taller the grass, the more loft you need in a wedge. A low shot is the best trajectory for a chip shot. For all short shots, in fact, the faster a golfer can get the ball on the green and rolling like a putt, the better the result will be. It's easier to judge how hard to hit something to make it roll a certain distance than it is to judge how hard to make the ball fly the correct distance.

Putting

When reading how much break to play for a putt, you're better off erring on the side of too much break than not enough. Strike the putt with medium speed and allow for plenty of break rather than hitting a firm putt with little break. And it's better to miss putts long rather than short as you can watch a long putt go by the hole and get an idea of how the ball will break on the return. Also, putts late in the day will usually break less and be slower than at the start of the day because the grass has grown during the day; wind makes putts roll faster and break more because the grass is drier; if you're confused about how a ball will break, notice whether the edges of the cup are tilted, which indicates break; and the grain of the green—the direction the grass grows—makes a putt break more in whichever direction the grass is growing.

Putting Indecision

We've already spoken about the danger of indecision for full shots, but what about putting? Sam Snead has always said, "Stick with the line you have in mind." But not only can there be indecision about the putting line, but about whether to try to make a difficult putt, too.

Jack Nicklaus has this advice: "When you are inside 20 feet make a definite effort to hole your putt but when you are outside that distance concentrate solely on the speed in a determined effort to put it within 'gimmee' range. Otherwise you are in danger of creating a three-putt pattern and nothing is more damaging to your mental attitude on the greens."

Long Putts

For lengthy putts, stand more upright to the ball so you can see the line better with an elevated view. The important thing about long putts is to strike them solidly moreso than having great accuracy.

Wind

For shots downwind and into the wind, play shots that fly lower than normal. You do this by playing the ball back in your stance toward the back foot and putting the hands more forward toward the target at address. Shots into the wind cause the ball to have more backspin, which makes it rise and thus not carry well. When you play to hit a lower shot, use more club than normal and try to punch the ball, keeping your hands low on the follow-through. Over time you will learn to judge whether the wind is a one-club wind, two-club, and so on. If you have a shot distance that normally calls for a 4-iron, the wind may force you to hit a low 3-iron. When playing downwind, the wind makes shots fly farther, but there is less control because the wind takes spin off the ball. When downwind, plan for the ball to hit and roll more and adjust your landing spots around the greens. For cross-winds, again, depending on the strength, you will have to adjust your aim. For a right-to-left wind, for example, aim more to the right. Expert players who can control the curvature of the ball might, in that case, hit a fade that "holds" against the wind and comes down at their target spot.

Taking More Club

The times to hit more club than you normally would for a certain distance are into the wind, when the green is elevated, when the air is damp and heavy, and when you're in between clubs, in which case use more club, choke down, and use a shortened swing.

Rough

Poor players and newcomers should stick with using a short iron to get out of high grass and only try something else if the ball is sitting up well. A 5-wood or utility wood is excellent for getting out of rough and gaining good distance as well.

Anger

If you've hit a poor shot, do what all the great champions do: nothing. Don't swing in anger or blame the ground or the club. Stop, take a deep breath, and keep your composure. Focus on swinging with good rhythm and balance on the next shot. Try to find the positive aspect in your play. On the other hand, don't play in a trance. You usually play your best when you're a little on edge or nervous. Being a little on edge puts your body and mind on alert. Jittery feelings, as might be experienced on the first tee, can be alleviated by taking deep breaths, trying to yawn, and stretching your muscles. Think about the shot at hand and put the situation and the surroundings out of mind for that moment. Byron Nelson's advice is, "Every great player has learned the two Cs—how to concentrate and how to maintain composure. If you really want to learn them, the two Cs aren't difficult to master."

 Chapter 6

PUTTING A SWING TOGETHER

To the uninitiated, the golf swing must appear quite comical and ludicrous, yet intriguing at the same time. One group of these nongolfers, the ones who will never give the game a try, refers to the swing—and the game in general—as flogging, finding themselves quite funny for transforming the name "golf" into something that fits their image of the sport.

Other nongolfers, the ones who give the game a try at some point in their lives, keep their thoughts to themselves for fear that their insults and wisecracks may come back to haunt them once they succomb to the golf bug.

And then there's another group that has no inkling at all as to what the game is about, other than what they've been exposed to in the funny pages. They're the ones who yell "Fore!" in the middle of someone's backswing as a carload of these comics drives by the local golf course.

Veteran golfers, and those who are playing the game for the first time, know very well that the golf swing is serious stuff. It's probably the most difficult sports movement to perform well, and it takes the longest to learn. Numerous professional athletes in such major sports as football, baseball, and basketball have made golf a free-time activity, and later commented that golf was the hardest game they'd tried. Its difficulty can make the most-accomplished star in these sports feel very humble.

> "Golf to me is not only a way of life, it's a creative outlet, a constant, never-ending challenge; frustrating, but never dull, infuriating, but satisfying."
>
> MICKEY WRIGHT

Why golf should be so unbearingly hard to play is not easy to understand at first. It may seem backward to say this, but perhaps golf would have more people playing it if they realized it was harder than they thought. At first glance they think golf is too easy and not worth their time. But, in reality, deep down most people probably realize the time and effort needed to learn the golf swing and wisely take up some simpler activity, such as watching golf played on television.

LEARNING IN STAGES

Think of the term golf swing for a moment and you'll likely create an image in your mind of an action that has only a single movement. And technically that would be accurate. But to train your body to make a proper continuous motion, the best strategy for a new player is to learn the swing in stages. According to the late champion golfer Julius Boros, the golf swing should be thought of as an efficient machine. "Each part of it is dependent upon the other parts; if one part is functioning incorrectly, the others will be affected. But working together they deliver the same effective result time after time. This is your objective. Build the most efficient machine you can. You'll be surprised how much more enjoyable the game will be if you do."

The golf swing is really a series of checkpoints or stages connected in a free-flowing action performed with feel, speed, and pace. It begins from an almost static, still position and continues with a slow, steady buildup of energy and power to propel the golf ball the maximum distance and the straightest direction. It ends in stillness, the golfer posed in the best way to view his handiwork, or ineptitude.

It is said of some golfers, the most notable example being Sam Snead, that they possess natural talent to swing the club. There's actually not a lot of naturalness to the golf swing. The golfer is bent over, with knees flexed and arms dangling. From this position that is reminiscent of a football quarterback ready to take the snap, the golfer must break from a still position and contort his back, spine, shoulders, hips, and knees in ways that apply varying degrees of stress on each part. The aches and pains are compounded by the additional factor that if the golfer doesn't swing with the correct method, there's further tension on the body. Even the feet and hands can suffer discomfort. If the grip is held incorrectly,

Early golfers had very loose swings that were mainly the result of the equipment they used.

for instance, blisters and calluses develop.

This physical element takes on lesser importance as the new player develops "golf muscles." These aren't muscles you build up to rock-hard, bodybuilding proportions. Rather, beginners who haven't used the muscles required to swing the club need to start gradually, thereby strengthening the key muscles so they can withstand increased practicing without undo strain. It is the absence and/or weakness of golf muscles at the initial learning stage of the swing that causes beginners to feel clumsy and uncoordinated.

Where does natural talent enter the picture? It is hard to think of someone being born with the ability to swing a golf club, and it's an exaggeration to think they have been. More likely the natural talent can be attributed to good hand-eye coordination, developed, quite likely, by participation in other sports, such as baseball. Combine that with a supple, durable, and flexible body and you have the formula for natural talent.

FRUITLESS SEARCH FOR PERFECTION

The search for the perfect swing has been an intense chase in golf's history, but never moreso than during the last fifty years. No matter the effort, however, it is an unattainable goal. Yes, perfect shots have been struck, even by the least professional of players. But golfers are not machines who can repeat a perfect swing on every shot. There will be those who try to solve the perfection riddle, but their ultimate "reward" will be frustration. As the late English golf writer Peter Dobereiner once wrote, ". . .the perfect swing does not exist. It is a dream, without substance and divorced from reality." But the attempt to find perfection is what has increased the playing proficiency of today's players to a high degree.

The early golfers 500 years ago weren't too concerned with the perfect swing. Their ability was determined by the equipment with which they played. The clubs of that time were built by craftspersons more accustomed to making spears and weapons of war. The clubs were not far short of being "clubs" in the sense that they could inflict severe damage to a person's body. They were heavy and the long-nosed wooden clubheads had the curved appearance of scoopers and scrapers.

Harry Vardon was instrumental in the evolution of the swing toward the end of the wooden-shaft era.

To swing these cumbersome implements, the player had to grip the club tightly and turn his body slowly around, swinging flatly, making a loose pivot in what came to be known as the St. Andrews swing. As clubs got lighter in the 1800s, craftspersons such as Allan Robertson started using iron clubs that helped golfers play with more accuracy and swing with more speed. He showed that ball flight could be controlled.

But golfers were still swinging from a hunched-over, wide-footed, stiff-legged swing. It wasn't until Harry Vardon in the late 1800s that an emphasis switched over to the classical golf swing players are familiar with today. Vardon, in addition to popularizing the overlapping grip, stood straighter and opened his stance. He made full hip and shoulder turns and had a classic finish with his weight shifted to the left side. His swing motion was more upright than what others had done.

Americans exposed to Vardon's technique during his tours of the country benefited immensely from his style, which was passed along from teacher to pupil. U.S. stars such as Bobby Jones, Walter Hagen, and Gene Sarazen continued the technical work done by Vardon.

The truly modern golf swing took off with the talents of Sam Snead, Ben Hogan, and Byron Nelson from the late 1930s to the 1950s. The ideas of a shoulder-width stance, upper- and lower-body resistance, and the late hit, among others, were more fully developed in these players than in anyone before.

While Snead was praised for a natural swing that was the most durable of golf's champions, Hogan was and continues to be held in mysterious, reverential tones as having come the closest as anyone to golf perfection. He used some unconventional techniques to develop a motion that prevented him from hitting a hook. And he had the extraordinary talent to maintain the angle created by his left arm and the clubshaft the longest of anyone during the downswing for maximum distance.

Although Jack Nicklaus emerged in recent years as the most-accomplished golfer ever, he didn't add much to the evolution of the golf swing. He stood out from the rest more for his strength, plus his mental ability and the preparation he took in planning for a tournament and shot strategy.

MANY STYLES TO THE SWING

With so many golfers searching for the one best method of swinging the club, it's no surprise that the golf swing is a very individual action. There is a basic way to swing, especially when it comes to the fundamentals, but no one can point to a single method and say this is the ultimate, pure way.

There have been notable players of an older vintage, such as Lee Trevino, Miller Barber, and even Arnold Palmer, who accomplished much with swings that experts would say had flaws in them. There are exceptional players of today, such as Jim Furyk and Allen Doyle, who are excelling with swing motions that are unique to them. They possess what golfer Jimmy Demaret once said of Vice President Spiro Agnew, "You have a slight swing in your flaw." But what it comes down to is these golfers took what felt correct to them, and through constant practice, made their technique work time and time again.

In this book you will be told the basic swing elements that will allow you, through hard work, to play golf with consistency and, if you're fortunate, proficiency. To learn the swing it all starts with the fundamentals in the preswing position. (Please note that instructional tips will be written for right-handed players. Those golfers learning from the left side will have to reverse directions.)

THREE TYPES OF GRIP

For all of its importance, the grip is, astonishingly, one of the most misapplied fundamentals that teachers see in their students. But because it is the only connec-

The overlap grip is probably the most common of the types of grips.

tion golfers have with the very object that hits the ball, players must be connected correctly with the club to have any real chance of golf success.

To confuse you right from the start, there are three primary types of grips. They will be reviewed in the order of popularity.

Overlap

The overlap grip, also known as the Vardon grip because British legend Harry Vardon was the first player of note to use it, can be used by players of any size or shape, although golfers with large hands will benefit most. To apply it to the club, stand straight with a club leaning against the front of your left thigh. Your arms should be hanging naturally by your side, with the elbow folds almost completely facing the sides of your body.

Now, simply move your left hand over to the club and grasp it near the top. Try not to change the angle of the hand as it had been by your side at the start. If you've done it correctly, when you open your left hand the grip should be running diagonally from the base of the little finger to the middle joint of the index finger. With the full-swing grip, the club is held more in the fingers. When we get to putting, the club is held more in the palms.

Close your left hand and make sure the left thumb is slightly right of center on top of the grip. Next, it's time to apply the right hand. Hold the club in front of you with your left arm stretched out and the forearm parallel to the ground. Put your right hand on the club at the base of the grip and slide it up to meet the left hand. The right hand should be situated so that the thumb pad of the right hand sits atop the left thumb, the lifeline of the right hand goes against the right side of the left thumb and the right little finger wraps around the groove created by the first two fingers of the left hand. When the right hand is holding the club, the right thumb should be slightly left of center on top of the grip.

Interlock

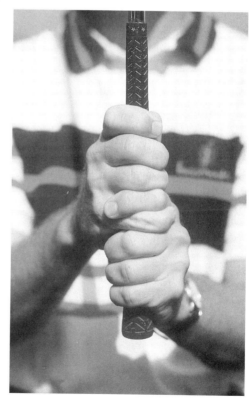

How would you like to use the grip favored by Jack Nicklaus and Tiger Woods? If so, this is the one for you, but make sure it fits your needs. The interlock is applied to the club in the same fashion as the overlap except the little finger of the right hand fits with the left hand by wrapping between the index and middle fingers.

The interlock gives the player a more unified feel than the overlap since the hands are linked together, but it's primarily used by golfers with small hands, as explained by Nicklaus. "There is a good chance that golfers with small hands will discover that the interlock grip fuses their hands together and holds

One finger of each hand intertwines in the interlock grip.

them on the club much more securely than the popular overlapping grip. My hands are small and the interlocking grip is the one I use today. It gives my hands a wonderful feeling of unity throughout the swing, a unity that the other grips could not supply."

Baseball/Full Finger

The hands sit on the grip for the baseball grip as they would for the interlocking style, but the hands are not connected; they just butt up against each other similar to how you would hold a baseball bat.

Each finger is wrapped around the club. Because there is more of the hands touching the club with the baseball grip, the concensus is that it's a preferred grip for beginners and weaker players.

The baseball grip provides more control. New players can start with the baseball grip and then progress to one of the other grips if desired.

No matter which of the three grips you use, one checkpoint they have in common can be seen by looking in a mirror. Be sure that the "Vs" formed on both hands by the index fingers and thumbs point toward the right side of the face. This is a neutral position and should be your starting point for the swing because it gives you an ideal chance to have the clubface in the best position at address and impact.

Hold the club with light pressure, so that someone could move the club around if you held it straight out but couldn't take it from your hands. Make sure you don't hold the club so tight that your wrists and hands can't hinge properly during the swing. "The feeling you should have is of the tips of the fingers, or the end two joints, holding the club firmly so that you aren't going to let go and it isn't going to move," explains professional star Nick Faldo. "But the rest of the hand needs to be loose and free, with real emphasis on getting the wrists relaxed and able to generate speed."

Everything in your swing could be done to perfection, but it would be ruined if you had your hands on the club incorrectly. Getting off to a proper start is essential. Use the correct grip and resist the temptation to put your hands on the club in whatever way feels comfortable to you. When you have your hands on the club correctly, there might be a period when it feels uncomfortable, but that will pass. Stick with it and you will soon feel at ease and see the positive results of your correct grip.

ADDRESS: SETTING UP TO THE BALL

Now that you've got your hands on the club in a fundamentally sound grip, it's time to do something with it, but you're still not ready to make your first backswing. You're connected with the club, now you must "connect" with the ball. You do that by positioning your body in a comfortable stance and posture that sets you up for the actual swing.

Setting up to the ball is called the address position. The thinking behind this swing stage is similar to that of addressing a letter, in which you prepare the letter with directions for delivery. In golf's address position, you stand up to the ball to send it in the direction you want it delivered.

For you to learn the standard address position for most shots, we'll have you stand about 18 inches to the side of the ball with a 5-iron. Put your hands on the grip in the way described earlier and extend your arms in front of your body parallel to the ground. Lower your arms and club at the same time as you also bend from the hips. Stop the clubhead about six inches above the ground. Now flex your knees and continue lowering the club.

This should lower the club to the ground behind the ball. A well-used image for the look of the address position is the feeling of barely sitting on a bar stool with your feet still on the ground. The late Davis Love Jr., a well-admired instructor, said the address position was "like sitting down, but not quite." Take note that you are doing these checkpoints correctly:

Back straight and not arched;

Body weight evenly balanced on both legs and both feet;

Shoulders tilted slightly right;

Shoulders lined up over the knees and the middle of the feet;

Left foot turned slightly outward and right foot pointing straight; and

Arms should hang from a near vertical position under the shoulders.

Don't reach for the ball, but don't have the hands and arms touching the body.

The sole of the club should be square with the ground; don't have the toe of the club pointing up or the heel raised off the ground. The sole should be level from toe to heel.

These nuances, although sounding overly picky, all aid the proper functioning of the swing later on and should be in place if you have your knees flexed, club resting on the ground, and rear end sticking out. You'll discover that subtle body positions can greatly affect how your swing functions.

Try not to be discouraged if during the first few times through this routine you'll feel like a mechanical windup toy. But like most swing components, you'll later move comfortably, smoothly and, most important, quickly. When you become an experienced player, you may not even need to go through this step-by-step address process. You'll step right into it as a matter of course.

That's the goal, to make every part of the swing, from grip to follow-through, second nature. New golfers will have an overwhelming desire to reach this state of natural golf ability so when they play with experienced golfers they won't be self conscious.

BUILDING WITH THE MINI-SWING

You've got the grip and address and you're standing over the ball in the ready position, so let's not leave you hanging. At last it's time to learn the swing and ingrain good habits to make your swing dependable and durable.

There's a nucleus to the swing that's worth learning first. If you perform it correctly, you've done more than you know to make yourself a good golfer. This nucleus, or mini-swing, is like the nucleus of an atom: it carries all the potential for power. The mini-swing covers the swing from the time of address to a point halfway back on the backswing to halfway through on the follow-through.

You would do well to fully concentrate on the mini-swing because doing it badly means your accuracy, control, and distance are negatively affected. All proficient players perform the mini-swing well. In analyzing the main difference between a professional golfer and a poorer player, it's the mini-swing, in most cases, that sets the professional apart.

What's so important about the mini-swing, and why can't you just focus on a bigger swing first? Because the mini-swing is the middle portion of the swing and will be a part of every full swing you take. And consider that the mini-swing has all the traits of a good, full swing: a backswing in which power is stored, a downswing that returns the clubface square to the ball for accuracy and releases power at the perfect moment, and a follow-through that has the golfer balanced on his left side and facing the target.

The mini-swing contains what golfing great Johnny Miller believes are the five basic moves to the swing: the one-piece takeaway, the early set of the wrists, the hinging of the right arm and wrist, the work of the knees as the first move in the downswing, and the release of the angles formed by the arms and wrists.

The Mini-Swing Start

Once again holding the 5-iron, apply the correct grip and step into the address position. Your first thought may be where to put the ball within your stance. Should it be toward the right foot, in the middle of the feet, or toward the left? This ball position varies slightly depending on the shot you're playing, but for longer shots, such as the woods and long irons, the ball should be opposite the left heel. As you play the middle to shorter irons, the ball should be between the left heel and the middle of the stance.

As for the width of the stance, the widest you will have your feet is when playing the driver. For that club, the inside of the heels should be as wide as your shoulders. As the clubs get shorter, you should draw your right foot closer to the left in short increments so that by the time you're playing a pitching wedge your feet are about a foot apart.

Begin the mini-swing by focusing on the left side of the body, from shoulder to foot, and start to turn this side to the right as you swing the club back with your arms, shoulders, and hips moving together as "one piece." Don't try to stretch your arms away, just extend them with the left arm remaining straight. To get the club started on the right track, imagine a line extending from the target to the ball and continuing on through to the right as you face the ball. This is the ball-target line. As you swing the club back, and even throughout the swing, the shaft should always point at that line or be parallel to it.

Move smoothly and without jerkiness. Keep your visual focus on the back of the ball, not on the clubhead as it moves.

The Middle

As the hands start moving upward, the wrists should gradually cock or bend, letting the club point skyward. Halt the backswing as your hands reach chest high. At this point the left arm should still be straight and parallel with the ground, and the left wrist flat. Your body weight will have switched toward the right side and the club will be "on plane," meaning the butt end of the shaft will be aimed at some point on the ball-target line.

At this stage please notice one of the key elements of the swing: the angle formed by the clubshaft and left arm. At the halfway point of the mini-swing, this angle should be 90 degrees. Retain a vision of that angle in your mind because you will want to refer back to it during the downswing.

The Finish

The controlled process of taking the club back now gets a little frenetic. The backswing should have built up some tension or coil in your upper body. This is the energy you need to apply to the ball. The downswing-to-follow-through portion takes much less time than the backswing.

Once again the left side is the key, turning back toward the left. Your hips turn open, but you do not slide them or your legs toward the target. As your left side turns open, the left shoulder works as a hinge and "pulls" the arms through. Allow your right elbow to swing down closely to the body, tucking it toward your side, a feeling many teachers have described as trying to stick the elbow into your right pants pocket. This keeps the club on track for "squaring up" with the ball at impact.

Perform the mini-swing in slow motion many times to make sure you are in the correct positions throughout. In particular, at the moment you strike the ball, be sure that your hands are positioned ahead of the ball, more on the target side of the ball, and also observe that the clubshaft is leaning toward the target. This is the ideal impact position and must be practiced often to make it your regular swing pattern. During the downswing, visualize the clubface returning to strike the ball in the same position it was at address.

Now, let's refer back to that 90-degree, left arm clubshaft angle mentioned at the top of the mini-swing. Please note that you ideally want to retain this angle for as long as possible on the downswing. It is difficult to consciously hold the angle because the downswing happens too swiftly and it needs to occur freely and without tension. But if you can hold the angle at the start of the downswing, your chances are good that it will release at the proper time at impact. When you lose the angle early in the forward swing, you've lost the energy stored up for release. You can have a loss of several yards distance because of it.

The mini-swing concludes with a mirror image of the backswing: Right arm parallel with the ground, club pointing up toward the sky as the shaft and right arm form a 90-degree angle, the right hand has "passed over" the left after striking the ball, body weight more on the left side than right, and the head should remain level with the point at which the ball sat. The clubshaft should point at a spot on the ball-target line. There should be some bend in the right knee and the leg beginning to balance on the toes. The force of the swing should have almost completely turned the body to face the target. Stop the swing when your hands are about chest high on the left side of your body.

After reading all the nitpicky descriptions of how the body and club should be positioned during each part of the mini-swing, it may give credence to the opinion that golf is a silly game. There's nothing silly about it, and in fact it's more science than silliness. Failure to put your body in even just one correct position can mean just that much less success you'll have. It won't mean utter failure, and you can still enjoy the game, but it will knock down your proficiency level just a notch.

That's the complete mini-swing, a motion that could, quite surprisingly, be used as a regular swing, although the user would have to put up with some funny comments. At the least, the mini-swing should be learned as a way to get out onto the golf course and experience the thrill of hitting the ball around. Beginners should definitely have the mini-swing under control before venturing out on the course. They must be able to move the ball down the fairway without difficulty to make sure they fit in with regular golfers and don't cause delays or holdups.

THE FULL SWING: GOING ONE STEP FURTHER

You've just read about the mini-swing, the heart and core of the golf swing. The full swing, which is what you're striving to master, is just an extension of the mini-swing by making longer backswing and downswing movements. Think of the full swing as an enlargement of the shorter swing.

The backswing is the calm before the storm, so to speak. Your goal is to load up as much power and energy as possible as you wind your upper body. The legs and feet remain your anchors to the ground as the upper body coils around. Then you use a controlled release of all that energy during the downswing. At just the right moment the power is unleashed on the ball so that it travels the maximum amount of distance and control.

Let's take a run through the full swing. Position yourself at address, and then take the club back as you did for the mini-swing. This time, however, continue your body turn past the mini-swing stopping point, coming to a halt when you feel your shoulders have turned 90 degrees to their starting position and the hips 45 degrees. Your left arm will point diagonally away from your body and upward.

This is the top of the backswing, and again, there are many positions to doublecheck to make sure you've performed it well. First, the left knee should point at or just to the right of the ball. Second, the shoulders/back should have

The full swing begins with the address position; at the top of the swing, the club should be just short of parallel or parallel with the ground; as the downswing begins, the 90-degree angle created with the left arm and club shaft should be retained for as long as possible; at impact, the left arm and clubshaft are in a straight line, similar to the address position; at the finish, the golfer faces the target with most of the body weight on the left leg.

turned behind the ball. Third, the back should face the target. Fourth, the club should be parallel or slightly short of parallel with the ground. Fifth, the club should point toward the target. And sixth, the right hand is hovering over the right shoulder.

There are three main points to consider about the backswing that have been debated for many years in teaching circles.

First, the action of the head has been bandied about, with the early teachers believing that the head should be kept still and not allowed to move at all. "Keep your head still" was one of the most common commands in golf. It is now accepted today that there has to be some minimal head movement as long as it's controlled. If the head were kept completely still, the golfer's body weight could reverse over to the left side during the backswing instead of going to the right as it's supposed to. It's okay to move the head toward the right, because it must move that way due to the movement of the spine and back away from the ball. After all, the head can't become disjointed from the shoulders. The key thing to remember is never let the head move ahead of the golf ball during the downswing until after impact has occurred. Doing so puts your weight out of balance, too far forward at impact. The head will move up and forward as the swing is completed in order to follow the rest of the body.

Second, a lesser debate has occurred regarding the left heel. (Yes, swing science has instructors quibbling about heels!) Should the left heel come off the ground during the backswing or remain "planted"? Before expanding on that, take a look at your own heel at the top of the swing. Note whether it's grounded or raised. Now, make your own decision, based on these opinions, whether you should continue as you presently do it. Flexible golfers are better off leaving the heel grounded. It eliminates additional movements you don't need and keeps the swing under control. You maintain a firm foundation and feel "grounded."

On the other hand, it's not harmful to raise the heel off the ground. If it comes up, it's not a swing fault as long as the left leg hasn't spun so far to the right that most of your body weight is on the right leg and hardly any on the left. What is helpful about raising the heel is that it allows for a bigger shoulder turn, which should translate into more yardage. Raising the left heel is sometimes a necessity for those people who aren't flexible enough to keep it planted; senior golfers especially will need to lift it. A good rule of thumb about the heel is to keep at least half the foot on the ground and only lift the heel an inch or so.

"No one has ever conquered golf and no one ever will."

BEN HOGAN

Just keep in mind that whether you lift the heel or keep it grounded, your body weight must switch to predominantly the right side at the top of the swing.

The third debated point is the left arm. "Keep the left arm straight" has been commanded probably as much as "don't move the head." And like our previous two points of debate, there has been some lessening of concern about the left arm in recent years. At one point, teachers stressed that the left arm had to remain rigidly straight from the address position until after impact. The problem here is that some people don't have the flexibility and the strength to keep the arm straight, particularly at the top of the swing. The benefit is that the left arm can be an excellent pivot point or lever when it's held straight. And it means one less movement you have to make on the downswing to straighten it out. One of the best examples of the benefits of a straight left arm is professional Davis Love III, the 1997 PGA Championship winner. His full arc creates a lot of distance potential.

But a look at most fine players at the top of the swing shows they have a slight bend in the arm at the elbow. Then, during the downswing, the arm straightens out again for the impact position. So, if you are flexible enough to keep the left arm straight at the top, that's wonderful and of great benefit to you. But don't be tied into a straight left arm if it can't be done. You'll get it straight at the key moment as you swing down.

LETTING THE POWER FLOW

You've been left at the top of the swing in our full-swing discussion, so it's time to get on with the grand finale to the swing's most difficult portion to perform well the point of impact.

Many amateurs can look quite sensational during the backswing, appearing as fundamentally sound as the best professional. They can get their body and the club in beautiful position, and look like they're ready for the tour. But the motion from the top of the swing to impact is where amateurs and poor players most often "lose it."

Why does it happen? Isn't the downswing just a case of duplicating the backswing, just swing the club back the other way? Yes, that's basically it. Releasing all the coiled-up power is the object of the downswing, and the arms and body should follow the same pattern forward as they took on the backswing, with only minor differences.

One of the most important of these differences is that the downswing occurs at a faster pace than the backswing, probably twice as fast. This must be done so that the release of power and energy occurs at its greatest speed. It does no good to swing forward slowly. There would be no "hit" applied to the ball, just a nudge from a decelerating club. So, use as a swing thought the idea of swinging "back slow, forward fast" as a guide. But it can't be done with a lurching motion. As the club is swung forward it's done with acceleration in mind, the unwinding of the body and club done at an increasing rate of speed.

The backswing and downswing aren't completely separate movements at the point they come together, known as the transition. The backswing is just coming to an end when the forward swing begins. It's the same as any motion that has a force going backward before going forward, just as a baseball pitcher rears back to throw but has started coming forward before he's finished winding up. This action helps propel the body forward at a greater rate of speed rather than coming to a halt and having to restart going forward from a dead stop. Arnold Palmer believes the acceleration of the club is one of the five fundamentals inherent in all good golf swings, including grip, address, takeaway, and a quiet-moving head.

The redirection from the backswing to forward swing can't be taught through any drill or conscious thought because it has to become a natural part of a golfer's individual action. Through constant practice the player will learn the trick of moving the left side forward while the arms are still going backward. The speed of the downswing is related to the tempo or pace of the backswing, because there should be some similarity, although the downswing will be quicker. Regarding tempo, Jack Nicklaus felt the backswing and downswing should be carried out at pretty much the same tempo. "The clubhead will always travel much faster coming down than going back, but the hands will not. Thus they should establish the tempo. If you have a fast backswing the downswing should also be fairly fast, otherwise you will lose momentum and therefore distance. If your backswing is slow and the downswing too fast you are likely to lose control of the club at the top of the swing and thus have trouble hitting the ball straight. So work at maintaining a uniform speed."

Nick Faldo described the swing transition this way: "The feeling is of holding back the right side and right leg and starting down with the left knee separating away from it. It's a wonderful sensation once you get it, but not an easy thought for Mr. Average. In harmony with this, the arms have pulled down, ready for a rounded attack into impact."

The key to starting the downswing occurs just as the club and arms are nearing the top of the backswing. There is a feeling that the left foot has taken firmer control as an anchor to the ground and stabilized. The left knee and hip move to the left, rotating in tandem. The turning of the left side helps set up the transfer of weight from the right side to the left. As the lower body unwinds, the shoulders and arms pull the club downward as the left wrist and arm/clubshaft angle is retained for as long as possible.

Champion golfers Byron Nelson and Ben Hogan believed the left leg was of primary importance to the downswing. "The key to starting the downswing properly is the left knee," Nelson said. "During the backswing it moves laterally to the right. Your downswing should begin with this knee, still flexed returning laterally to the left. This movement will anchor your left heel and cause your legs and lower body to slide to your left, establishing that pull pattern with your whole left-side arm-hand unit."

Hogan believed "the hips initiate the downswing. They are the pivotal element in the chain action. Starting them first and moving them correctly—this one action practically makes the downswing. It creates early speed. It transfers the weight from the right foot to the left foot. It takes the hips out of the way and gives your arms plenty of room to pass. It funnels your force forward toward your objective. It puts you in a strong hitting position where the big muscles in the back and the muscles in the shoulders, arms and hands are properly delayed so that they can produce their maximum performance at the right time and place."

Lee Trevino's swing is appreciated for its nontextbook movements. The trick was training himself to repeat the same movements consistently.

During the point of impact, the hips have opened up to the target and point to the left of it. As the hands reach the bottom of the swing arc, they have uncocked so the club has been released at the perfect moment to strike the ball. The left arm and the clubshaft, ideally, are lined up in a straight line at the moment of impact, leaning toward the target.

In the ideal impact position you hit the ball first and then the turf. It may seem odd to do so, but you swing down on the ball to make it go up. The clubface traps the ball against the grass and the loft of the club makes the ball fly in the proper trajectory. That's why, when making practice swings, you should observe where the bottom of the swing arc is hitting the ground, then position the ball just to the right of that spot so the club makes contact with the ball first.

A great benefit of this ball-first impact is that the ball flies through the air more accurately with less variance. Plus, you impart backspin to the ball so that when it hits the green, there is little roll. Backspin allows you to land the ball close to the hole because there's less chance of it bouncing away a great distance. Watch the pros play and notice that their divots always start after they've made contact with the ball.

Observe that at impact the body and club should appear to be in the same position they were at address, except the hips are open about 45 degrees and pointing left of the target. Here's where your practice with the mini-swing will come in handy. If you've learned the correct impact hit, you'll have similar impact positions during your full swing: the shoulders square to the ball-target line but on the verge of opening up, the left shoulder higher than the right, the left wrist flat and not bowed or concave, the arms straightened, the clubshaft leaning forward toward the target, the clubface square to the ball-target line, the upper body and head level with the ball's original position, and the wrists uncocked.

Following impact, the left side of the body continues to turn and rotate, and the left shoulder moves under the chin. Your arms continue swinging forward with the feeling that they are moving straight down the ball-target line. If your arms swing around to the left or out away from your body, it causes the ball to go off line. Strive for the feeling after impact of having the right arm straighten and point ahead of where the ball was. Then continue swinging the arms straight toward the target. If you fail to do this, you haven't fully applied all of the swing power that had been built up.

There's not a lot you can change once the ball has been struck and you're ready to complete the swing with a follow-through. Mickey Wright, one of the finest women players of all time, described the follow-through as "the completed, relaxed expenditure of the momentum of the clubhead generated during the swing itself."

If you've done things correctly to that point, the rest of the swing is easy to complete. The body continues to rotate to the left, with almost all of its weight on the left side. The left leg stiffens and the right leg bends at the knee, with the right foot balanced on the toes. In fact, there should be so much weight on the left side that you could lift the right leg and not lose your balance. If you're not able to do that, then you haven't fully transferred your weight. You've held back on your coil and power. Practice the feeling of getting all your body weight to the left side after impact. Your arms continue moving up and around, finishing so that your hands are over the left shoulder. Your body fully faces the target so that you're staring straight toward the direction you've hit.

PRACTICE IN SLOW MOTION

Because the downswing happens so quickly, practice it by swinging in slow motion over and over again. Practice without a ball in front of you so that you don't focus on the ball but instead can concentrate on the correct movement. Take your time and get used to the feel; you'll be happy later that you allowed your body to get acclimated to this motion. Gradually build speed into the downswing until you feel you have it under control. Your goal should be to swing as hard as possible without causing yourself to lose balance or fall off your feet. When you have the hang of it, start hitting balls.

That explains the swing process, but hardly in a nutshell. There is no substitute for hands-on teaching, which is why in Chapter 9 you'll learn how to take a lesson. Explaining the golf swing in the written word is a big challenge because the game requires a lot of feel. Golfers have to know how certain movements are supposed to feel before they can see the light about what is correct and what isn't.

It doesn't help a new golfer's confidence to watch the swing of a golf professional and be amazed at how easy the process seems. There's little wasted movement by tour pros and, most telling, they don't take hard, uncontrolled swings. As Julius Boros once remarked, "People often ask me, 'How do you hit the ball so far when you swing so easy?' The answer is simple. I hit hard. Notice I didn't say I swing hard. The distance your ball travels is governed solely by the amount of power you unleash at impact."

Professionals keep the swing smooth and let all the proper angles they've set up throughout the swing work to make the ball go far and straight. You can accomplish much the same with similar tempo and control, and by remembering a swing thought Mickey Wright used about trying to feel the clubhead as she swung: "A swing is a conscious feeling of the weight and position of the clubhead at all times throughout the swing."

ANSWERING SOME QUESTIONS

The following Q&A should help answer some other swing questions for the new golfer.

Should I PlayLeft-handed or Right-handed?

The common thinking long ago was that a right-handed person should play as a rightie and left-handed as a leftie. But in recent years another kind of thinking came along, based on the fact that a golfer's lead arm on the downswing (the left for a right-handed player, for instance) should be the strongest arm. That got people thinking that right-handed persons should play left-handed and vice versa. Another way of thinking is to play golf in accordance with other activities.

If you bat leftie in baseball, then play golf as a leftie. If that doesn't help satisfy the question, then consider how well the player shifts his weight from both sides. If a left-handed person can make a better weight shift as a rightie, then play from that side. If it's better as a leftie, play as a leftie.

If I'm Making a Change in My Grip, Should I do it Gradually or All at Once?

The grip should be fixed completely right off the bat if it is really ineffective. It has to be in the fingers for the full swing. But circumstances vary. It is not easy to change somebody's grip. They lose all their golf balls and lose interest. For that reason, it could be better to change a grip gradually. It should be done according to the ability of the player.

How Long Does it Take for a Grip Change to Take Effect?

Grip changes are the hardest for any player to do because it is their first sense of feel. Normally, the first response to a grip change is very negative. In terms of the actual feel in a golfer's hands, however, the result may begin to tell them something else. So, the more successful they are in getting the result, the better they begin to feel. And it is not so much the feel in their hands that has changed, but the ball is telling them one thing, so they are relating in more of a positive way. Golfers should know up front that a new grip is going to feel terrible; they might as well accept that it's not going to feel good.

I Have Trouble Getting the Club Started on the Takeaway. Any Advice?

Grip, posture, and takeaway dictate a lot about whether the swing is going to be successful or not. A simple thought to getting the club started is to think of the left shoulder. Picture the left shoulder pushing the club back. You must trust that if the left shoulder is moving back, the rest of the left side is also moving. Keep the left arm straight at address, and by pushing the club back with the left shoulder you'll feel good extension for the first couple of feet of the backswing and should avoid a jerky feeling.

ON THE PUTTING GREEN

In time, you will become good enough with the full swing that you can focus on the game's great equalizer: putting.

A small percentage of players become great ball strikers, but the opportunities expand when it comes to putting. An awful full-swing player would get trounced against a better player, but if that same poor player was a magnificent putter, she would have a chance to beat the player with the better swing.

And consider what good putting can do for the final figures on your scorecard. A golfer who bats the ball all around the course and is equally sloppy on the putting green, taking three or four putts each time, will be a 100-plus shooter and will always be a 100-plus shooter. But good putters can bring scores down in a hurry, even if they can't get to the green in short order. Taking no more than two putts a hole can mean chopping off 18 to 36 shots a round and be the difference between enjoying golf and giving it up.

Conversely, an excellent shotmaker would be frustrated to no limit if he consistently took more than two putts a hole, but he would be in the top level of players if he holed a lot of putts and rarely three-putted.

No matter a golfer's ability, poor putting can pull his entire game down. Putting should be so simple, but it can cause great frustration and affect the desire to improve.

Putting is a totally different kind of motion and feel in comparison with the full swing. It requires touch, imagination, and gentleness, compared with the aggressiveness and strength required to do the full swing well. The only swing area comparable with putting is the short game, which also requires touch, feel, and imagination. You don't have to be muscular to be a great putter, you just need soft hands, a good judgment of pace in the putting stroke, and the smarts to understand how a putt will break, commonly known as reading the greens.

One of the game's all-time greatest putters, Dave Stockton Sr., said it well when he talked about how he develops the touch for good putting. "Putting is not about strength, so it doesn't require flexibility exercises or weight lifting. It is a matter of hand-eye coordination, and you should do anything you can to help develop and refine it. I feel putts better if I shoot pool the night before. I also do needlepoint, occasionally, which also helps. Fly-fishing would be another good exercise."

Putting is easy to practice, too. Nearly every golf course has a practice putting green next to the clubhouse. Public courses allow anyone to come and putt around. And as long as your back can handle it, putting can be done for countless hours. Make it a point to putt even on days you're not playing, or during a lunch break. Just little segments of practice time can be valuable and help create the confidence and faith so important in the putting stroke. The more you practice the less you feel mechanically minded, which is always a plus for a skill that must feel natural and flowing and be done with a positive mind-set.

Chapter 3 described the kinds of putters available for use. Settle on a type that feels the best to you, regardless of its appearance or style. Putting is very much based on being in a comfort zone, so consider that your No. 1 priority in picking a flatstick.

Also of importance is considering where the sweet spot is on the clubface. This is the location where the ball comes off the putterface with the most solid feeling because it has the most weight behind it, or it is the balance point, as with a heel-toe balanced putter. Sometimes the directional marking on a putter will be at the sweet spot. Other times you have to discover it yourself. You can do this by holding the putter in front of you with your left hand so that it dangles with the putterface toward you. Strike the clubface a couple of times with the right index finger. Start in the middle and see if the putter twists or rebounds straight back. If it twists, keep tapping in other spots until the putter returns without twisting. That's the sweet spot and it's the location you should always use to make contact with the ball. If it's not marked with the directional line, put a thin piece of tape there so you know where to strike the ball during practice.

GRIPPING THE PUTTER

In discussing the full-swing grip earlier, we mentioned that the club is held in the fingers of the hands. The putting grip is the opposite and is mainly held in the palms. To grip the putter, hold the handle diagonally across the left palm from the base of the index finger to the bottom-right palm. Simply close the hand and rest the thumb on top of the grip. To put on the right hand, the thumb pad of that hand sits on top of the left thumb, the right thumb sits on the shaft, the right little finger is up against the middle finger of the left hand, and lastly, the left index finger rests on top of the fingers on the right hand. This grip setup has your hands in "opposition" with each other. In other words, they face each other equally so the putterface is less likely to open or close during the stroke.

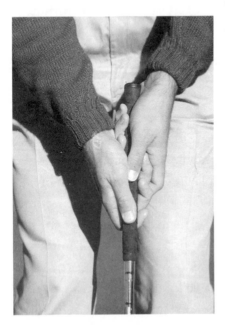

A feature of the putting grip is having the hands in perfect "opposition" to each other.

The feel of a putter is different for everyone. This grip is an ideal, textbook variety. Over time, you might find one that's different, as Lee Trevino did. "I put all ten fingers on the shaft, merely sliding my right hand down a fraction so that the right little finger does not

The putter is held more in the palms than in the fingers, as in the full-swing grip.

overlap the left forefinger but instead is on the shaft. This gives me the feeling of having more control with my right hand by having that little finger on the leather."

Your grip pressure should be similar to the full-swing grip. There should be no tension in the fingers, arms, and shoulders. You should be comfortable, not rigid. This loose feeling helps move the arms and shoulders back and forth in a pendulum motion. The rest of the body, in particular the head, remain still.

As for posture, have a slight flex in the knees and bend over from the hips so your eyes are positioned directly over the ball. (Determine if your eyes are over the ball by holding a ball from your eyes and letting it drop. Watch where it lands and use that for ball position.) Put an even amount of weight on both legs. Your hands should be under the chest, with the back of the left hand facing down the line of the putt to the hole. The feet are no wider than the shoulders and the toes form a straight line parallel to the putting line, which is the path you expect the ball to take toward the hole.

Not only should the ball be positioned under your eyes but it should also be at the point where the putter bottoms out. You can find this by taking practice strokes in slow motion and noticing where the bottom of the swing arc occurs. Keep that spot in mind and position the ball there; in most cases, the ball will be between the middle of the stance and the left foot.

Aim is always important in any shot you play, but it's especially so on the putting green. A slight miscalculation with putting aim can mean the difference between a make and a miss by just a quarter-inch or so. And that's even with making a good stroke. Most putters have a hash mark or directional line on the top side for alignment. When you have a path in mind, use that mark to square the clubface on the perfect line.

The regularity of a good putting routine will put you at ease. It begins with quickly moving to your ball upon reaching the green, being sure not to step on the line other balls will take to the hole. Mark your ball, clean it, and study your

The arms and shoulders form a triangle that rocks back and forth during the putting stroke.

putting line right away if you'll be putting first. If you're later in the order, try to sneak peaks at the putting line while others are putting, but don't disturb their routines or get in their line of sight.

When it's your turn to putt, replace the ball, take any final looks you need to determine the break, and stand to the side of the ball. Take a couple of practice strokes, move into your stance, and then aim the clubface behind the ball. Glance at the line, recheck your aim, take one more look, make a final check, and stroke the putt. This entire procedure, once it becomes ingrained as a natural process, will go quickly and be quite effective as you become a good putter. All the preparatory work before the stroke will be done quickly, leaving you free to visualize making and reading the putt and making a good stroke.

When you are ready to make the stroke, line up the putterface first, being sure to have the ball directly in front of the sweet spot, then step in with your feet for stance and posture. Have your toes, knees, shoulders, and hips line up with the direction you want the ball to go. When you're ready to stroke the putt, be sure to picture in your mind how hard or soft you need to hit the ball to make it go the proper distance. Imagine having the ball "die" about a foot past the hole.

The putting stroke is a smooth motion, similar to the smoothness of the take-away on a full shot. Every part of the body should be still, except for the triangle formed by the shoulders, arms, and hands. The great Scottish teacher and player Tommy Armour observed, "To become a good putter the main requisites are to keep the head dead still and make the putter blade go accurately toward the hole." The triangle swings the putter back and forth like a pendulum, maintaining the angles formed by the elbows at address. Keep a bit more grip pressure in the left hand during the stroke and don't let the wrists bend or flex, especially the left wrist. Doing so would certainly cause the putterface to misalign at impact.

The right hand is a support to the left, helping keep the triangle in perfect union. The right elbow should stay closely tucked to the body and not flare out like a chicken wing.

Proper acceleration is key to good putting. There should be no stopping or stalling during the stroke. Keep the putter moving on an even level, not quick on the back and slow to the front. Avoid making a big backswing and short follow-through, which doesn't deliver much punch to the putt and is just the reverse of what most putters do. Some take the putter forward as much as they take it back; others take the putter short back and more through, sort of a popping stroke. These two are much more desirable than a long backswing that barely gets past the ball coming through.

The transition between the back and forward putting motions is well described by American champion golfer Tom Watson. "The putting stroke must be made with rhythm. The change of direction should be smooth and unforced, just as it is with the pendulum of a grandfather clock. The overall speed of your stroke can be fast or slow—mine is pretty fast—so long as it is rhythmic. The transition from the finish of the backswing to the start of the forward stroke should be made at the same speed, like a pendulum."

Try to make the putt roll end over end, not wobble from side to side. This helps the ball stay on line better. To roll the ball practice with a range ball with stripes on it. Put the ball in a way that the stripes are aimed straight down the intended putting line. Then stroke the ball so the stripes roll straight instead of sideways.

READ ANY GOOD GREENS LATELY?

Being decisive is an important key to reading greens, which is the practice of using your sight, hearing, and touch to study how a putt will break. You must develop a good ability to read greens, because a great putting stroke with poor directional judgment does you no good. Making any putts would truly be potluck.

Green reading begins as you approach the putting surface. While heading toward your ball to mark it, notice how the green is sloped. See if the green is flat, or sloped from left to right or right to left. See how tall the grass is; if it's shaggy, you know the putts will roll slowly. Feel with your feet as you walk if the greens are hard or soft. Hard greens tend to be faster than soft greens. As you walk around the green, you'll sense whether you're walking uphill or downhill. And a crunchy noise as you walk hopefully doesn't mean creaky joints; it's a sign that the green has dried out and will be fast and unreceptive to holding shots.

A putt curves or breaks in one of four ways. It could roll straight, it could break left to right, it could break right to left, and it could have a combination of all three shapes. Some putts go uphill, others downhill, and others go up or down and have break. You "read" or determine the break by studying the slopes and tilts to the greens.

If the slope goes from left to right, aim the ball to the left so it sweeps back toward the hole. If the green slopes right to left, you need to aim the ball to the right of the hole, the amount determined by how much the green slopes. You'll determine this amount over time by practicing and playing; the amount of break is also decided by how hard you want to hit the ball. If you want to die the ball into the cup, and thus hit the putt softer, you have to allow for more break. If you want to hit a firmer putt, play less break.

If you miss the putt to the right of the hole on a right-to-left breaking putt, you've missed it on the high side, or "pro side." If it misses to the left of the hole, you lost the putt on the low side, or "amateur side." The same terms apply on left-to-right putts; they're just reversed.

Breaking putts that go downhill must be hit softer than flat putts, so allow for more break. Uphill breaking putts must be hit harder, so allow for less curve. So if the putt isn't flat, you must not only allow for the break of the putt but also for the speed of it as well. As mentioned, for any putt, make the effort to leave the ball a foot beyond the hole if it misses. "You usually miss the hole farther by being short or past it than you ever miss it to one side or the other," said Tommy Armour. "So try, in any way that you can figure out, to get your putts as nearly as humanly possible the right length."

As you get ready to stroke the ball, feel confident that you've picked the right line and have everything in place. Your last thoughts should include the picture that the entire ball is going in, not just part of it. Imagine the ball being swallowed by the hole.

Be assured and confident in all your putting technique, as champion golfer Byron Nelson describes the importance of decisiveness on the greens. "Being decisive is particularly important in putting. Look at the line of a putt, decide how much it will break and how hard you want to hit it, then make the stroke. I've seen very few players get set over a putt, back off, change their minds, and then make the putt."

THE SHORT GAME: GOLF'S GREAT SHOT SAVER

"A good short game is the greatest stroke saver I know. A good short game depends 90 percent on whether you think you have a good short game and can get that ball into or close to the hole. A good short game is feel and confidence." So said golfing great Mickey Wright, who realizes that missing greens is a part of golf. It's what a golfer does with those missed shots, however, that determines how badly they mess up a player's score.

Beginners very likely play half their shots from 50 yards on in around the green. A sharp short game, which includes pitch shots, chip shots, sand play, and putting, can make the difference between an average round and a great one. Here is how you can play a few shots from around the greens.

First, realize that the short game requires a lot of feel from the golfer, who must have good judgment on how hard to hit shots and at what trajectory. This isn't a talent that comes easily, so don't be discouraged if you don't have it from the start. Through constant practice and experience on the golf course, and by using proper technique, feel for the short shots will come in due time.

A chip shot is any shot played from grass around the green and it's usually hit with a low ball-flight. A pitch shot is a longer shot and hit much higher. Nearly every club in your bag can be used for a chip or pitch, but most times you'll use a 7, 8, 9-iron, pitching wedge, or sand wedge.

There are three basic types of pitch shots.

The first is the run shot, a low shot used when there is no trouble in front of the green and the flag is in the middle or toward the back of the green. You play the run shot by narrowing your feet width, opening the stance by pulling the left foot back off the target line, putting your weight on the left side and playing the ball in the middle of your stance. Aim the clubface at the hole and swing the club back similar to the mini-swing backswing, although your lower body shouldn't move very much. Maintain your wrist angle on the downswing and let the club

"If you have a chance, practice a little just after you have finished playing a round. At that time you clearly remember where you had the trouble and you can work on those shots."

TOM WEISKOPF

land on top of the ball. This pinches the ball against the grass and springs it forward on a low flight. Keep your hands moving so the club and hands are ahead of the ball at impact. Finish the swing with your hands about waist or chest high. The ball should fly low and, upon landing, roll for many yards. You can play this shot no matter if your ball is in short or tall grass.

The second shot is the walk shot, a medium-height shot that works best to a flag in the middle or back of the green as it doesn't roll very much. The walk shot is very much like a regular wedge shot. You play it by standing with a square stance and the clubface aimed at the target. Your weight is balanced on both legs, and the ball should be positioned off the left heel. Use almost no leg movement as you swing the club back until your hands are waist high and the club is pointing upward. Hit the ball with a descending blow, trusting the loft of the club to get the ball up. Finish with a mirror image of the backswing, the club pointing skyward. Use this shot out of any grass situation.

The third shot is the sit shot, a high shot that lands softly with little roll and is ideal for tight situations when there isn't much green between the fringe and the flag. It's great for hitting over tall objects, too, but you can only play it when the ball is sitting with a good lie on short grass. It's a great shot saver, but it's very tricky to play. You play the shot with the clubface open, as if it's aimed right of the target, and your stance open, meaning the left foot is moved away from the ball-target line. Position the ball off the left heel, with your weight evenly on both legs. Swing the club back along your stance line; it will feel like the club is swinging away from you. Take the club up abruptly and down the same way in a U shape. Allow the club to hinge up on the backswing and follow-through. Because this shot is very precise, take a couple of practice shots to see where the club bottoms out, then make sure the ball is positioned in that spot. Failure to do this could make you hit the ball fat or thin.

You can use a pitching wedge for the run and walk shots, but use a higher-lofted club like a sand wedge for the sit shot.

An often-used chip shot is taking a 7- or 8-iron for hitting a ball on the fringe. The stroke used here is very much like the putting stroke. You can either hold the club like a putter or use the full-swing grip. Line up the shot as you would a putt, because this kind of chip shot is very makable. At address, put more weight on your left side and position the ball off the left foot. Angle the club forward so the hands are ahead of the ball. Then make a putting stroke, letting the club fall on the ball so it pinches the ground shortly then springs forward on a low trajectory. Try your best to let the shot roll as much as possible toward the hole so it rolls like a putt.

A sand wedge, of course, is the club of choice for hitting the basic bunker shot. When you're faced with a shot from a greenside bunker, the first objective is simply to get out. There is no need to get cute with being extra precise, unless you have pro caliber talent. Having a positive attitude is a key requirement to the successful bunker shot. Another is making sure you have a sand wedge that is designed to bounce off the sand rather than dig into it. And lastly, you need the technique to get out of the sand in one swing.

When you face a bunker shot of up to 30 yards, play it by first examining where you want the ball to land. Step into the bunker from behind the ball and take a stance similar to the sit shot, with your left foot pulled back and clubface open. Your feet should be in line with the landing spot you've chosen. Wiggle your feet in the sand for solid footing, but don't test the sand any further, because that's against the rules. You also cannot ground the club in the sand, meaning the club cannot touch the sand until impact.

Position the ball off your left foot and flex your knees slightly. There should be about 80 percent of your weight on the left leg. Make sure the club is hovering above the sand and keep your body still over the ball. Swing the club along the stance line so the club travels away from you. Keep your legs "quiet" so they don't move very much. Swing mainly with your arms in a U shape. As you swing down, try to make the leading edge of the clubface enter the sand about an inch or two behind the ball. Attempt to take a thin sliver of sand that begins behind the ball and finishes an inch or two in front of it.

The ball should come out with medium height. Depending on how well you nipped it, the ball will either roll a short distance or take a hop or two and stop dead. The ball won't react very well, however, if you had to hit it to land on a downslope.

All of these score-saving shots around the greens point to the fact that there is no substitute for a great short game. It can truly increase your enjoyment of the game as you knock off strokes from your score. Corey Pavin, the 1995 U.S. Open champion, said, "Chipping is critical for the simple reason that even expert golfers miss several greens per round with their iron shots. The only way to score well is to consistently chip the ball so close to the hole that you can't help but make your share of par-saving putts. Poor chippers invariably attribute their high scores to their poor driving or putting, all the while ignoring the fact that their sloppy short game is the true reason they shot a high score."

 Chapter 7

THE BENEFIT OF HANDICAPS AND COURSE RATINGS

HANDICAPS: PLAYING OTHERS ON EQUAL TERMS

In the world of sports, golf is one of the few that has a method for putting players of different abilities on equal footing when they compete against each other on the same playing field. The handicapping system allows a poor player the opportunity to play, and even beat, a better player in competition.

Only in a few sports, such as golf, bowling, sailing, and horse racing, is one side given a head start or the situation of all competitors adjusted so that everyone begins on equal terms. A golfer's handicap—a number that indicates their level of ability—brings a 30-handicapper to the level of a scratch player so the two can enjoy a round together and have a little competition at the same time. It makes the poorer player feel he has a chance against a superior opponent.

Before getting into some further explanation of handicapping, let's look at its background. The creative Scottish people, who did so much to form the game of golf, also were responsible for the handicap system, which is first referred to in documents of the late 1600s. The Scots applied the concept to golf after seeing it used in horse racing. Before a race, a jockey was handed his odds for winning a race in a cap, thus "hand-in-cap" soon became handicap.

The Scots chose to assign odds to golf matches as well. A golfer was given a certain number of strokes against another player. This adjustment of strokes went hand in hand with bets being placed on who the bettors thought would win.

In early handicapping, the most common odds gave the lesser player a set pattern of strokes from the better player. There was third-one, in which the player got a shot every three holes; half-one, a shot on alternate holes; one more, a shot every hole; and two more, two strokes on every hole. "Getting a shot" means a golfer may subtract one stroke from his actual score on a hole. If a 6 was made on a par 5, the player could record a 5 on the card for use in the match.

The term handicap entered into common golf language around 1870 as handicap tournaments became more popular. A committee assigned strokes to the players, who were given a chance to disagree if they weren't happy with the total. In the 1880s, the predecessor to today's method for determining a handicap was started; a player's best three scores of the year were averaged and the course rating or scratch score was subtracted to provide the handicap. The best-three-scores system was adopted for use in America by the USGA in 1911.

The USGA set up its own handicap system in 1912. Handicapping helped it establish tournament fields, such as not allowing players with handicaps higher than 6 to compete in the U.S. Amateur (the present figure is a 2.4 Handicap Index or better).

Refinements over the years were made to improve how the course-rating system and figuring of the correct handicap could work together, but some of the changes served only to make the system more confusing. The idea of "current ability" was introduced in which a handicap was figured based on a player's best ten of his last fifteen scores. That was later changed to numerous other formulas before the best ten of the last twenty scores was commonly accepted.

There is a lot of incentive to having a handicap. It is needed not only to participate in most tournaments but also to raise the status of a golfer in the eyes of other players. And keeping a handicap is a great way to gauge how well a golfer is improving or regressing, whatever the case may be. Unfortunately, a National Golf Foundation study in 1997 revealed that less than 20 percent of all golfers maintain a handicap.

PURPOSE BEHIND COURSE RATING

Working in tandem with handicap strokes is course rating, known as the evaluation of the playing difficulty of a course. Because a player's handicap is based on his ability to play the course, it was necessary to devise a method for rating the toughness of a course. At first, a course rating was done by calculating how many shots it would take a better player to reach the putting green, then adding two more shots. This not only helped develop a hole's par, but the strength of the course, too.

When the handicap system was first developed in the United States in 1912, the USGA decided that a course's rating should be determined by the expected score the present U.S. Amateur champion, Jerome Travers, would make.

But in time a course rating was determined by a team of evaluaters from state or regional golf associations. Clubs cannot rate their own course. A course rating is listed in decimal form and is primarily based on a yardage formula, but evaluators also take into account other course difficulties, such as topography, fairway width, rough, amount of out-of-bounds, water hazards and trees, bunkers, size of the greens, green speed, and how the course affects a player psychologically.

The tougher the course, the higher the course rating. Shinnecock Hills Golf Club in Southampton, New York, for instance, has a course rating of 74.6 from its longest set of tees. Easier golf courses usually have course ratings in the mid to high 60s.

WHAT IS A HANDICAP INDEX?

For many years, a golfer's handicap was listed as a whole number (see how it was determined under the heading Handicap Systems later in this chapter). Golfers now utilize two handicap figures: a home handicap, which is still a whole number, and a USGA Handicap Index.

The home handicap is a straight handicap total for use at a golfer's regular home golf course. The Handicap Index, on the other hand, is the number to use when a player is away from home at a different course. The Handicap Index is expressed in decimal form and is devised for use with the USGA's Slope Rating/course handicap table.

When a golfer goes to a different course, she needs to check the course handicap table that should be posted somewhere in the clubhouse, golf shop, or locker room. The player needs to know from which set of tees he'll play that day, because the allocation of strokes is different due to the change in difficulty from each set of tees. By checking where her Handicap Index falls on the table, a golfer knows how many handicap strokes she can get on that course for the round. And by looking at the course scorecard and seeing how the handicap holes are distributed, a golfer can see on which holes he will get a stroke.

THE NEED FOR COURSE RATINGS AND SLOPE

The difference in difficulty from one course to the next is the reason course ratings were created initially, and they were later followed by the Slope Index.

A course rating is a number representing the score an expert, or scratch handicap, golfer would be expected to shoot from a selected set of tees. As an example of how it's used, let's look at the Stadium Course at the Tournament Players Club at Sawgrass, in Ponte Vedra Beach, Florida, which is the site for the Players Championship on the PGA Tour each March.

From the regular tees, which total 5,761 yards in length, the course rating is 68.7, the score a scratch player would be expected to shoot from that set of tees. However, from the longest set of tees, called TPC, the course totals 6,857 yards and the course rating is 74.0. A more difficult course than the Stadium Course would have higher numbers, and an easier course lower numbers.

For many years, golfers used the course rating to figure how many handicap strokes they would get on a course. However, because every golfer can't be expected to play like a scratch golfer, the USGA put together a second ratings chart starting in 1987 called the Slope Index, which helps even out things for the average player. The system was first put in use in 1983, but became mandatory in 1991 if courses wanted their players to have official USGA handicaps.

Slope does what its name suggests by curving the handicap strokes a player gets to adjust to the difficulty or easiness of a course compared with the player's regular course. To explain, let's use the Stadium Course again. If a player with a Handicap Index of 12.2 at his home course played the more difficult Stadium Course from the TPC set of tees, it would not be fair to only allow her twelve shots. Upon arriving at the Stadium Course, the golfer looks at the course's Slope Index sheets in the clubhouse or locker room and refers to the TPC tee Slope Index. It would read 135; according to a Slope Index rating of 135, a player with a Handicap Index of 12.2 gets fifteen shots due to the course difficulty. The player would get fewer shots if he was playing a course that was easier than his regular course.

HANDICAP SYSTEMS

Many public and private courses have electronic handicapping systems set up for use by members of their men's and women's associations. The most common setup is a computer located in the men's and women's locker rooms or a single computer in a central location. A software program for figuring handicaps is loaded onto the computer. After a round of golf, the player enters his score (using the Equitable Stroke Control system) and the program does all the figuring. A list of adhesive labels is run out frequently during the season so the player can carry his USGA Handicap and Handicap Index around to refer to wherever he plays.

One of the prominent systems in use is the GHIN, the USGA's Golf Handicap and Information Network begun in 1980. In addition to tabulating handicaps, the GHIN is capable of pairing players for a competition, printing scorecards, and marking the holes on which a player will receive strokes. The GHIN also has the capability of assisting in a Rules of Golf question.

If you do not have access to a computer handicap system, a makeshift handicap can be computed by the golfer. But be forewarned that it takes a lot of bookkeeping to maintain a handicap, and some competitions that want a USGA-caliber handicap might not accept one that's self-computed.

A handicap can be figured based on the lowest ten differentials from a golfer's most-recent twenty scores. A differential is the difference between a golfer's score and the course rating. If a player shot an 89 and the course had a rating of 73.5, the differential is 15.5.

Once the ten lowest differentials are determined, they are added together and compared with a USGA handicap differential chart. The chart uses more than twenty ranges to specify handicaps. If the ten differentials added up to 113.5, for instance, according to the USGA chart the golfer would have a course handicap of 10.

The USGA has set Handicap Index limits of 36.4 for men and 40.4 for women.

HOW TO USE A HANDICAP

Once you have a USGA handicap, the question is what to do with it. The main use for a handicap is its equalizing ability in competition, which can take two forms.

First, when friends go out for a casual round of golf, they can use their handicaps to set up a match. For example, if Player A is an 18-handicapper and Player B is a 10, they can use their strokes in one of two ways to play each other in a match-play format. They can both use their handicaps to get a shot on the appropriate holes, or they can subtract the lesser handicap from the greater and have the weaker player receive that number of strokes. In this case, Player A would get eight shots from Player B, meaning on the No. 1 through No. 8 handicap holes on the course, Player B would subtract one shot from her score. Providing the golfers played their regular games, they would have a close match by the end, the handicap system would have done its job and Player A, although having a higher handicap, would have a good chance of winning.

Things would be a little more complicated for a foursome. If the group members had handicaps of 5, 8, 12, and 15, the common practice would be to have the 5-handicapper play at scratch and not receive any strokes, the 8 would get three shots, the 12 would get seven, and the 15 would get ten. The idea is to always work off the player with the lowest handicap.

If a player is to receive more than eighteen strokes in an eighteen-hole match, he gets double strokes on holes equal to the number above eighteen. So a golfer getting twenty-four shots, for example, would get two shots on handicap holes one through six and a single shot on holes seven through eighteen.

Individual hole handicapping is printed on the scorecard. The allocation of handicap strokes is done by an evaluation process of the golf course. Each hole on a course is looked at to see which ones a golfer would need strokes on the most. So the hardest hole on the course is usually the No. 1 handicap hole, and the rest of the holes progress from there up to the eighteenth handicap hole, usually the easiest hole on the course.

Golfers like to evaluate the hole ratings during a round to see if they agree with how the evaluators did. Most disagreements arise over long, difficult par 3s, which usually aren't rated among the toughest holes. The reason goes back to the purpose of allocating strokes among the individual holes. A hole on which even the best player is likely to make a bogey, just as an 18-handicapper would, is not worth ranking highly because everyone is likely to make bogey or worse and the hole would be a wash. So some times a demanding hole doesn't mean it will be one of the first few holes on which to get a shot. As one handicapping expert once said, "The philosophy of handicap stroke allocation is that a stroke should be given on a hole where a player most likely needs that stroke to obtain a half [tie] in a match."

A second competitive format is a tournament involving many players in a stroke-play event. Players keep their scores as usual, holing out on each hole, and turn in a gross score, or the number they actually shot. Then the committee in charge subtracts the player's handicap total from the gross score to compute a net score. The tournament standings would be based on everyone's net score, although most events also give a prize to the gross winner. This common tournament format gives the lesser player a chance to be the top dog. For example, a 25-handicapper who shoots a 95 would be given credit for a 70. A 4-handicapper who shot a gross 75 would be given a 71 and would finish second.

It's plain to see that handicaps put golfers of varying degrees of talent on a similar starting point. They aren't that useful when scratch or near scratch golfers go head to head as their abilities are so close.

POSTING SCORES

The general rule for which scores a golfer may post is that all scores should be recorded.

An important factor is that the score should have Equitable Stroke Control applied to it. The ESC is a method of adjusting a score so that an extremely high score on a hole doesn't drastically affect the player's overall score such that it becomes an unfair representation of his ability or current handicap. A player who usually shoots par, but has a round with four quadruple bogeys, would be posting a score out of the ordinary from her usual play unless the ESC was applied to the score. The ESC also serves to control sandbaggers, those golfers who try to inflate their handicaps so when they enter tournaments and play up to their regular standards, their false handicap can put them way in front of the competition.

The ESC is a way of thinking that came about in the 1800s, but wasn't adopted for use in the United States until 1973. It took a while for it to gain total acceptance in America, but it must be implemented for any score intended to formulate a handicap.

Under the ESC, golfers are assigned a maximum score that can be recorded on any hole, no matter what the par. That maximum number is determined by the golfer's handicap, as follows: Golfers with a handicap of 40 and above can take a maximum of ten shots; 30 to 39, no more than nine; 20 to 29, a limit of eight; 10 to 19, seven or below; and 0 to 9, a maximum of six. (The USGA has amended the ESC for 0-to-9 handicappers so that they can record a maximum score of double bogey on any hole. The modification is optional in 1998 and is mandatory effective January 1, 1999.)

A player need not have played an eighteen-hole round to post a score. Two nine-hole rounds played on different days can be added together, even if it's the same set of nine holes. Just add the scores together and combine the course ratings and average the Slope Index. But two nine-hole scores can't be combined if an eighteen-hole round was played between them. They must be back-to-back nines.

A score can also be posted if a golfer played less than eighteen holes but got in at least thirteen. On the holes that weren't played, simply mark down the par plus add a stroke on holes where you would have received a handicap stroke.

Scores cannot be posted from events that limited the amount of clubs that can be used, such as a one-club tournament. You cannot report scores for which you used winter rules, unless the club or tournament committee gave its approval. You also can't report scores from eighteen-hole courses that are less than 3,000 yards; if most of the holes were played under a scramble format; and if the round was played out of season, which the club will rule on when it's ready to close for the winter. Rounds played while golfing in Sun Belt states can be posted even if your home course is considered out of season.

If you pick up on a hole, write down the score you would have most likely made, as long as it doesn't exceed the ESC limit. If you take a mulligan on a hole, you must mark down that you scored par plus any handicap stroke(s), regardless of what you actually scored. And lastly, if you played a round by yourself, the score can be posted, but not if you played two balls all the way around.

USGA DEFINITIONS
Primary Handicap Terms

Equitable Stroke Control (ESC)   The downward adjustment for handicap purposes of unusually high scores on individual holes.

USGA Handicap Index   A number that represents the ability of a player on a course of average difficulty. It is expressed as a whole number plus a decimal fraction.

Course Handicap   The number of handicap strokes a player receives from a specific set of tees at the course being played. A course handicap is determined by applying the player's USGA Handicap Index to a Course Handicap Table or course handicap formula. It is expressed in whole numbers of strokes.
USGA Slope Rating: *A measure of the relative playing difficulty of a course for players with handicaps above and below scratch.*

WHERE TO GO FOR HELP

The USGA is the best source for handicap information. It has numerous books, pamphlets, and multimedia sources that detail every scope of handicapping, available for a fee. A listing of these materials can be obtained from the USGA by phoning its order department, 1-800-336-4446 or (908) 234-2300.

 Chapter 8

GOLFER, KNOW THY RULES

One of the game's great sources of comic relief is the Rules of Golf, that infernal collection of demands and restrictions on a golfer's freedom to play golf any way he wants to. You might ask, How can something so seemingly convoluted and nonsensical be a source of amusement?

It's simple. Just by the fact that the golf ball lands in some ridiculous places, and there has to be a rule that tells a golfer what to do in that situation, there are plenty of opportunities for laughter when a rule has to be applied. Even professional golfers can hit the ball all over the lot, ending up in some unusual places.

For instance, take the time a ball struck by Hale Irwin hit a female spectator at a PGA Tour event and the ball finished in her bra. When the tour rules official arrived on the scene, he told Irwin that he had to retrieve the ball and drop it on or near the spot where the woman stood. The ruling put Irwin in a ticklish situation, but the woman did the ball removal for him.

Or there was the time at another tour stop when Curtis Sifford overshot a putting green. When he saw the shot heading long, he yelled "Fore!" to get the attention of the fans. Hearing his call, the spectators moved and in the jostling, one woman's hot dog fell on the grass. Incredibly, Sifford's ball ended up on the hot dog. He was allowed to clean off the mustard, move the hot dog, and drop the ball at the spot where the hot dog had been.

Even the great players need to call upon the rules now and again. Arnold Palmer read the local rules sheet to determine his options from this ditch during a PGA tour event in the 1960s.

Australian Kel Nagle once was credited with shooting a 105 for eighteen holes because he had written his front-nine score—34—in the spot meant for his score on the ninth hole. The rules say he had to take the score for which he had signed, even though he had scored much less.

And in another ruling, Chi Chi Rodriguez once sliced a ball onto a small island that was in a water hazard along a hole he played in a Canadian tournament. He was allowed to play the ball from the island, but to avoid getting his shoes and pants wet, he had his tall, lanky caddie carry him back and forth to the island in the calf-deep water. Chi Chi stayed dry and made a birdie on top of it.

The list could go on and on. But along with the comedy is a lot of seriousness and confusion. The rules are like tax codes and mortgage agreements: the more they are explained, the harder they can be to comprehend. To fully understand the rules, you need to put them to use and see them in action. Only then can you connect with the many terms, phrases, and rulings that on paper seem quite ponderous and almost impossible to digest.

The Rules of Golf aren't meant to confuse golfers. When understood and used at the appropriate times, they can be a golfer's best ally in making sure they shoot the best—and most honest—score possible. When rules aren't understood and are applied incorrectly, then the golfer is his own worst enemy and in all likelihood raises his score needlessly.

> "Golf is a really funny game. Sometimes you can be hitting the ball very well, but you just can't get the ball in the hole. So many things you've got to think about. But if you can just try and keep it simple to just play your game, be as positive as you can and just have the belief that you're going to win, you're going to win one or a couple. Hopefully you can be a little stronger than the other guy and hopefully you won't make as many mistakes as the other guy."
>
> ERNIE ELS

The rules makers have worked for decades to improve the language of the rules to make them as easy to understand as possible. There are very few wasted phrases or words. Everything you see in the rules are meant to be as specific as possible in explaining how to apply them.

And apply them you must if you want to report a score that's as close to accurate as can be so you are aware of your true abilities. Rules help decide the correct order of finish in tournaments so the proper winner is crowned. Rules are important to make sure any wagers and bets are done correctly. And when the correct score is reported because of a ruling, accurate handicaps are possible.

There are many advantages to knowing the rules, but it's probably safe to write that most golfers don't fully abide by the rules or even pay any attention to them. Few people are harmed by that as long as the golfer who lacks a rules conscience doesn't try to bring an incorrect handicap or sloppy rules behavior into a situation where everyone else is strict in following the rules. There's just no way the two can mix.

As you learn the rules, and later make use of them on the course, it's important to keep a few thoughts in mind. First, a ruling may be made differently depending upon the type of format you're playing. A rule can go one way if the format is stroke play, and another way if it's match play. Watch for wording that specifies the differences. There are also references to team play, primarily under Rules 29 to 32. Second, it's important to note who was involved in the rule. It makes a difference, for instance, if a ball in motion was stopped by the player's caddie or the caddie of another player. And third, be aware of where the rule incident took place. Rules are not necessarily applied the same for a ball in the bunker, for instance, compared with a ball in the fairway.

WHY HAVE RULES ANYWAY?

Elsewhere in this book you'll read comments about how one of the benefits of golf is getting the player away from the craziness of the world, both the restrictions enforced at work and the daily demands of life at home. Golf is a release from structured life. So why is it necessary for golfers to have their "freedom" mucked up with a book full of thirty-four rules and other nitty-gritty details?

Well, for the same reason there are traffic laws. There have to be guidelines all golfers go by to maintain a sense of orderliness and smoothness on the course. We'd all love to do our own thing, but if we did, the chaos that would follow wouldn't allow us to enjoy the game very long. Rules let all golfers play together in peaceful coexistence and set the ground rules for play and the type of equipment they can use.

This, surely, was one of the main intents the first rules makers had when a list of thirteen original rules were introduced in 1744 by the Honourable Company of Edinburgh Golfers in Scotland. Here's how that first set read:

1. You must tee your ball within a club length of the hole.
2. Your tee must be upon the ground.
3. You are not to change the ball which you strike off the tee.
4. You are not to remove stones, bones, or any break-club for the sake of playing your ball, except upon the fair green, and that only within a club length of your ball. [A break-club is any object that might cause a club to break when swinging at the ball.]
5. If your ball come among water, or any watery filth, you are at liberty to take out your ball, and bringing it behind the hazard, and teeing it, you may play it with any club and allow your adversary a stroke for so getting out your ball.
6. If your balls be found anywhere touching one another, you are to lift the first ball till you play the last.
7. At holing, you are to play your ball honestly for the hole, and not play upon your adversary's ball, not lying in your way to the hole.
8. He whose ball lies farthest from the hole is obliged to play first.
9. If you should lose your ball by its being taken up, or in any other way, you are to go back to the spot where you struck last, and drop another ball, and allow your adversary a stroke for the misfortune.
10. No man, at holing his ball, is to be allowed to mark to the hole with his club or anything else.
11. If a ball be stop'd by any person, horse, dog, or anything else, the ball so stop'd must be played where it lies.
12. If you draw your club in order to strike, and proceed as far in the stroke as to be bringing down your club—if then your club shall break in any way, it is to be accounted a stroke.
13. Neither trench, ditch, nor dyke made for the preservation of the links, nor the scholars' holes, nor the soldiers' lines, shall be accounted a hazard, but the ball is to be taken out, teed, and played with any iron club.

Two years after this set of rules was devised, the golfers at St. Andrews, Scotland, adopted them for use. After the 1850s, control of the rules was turned over to the Royal and Ancient Golf Club in St. Andrews.

That set of thirteen rules doesn't make for exciting reading, but it shows that rules verbiage was dry from the beginning. However, these rules still have some relevancy to the game we play today. The old Rule 8 is close to the procedure golfers follow on the course these days, and Nos. 2, 3, 7, 9, and 10 are still part of the thirty-four rules in the present book. How did we get to thirty-four rules from thirteen? The total was forty-one in 1980, but since has been reduced. The primary reason for the increase is that, as the ability of players changed and evolved, as did equipment and course architecture, numerous rules situations arose that needed codifying.

The rules continue to undergo changes, but at a much slower pace. From the first set administered by the Edinburgh golfers, the rule book today is under the charge of the Royal and Ancient Golf Club of St. Andrews, Scotland, and the USGA. The two bodies meet every four years (the next meeting is scheduled in 1999) to work together on all modifications and changes. They share duties for governing the rules around the world: the USGA for the United States, Mexico, and Puerto Rico, and the R&A for the rest of the world. The two groups first met in 1951, having worked on separate rule books up to that point. The 1983 meeting was one of the most productive, as a smaller version of the rules was released. The two sides have minor differences, but for the most part have a unified code of rules.

Despite attempts to make the rules as easy to digest and use as possible, there are still hundreds of confused golfers each year who don't understand how a rule should be applied. The USGA alone receives more than 10,000 calls, letters, and E-mail messages a year asking for the association's opinion on whether a ruling was done correctly or to help make one on the spot for a tournament being held. Every so often one of these inquiries helps the USGA add to its other rules reference book, *The Decisions on the Rules of Golf.* Oh yes, there is another book, and this one's more detailed than the regular rule book. The decision book has specific references to rulings about some of the most far-fetched occurrences on a golf course. Here's one example:

Decision 18/3 refers to "ball in fork of tree moves in relation to ground but not in relation to fork." The question is: A ball rests in the fork of a branch of a tree. The player climbs the tree to play his next stroke. The branch bends under his weight. Although the ball has moved relative to the ground, it has not moved relative to the fork. Is the ball deemed to have moved? Answer: The ball is deemed not to have moved as it did not move in relation to the fork of the tree in which it was lodged.

No kidding, that was an actual incident that now is a part of the decision book. All of these types of rulings—and there are more than 1,000 of them—are kept in one collection so if another golfer has the same thing happen to him—as great as the odds might be against it—there is a reference to it in the decision book. Even if a golfer never needs to use the decision book for a ruling, it makes a heck of an entertaining read to see what's happened to other players.

All the nitpicks and inquiries into the rules indicate there is a fair amount of players who want to do things the right way. It's important to them that they play honestly and in proper fashion, and they're probably having fun at the same time. Playing by the rules doesn't have to be a negative situation. It can become a great habit. Golf, after all, is probably the only sport that has the player be the first referee, rather than have an official make the first call. Referees are brought in later when the player can't make a ruling himself.

Through the centuries golf has developed a unique and marvelous code of integrity, honor, and fair play. The Rules of Golf play a major role in continuing that honor system to each generation of players, who deal honestly with themselves and realize that cheating only hurts their own game and takes them down a notch in the eyes of their friends. And those friends may not be friends for long if they don't want to put up with unethical behavior. You may be the worst golfer around, but if you're a good sport and play by the rules, you can find a game any time.

OBTAINING THE RULES AND RULES EDUCATION

The rule book is actually a handy 4-by-6¼-inch booklet; the 1998 copy has 144 pages. The book is the perfect size for a golf bag or back pocket, always ready for reference at a moment's notice. A rule book should be standard equipment for any golfer's bag. It's probably the best dollar you'll ever spend on golf. Rule books are available through the USGA for $1.00 and a shipping and handling charge of $1.25.

The contents of a rule book include sections on etiquette, definitions, the rules of play, rules about other forms of play besides individual competition, tournament administration, local rules, conditions of the competition, design of clubs and the ball, lightning safety, and the USGA's rules of amateur status and policy on gambling.

That's a lot of good, pertinent information in such a small book. But there's no reason to stop there when the USGA has so many other rules publications. There's a deluxe, large-type edition of the rules for $5, the *Decisions on the Rules of Golf* for $15, the six-page *Golf Rules in Brief* for 75 cents, and a safety and etiquette pamphlet for $1.50. All are available through the USGA's order department in Far Hills, New Jersey, phone 1-800-336-4446 or (908) 234-2300.

Hard-core rules nuts can get further education by attending one of the rules workshops conducted jointly for the past fifteen years by the USGA and the PGA of America. The seminars are run from November through March in various parts of the country, and range from introductory level to regular level to tournament officiating. The workshops are very popular and tend to fill up quickly. The USGA, (908) 234-2300, and the PGA of America, (561) 624-8400, can provide further information.

The Best Rules to Know

From reading the rules a golfer will learn the things that can and can't be done. Unfortunately, the rules don't spell out things in plain language to make the dos and don'ts completely clear. In the next two sections, we'll touch upon some specific instructions about procedures and actions that are and aren't allowed. First are the things that can be done.

Touching the Ball   Unlike what you might see with your regular group of care-free golfers, players are not allowed to touch or move the ball from the time it's hit off the tee until it's on the putting green. On the tee, the golfer can touch the ball and place it either on a wooden tee or maneuver it on the grass with the club. On par-3 holes, some golfers like to hit off a small tuft of grass they've created by striking the ground with the toe of the club. The ball must stay within the boundaries of the tee markers. After the ball is hit, there's no moving or touching it until reaching the putting green, unless golfers are playing under a lift-and-clean rule in muddy conditions. The ball should be played as it came to rest, no matter whether it is in the rough, the fairway, an old divot, or against a tree.

There are two exceptions. First, if a poor player or beginner is having a tough time on a hole during a team tournament and his score doesn't count, she should pick up before reaching the green. The second exception occurs during a rules situation. If a ball comes to rest in casual water or ground under repair, if it's in a water hazard, or if it's in a relief situation from an obstruction, a golfer is permitted to touch the ball.

Mud   When conditions are muddy, a local rule may allow the golfer to lift and clean the ball and then place it back on the spot it had come to rest.

Waggle   You can put the ball back on a tee after knocking it off during the pre-swing waggle, and it doesn't count as a stroke.

Practice swing   If you hit the ball during a practice swing, it's not counted as a stroke, but you must add a penalty stroke for moving a ball in play. Replace the ball and play away.

Putting a distinguishing mark on your ball helps I.D. it if needed.

Marking the ball   There is no penalty for not putting a mark on your ball to distinguish it from other players', but it's a good idea, especially during a tournament. Players can put an arrangement of dots, their name, or some other marking on the ball to make it different from anyone else's. This ensures that if two balls of the same type with the same number are hit next to each other, at least one player will know which ball is his. If neither player knew whose ball was whose, they would have to declare both balls lost and have to hit over again with a penalty stroke. If a person played a wrong ball, there would be a two-stroke penalty in stroke play and loss of the hole in match play.

Debris   When things such as paper cups, broken tees, or cigarette butts are near the ball, they can be removed, even in a hazard.

Advice   You're allowed to ask another golfer for information that's normally available to players, such as where the yardage markers are located or how long a hole is, or the par of a hole.

Holing out   Always finish out the hole by making a putt to hole out, but it's not necessary during match play to hole out if your final putt or shot is conceded by your opponent (Rule 3-2, 16-2).

Loose impediments   These can be removed from around the ball as long as the ball doesn't move from its position and the ball isn't in or touching a hazard (Rule 23-1).

The club cannot be soled in a hazard, such as a sand bunker.

Damaged ball   If your ball is damaged during play of a hole, and your playing partners agree, you may put a new ball in play, but only on the hole in question or between holes (Rule 5-3).

Water hazards   If a ball goes in a water hazard, it can be played as it lies, a new ball put in play with the addition of one penalty stroke (keeping the point at which the original ball last crossed the edge of the hazard directly between the hole and the spot on which the ball is dropped), or another ball played from where the last shot was just played. If the ball is in a lateral water hazard, those same options apply but the ball drop must be done within two club-lengths of either where the ball last crossed the hazard edge or at a point on the opposite hazard edge the same distance from the hole (Rule 26).

Unplayable lie   If you elect to declare your ball unplayable outside of a water hazard, meaning it's in such a spot that it's impossible or unwise to swing at it, a golfer can opt to pick up the ball and drop it either within two club-lengths no closer to the hole, drop any distance behind the point where the ball lay (keeping that point directly behind the hole and the spot on which the ball is dropped), or replay the shot. If you feel your ball is unplayable in a bunker, the ball must be redropped within the bunker. It's not a free drop, however. You must add a penalty stroke (Rule 28).

Leaves are loose impediments that can be removed from around the ball.

Provisional ball   Playing a provisional can save a golfer from wasting time by retracing his steps and replaying a shot. If you think a ball has gone out-of-bounds or is lost outside a water hazard, you can play a provisional ball.

To do this you must announce your intentions to your group and hit the provisional before looking for the first ball. If you find the original within five minutes of reaching the area the ball is in, or if the ball is in a water hazard, you can't play the provisional. But if the first ball is lost outside a water hazard or went out-of-bounds, you add a penalty stroke and play the provisional (Rule 27).

Ground conditions   The rules give golfers an out when their ball comes to rest on less than ideal turf, such as ground under repair and casual water. To take relief, find the nearest point that clears the ball from the poor lie, not closer to the hole, and then drop the ball within one club length of that point. If the relief is needed in a bunker, the ball must be redropped in the bunker, otherwise there's a penalty stroke for dropping outside the bunker. To drop on the putting green, find the nearest spot that gives relief and isn't closer to the hole (Rule 25).

Local rules sometimes allow golfers to lift, clean, and place balls that pick up mud.

Obstructions   An obstruction is anything artificial on the course. Movable obstructions are things such as bunker rakes and cups. Immovable obstructions are things such as cart paths and irrigation control boxes. Golfers can get relief from both types without penalty strokes. Rule 24 describes how relief is taken, sometimes by placing the ball and other times by finding the nearest point of relief and dropping the ball.

Ball moved   The ball can be replaced without penalty if, while at rest, it's moved by someone other than the player and his caddie or by another ball in motion (Rule 18). But if a golfer's ball is moved, while at rest, by the golfer, his caddie, or the player's partner, or if it moves after it's been addressed, it must be replaced and a penalty stroke added.

If a ball you've hit is deflected or stopped by a ball at rest, you play the ball where it comes to a stop. It's a two-stroke penalty, however, on the putting green against the player who putts a ball that strikes another ball on the green (Rule 19).

Practice   Golfers are allowed a practice swing, but not a practice stroke, while on the course. That means taking a practice swing without the ball. Practice chipping and putting on or near the putting green of the hole just played is allowed if it doesn't affect pace of play (Rule 7). Practice is not allowed from a hazard.

Teeing Off   In order for all golfers to play the same course, particularly in a tournament, players must tee off from the same set of tees. Golfers are allowed to tee the ball anywhere within a rectangular area that is defined on the two lengthy sides by the tee markers and two club-lengths in depth. The ball must be within this area, not the golfer. If the ball is hit after being teed outside the area, an opponent can make the player hit again in match play. In stroke play, there is a two-stroke penalty and the shot must be replayed (Rule 11-3).

Order of Play   On a tee, the first player to hit is the one with the honor. During match play, the winner of the previous hole hits first, and in stroke play the player with the lowest score on the previous hole plays first and the other players hit in order of score. A match play opponent can ask an opponent who played out of turn to hit over again, but there's generally no penalty for doing so in stroke play (Rule 10).

SOME THINGS GOLFERS CAN'T DO
Don'ts

Leaves   A fallen leaf is a loose impediment. However, they can't be removed from around a ball when the ball is in a hazard, such as a bunker. Leaves can be removed when the ball is outside a hazard.

Winter Rules   The USGA does not recognize winter rules as part of its regular rules. Winter rules are sometimes referred to as preferred lies. The primary rule is that a player can move the ball on the fairway and fringe area a maximum of six inches, no closer to the hole, to create a better lie. Many golfers use this leeway as a matter of course. They don't play golf unless they can "bump" the ball into a better position. It's a sign they don't have much confidence in their swing or ability to hit from any lie. They don't realize that bad and good lies even out in the long run.

Golfers should refrain from using winter rules, unless the club posts a sign stating it's okay to do so. In those instances, it's usually during the off-season when course conditions are spotty, or during the regular season when dry or overly wet conditions have been dominant. It's not a bad idea for beginning players to move the ball around into a nice lie, but playing the ball "down" all the time will make a golfer a better player.

Advice   Golfers cannot ask other players what club they used to play a shot prior to their shot or ask other questions that would help plan club selection and shot strategy.

Fourteen Clubs   You cannot have more than fourteen clubs in your bag. If you do, it's not enough to turn the extra clubs upside down and say they're out of play. They must be taken out.

Yardage Gauges   The artificial devices that help measure distances to the putting green cannot be used during competition.

Conceded Putts   You cannot concede putts to yourself, but you can to other players during match play.

Tee Markers   The location of the tee markers cannot be moved or altered. The course must be played from the length at which it was set up.

Switch Balls   Golfers can't put a new ball into play while playing a hole unless the ball becomes unfit for play. Switching to a new ball has to be done between holes. So technically, the habit some players have of switching to a "putting" ball on the greens or a "water ball" when they face a shot over water is not allowed by the rules, but it's done often in casual play.

Natural Objects Things such as rocks, twigs, grass, leaves, pine cones, or anything natural cannot be removed from within a hazard. They can be moved outside of hazards as long as it doesn't cause the ball to move. If the loose impediment is within one club-length of the ball when it is moved and the ball alters its position, it's a one stroke penalty and the ball must be replaced before continuing (Rule 18-2c).

Waive Rules The Rules of Golf cannot be waived by agreement of the players within a group.

In a Hazard No part of the club can touch the ground in a bunker or in a water hazard prior to the shot. If the club is grounded, it's a two-stroke penalty. The club can be grounded within a waste bunker—the very large and unkept bunkers seen quite often on sandy courses, such as those in Florida.

Putting Prior to stroking a putt, the surface of the green cannot be tested by scraping it or rolling a ball (Rule 16-1d). You also can't strike the flagstick with the ball while putting on the green, and you can't tap down spike marks that are on the putting line prior to stroking the ball. Ball marks and old hole plugs can be repaired at any time, and spike marks can be tapped down after a group is done putting.

Out-of-bounds A ball cannot be played from the OB area. If a shot goes OB, a second ball must be put in play from where the first was hit and a penalty stroke added.

Hitting the Ball Rule 14 says the ball has to be swung at with a club, it cannot be scraped along or pushed. Within the same rule it notes that if the ball is struck more than once during the same swing, the player must count one stroke and add a penalty stroke.

Line of Play The area of a golfer's intended swing or line of play to the hole cannot be improved by bending, moving, or breaking anything that's fixed or growing except what occurs in taking a stance or making the swing.

Ball Moves The ball cannot move during the address position. If it does, a penalty stroke must be added.

Wrong Ball You can't play a wrong ball and get by without a penalty, unless the ball is in a bunker or water hazard. If the wrong ball is played in match play, the penalty is loss of hole; if in stroke play, it's a two-stroke penalty and the correct ball must be played (Rule 15).

COMMON RULES VIOLATIONS

Having seen what can and can't be done, here's a list of the ten basic rules that are most commonly violated by golfers in casual play. This list was put together for *Golf Digest* magazine by the late Joseph C. Dey and Tom Meeks, rules experts with the USGA, in the 1980s.

1. Giving advice and indicating the line of play (Rule 8).
2. Taking a drop from a cart path (Rule 24).
3. Taking a ball out of a water hazard and dropping it along the "line of flight" (Rule 26).
4. Improving your lie or position by moving growing things beyond the limit allowed (Rule 13).
5. Tamping down the line of putt (Rule 16).
6. Procedure for a lost ball (Rule 27).
7. Taking relief from immovable obstructions and ground under repair (Rules 24 and 25).
8. Playing a provisional ball (Rule 27).
9. Procedure for an unplayable lie (Rule 28).
10. Undue delay in looking for a lost ball (Rule 6).

Other procedures that are often done incorrectly include accidentally moving the ball at address, marking the ball improperly on the green, bumping the ball, and touching the sand in a hazard with the clubhead at address.

> "After a bad grip, the most common fault I see among golfers is an incorrect address position. Think about it for a second: If you start out in a bad position, what are your chances of making a good swing?"
>
> **KEN VENTURI**

RULES AND GOLF EQUIPMENT

Within the rule book is a section devoted to specifications for equipment construction that's mainly targeted for equipment manufacturers. Because so many competitions are held under the Rules of Golf, equipment must meet the USGA standards to be conforming and approved for use.

When a new ball or club design is ready, a sample is sent to the USGA for testing. Nine pages are devoted in the rule book to the design of clubs, including grip styles, putters, the shaft, clubhead shape and dimensions, clubface markings, and groove shapes.

As for balls, the USGA puts a limit on how far they can go, called the Overall Distance Standard. A USGA-approved ball must weigh no more than 1.62 ounces and be not less than 1.68 inches in diameter. It must be spherically symmetrical, meaning it must fly the same way no matter how it sits on a tee or the ground. The ball's initial velocity must not be more than 250 feet per second, with a tolerance of 2 percent, when it's hit by a mechanical machine swinging at 143.8 feet per second (known as the initial velocity standard). And the Overall Distance Standard dictates that the ball must travel no more than 280 yards (carry and roll), with a tolerance of 6 percent, when struck by a clubhead moving at 109 miles per hour.

When a ball passes all the tests, it goes on the USGA's conforming list, which has more than 800 models. There are no guidelines about the number of dimples or their shape, the ball's color or how big the ball can be or how light it can be. But obviously the ball manufacturers are not going to vary too far from the standard features in these areas.

Having a standard of rules that establishes what can and can't be done in the making of equipment is one of the few ways to maintain the integrity of the equipment companies and ensure their products are remaining true to tradition and fair standards.

GLOSSARY OF RULES TERMS AND PHRASES

Understanding the rule book depends a lot on knowing the terminology and words that are interspersed throughout the rules and other sections. It's important to know the meaning behind these words because there are subtle differences in how a rule is applied depending upon the context of the word.

For example, what constitutes a stroke has to be clearly understood. It's not a stroke if a golfer starts the backswing but stops halfway back for some reason and starts over. But if the golfer has started the downswing and has the intent to hit the ball and send it forward, and misses the ball or tops it, the swing is considered a stroke.

Or when it comes to water hazards, there are the regular kind and the lateral kind. When a golfer's ball goes into water, the procedure for continuing play is not the same for each kind of hazard.

Here are many of the terms and words found within the rule book.

Address   The posture a golfer assumes prior to swinging the club. A player has addressed the ball when he's taken his stance and grounded the club behind the ball. When in a hazard, the address position is considered taking the stance only.

Advice   Any information that may help another player make a decision on club selection or the type of shot strategy he'd use. Golfers can only receive information of this type from their caddie, partner, or his partner's caddie.

Albatross   Term for a double eagle; two under par.

All square   Occurs when two opposing sides are tied in a match.

Amateur   A golfer who doesn't play for prize money or other compensation.

Away   Being the player farthest from the hole. This golfer hits first in his group whether on the fairway or the green.

Backswing   The part of the swing from address to the top.

Ball   It can weigh no more than 1.62 ounces and not measure less than 1.68 inches in diameter.

Ball holed   The ball is considered holed out after it falls below the level surface of the hole and is within the circumference of it.

Ball in play   Occurs when a golfer plays a ball from the tee. Unless the ball goes out-of-bounds, is lost, or is substituted with another ball, it remains the ball in play until holed out.

Ball lost   A ball is lost if it hasn't been located within five minutes of the start of searching, or if the player has put another ball in play by hitting a shot from where he last played or from where he believes the original ball to be.

Ball mark   The depression made when the ball lands on the putting green. The mark may be repaired without penalty.

Ball moved   A ball has moved when it moves from its original position and comes to rest in a different spot.

Best ball   A playing format also known as better ball. The best individual score among teams of two or more players counts toward the final score.

Birdie   Making a score on a hole that's one stroke less than par; one under par.

Bogey   Making a score on a hole that's one stroke more than par; one over par.

Bunker   A depression in the fairway, rough, or near the green. It's usually filled in with sand, but can also be a grass bunker. Golfer must play out of it if the ball lands there. Also called a trap. Since a bunker is considered a hazard, you cannot ground your club in one.

Bye   Exemption from playing a match in a match-play tournament.

Caddie   The person who totes a golfer's clubs on the course during play and provides advice on club selection and shot strategy. For rules purposes, a caddie carrying for more than one golfer is considered the caddie of the player who is hitting a shot.

Carry   The distance a ball travels from where it was hit to the point of landing. Carry also means the amount of ground a ball has to go over before reaching a targeted area.

Cart path   A road, usually paved or gravel, that routes through the course and is intended for use by motorized carts.

Casual water   The temporary pooling of water other than a water hazard. Casual water either rests above ground level or is brought to the surface when the player takes a stance. Snow and natural ice can be considered casual water or loose impediments. Dew and frost are not casual water. Golfers get a free drop away from casual water.

Cavity-back irons   Clubs with weight distributed around the clubhead perimeter due to the weight removal on the back of the clubhead. Great clubs for players who often miss the center of the clubface.

Clubface   Portion of the clubhead that makes contact with the ball; has groove markings.

Committee   Persons in charge of running a competitive event; if a tournament is not being held, the committee is the group of people in charge of the course.

Competitor   Player in a stroke-play event. A fellow competitor is a golfer the competitor plays with.

Course   The entire area where play is allowed.

Course rating   The score a scratch-handicap player or expert would shoot from a certain set of tees. The more difficult the course, the higher the course rating.

Dormie   Term used in match play. A player is dormie when he leads a match by the same number of holes left to play.

Double bogey   Scoring two strokes more on a hole than the par score; two over par.

Double eagle   Scoring three strokes less on a hole than the par score; three under par.

Down   The side or player losing a match.

Downswing Portion of the swing from the top to shortly after impact.

Drive A golfer's first shot played on a hole, most often with a driver.

Drop Must be made after a ball has been lost, gone out-of-bounds or into a water hazard, become unplayable, or is in ground under repair. The drop is made by extending the arm straight out to the side and letting the ball fall from shoulder height.

Eagle Scoring two strokes less on a hole than the par score; two under par.

Equipment A player's clubs, bag, hat, pullcart, and golf cart are considered the player's "equipment." It is anything worn, carried, or used by or for the golfer. The ball, a tee, and a ball marker are not considered part of the equipment.

Fairway The short-cut grass area that is the intended route from tee to putting green.

Fellow competitor The relationship of one player to another in a stroke-play tournament.

Flagstick Consists of a pole and flag placed in the hole to indicate the location of the hole on the green; also known as the pin.

Follow-through Segment of the swing from just after impact to finish.

Fore! Warning yelled by players that an errant shot is heading toward a group in the landing area.

Forecaddie Person standing in the rough along the landing area to mark where wayward drives finish. A forecaddie is considered an outside agency.

Forward swing The swing from the top of the backswing to follow-through.

Four ball Competition in which two golfers play their best ball against the best ball of two other players.

Foursome   (1) Four golfers playing together; (2) format in which two-man teams play against each other in an alternate-shot format.

Fringe   Closely mown grass immediately surrounding the putting green; also called apron.

Front nine   The first nine holes in an eighteen-hole round; also called the "out nine."

Gimme   A very short putt, often conceded by a playing partner, which is against the Rules of Golf.

Green   Extremely short-cut grass that has the hole and flagstick located there and is used for putting.

Grip   (1) Placing the hands on the club before swinging; (2) rubber or leather wrapping on the club at the part the golfer grips it.

Grooves   Lines and/or markings on the clubface that spin and control the ball.

Gross score   A player's score without the use of handicap strokes; what the player actually shot.

Ground under repair   Ground of such poor quality that it's been marked by course officials. It can include grass clippings and dirt piled for removal. Players are allowed to make a drop away from these areas without penalty.

Grounding the club   During the address position, the club is grounded when the sole of the club touches the ground behind the ball.

Half/halved   Either a hole or match that is tied in a match play event.

Handicap   Total strokes a golfer receives to equalize competition between poor (high-numbered handicaps) and better (low-numbered) players.

Hazard   Consists of bunkers and bodies of water (not casual water); you cannot ground your club within a hazard and you usually must take a penalty stroke for hitting into water.

Heel-and-toe weighting   Club construction method that distributes weight around the perimeter of the clubhead so mis-hit shots are not affected as much.

High handicapper   A golfer getting a high number of handicap strokes, such as thirty or more; most likely a beginner.

Hole   Opening on the putting green that is 4¼ inches wide and 4 inches deep; also called the cup.

Hole-in-one   Holing out with the tee shot on a par-3 hole.

Holed out   A ball that falls below the level surface of the hole.

Honor   Playing the first shot on a hole by hitting a tee shot. The honor is determined by flipping a coin or a blind draw on the first tee; it's by lowest score the rest of the round.

Imbedded lie   A ball that sticks in wet or muddy turf.

Impact   The moment when the clubface and ball meet during the swing.

Intended line   An imaginary line starting from the ball and extending to where the player wants the ball to go.

In the leather   A ball that's very close to the hole. The original meaning was a putt within the length of a leather grip, but now it's thought to be the length of the clubhead to the bottom of the grip.

Iron   Clubs numbered from 1 to 9 and the wedges; the low-numbered clubs hit the ball the farthest.

Lateral water hazard   All or part of a water hazard that is usually to the side of the golfer as he plays the hole; usually marked off with red stakes or lines.

Lie   (1) How well the ball sits on the turf; (2) current number of strokes played on a hole, as in "What do you lie?" (3) angle the back of the club-shaft makes with the sole of the club.

Line of play   Direction the golfer wants the ball to travel to the hole. It's considered the line from where the ball lies to the hole, plus a reasonable area on either side of the intended line.

Line of putt   Direction the player wants the ball to roll after making a putting stroke, plus a reasonable margin on either side of the intended line.

Local rules   Additions to the Rules of Golf or special rules applied by the committee that are unique to a golf course.

Loft   The amount, in degrees, that the clubface is angled backward from the leading edge or sole to the top edge.

Long iron   The 1-, 2-, and 3-irons; irons with the least amount of loft.

Loose impediments   Natural objects such as stones, leaves, twigs, and grass, so long as they are not growing or solidly embedded. Sand and loose soil are loose impediments on the putting green; at the player's option, snow and natural ice can be either casual water or loose impediments.

Lost ball   After a five-minute search, a ball is lost if it is not found or identified. Also, the original ball is lost even if the golfer didn't try to find his ball and put another ball in play under a Rule of Golf. And if the player has played a shot with a provisional ball from where the first ball might be or from a location closer to the hole, the ball is then lost.

Low handicapper   A golfer who receives a low number of handicap strokes, such as under ten; usually an experienced player.

Marker   The person appointed to write down a player's score in a stroke-play tournament. The marker walks with the player around the course.

Match play   Format in which one person or team competes against another person or team in a nine- or eighteen-hole match; the side that wins the most holes wins the match.

Medal play Competition in which the number of strokes taken determine the outcome. Professional medal-play tournaments consist of three or four rounds; the golfer with the lowest score wins. Also called stroke play.

Medalist The lowest scorer in a medal-play tournament.

Middle iron The 4-, 5-, and 6-irons.

Mixed foursome Event in which women and men compete simultaneously.

Mulligan Playing a second ball from the same spot as the first when the first shot is not acceptable; usually done on the first tee; violates the Rules of Golf.

Nassau Popular bettor's game usually played for three points, one each for the front and back nines and one for the entire round, played in match-play style.

Net score Score after a golfer's handicap has been subtracted from the gross score.

Observer An official who accompanies a group and advises on rulings or reports them.

> "Golf is the greatest game of them all. You can play it by yourself and revel in the beauty, solitude, and peace that the game offers. You can play it with your friends and enjoy the camaraderie, good-natured give-and-take, and thrill of competition. You can play it when you're 8 or 80 and you'll learn something new every time out— about golf and maybe about yourself."
>
> NANCY LOPEZ

Obstructions Anything artificial, such as roads and paths, and anything man-made, such as ice. Out-of-bounds fences and markers are not obstructions. In certain situations, you can move a ball away from an obstruction.

Order of play The committee establishes the order of play off the first tee in a tournament; the honor is set by a coin flip or blind draw otherwise.

Open tournament An event open to both amateurs and professionals.

Out-of-bounds Also called OB. Ground that has been ruled out for play, usually bordered by white markers. A shot finishing out-of-bounds must be replayed from the spot of the original shot. Distance is lost and a penalty stroke added, which is the reason the phrase "stroke and distance penalty" is used.

Outside agency Includes a referee, marker, observer, or forecaddie, anything not part of the competitor's side. Does not apply to water or wind.

Par The score a good player would probably make on a hole, including two putts (such as, on a par 4, reaching the green in two shots and taking two putts). An eighteen-hole course usually has a par of 70 to 72. The USGA suggests that par 3s be up to 250 yards for men and 210 for women, par 4s be 251 to 470 yards for men and 211 to 400 for women, and par 5s be 471 yards and over for men and 401 to 575 for women.

Partner A player teamed with another golfer on the same side.

Penalty stroke(s) One or two strokes added to a player's score when there's been a Rules of Golf violation, such as hitting a ball out-of-bounds.

Play through Procedure of letting a faster group pass a slower group. The slower group should initiate the courtesy.

Plugged lie A ball that remains imbedded within the hole it created upon landing in very wet ground.

Preferred lie Placing the ball in an improved lie; usually ruled during tournament play when weather has caused muddy conditions.

Professional A golfer who plays the game for monetary compensation.

Provisional ball A second ball played from the same spot as the first when the original ball is believed lost outside of a water hazard or may be out-of-bounds.

Putt One stroke taken on the putting green.

Putter   Club used to strike the ball on the putting green or from surrounding short-cut grass.

Putting green   Very short grass that surrounds the hole and flagstick.

Quadruple bogey   Score on a hole that is four strokes more than par; four over par.

Referee   Official accompanying a group to assist in rulings. The referee cannot tend the flag, mark ball positions, or stand to assist in shot direction.

Relief   Getting to drop a ball that rests in a hazard or is affected by an obstruction.

Rough   Tall grass that is adjacent to the fairway and surrounds the green.

Round   A complete set of holes, either nine or eighteen.

Rub of the green   A ball accidentally stopped or deflected in flight by an outside agency, such as a forecaddie.

Sandbag   A golfer playing poorly on purpose to get a higher handicap to use to his advantage in competition.

Scorecard   Card that lists hole pars and local rules and has space for the player to write in scores.

Scratch play   Playing format in which no handicap strokes are used.

Scratch player   A 0-handicap golfer; someone with great golf skill.

Shaft   Part of the club that connects the grip and clubhead, usually metal but can be graphite or titanium.

Short iron   The clubs with the most loft; the 7-, 8-, 9-irons, and wedges.

Shot   Swinging the club to hit the ball forward.

Single   One golfer playing alone.

Skins   Betting game in which a set amount of money is won by the player with the lowest score on a hole. If players tie for the lowest score, the money is added to the next hole's total.

Sole   (1) Letting the bottom of the club touch the ground at address; (2) the bottom portion of the club.

Staked trees   Newly planted trees that are tagged and held up by a stake; a local rule usually allows players to drop away from staked trees with no penalty.

Stance   Position of the feet prior to swinging the club.

Stipulated round   A round of nine or eighteen holes played in their proper sequential order.

Stroke   Forward movement of the club with the player's intent of hitting the ball.

Stroke hole   Hole on which a player receives a handicap stroke.

Stroke play   Competition in which the strokes taken for a round determine the standings; golfer with the lowest score wins. See medal play.

Stymie   (1) A situation where a shot to a certain target location is blocked by a tree or other object; (2) an obsolete Rule of Golf for the putting green. A golfer was stymied if a playing partner's ball was between his ball and the hole. Golfers could not mark their ball at that time.

Summer golf   Playing the ball as it lies throughout the course; playing by the official Rules of Golf.

Sweet spot   The place on the clubface, usually the center, where the ball comes off most solid.

Swing   The movement made with a club to advance the ball forward.

Swing length   Distance the golfer swings the club back on the backswing.

Swing plane   An imaginary "plane" that connects the shoulders and the ball and is the path the club is swung along from start to finish.

Swing speed   The speed, in miles per hour, that a player swings the club at impact.

Swing weight   A golf club's weight distribution about a fixed fulcrum point. The higher the swing weight, the more the club feels heavy in the head.

Takeaway   The early part of the swing starting at address until the hands reach hip height.

Tap in   A putt of very short length, six inches to a foot.

Target   Where the golfer intends the ball to finish, used as an aiming guide.

Target line   Imaginary line from the ball to the target, used to help aim the club and body.

Tee   (1) Usually a wooden peg used to hold the ball up off the grass while teeing off; (2) rectangular area of short grass from where a golfer begins play on a hole.

Tee markers   For each set of tees, there are a pair of markers that indicate the spot from where golfers should begin play on a hole. Specifically, golfers must play from a rectangular-shaped area that is two club-lengths in depth, with the front and sides determined by the placement of the tee markers.

Tee off   Playing a shot from the teeing ground.

Tee time   An assigned time for a group to start its round.

Teeing ground   This describes the entire area of the tee and is the place where play of a hole begins.

Tending the flag   While a golfer putts from a distant spot on the green, another golfer or caddie holds the flag while it is still in the hole. As the ball approaches the hole, the flag is removed and the holder moves away so the ball is not affected.

Threesome   Group of three players.

Through the green   The entire area of the course except for the tees, putting greens, and hazards.

Toe   (1) The broad part of the clubface opposite where the shaft and clubhead join; (2) hitting the ball on the toe of the club; a swing flaw.

Trap   See bunker.

Triple bogey   A score on a hole that is three strokes more than the par; three over par.

Twosome   Group of two players.

Unplayable lie   Occurs when a ball is located in such a spot that the player cannot make an effective swing at it. The player may declare the ball unplayable and take a penalty stroke for moving the ball clear by two club-lengths, no closer to the hole.

Waggle   Short, back-and-forth movements with the club prior to taking the club back.

Water hazard   There are two kinds. First, a regular water hazard is defined by yellow stakes or lines, and second, a lateral water hazard is shown by red stakes or lines. As a general rule, lateral hazards are to the sides of the golfer's line of play and regular hazards are between the golfer and the hole. The parts of a water hazard include the water, plus the turf on the edges. The hazard boundaries extend upward and downward and any stakes or lines that define the margin are part of the hazard.

Wedge   Clubs with a lot of loft used for short shots.

Weight shift   Transferring a golfer's body weight from a centered position to the right side, then centered and moved to the left during the swing (for a right-handed player).

Whiff   Missing the ball entirely while swinging; counts as a stroke.

Winter rules   Moving the ball six inches from its spot in the fairway or fringe of the hole the golfer is playing, no closer to the hole, to get a better lie. This is a violation of the Rules of Golf.

Woods   The long-shafted clubs used for shots off the tee and fairway when great distance is needed. Modern woods can be either wooden or metal headed. These clubs hit the ball the farthest of any clubs.

Wrong ball   Any ball besides the one in play, a provisional ball, or one played under Rule 3-3 or Rule 20-7b.

X'd-out ball   Low-priced balls that the manufacturer says have imperfections.

 Chapter 9

THE ROAD TO LEARNING AND IMPROVING

The golf swing is not unlike any other skill being learned in that there are hands-off and hands-on approaches, which have varying degrees of success. Getting the hands-on treatment is ideal, but hands off isn't bad, either, as long as the source of instruction is of good quality.

Because of the feel required to play golf well, the hands-on approach, through a golf school or with a personal instructor, is the most useful way to learn. Nearly all the great golf champions had someone they went to on a personal one-on-one basis, someone who instilled in them, through constant attention, the skills that made them great. Jack Nicklaus had Jack Grout, Tom Watson had Stan Thirsk, LPGA great Betsy Rawls had Harvey Penick. Other great players had a variety of teachers who physically placed their hands on them to put them in the many proper positions and ingrained good habits.

The hands-off approach through books, videos, and observation can be effective as well. Greg Norman has often spoken about learning the game by reading Jack Nicklaus' instruction books of the 1960s. Ken Venturi got to watch Byron Nelson and other great players while growing up in the San Francisco area, picking up on their best swing habits and making them part of his own game.

However a golfer approaches the learning process, the main factor is to follow swing advice that is solid, useful, and established in practice and theory. Study the advice well and ingrain it with good, quality practice sessions. And there should be occasional checkups from an experienced teacher who can make sure all the swing elements are being done correctly, thereby offering corrective measures when necessary.

Johnny Miller, the champion golfer who now serves as a television golf commentator, recognized the value of both hands-on and hands-off approaches in saying, "There are two ways, really, that you can gain knowledge. The first is to go to a good teaching professional. The second way is from books. My father saw to it that I had the opportunity to take advantage of the great players' knowledge by exposing me to the best books during my early years."

THERE'S NO SUBSTITUTE FOR PRACTICE

Golf is one of the few sports—in fact, there may not be any others—that the place to effectively practice it is not on the actual field of play. Baseball players both practice and play on the diamond; football players do both on the football field; hockey players do both on a rink; basketball players do both on a court with a hoop. When golfers play on a golf course, they're not really practicing; they're playing, seeing if what they've practiced can hold up in competition, even if they do hit the same shot a couple of times. No, golfers play on the golf course and practice on the practice range or driving range.

To provide an idea of how important it is to practice, not just golf but any skill, a study released by Johns Hopkins University in 1997 revealed that it takes up to six hours for the brain to permanently store a new skill once it has been introduced. In measuring blood flow in the brain, it was concluded that it takes five to six hours for the memory of a new skill to transfer to a permanent storage site in the back of the brain from a temporary one in the front. Even trickier, the study said, was that if another skill was introduced before the first one was stored, it could cause the initial one to be lost in transfer or erased. This time frame was called a "neural window of vulnerability." A psychiatrist in the study said it is not enough to simply practice something. You have to allow time to pass for the brain to encode the new skill. It was suggested that after a practice session, there should follow a five- to six-hour period of routine activity during which no new learning was done.

Although golfers don't need a reason to take a break, this information about the learning process is solid evidence that learning a skill like golf takes hours and hours of practice and time to let things sink in. Not all golfers can be as fortunate as Sam Snead, Fred Couples, and others on the professional tour who have great natural talent. Most golfers have to rely on receiving a piece of swing information, practicing it, and then taking a break before picking up where they left off. And the practice range is the place for this, not the golf course.

A catchphrase these days, "perfect practice makes perfect," is a play on the "practice makes perfect" line. The meaning here is that golfers ought to have direction while they practice. Constant practice of the wrong movements does no good. That's probably worse than no practice at all. Don't ingrain the wrong habits. Practice with the proper methodology to make your swing work its best. For new players, it is this repetition of correct movements that builds confidence and assurance in a sport that requires a lot of both. "Practice is the only way I know to build true confidence in your ability and trust in your equipment," Sam Snead once said. "Older golfers especially need all the confidence they can possibly develop."

The enthusiasm for golf has extended to the driving range, including double-decker hitting stalls.

Snead had a well-developed practice philosophy comprising four tips: (1) Practice frequently in short doses; (2) practice like you play, practice shotmaking; (3) emphasize the fundamentals, and (4) practice your short game.

Practice driving ranges are found in two locations: a stand-alone range in some part of town and a range that's part of a golf course facility. The second type of range affords more privacy than the stand-alone kind because golfers are more likely to go to a golf course to play, not practice. Ranges at private clubs are more isolated still. At those facilities, practice balls are sometimes available free as part of the club's membership dues. Other nice benefits are balls that tend to be of a better grade than elsewhere, and golfers can always hit off actual grass.

A public range, because of heavy use, often has players hit off mats, which have a strip of artificial grass for striking the ball. Some ranges allow play off grass, and some allow both, but you're likely to find mats at most ranges. That's unfortunate for the golfer who doesn't get the feel of hitting off turf and instead feels the jarring effect of hitting off a surface that doesn't give very well. Mats are helpful, though, for the driving-range owner because constant traffic could likely wipe out the turf and leave bare dirt.

The best practice sessions take place during the off days from actual play. The ideal playing-practice schedule is one with continuous playing time, not bursts of play followed by huge gaps in which the clubs are left untouched in the car. For example, a preferred plan might be playing one round of golf on weekends and nine holes sometime during the week. In between you would practice at least two times so that you don't focus all your playing time in one short segment. A poor plan would be a six-hour session one day and no practice again for two weeks. Under that schedule, players tend to forget the swing traits they were working on and have to start over again.

Golfers build swing consistency by playing a little bit at a time more often rather than a heavy schedule of play on a sporadic schedule. Staying in touch with your swing helps keep it working smoothly and helps you learn new movements. Good habits are developed with frequent practices.

At a driving range, there is usually a hitting area for full-swing shots with woods and irons. You will see the mats or grassy area for hitting, and out in the field will be signs posted at various distance spots, such as 50 yards, 100, 150, 200, and 250.

In cold weather regions, indoor practice areas are popular golfer hotspots.

Most driving ranges don't go beyond that length because it's rare to have an amateur hit the ball that far. Sometimes these distances seem too generous and hardly legitimate, but not to worry. They are in the ballpark distance-wise, and the signs should be used as targets more than a gauge of yardage. You can use the course to get accurate readings of how far you hit each club.

The range may also have a practice putting green and another green and bunkers for short-game work. That's not a common setup, however, for public ranges, but it is at private clubs. Range balls come in baskets of various sizes, but no more than three. Small buckets have around thirty-five balls for a price of $3. Large buckets have seventy-five balls for $4 or $5. A third size would fall somewhere in the middle.

Driving ranges sometimes have teaching professionals or instructors who give lessons for a fee, usually over a half hour or an hour. Be aware that teachers have varying degrees of expertise. Some may be no more than a good player in the area who gives advice. Others may have PGA of America membership and thus be extremely capable of helping any caliber of player. Make sure you know the ability of the teacher you're seeing so you, first of all, are paying the proper price, and second, can feel comfortable that the words of advice being passed to you can be trusted.

If you go to the range to practice, and do not see a teacher, slowly build up your visits until you can devote ninety to 120 minutes for a session. That gives you time for an ideal practice session, which would include forty-five minutes hitting irons and woods on the range and another forty-five minutes working in the short-game area. The practice concludes with thirty minutes of putting. This time frame gives you a good balance of hitting full shots and what are referred to as "feel shots": the chips, pitches, and putts. Feel shots are so important during a round of golf that they deserve special attention in practice. In fact, if you can't devote the time to a full session, it's a good idea to cut back on full shots and spend most of your time on feel shots. Sometimes you will need to work on trouble areas, such as when you're having difficulty with the driver, but focusing on feel shots is valuable once you're on the course as they can greatly cut down on the wasted shots that inflate scores.

An excellent way to ensure a productive practice session is to set up a workstation. After purchasing a pail of balls, head for an open mat or locate a level piece of ground if you can hit off turf. If you want isolation to focus better, go to the far end of the range because most people will walk as little as possible to get to a spot. On grass ranges, those areas usually have the nicest grass. Pick out a target and place one of your clubs on the ground aimed at the target. Put a second club parallel with the first, a foot to the left as you face the target. Then put a third club perpendicular to the second, extending down from the middle. The second club is for aligning your feet to the target, and the third helps point out correct ball position. Remember that the ball should be played between the

At the range, it's a good idea to set up alignment clubs for proper aim.

left heel and the middle of the stance, depending on which club you're using. Remove the first club and you're ready to make some swings.

Another good practice tip is taking a practice swing prior to every actual shot. Make a good swing then try to duplicate it with the ball. This makes sure you don't rush through the session.

Don't be bashful about trying to get better by any means possible, even it it means putting the ball on a tee to help get it in the air. Be orderly about your practice. Don't hit the ball from all over the turf. Develop a divot pattern that makes one circular-shaped divot spot instead of a scattered approach that forces you to move around. Always hit balls from the back of a divot hole rather than the front since an elevated ball on a divot causes scooping, digging, and lifting.

Take special note that a productive practice does not mean hitting balls as quickly as possible. Practice is not a race to see who can hit the most balls, or how many you can hit in an hour. Each ball you hit should be done with the same pace and routine. When playing full shots, have a definite goal or swing position on which you're focusing. Come prepared with a practice plan to work on certain swing thoughts or a new skill someone just told you about. Maybe you just read a tip in a magazine article and feel the need to work on it. For each range shot, follow a regular preshot routine that you would use on the golf course, being sure to always have a target in mind, as expressed by Mickey Wright: "Never, never, ever hit a practice ball without a target." Do all the fundamental parts correct with grip, stance, ball position, and aim. This is the best way to build up golf muscles and muscle memory. Make each ball a quality practice shot and swing. Some people have the wrong thinking that hitting 100 balls in an hour means they had a good practice. But hitting and absentmindedly raking another ball over as quickly as possible wears you out and does more harm than good. Be dedicated to hard work, but be smart enough to pace yourself and not burn out before the next practice session.

On the full-swing range, start by hitting short irons and work your way up through the middle and long irons to the woods. Finish the forty-five minutes by hitting a few wedge shots, then move to the short-game area for a variety of shots around the green and from the bunkers, and then finish off with putting. At any stage, if you feel tired, take quick breaks. Take easier swings or hit wedge shots instead of driver shots. Don't get stuck on one particular club. If you're wanting to practice a particular swing movement and ingrain it thoroughly, swing either a 5- or 7-iron. Those clubs have proven to be the best for learning swing technique because they get the ball airborne easily. Many range users flail away with their driver—a tough club to hit well for the beginner—instead of working with an easier club to hit.

> "What makes golf different from, and I think more difficult than, other sports is that it is one of the few sports in which a player must initiate the hitting action. In most other sports a player reacts to the action—a pitch, a serve—of another player."
>
> KEN VENTURI

If you've been playing well on the golf course or been hitting well on the range, don't increase the length of your practices. It may seem like a good idea when you're swinging well to practice longer, as if doing so will make your swing fault-proof. Just continue with regular practices and enjoy the streak of good play. Adding to the practice time may make you tired and bored, and if you start hitting bad shots, the confidence you just had will quickly fade away.

A recent trend in driving ranges has been the growth of indoor ranges, primarily in the northern part of the United States. They're designed for year-round use when weather conditions force players to stop playing outside. Because they are indoors, these ranges have additional features that outside ranges might not, among them a food court and electronic swing analyzers, which attract players during the off-season with their ability to analyze swing faults and help the player improve prior to taking his game outside again in nicer weather.

And if any kind of driving range isn't available, there's always the good old-fashioned practice method: an open field with a shag bag full of balls. Find a field of grass that doesn't prohibit golf practice and take fifty balls or so with you.

Empty the bag, walk it out 100 or 150 yards and drop it as a target, then hit wedge shots and other clubs. When done, pick up the balls and go. The ambitious golfer can always find some method of getting in his practice time.

Drilling things home in practice

No matter how determined you are to be a diligent practice golfer, you will have moments where hitting balls feels like torture and leaves you disinterested. At those times, you need to make a game of practicing by either visualizing a different environment or performing drills that take away swing faults.

Drills make your practices perfect and are a good substitute for not having an instructor standing next to you ready with a hands-on approach. The best drills don't take much time to prepare and they give you an accurate feeling of how a swing movement should be performed. Some drills can be done without a ball or club and others require some setup time. Try some of these drills to see which ones work best for you, and then make them a part of your practice time. For the full-swing drills, practice with a 5- or 7-iron.

Full-swing drills

To learn the swing motion/pivot   Practice without a ball in front of you so you don't waste money on range balls. Use the swing taught in Chapter 6 and swing the club at home for a few weeks before going out to hit balls at the range. Use a full-length mirror or reflective glass to watch that you're making the correct motions. When the sun is out you can see by your shadow if a lot of your movements are correct.

To ensure your body parts move in proper sequence   Use one of Harvey Penick's favorite drills, the slow-motion drill. Get in the correct address position and swing the club as you would for a full-swing shot. But do it in slow motion, stopping at the top of the swing and at impact to double-check you've created the correct angles with your arms, wrists, shoulders, and legs.

To save money in range costs   Invest in a hitting net for your backyard. The cost will be recovered over time in the amount you'll save from paying for range balls, and you'll have the convenience of hitting any time you want.

To eliminate a loose grip at the top of the swing   Place a penny between the base of your right thumb and left thumb within the grip. Swing the club and at the top of the swing make sure the hands are close enough together so the penny doesn't fall. Your grip will remain snug for better contact at impact.

To learn to swing the arms together   Tee up a ball and stand at address with your left arm behind your back. Swing easy with the right arm and just try to make contact with the ball. Do the same thing with the left arm, with the right behind the back. You may whiff the ball at first, but hang in there. Continue this for about fifteen minutes and then swing the arms together.

To swing the club back smoothly on the takeaway   Stand at address after putting a tennis ball behind the clubhead. As you take the club back, try to keep the ball in contact with the back of the clubhead for as long as possible until the club pulls up naturally. This promotes a low, smooth takeaway and increases the swing arc of your arms.

To swing with good tempo, Part I   Picture yourself swinging your clubs at half speed. Begin by using your short irons and work up to the longer clubs. With each one, imagine the speed you would need to hit the ball half the distance. This drill is helpful for those golfers who swing faster than they think they do; they'll be surprised how much more solid they make contact.

To swing with good tempo, Part II   Tee up three balls in a perpendicular line to you, each about a foot apart. Swing a 5-iron, hitting the first ball with one-third your strength, the second with two-thirds, and the last full power. If you're like most golfers, the two-thirds speed shot will give you the best results, and provide a lesson in how you don't need to swing hard to play well. Use the two-thirds speed to hit most of your shots and you'll know there's still power in reserve.

To remain flexible and learn swing movement at the same time   Take an exercise bar, broom handle, or driver and put it behind the back along the shoulders, with the arms draped over the ends. From the address position, make a backswing turn so the turn-bar object points at the ball at the top of the swing. Then swing all the way through to the finish so the other end of the bar points at the ball.

Repeat this motion at least ten times a day and your flexibility will improve, especially in the upper body.

To learn a proper weight shift   Stand in the follow-through position and start the swing in reverse fashion. Swing down to the address posture and then make a normal swing, focusing on getting back to the follow-through posture from which you started.

To avoid scooping the long irons   Make a divot on the target side of the ball. You do this by keeping in mind that the club must be descending at the point of impact, not rising up. Make some practice swings and notice where the club bottoms out, then position the ball so it's just to the right of that spot.

To learn how to cock and uncock your hands and wrists   Stand at address with a ball in your right hand and another ball in the regular position on the ground. Swing the right arm back as usual, and on the downswing straighten it out and throw the ball, trying to strike the ball on the ground. This drill lets the right side of the body release the power from the backswing.

To ensure proper aim   Stand behind the ball and pick out a target. Take a club and place it on the ground a few inches away from the ball and pointing to the target. Then imagine that your toes, feet, knees, hips, shoulders, and arms need to be parallel with the clubshaft. This same technique is perfect for any full-swing, chipping, or putting practice.

To get the feel for a proper downswing   Practice it in slow motion many times. Remember to keep the left arm-clubshaft angle for as long as possible before impact. Gradually increase the swing speed until it's at your normal pace. Make it a goal that you swing as hard as you want and not lose your balance. That's when you know you've reached your ideal swing speed.

To learn the feeling of extending the arms after impact   Practice with only your right arm, using a 5-iron. Put the left arm behind the back and choke down on the club with the right. Try your best using only the right arm and you'll see how it should fully extend and straighten at impact and beyond.

To increase awareness of shot strategy   Have a scorecard of the course you play most often and pretend to play a round of golf on the range. For example, if the first hole is a par 4, hit a driver, gauge how well you hit it and how much you would have left to the green, then hit the correct club, whatever that may be. Then continue with the second hole and so forth. Give yourself two putts for each hole. You won't be able to keep an actual score, but the game teaches you how to switch back and forth between different types of clubs.

Short-Game Drills

To have feel for chipping and pitching the correct distances   Go to a practice green and put four objects, such as a headcover, at 10-yard increments on the green. From the fringe, use a variety of clubs to hit balls to each object, experimenting with each club and aiming to make the balls finish next to the object. Vary the order of the objects you're hitting toward for the most effective practice.

To understand how to hit pitch shots of different heights and trajectories   Take a large barrel or trash can and prop it up at different angles, ranging from pointing at you to pointing skyward. Stand about 30 yards away with a wedge and try to hit balls into the container at the right angle.

To improve your aim   Place your golf bag on the ground and angle it away from you. From a distance of 20 yards, use your clubs from the 7-iron to the pitching wedge and try to hit the bottom of the bag with a group of five balls. Keep working at it until you hit the bottom quite often, then decrease the target size by moving the bag further away or find a narrower object.

Sand-play drills

To take out the right amount of sand   Draw a line two inches behind the ball and practice making the club enter the sand at the line and exit two inches on the other side of the ball.

To learn how deep the club should enter the sand   Imagine taking a thin cut of sand. Draw an oval in the sand and practice taking just that amount of sand out of the bunker. Once you get the hang of it, put the ball in the center of the oval and continue practicing.

To mentally picture how much sand to take   Use the image of how you would cut the skin off to peel an apple and use that same thought in dislodging the sand. Or picture the ball sitting on George Washington's image on a dollar bill and remove that much sand.

Putting drills

To get a feel for what each arm does in the stroke   Putt with each arm alone from a distance of no more than five feet. For example, with the right arm alone, hold the left along the left leg. Take the club back slowly and swing through toward the hole. Don't get wristy. After practicing with the arms apart, bring them together as a unit.

To stop leaving putts of any length short   Stick a tee out of the back part of the hole so that it is angled toward the direction of the ball like a backstop. Try putts from short range and strike them hard enough to hit the tee and fall in the hole.

To get a feel for putting different distances   Stick three tees at three-foot increments on the green. Using six balls, select a tee to hit toward and putt the balls so they finish near it. Alternate the tees you play to so you get used to stroking putts of different lengths.

To get more feel for distance   Stand at one location on the green, preferably in the center, and pick three spots on the fringe of varying length. Stroke putts to each spot, trying to make the ball stop rolling at the edge of the fringe.

To help picture how putts are affected by break   Go to the practice green and locate a putt of about 10 feet that has plenty of curve to it. Picture how the putt will break and then put four more balls at two-foot increments along the line you've visualized. Then start with the shortest putt and hit each ball into the hole, seeing how you did picking out the break. If you've misread the putt, start over and try again.

To avoid swinging the putter away from the ball incorrectly   Put a board on the other side of the ball from you, about a half-inch outside the toe of the putter when it's at address. Make your normal stroke and be sure not to hit the board.

To learn a balanced putting stroke   Find a level putt on the green of about five feet and put down a ball. Put one tee level with the ball but a couple of inches from it, another tee five inches in front of the ball and another five inches behind the ball, all in a parallel line. Then make the putting stroke so the putter goes back and forth level with the two outside tees. This teaches you to swing the putter backward the same distance as it's swung forward for a balanced stroke.

To practice long putts of more than 20 feet   Make a game of it using a points system. Find putts of varying length and use five balls. Each time you make a putt, give yourself two points and one point for each ball that finishes within two feet. Keep track of your point totals and try to improve each time; compete with a friend to make things even more interesting and competitive.

To practice uphill and downhill putts   Practice a 20-foot uphill putt five times. Don't worry about making it, just memorize the feel of how hard the putt was stroked. Put a tee where you just putted from and reverse directions, hitting downhill from the hole to the tee. Make the putts finish close to the tee or hit it. By reversing directions you'll discover how feel is crucial to the stroke.

LEARNING FROM THE EXPERTS

One of the greatest ways to learn any skill is imitation. That's why a difficult sport to learn like golf should be introduced to a person's motor skills at a young age. Children are among the best imitators in the world, and have a great ability to mimic what they see. When they watch a golf instructor or parent swing, they can pretty easily match the swing motion.

Unfortunately, as people age, it is harder to learn by watching others. Adult golfers get into their mind a preconceived notion of what the swing should feel like and it's hard to make them change, just as it is more difficult to learn a musical instrument at an older age rather than as a youth. Having said that, golfers of all ages can pick up important tips and suggestions about their golf swing by watching the players who make the game look so easy and learnable: the professional golfer who travels the world to earn a living in these prosperous times on the pro tours.

As Johnny Miller observed about learning by watching, "It's important to realize that in emulating the great players, you should not try and carbon copy the great

> "If there is a secret to golf, it is to know one's capabilities. My advice is never to overextend even if a particular hole or situation seems completely hopeless. Play within yourself, and you will be surprised how often the cup seems to come to you."
>
> CARY MIDDLECOFF

players' swings or technique in the various parts of the game. What you do is study what each player does supremely well, and apply the principles of what you learn to your own game. In most cases, you will adapt these to some extent. After all, no two people will have identical physiques or temperaments."

There are three places to learn from the golf pro: at a tournament site, on television, and in a video, book, or other media outlet. In this chapter, we'll fully discuss how to watch the professional at a tournament or on TV.

Attending a pro tournament in person is probably equal parts mayhem, solemnity, carnival, and physical exertion. The mayhem comes from battling huge throngs of people trying to catch a glimpse of players as they play their round. Unlike television, which can hop the viewer around from one course location to the next, an in-person visit puts you in one spot. If you're in the same spot as hundreds of other people, you won't see much unless you're in the front of the pack.

The carnival comes from the atmosphere that exists away from the golf course. Merchandise booths, food tents, and the corporate village, where companies wine and dine their clients, combine to create a circus feeling that is unlike what's taking place on the course.

Before discussing how to learn from watching the pros, let's first examine the ins and outs of attending a professional golf tournament.

The majority of tour stops start at the beginning of a week with three days of practice on Monday, Tuesday, and Wednesday. Sometimes a PGA Tour event begins the actual tournament rounds on Wednesday, but the vast majority begin on Thursday and continue for four days through Sunday. Events on the LPGA Tour and the Senior PGA Tour fluctuate from Thursday starts to Friday starts, four-day tournaments to three day. Every major tournament is played over a four-day stretch for a total of seventy-two holes. Three-day tournaments last fifty-four holes.

The caliber of player in the tournaments is very changeable. Major events, such as the U.S. Open on the three major American pro tours, will have all of the best players possible. Tournaments that offer large amounts of money, obviously, will have great fields, but the converse is true about tour stops at the low end of the money scale. Regardless of whether the tournament has the big names of the sport playing or not, spectators can be assured they are going to see high-caliber golf. The talent pool available on every tour runs so deep that any player in a pro tournament is someone from whom the amateur can learn.

Tiger Woods is just one of dozens of popular players who attract fans to pro events.

When you know of a tour event you plan to attend, advertisements will explain how to purchase tickets. Tickets can usually be ordered and received well ahead of the event, which is necessary for the major championships as those events are quite often sold out months in advance of the tournament dates. Tickets for other events can usually be bought on the day you plan to attend. The cost for practice rounds is less than the tournament rounds, ranging from $5 to $30. Tickets for the actual tournament rounds range from $10 to $50 or more, depending on the event. You will want to watch for tournament information to determine the best day to attend because some practice days have extra events such as teaching clinics, shootout competitions for the pros, and pro-ams, a well-known format that has a professional paired with four amateur players in an eighteen-hole round. The pro-am usually takes place on Wednesday of tournament week and runs throughout the day.

There is an extra charge for parking at most events. The local paper usually publishes a routing of how the public should travel to the golf site; parking can be right next door to the course or miles away, in which case the spectators are bused back and forth to the course.

To get the most out of your day at the course, don't think of it as you would attending a football game, where you'd sit on your haunches. You're going to do a lot of walking around. Arrive in comfortable shoes and clothes that keep you at a good temperature depending on the weather. If it's hot, make sure to bring a hat and sunblock. Gallery members usually, at some point, find a vantage point to watch players come through, and having the sun beat down on you takes its toll on your skin.

There are some things that are not welcome at a tour event: coolers, radios, mobile phones, strollers, bulky box periscopes, signs, ladders, large folding armchairs, and beepers. If you must come with beepers, you won't be able to get close to any of the players, except at the practice range. Mobile phones and beepers set on vibration are allowed, but users should not make calls near the players. Cameras are permissible during practice rounds, but definitely not during tournament rounds. If you use one during practice, make sure you don't click the shutter until after a player has struck the ball, except near the driving range.

In most cases, there is no need to talk with a player while he's playing a practice round or tournament eighteen. Players who hit a wayward shot near the spectator areas may initiate a dialogue with the crowd, so it's usually best to see what mood the player is in for talking. They appreciate applause or acknowledgment of a good shot and will recognize such cheering. But shouting as if you're at a pro baseball or basketball game, especially something like the "You the man" catchphrase of the past ten years or so, is definitely a faux pas that singles you out as uncool and unaware of proper fan behavior. Outbursts only fit in if the cham-

Spectators get an up-close view to observe the putting techniques of professional players.

pion is walking up the final hole, or if someone makes a rare shot. If you're with a companion and need to speak under normal circumstances, do it in a whisper.

Golf should mostly be played as a quiet game, but there are times to let loose. Remain still and quiet as a player prepares for a shot and during the shot. Observe the "Quiet, please!" paddleboards held up by the gallery marshal. It is amazing how much voices travel at a golf course, especially downwind. After the shot is played, you may react in whatever manner is necessary, depending on the outcome of the shot. Applause and shouts of happiness are okay for good shots, groans for poor ones or near misses are also fine. In the matter of clapping, only good shots or results should earn your applause. Don't clap if a player stubs a shot or hits one in the water, a bunker, or out-of-bounds. And don't applaud if she makes an over-par score on a hole. Playing bad holes is not what the player is trying to do, so don't applaud his ineptitude. When she makes par or better, polite applause is justified. Likewise, a shot that finishes far from the hole is generally not well accepted by the pro, so keep your hands quiet. By applauding at the right time, you'll show you have the smarts of an experienced golf observer.

There are three locations to view golf action. The first is the practice range, which often has a grandstand set up for gallery seating. A second is finding a vantage point at a spot on the course that allows viewing of various spots, such as a putting green, a tee, and another hole. A third is following a specific group around the course. During the first couple of tournament rounds, players are often grouped in threes. The first group tees off around 7 A.M.; the last as late as 3:30 P.M. Most tour events have a morning and afternoon session; groups tee off on either the first hole or the tenth, and then cross over to play the other nine. The same occurs in the afternoon. In major championships, all groups tee off on the first hole and play the holes in order. Daily pairing sheets are printed that list the groups, their starting times, and how the course is laid out. Get familiar with the course design so you can go straight to the areas you're needing to get to.

The most exhausting viewing method is walking around the course with groups you're interested in seeing. Gallery ropes are set up around the course to indicate where spectators can and can't walk. Often these ropes have the fans doing a lot of walking up and down hills and around trees and bunkers. The walk can be more difficult than what the players go through. Don't ignore gallery ropes and go on parts of the course where you're not allowed, such as greens, tees, and bunkers. If it's too crowded around tees and greens, move further toward the fairway to get a better view. Stay ahead of the players as they go around the course and you'll stay ahead of the other fans. Pairings are usually done so that there are groupings of popular players at certain times in the morning and the afternoon. By following a series of groups that have Greg Norman, Tiger Woods, and Phil Mickelson, a fan can hop around from hole to hole to see as much of each player as possible.

Always be on the alert for where the golfers are hitting. It's not good planning to stand where the golfers are hitting their drives or in a spot where you can't see them. You're likely to get hit by a ball at some point, and a flying ball that's been hit by a pro golfer packs a powerful punch. Getting hit by a ball is a possibility you accept as a ticket buyer and the course and tournament are not responsible if you're nailed. Don't touch a ball if it comes in your area, but do keep an eye on where wayward shots end up. You may be a crucial eyewitness when a marshal comes over to locate the ball.

Give players plenty of room to pass by wherever they are walking, near the range or from green to tee. Be sure to follow the orders given by the marshals, and observe the gallery crosswalks on most fairways, which are the places spectators can cross over to the other side of the hole. Marshals only allow crossing over when a group has passed by or if no group is on the tee ready to hit. If you're following a group, wait to move to the next tee until after everyone in the group has putted out. If you're watching a popular player such as Greg Norman or John Daly, don't run off after he's putted. Such a departure en masse makes it more difficult for the other players to putt.

If threatening weather is in the area, leader boards throughout the course will post weather warning signs. When this occurs, play may be suspended and a siren will sound. Spectators need to find shelter, but must avoid bleachers, high places, open fields, bodies of water, any metal objects, tall trees, isolated trees, telephone poles, power lines, and golf carts.

As for autographs, fans are really at the mercy of how the professional feels about them. Some prefer only to sign at designated autograph booths near the clubhouse. Others sign no matter where they are asked, and still others find autographs to be a complete nuisance. Most pros understand that the fans are a necessary element of the game and help provide for their livelihood. They oblige autograph requests as much as possible. You can tell from a player's body language if they're the affable type or not. The spectator has a role, too, in getting a signature. He shouldn't be pushy, rude, or demanding of the player or other fans. There is a limit to how many autographs a player can sign, and if you're shut out, so be it. There's always next time. Try to get the player as she's going to and from practice or after she's done with a practice round. Some players also sign as often as possible during a practice round if the timing feels right.

If you decide not to follow groups around, go to a strategic location that affords a good seating spot and lets you see action on various holes. A look at the course map will indicate a great viewing place, where there could be a par-3 hole, a par-4 green, and another tee all in close proximity.

Lastly, no one should go to a tour event without spending some time at the practice range. This is where the pro player spends a lot of his time, improving on an already impressive looking swing. And this is the place where the spectator can do her best viewing and learn the most about the golf swing.

Learning by watching a tour player at the driving range is similar to learning by watching him on television. The best plan is to look for a player about your same height, size, and build. There are slight differences in the way golfers of different physical shapes swing. No matter the size, however, nearly all pro golfers swing with great rhythm and tempo. That's a strong lesson to learn. It is common for spectators to leave a tour event and comment to a friend, "Those pros make it look so easy. They didn't swing very hard at the ball at all!"

Remember, the best swings are those that set up all the proper angles and deliver them to the ball at impact in the proper sequence and timing. The swing isn't a race to complete. Professionals illustrate that point very well.

Another point to observe is the preshot routine pros employ. The routine is repetitive and useful. Notice how a pro assesses the shot, checks the wind condition and location of the flagstick on the green, finds the yardage to the hole, selects a club, visualizes the shot, then takes a stance, waggles the club a time or two, gets to feeling set, and makes the swing. By using this sequence over and over, the pros have made it all happen very quickly, at least most of them. There are slow players out there, and their habits should be avoided. A decisive player like Tom Watson has long been a great example of playing with dispatch.

Composure and calm are traits you'll see in most pros. Sure, there are some that lose it when things don't go their way, but learn from the pros who accept bad shots or adversity as part of the game, remain calm, and try to do better next time. Rarely will a professional hit two bad shots in a row. She recovers from a poor one and avoids making the same mistake twice. A pro's mental toughness is something that separates him from amateurs, and even from one another. Imagine how her thought process is working in tense situations and imagine yourself making those same decisions.

If you're watching a televised golf event—and there is never a shortage of TV golf these days—pay special attention to the slow-motion replay shown at various times during the broadcast. Unfortunately, the commentator's description of the swing is often too advanced or unclear for the average player to understand, but little swing tidbits can still be ascertained. Have a club sitting nearby so you can practice a new grip or address position while the pros play. And television shows a great deal of putting. There are many different putting styles, but one point on which to focus is the way all the good putters accelerate the club through impact. The putter swings back and through with good pace and is always kept moving toward the target. The motion isn't a quick-back, slow-through stroke.

Whether you go to see the pros in person or watch them on television, remember the overall goal is to have fun and enjoy the experience of learning from the best players in the world.

GETTING HANDS-ON EXPERIENCE

Attending a golf school is probably the most expensive way to learn how to play, but along with lessons from a teaching professional, a golf school is the best place to go for hands-on experience.

Golf schools range in cost from a few hundred dollars to several thousand, depending on where you go, who the teachers are, and whether lodging and meals are part of the package cost. There are dozens of golf schools, most of them advertised in major golf publications, newspapers, or golf courses.

In selecting which school to attend, consider a number of factors. Going at the beginning of the golf season is good in that it can get the student prepared physically and mentally for a new year, but it can also be a tiring experience because the body hasn't used its golf muscles in quite a while. If you select an early-season school, be sure to pace yourself and have plenty of bandages for blisters and pain relievers for sore muscles. Before the school, practice swinging a club at home for a few days to get the feel of the club again.

A school in mid-season can straighten out an errant game and still allow enough time to enjoy the rest of the golf season with improved play. A school at year's end can be useful only if the player continues to do things on his own at home whenever possible, so that when the new season comes around he can still call upon some of his new skills and advance from there.

A prospective student should also consider the lodging and travel options. Someone who lives in the North and travels to the South for a school will have to pay for airfare, lodging, meals, the school, and anything else that's tied in with the trip. However, some schools have a commuter option. For example, a golfer in the Chicago area might find a three-day commuter school to attend, which means she can stay home and travel to the school and avoid the lodging and meal cost, plus not have as big a tuition fee for the school. That's just an example of the flexible schedules and rates that most schools have.

And another consideration is the teaching staff and the type of methodology taught. There are some radical methods that make the student feel completely out of the loop. Some of the major schools, such as Golf Digest Schools, have staffs that are well respected and have been evaluated for their expertise. But it doesn't hurt to phone the prospective school and discuss with someone the types of teachers used (some schools utilize famous teachers or tour pros at times), their teaching style (some teachers are confrontational, others more passive), what their swing beliefs are, how much attention each student will receive (a ratio of one teacher for every six students is an ideal maximum), and an example of the daily schedule and what other activities are available. Ask also what the student is expected to know. Is a working knowledge of the swing and the game required, or can a total beginner attend? The student needs to know he won't have the instructors talking over his head. Students pay a lot for a school and deserve to know what they'll get for the money.

> "You want a clear mind and a firm, decisive stroking action when putting. All I think about is accelerating the putter through the ball and making solid contact. I want to meet the ball with the sweet spot of the putter. By thinking about making solid contact, your mind is fixed on a positive thought, which prevents you from thinking negatively."
>
> TOM WATSON

The average school lasts about three days and covers everything from the grip and swing fundamentals to chipping and putting. Practice tips and drills are introduced to help the player improve. The student is evaluated for swing problems and a course of action is planned during the three days to overcome the flaws. Better schools will include a manual to jot down notes, a videotape of the student's progression through the three days, a playing lesson, and even a small goodie bag containing take-home items.

The school might include an introductory dinner the night before instruction begins, during which the teacher is introduced and explains how the school will unfold. Over the three days there will be sessions on the full swing, chipping, sand play, putting, strategy, and how to practice the new skills introduced. The student, meanwhile, will be told to pace himself to avoid burning out the first morning by hitting as many balls as possible. She'll be reminded to keep her mind clear during swing discussions and avoid becoming more confused than she already is. An action plan for overcoming the player's main swing flaw will be put together. And the school eventually becomes a learning place that the student controls what he gets out of it more than the teacher. A superb learning attitude goes a long way in making the school the best experience ever and something with lasting value.

GOING STRAIGHT TO THE SOURCE

One of the original sources of golf instruction is the golf professional. Actually, prior to the pro were clubmakers, who were relied on for not only making clubs but also for having the best knowledge of the swing. Golfers could also seek out any player who was considered at the top of the talent pool, and then from the late 1800s on there were the golf professionals who demonstrated more consistently than anyone before how well the game could be played. It was only natural that lesser players pick the pros' brains for swing tips and advice for whatever was ailing their game.

In the United States, the golf professional became a familiar figure at the private country clubs of the early 1900s. When professionals banded together to form the PGA of America in 1916, it was with the intention of promoting their profession and helping the cause of the professional move forward. One of the main causes is teaching so golfers can improve their swings and thereby enjoy the game more earnestly. This is the same goal of the 900 women who are members of the LPGA Tour's Teaching and Club Professional division.

Please realize that there is a difference in the teaching pros available for use. An instructor can only be called a PGA club professional if he has completed the apprenticeship work and gained PGA of America membership (the PGA of America has 23,000 members worldwide, 642 of which are women). If the instructor has done so, you can be assured she has studied the golf swing and learned how to give others instruction. Their teaching philosophy is sound and trustworthy.

However, there is another teaching segment unassociated with the PGA of America that simply goes by the titles golf instructor, teacher or coach, and sometimes, falsely, as teaching professional. These individuals may not have any formal training at all as instructors and in some cases don't have the qualifications to be helping people with their swing. If you use a non-PGA member, be sure he has the technical expertise and knowledge to be of real use.

If you see an instructor or PGA professional for a lesson, it will be a half-hour or hour session. Lesson fees are usually in the $30 per half-hour range, some lower and some much higher. If you need to schedule a series of lessons, see if the teacher has a discount plan to save on costs. Some of the world's best-known teachers, such as David Leadbetter and Butch Harmon, receive $100 or more for one lesson. Because the cost for even a low-end teacher is substantial, that's all the more reason to make sure the person you're working with is worth the money. And it's important to pay close attention to what information is being passed along to make the best use of the time together.

When you've decided to see a teacher, either because of a recommendation or the teacher's credentials, the teacher will schedule you to come and jot down your name in an appointment book. When the lesson time comes, it wouldn't hurt to have spent thirty minutes or so on the driving range getting warmed up so you're all set to go. During a first meeting, the teacher will want to know some things about your golf background, and especially, what swing problems you've had and what you hope to get out of the game. Think ahead of time of where you want to be swing-wise one year from now, even five years from now. The teacher will most likely watch you hit balls for a few minutes, observing your fundamentals and looking at ball flight and the swing itself. Make sure you swing with your natural shot; don't alter your swing in any way to hide a swing fault or avoid embarrassment because of how you look. Realize that golf teachers see swings of every shape and kind and that yours is probably not even close to being the worst she's seen. You're trying to get better, not win first place in a beauty contest. Let the teacher see your entire game and move forward from there.

During the first session, the teacher may not have you work on more than one thing. If he sees that you release the club too early and have lost power at impact, for instance, he would point that out to you first and explain the problem, then have you do an impact drill. The teacher may ask you to do that drill for the rest of the session and then do nothing but that drill for a week before your next session. To you it will feel like you're regressing and have gotten worse. But keep in mind that in most golf learning, the player has to take a step or two backward before making a major leap forward. Keeping the faith and having patience are often the two biggest things you need to have to get better with an instructor.

If you're fortunate, going a couple of sessions with the teacher may be all that's needed to solve your problem and head you on the road to solid golf. The teacher won't need to see you again until another swing problem occurs or perhaps for a checkup at the end of the year. That's a typical occurrence for established players. If you're a new player just taking up the game, you'll need to schedule a series of lessons with the pro, or, to save money, you might want to join a series of beginner meetings instead. Clinics for new players last six to eight weeks and are for a set fee, which makes this way of learning more cost-efficient than a series of one-on-one teacher meetings. Beginner classes usually involve groups of around six players, who learn the fundamentals and all phases of the game.

Lessons can be arranged to learn not only the full swing but also the short game and putting. Instructors follow the same pattern no matter what game segment is being taught; there's always an initial meeting to discuss the golfer's past history, then a diagnosis, and lastly a remedy or cure. Payment is made to the teacher after the lesson, but tipping is not necessary unless you've done a long series of lessons and feel satisfied enough with the progress made to add something extra after the last meeting.

Along with the work involved in taking the lesson, one of the hardest parts of instruction sessions is knowing the right person to see in the first place. You're looking not only for a person with swing smarts but also someone who can communicate well and is people oriented. Some teachers' style is confrontational and challenging. Others are more laid-back. You need to find someone with a good match to your style. And women don't necessarily need a female, or men a male, teacher. Good teachers come in both varieties.

Sometimes you can't tell if a teacher is right for you unless you try him. Things may look promising, but you can only tell with an actual lesson. Afterward assess if you had your questions answered satisfactorily, the time together was enjoyable, things meshed properly, you learned something, and you improved. If the answers are favorable, then you've found your swing person.

A common approach to finding a teacher is to use the one located at the course or driving range you use. Another way is to use one recommended by a golfing pal. Yet another good method is by contacting the LPGA Tour—(904) 274-6200, Daytona Beach, Florida, Internet site: http://www.lpga.com—for its suggestions of good teachers in your area, or contact the PGA of America.

There are forty-one geographical sections of the PGA of America. Each is assigned to service the PGA golf professionals and assistants within their region. In addition to conducting events in which their members play, the sections provide grass-roots support for programs geared toward juniors and amateurs, and they arrange workshops, seminars, and other educational programs for the PGA member and apprentice.

The sections report on their activities to the main PGA of America office at 100 Avenue of the Champions, Palm Beach Gardens, FL 33418; phone: (561) 624-8400; fax: (561) 624-8448; website: http://www.PGA.com. Phone the section office nearest you to ask about reputable teachers you can see.

Aloha
770 Kapiolani Boulevard
Room 715
Honolulu, HI 96813
Phone: (808) 593-2230; (808) 593-2232; (808) 593-2235
Fax: (808) 593-2234

Carolinas
3852 Highway 9 East
P.O. Box 709
N. Myrtle Beach, SC 29597-0709
Phone: (803) 399-CPGA (2742)
Fax: (803) 399-1504

Central New York
822 State Fair Boulevard
Syracuse, NY 13209
Phone: (315) 468-6812
Fax: (315) 488-8268

Colorado
12323 East Cornell
Suite 21
Aurora, CO 80014
Phone: (303) 745-3697
Fax: (303) 745-5088

Connecticut
35 Cold Spring Road
Suite 212
Rocky Hill, CT 06067
Phone: (860) 257-GOLF (4653)
Fax: (860) 257-8355

Dixie
601 Vestavia Parkway
Suite 320
Birmingham, AL 35216
Phone: (205) 822-0321
Fax: (205) 822-2842

Gateway
12225 Clayton Road
St. Louis, MO 63131
Phone: (314) 991-4994
Fax: (314) 991-3543

Georgia
1165 Northchase Parkway
Suite 140
Marietta, GA 30067
Phone: (770) 952-9063
Fax: (770) 859-9305

Gulf States
P.O. Box 29426
New Orleans, LA 70189
Delivery: 5690 Eastover Drive
New Orleans, LA 70128
Phone: (504) 245-7333
Fax: (504) 245-7364

Illinois
1 Pete Dye Drive
Lemont, IL 60439
Phone: (630) 257-9600
Fax: (630) 257-9671

Indiana
P.O. Box 516
Delivery: 2313 North Hurricane Road
Franklin, IN 46131
Phone: (317) 738-9696
Fax: (317) 738-9436

Iowa
1930 St. Andrews N.E.
Cedar Rapids, IA 52402
Phone: (319) 378-9142
Fax: (319) 378-9203

Kentucky
P.O. Box 18396
Louisville, KY 40261-0396
Delivery: 4109 Bardstown Road
Suite 5-A
Louisville, KY 40218
Phone: (502) 499-7255
Fax: (502) 499-7422

Metropolitan
49 Knollwood Road
Suite 200
Elmsford, NY 10523
Phone: (914) 347-2325
Fax: (914) 347-2014

Michigan
32744 Five Mile Road
Livonia, MI 48154
Phone: (313) 522-2323
Fax: (313) 522-5626

Middle Atlantic
2721 Jefferson Davis Highway
Suite 101
Stafford, VA 22554
Phone: (540) 720-7420
D.C. area: (703) 551-4653
Fax: (540) 720-7076

Midwest
1960 Copper Oaks Circle
Blue Springs, MO 64015
Phone: (816) 229-6565
Fax: (816) 229-9644

Minnesota
12800 Bunker Prairie Road
Coon Rapids, MN 55448
Phone: (612) 754-0820
Fax: (612) 754-0891

Nebraska
9301 Firethorn Lane
Lincoln, NE 68520
Phone: (402) 489-7760
Fax: (402) 489-1785

New England
Hillview Country Club
149 North Street
North Reading, MA 01864
Phone: (508) 664-6555
Fax: (508) 664-3343

New Jersey
P.O. Box 200
Delivery: c/o Forsgate Country Club
Forsgate Drive
Jamesburg, NJ 08831
Phone: (908) 521-4000
Fax: (908) 521-4004

Northeastern New York
48 Howard Street
Albany, NY 12207
Phone: (518) 463-3067
Fax: (518) 463-8656

Northern California
2133 Las Positas Court
Suite A
Livermore, CA 94550-9774
Phone: (510) 455-7800
Fax: (510) 449-5753

Northern Ohio
38121 Euclid Avenue
Willoughby, OH 44094
Phone: (216) 951-4546
Fax: (216) 951-0508

Northern Texas
2000 N. Central Expressway
Suite 100
Plano, TX 75074
Phone: (972) 881-GOLF (4653)
Fax: (972) 423-7861

North Florida
200 Forest Lake Boulevard
Suite 3
Daytona Beach, FL 32119
Phone: (904) 322-0899
Fax: (904) 322-2567

Pacific Northwest
4011 Yelm Highway S.E.
Olympia, WA 98501-5170
Phone: (360) 456-6496
Fax: (360) 456-6745

Philadelphia
Plymouth Green Office Campus
801 East Germantown Pike
#F-6,
Norristown, PA 19401
Phone: (610) 277-5777
Fax: (610) 277-6151

Rocky Mountain
595 E. State Street
Eagle, ID 83616
Phone: (208) 939-6028
Fax: (208) 939-6058

South Central
951 N. Forest Ridge Boulevard
Broken Arrow, OK 74014
Phone: (918) 357-3332
Fax: (918) 357-3328

Southern California
601 S. Valencia Avenue
Suite 200
Brea, CA 92823
Phone: (714) 776-4653
Fax: (714) 572-1350

Southern Ohio
2186 Gateway Drive
Fairborn, OH 45324
Phone: (937) 754-4263
Fax: (937) 754-4663

Southern Texas
1610 Woodstead Court
Suite 110
The Woodlands, TX 77380
Phone: (281) 363-0511
Fax: (281) 367-3167

South Florida
10804 W. Sample Road
Coral Springs, FL 33065
Attn: PGA Building
Phone: (954) 752-9299
Fax: (954) 752-9659

Southwest
5040 E. Shea Boulevard
Suite 250
Scottsdale, AZ 85254
Phone: (602) 443-9002
Fax: (602) 443-9006

Sun Country
Mountain Run Center
5850 Eubank N.E.
Suite B-72
Albuquerque, NM 87111
Phone: (505) 271-1442
Fax: (505) 271-8626

Tennessee
400 Franklin Road
Franklin, TN 37069
Phone: (615) 790-7600
Fax: (615) 790-8600

Tristate
221 Sherwood Drive
Monaca, PA 15061
Phone: (412) 774-2224
Fax: (412) 774-5535

Utah
525 East 4500 South
Suite F-250
Murray, UT 84107
Phone: (801) 281-8123
Fax: (801) 281-8127

Western New York
P.O. Box 1728
Williamsville, NY 14231-1728
Delivery: 5725 Main Street
Williamsville, NY 14221
Phone: (716) 626-0603
Fax: (716) 626-5308

Wisconsin
4000 W. Brown Deer Road
Milwaukee, WI 53209
Phone: (414) 365-4474
Fax: (414) 365-4479

MAKING A VISIT TO A ONE-DAY CLINIC

A popular teaching format in recent years, particularly at professional tour events, is the one-day clinic. This method has two approaches: First is the type that participants attend and actually take part in the learning, and the second is the type where attendees watch from the sidelines as instructors demonstrate a topic. These clinics last an hour to ninety minutes and usually take place at a practice range. Seating is set up for spectators. The second type of clinic doesn't require anything more from the viewer than keen listening skills and the ability to take good notes.

If you're attending a one-day clinic, be sure to arrive early so you can warm up prior to the actual start time. Have your listening ears ready and don't be timid about asking questions if something leaves you confused. Come prepared knowing you most likely will be asked to make some kind of change in your swing and to do so through future practice time. You won't solve a swing problem in the short time of a clinic. Things such as grip, posture, and address changes will feel unusual at first and take time to become second nature.

Keep your mind clear and don't try to overload it with too many swing thoughts. A dozen ideas all at the same time make the swing feel mechanical and tight rather than free-flowing. When the clinic is finished, don't go straight to the course and play. Spend more time working on the swing fix by yourself so you can work more focused instead of thinking the instructor will be around any second to critique you. Practice what you've been taught for a while longer before taking your game to the course again.

HOW MUCH CONCENTRATION DO YOU NEED

Most proficient golfers speak about how the ability to focus and concentrate can be the difference between being a good golfer and a mediocre one. If you have devoted yourself to being the best golfer you can, then you have to totally involve your mind and body in the learning process. You must prepare to play, focus on each shot, and swing with control. Each shot must be a unique situation to you. And this applies not only to course play but practice. You can be the golfer you want to be if you learn the golf swing well and learn to channel your focus on eliminating bad thoughts. Swing with confidence and get the job done.

Emotions can vary widely in golf and how you use them is an individual factor. Ben Hogan was known for playing in near silence and had a reputation as a rude playing partner who only focused on himself. He wasn't that way off the course, but his total focus on playing golf is what made him, by most estimates, the best ever striker of the ball. Other players like Lee Trevino must talk a lot and jabber with anyone around him to stay loose, and yet he can shut everything else out when it's time to hit a shot.

The late, great Babe Didrikson Zaharias said that too many distractions can reduce your effectiveness as a tournament player. "When I've been thinking about too many other things besides golf, and my mind isn't clear and easy out there, then I don't plan my shots the way I should. I don't see the one right place where the ball should go. I'm just keeping the ball in play."

However, golf for you may not be an intense passion. You could be a golfer for the relaxation and exercise it gives you. You've had enough intensity at the office or at home, and the golf course is the place to escape from it. There is nothing wrong with that attitude and in many ways it's the best way to go because you have no worries or anxieties about your score or how well you play. You simply like golf as an activity and diversion.

> "Walk onto any practice area in America and you'll always find more players beating balls on the range than practicing their chipping. Most golfers view chipping as unrewarding drudgery. In fact, poor chipping is a primary reason the handicap of the average golfer has remained frozen at 18 for the last 25 years."
>
> COREY PAVIN

A round of golf doesn't need to be four to six hours of all-out concentration. The primary action in golf is the shot itself, so if you're a 100-shooter, think of golf needing sixty seconds of your complete attention 100 times a round. That's the time required to plan the shot and then execute it. Golfers should take mental breaks between shots as they're walking to the ball and not worry about what the next shot will be because they don't totally know the shot conditions they'll face until they reach the ball.

There are a lot of peaks and valleys in golf, and your goal should be to not let them be too tall or too deep. Remain on an even level as much as possible and keep in mind that all you can ask of yourself is to do your best. Golf is a game that gets the best of you one day, but it could be your day the next. By remaining level-headed you can keep your mind clear to make the best swings possible.

 Chapter 10

HEALTH—GOLFERS CAN GET INJURED

G olf has had a lot of slings and arrows directed toward it by critics who think it shouldn't be categorized as a sport. They compare golf with baseball, basketball, football, and hockey—the "real sports"—in which athletes look like athletes in their uniforms and clearly demonstrate they exert a lot more effort than golfers. Critics put golfers, auto racers, and bowlers in a separate, nonathletic category that's a notch below the other sports.

Obviously, these critics must not be golfers. They've never played golf while walking a hilly course in humid, 95-degree weather. That's not the same as playing a forty-eight-minute professional basketball game, but it's a taxing physical effort of another kind that requires great physical skill and endurance.

There's not a lot of difference in the amount of energy put out by either the expert golfer or the high handicapper. Poor players have a tough time physically because they take so many more strokes than good players and the majority of those strokes are preceded by one or two practice swings. Better players don't swing as often, but the swings they do take, combined with mental fatigue, amount to a substantial energy output. The better a golfer is, the stronger the mental ability must be to compete on the highest level.

Golf has similarities with the so-called real sports in that its primary physical action, the swing, is a single, quick, burst of energy and motion. The golf swing, along with the baseball swing, hockey shot, jump shot, and football pass, are fast movements that determine who leads the competition, whether it be measured in strokes, runs, or points.

But the clear difference in comparing golf to the other sports is that golfers don't run following the swing. Athletes in the other games are off and running most of the time after the hit or shot. Their constant activity as opposed to a golfer's apparent slowness is one reason golf isn't considered more as a sport by some. Golfers stand around a lot and don't go faster than a walk, unless you've won the U.S. Open and have decided to run around passing out high fives.

But let there be no mistake about golf. It's not a contact sport, but as one of the most popular pastimes, golfers experience plenty of aches and pains, varying from the nagging variety to the serious kind that can end a person's golf days.

How can a golfer get hurt by swinging a golf club? It's not hard to imagine or explain in nontechnical terms. Picture the golfer at the start of the swing, standing motionless in an uncomfortable bent-over position, bent from the hips, and putting stress on the back. As the club is swung to the top, the upper body twists and bends, putting tension on the spine. Then there is the quick pivot back to impact, putting stress on the spine and back muscles. The arms and hands are jarred by the impact of the club striking the ground, then more tension is placed on the upper body and spine as the golfer twists and unwinds in the other direction. Throughout the entire procedure there is subtle bending, flexing, and rolling of many joints in the legs and arms.

That's what the body goes through for every golf swing, and it's done over and over many times during rounds and practice sessions. Add in the time a golfer practices his putting, and there is added stress on the lower back while the player stands over the ball. Over time, the repetitive movements add up and body parts can be worn to the breaking point. There is either constant pain or an injury occurs. Small fractures can take place in bones. And all of this doesn't even take into account the constant pounding to the legs and feet of walking. Riders of golf carts aren't left off the hook, either. The continual bumps caused by riding over rough ground put pressure on the back.

The back, in fact, is the most commonly injured part of the body for men. Women are most often hurt in the wrist and then the back and the elbow. But, of course, every person is different. The following items describe some of the commonly seen golf maladies, plus comments on some general health care.

SOME COMMON PROBLEMS
Elbow tendinitis

This occurs when the tremendous force at impact transfers a shock to the forearm muscles, which then reverberate the force to the small tendons that attach to the bones at the elbow. The elbow most affected is the one that leads the downswing, such as the left elbow for a right-handed player. The risk of getting elbow tendinitis increases with the amount of golf played, as well as age. If the pain isn't too severe, it can be eased by swinging with a slightly bent left arm at the top of the swing and at impact. In other words, don't make the left arm as straight as a board because that puts stress on the elbow joint.

Another option is decreasing the grip pressure applied by the hands and keeping it that way during the swing. Golfers can also swing the club in a sweeping motion rather than dig down to take deep divots, and there's the choice of using graphite-shafted clubs for their absorbing quality or clubs that have the newer vibration-dampening devices in the shaft. Medically, a common approach to elbow tendinitis is using an elbow brace, the device that wraps around the upper forearm and connects with a Velcro-type closure. The brace acts like a shock absorber. Strengthening exercises also are a good idea. The forearm muscles can be toned up with a light weight or by squeezing a rubber ball.

Course chemicals

All that green grass on the golf course isn't there by accident. All the chemicals pumped onto the grass make a big difference. Some of those chemicals are potent, which is why many courses today do the courtesy of posting signs on the days chemicals are used. This lets golfers know what kind of an environment they're stepping into in case they have allergies and can suffer bad reactions. Some chemicals are known to cause headaches, rashes, and other health problems. To be safe, golfers should never put the ball in their mouths or lick them to clean them off, which used to be the common practice for many players.

Avoid wearing shorts on days where there is a lot of dew because the moisture could be contaminated and kicked up on bare skin, but if you do wear shorts, wear high socks. And be sure to clean off the hands after playing and before eating any food.

Wristbands

These bands, both the copper and metal alloy kinds, are two of the latest health rages, not just in golf, but in general. Although some in the medical profession are hesitant to endorse them, the bands are said to have a therapeutic effect. The copper bands are thought to help relieve arthritis and tendinitis conditions. It is believed the copper dissolves into minute particles that are absorbed by the skin and perform wondrous healing. The metal-alloy bands, with two small beads on each end, are said to correct a person's imbalance of positive and negative energy. This may be a placebo effect, if anything, but the bands appear to help some people while being of no use to others. At this point, they seem to be of use on an individual basis.

Biomagnets

Related to the new-style wristbands are biomagnets, which, again, have not been seen by the medical profession as anything but pure speculation. There have been no studies done to support the belief by its users that magnets ease aches and pains because of their polarity. Proponents say that injuries give off positive magnetic fields and the negative field of the magnets works to relieve pain by stimulating cells and increasing blood flow to the affected area. Toxins are eliminated and inflammation is reduced. The magnets also, the manufacturers say, stimulate an electrical current that activates the nervous system and blocks pain. Senior PGA Tour players Jim Colbert and Bob Murphy have taped a dollar-bill-sized amount of magnets on their back and neck to ease back pain. Michelle McGann of the LPGA Tour sleeps on a magnetic mattress pad. In all, approximately eighty touring pros use some kind of magnetic therapy, as of 1997. (People who have pacemaker implants should probably avoid magnetic therapy.) Many of these biomagnetic products, such as wrist and back wraps, are available in major sporting-goods and discount stores. Prices range from $75 for a back belt to $500 for a mattress pad.

Sunglasses

The newfangled, space-age shades of the past ten years, the kind that wrap around the face, have gone from being ridiculed to mild acceptance to greater acceptance. When they were first seen on the PGA Tour, they were worn by the younger generation—the "Joe Cools"—which didn't do much as an endorsement for using them. But when some of the more respected players on both the men's and women's tours started wearing them, people saw them in a whole new light. Sunglasses are quite acceptable as more than just a fashion statement. They keep out ultraviolet rays that can damage the eyes. If eyes are overexposed to the sun, conditions such as pterygia and pinguecula can develop, which are growths on the whites of the eyes that expand onto the cornea and obscure vision. Cataracts are another concern. As for playability, sunglasses reduce glare so the eyes aren't as fatigued. In the past, players often complained that sunglasses distorted colors and vision in general, which made them impossible to use when reading greens. But getting the right color lens can make a difference. Brown, vermilion/pink, and gray are good choices; green, blue, yellow, and orange are not so good. Any golfer that plays in the sun a lot, such as in the Sun Belt states, should consider using sunglasses for the future protection of their eyes. Just make sure the glasses are a quality pair with a coating to screen out ultraviolet light.

> "You will never master golf—and neither, I fear, will any pro. The fun of the game, the fun which I constantly enjoy and which you too can learn to savor, is in trying."
>
> ARNOLD PALMER

Wrist

The wrist takes a constant beating from the amount of vibration it gets from the club striking the ground. When it becomes sore, and a doctor doesn't feel there's anything structurally wrong, rest is the best solution to ease the pain. If you have to play, try using a wrist brace, or if it's a casual round, tee up the ball a lot, even off the tee, so you don't have to hit the ground so much. Putting ice on the wrist after play will control inflammation, but soaking the wrist in warm water prior to play will help loosen it up.

Back

Herniated and degenerative disks, muscle spasms, and arthritis are all symptoms of serious back problems that must be checked out by a specialist. But for 90 percent of back pain, people can recover without any serious treatment such as surgery. For any back problem that's not of a serious nature, there are a few measures that can be taken to relieve back pain. While putting, for instance, a golfer can stand more upright, stand closer to the ball, and narrow the stance so the lower back doesn't feel as much pressure. Getting a longer putter will prevent bending over putts. Warm baths and heat applied to the sore area of the back, along with rest, will loosen tight muscles. Overweight golfers can take a substantial amount of stress off their backs by losing weight from the abdomen. Strong stomach muscles help support the lower back. And stretching before and after play is really a must for improving back condition. One stretch involves taking a driver, broomstick, or exercise bar and resting it across the shoulders. The arms then drape over the object from behind. Next, turn from side to side, keeping the feet and lower body still and turning so that the shoulders pivot 90 degrees in each direction. Toe touches are also a good stretch, as is lying on the back with the knees bent. From this position, grab one knee with both hands and pull it toward the chest as far as possible; then switch and pull the other leg toward the chest. And still another stretch requires a short rope. Holding the rope in the right arm, lift the arm and bend it so the arm and the rope dangle behind the back; the left arm reaches behind the back and grabs the free end of the rope. The left arm pulls down to stretch the right side of the upper torso. The second part of the stretch is reversing so the left arm is above the head and the left portion of the upper body is stretched. All of these stretches should be done a few times at first, and then the number of repetitions gradually increased.

Heat

Playing in heat can be wonderful for loosening the muscles, but along with lightning, is one of the two most dangerous weather conditions in which to play golf. Golfers can play it safe by taking the proper precautions. The precautions begin by using the correct sunblock for protection against skin cancer, which can occur with golfers who play for years and years in ultraviolet light exposure. Sunblock containing PABA (para-aminobenzoic acid) and with a sun protection factor (SPF) of 15 or higher is best. Wearing light-colored clothing prevents the sun's rays from intensifying, and cotton fabrics are good for letting the skin breath. An apparel company called Sun Precautions has been a leader in making clothes with built-in ultraviolet light protection. A wide-brimmed hat, a visor, or cap, of course, are ideal for protecting the face and keeping cool. A wet towel kept handy for wrapping around the back of the neck is always great for staying comfortable. As for nutrition, golfers playing in hot weather usually feel more comfortable when they don't eat big, heavy meals prior to playing. Eat light, make sure to sprinkle a little salt on the food rather than use salt tablets later, and grab something handy like a nutrition bar or a piece of fruit to eat on the course. While playing, drink a cup of water on each hole. Stay away from soda, alcohol, and sugared drinks. Water and special athletic drinks are the best liquids in the heat.

GOLF—THE WALKING GAME

As mentioned earlier in this chapter, any criticism of golf as a legitimate sport has been due to its lack of running and moving around. Swing, walk, find the ball; swing, walk, find the ball. That's the tempo of golf, not the pace of a basketball game where players are in near-constant motion. Because it's a walking sport, people can't believe there's any benefit to playing golf. But walking is the way the game was meant to be played.

When the game started in Europe, taking a ride on some mode of transportation was the furthest thing from the players' minds. The nature of the game dictated that after hitting the ball, the player would walk after it to find it; not run, jog, or trot, although some records of the very early form of golf indicate players went to their next shot in haste.

From that early origin, golf has evolved to the disappointing situation we have today: Golf carts rule at most courses. Carts pour money into the golf course coffers, but there's little to recommend their use. They slow down play, particularly at courses where the carts have to be kept on the carpath. They've turned golf into an antisocial game because players in two carts can't talk with each other except for a few moments on the tee and the green. A great amount of discussion time walking the fairways is lost. Gas carts pollute the air, and cause excessive noise. And they simply aren't a part of how the game was originally meant to be played. They make golf look like it's meant for the lazy and elite.

Golf is a walking game, and whatever each new golfer can do to make sure it stays that way is a valuable contribution to carrying on the traditions of golf. Unfortunately, there's one big obstacle to sending the cart to the background, and that is the mandatory cart rule that has grown like a big sore on the sport. It's important to note, however, that it's primarily an American problem. In other parts of the world, carts, or "buggies," as they are called, are rarely seen and golfers are free to walk and carry their bag in the traditions of old. The thought of taking a cart to play golf is repulsive to a non-American golfer, and the wonderful thing about it is the management of the golf courses outside the United States supports this dislike for carts.

It seems impossible that there would ever be a way to make the same thing happen in the United States, but at least important groups are trying to promote the idea of walking. Tests have proved that walking with a light carry bag, a pull cart or with a caddie provides twice the benefit of caloric usage as riding a cart. Another study said walking helped control cholesterol levels.

The USGA, in a continuing campaign to encourage walking, has issued a booklet called A Call to Feet: Golf Is a Walking Game. In the foreword, the USGA says it believes that walking is an integral part of the game, and adds "To reverse the inexcusable trend of riding in carts without a legitimate health concern, the USGA offers this publication so that the apparently forgotten merits of walking can be rediscovered."

The USGA says those merits are: (1) playing the game the way it was meant to be played; (2) enjoying the benefits from the exercise; (3) enjoying the course more; (4) enjoying the company of opponents or fellow-competitors; (5) playing better. Anyone can join the USGA's walking campaign, but in doing so, they must take an oath promising that they will never again use a golf cart, unless forced to or caused to do so because of their health.

GUIDES TO GOOD GOLF HEALTH

Because golf has not been a sport that has traditionally emphasized exercise, fitness, and good nutrition with its players, there hasn't been a lot of material available on how golfers can take better care of themselves. Hardly any tour professionals referred to taking care of their bodies, with the exception of Frank Stranahan and Gary Player. Up until the last ten to fifteen years, most of the general advice had centered on stretching before and after play.

But some researchers have studied the body's different muscle groups and seen how they do or don't affect the golf swing. Their goal was to come up with a set of exercises that would strengthen and tone the muscles directly involved with the swing.

The Centinela Hospital Medical Center in Inglewood, California—the "official hospital of the PGA Tour and the Senior PGA Tour"—came out with the first scientific exercise program specifically for golfers. Two books, 30 Exercises for

Better Golf in 1986 and Exercise Guide to Better Golf in 1994, have marvelous exercises for golfers. Because the exercises work specifically on golf muscles, they improve golf strength and flexibility, help drive the ball farther and make better contact, develop endurance, lower the risk of injury, and help play with consistency. Golfers can tailor exercises to their individual game and schedule them at their own pace.

Those books help prevent injuries, but golfers still come down with medical problems. It happens to even the best players: Jack Nicklaus, Fred Couples, and Seve Ballesteros have bad backs; Jerry Pate and Gil Morgan had rotator cuff injuries; and many senior players have hip trouble. The lower back seems to be a golfer's No. 1 problem, followed by the shoulders and the wrists.

Probably the first book devoted exclusively to golf medicine was Feeling Up to Par: Medicine from Tee to Green (F.A. Davis Company, Philadelphia, 1994), edited by three medical doctors, Cornelius N. Stover, John R. McCarroll, and William J. Mallon. The book has twenty-three other contributors in addition to the authors and has sections on training and conditioning; psychology; nutrition; vision; cardiovascular; joint replacement; injuries to the back, shoulder, elbow, wrist and hand; and the rehabilitation of an injured golfer.

Mallon, who is a medical consultant to and wrote the "Ask the Doctor" series for Golf Digest magazine, later wrote another golf-injury specific book, The Golf Doctor: How to Play a Healthier, Better Round of Golf (Macmillan, 1996). This book is similar in scope to Feeling Up to Par and also has sections on equipment modifications and exercises for golf.

 **Chapter 11**

TAKING YOUR GAME ON THE ROAD

In time, most golfers associate themselves with a local club where they play the majority of their golf. Depending on what type of course you play, the cost will vary.

Private-club golfers pay yearly dues to obtain playing privileges. Even if they only play one round a year, they must pay the full price to retain membership. The cost of playing at a private club is usually much greater than public expenses, and it's so high that there's virtually no way you could play enough rounds to get your money's worth. However, private-club golfers are really paying for the privilege of being at a course where it's less crowded than a public facility and access to the course is limited to an exclusive group of people.

The process of getting into a private club is dependent on the club's prestige and status. The less ballyhooed ones may require just a credit check on the applicant and a couple of sponsors who can speak to the person's character. The prestigious clubs have a more elaborate process that must be followed, as well as an escalating cost for joining to match their reputation. An applicant's name must be submitted for nomination by a sponsor, which is usually a club member. The name is posted for other members to observe; they can make comments to the admissions officer during the period before the name is voted on by committee. During the appraisal period, it's a good idea to play as many rounds of golf as possible with club members and/or attend the club for social events. Making yourself known to as many members as possible is a key public relations ploy for anyone wanting to join a club.

There are two payment options available for golfers playing public golf. They can buy a single green fee each time they play, or they can purchase a season pass that entitles them to play unlimited golf throughout the year. If you're a golfer who plays a lot, the latter method is best. Estimate the number of rounds you play, multiply that number by the cost of a regular green fee, and see how that figure comes out in comparison with the season-pass cost. Then make a decision based on the most cost-efficient method.

There are great advantages to playing most of your golf at the same course. First, there is the familiarity factor. Each time you play a course, you are more at ease with knowing where to play each shot and you feel comfortable about that course's procedures for getting a tee time. Second, if you do get a season ticket there, you'll save money. Third, your golf game will improve quicker if you select a difficult course to play most of the time rather than a pushover. Playing an easy course may help your score, but by pushing yourself to excel at a tougher layout, you'll get better faster. And fourth, you'll likely establish ties with a regular playing group and golf-shop staff.

Having said that, though, the real purpose of this chapter is to suggest that golfers who want to broaden their playing experience should take advantage of the many other excellent courses besides their own. It's perfectly fine to play most of your golf at one location, but there's a whole world of great golf to investigate and enjoy. One of the great feelings in golf is to discover a gem of a course in your area that you'd never played before. Playing other courses helps sharpen your concentration, trains your eye and senses regarding different architectural styles, improves your game by exposing you to different conditions and shot requirements, and helps you appreciate even more the diversity of this game.

There's no reason to feel timid about playing a course that's new to you. Chances are the course will have similar tee-time, dress, and other procedures to the course you play regularly. Simply make a call to the golf shop and explain to the worker that you plan on playing the course for the first time. If the shop person is doing their job and on the ball, they will be more than happy to help you and do everything they can to make your first round at their course a smooth and enjoyable one.

How do you find a hidden gem in your area, or at a business or vacation destination? You can try the phone book, the PGA of America section in that area (see the listing in Chapter 9), or the area tourist bureau or chamber of commerce. What will also help is the following partial list of quality public and resort courses in the United States and Canada. So, here's to enjoying the excitement of broadening your golfing experience. (Courses are listed by name; P for public course, R for resort, or SP for semiprivate; number of holes; and town. Some golf clubs have a combination of three nine-hole courses, three eighteen-hole courses, or an eighteen-holer and a nine-holer, for example, to add up to the number of holes listed.)

U.S.A.
Alabama

Auburn Links, P, 18, Auburn; *Bent Brook*, P, 27, Bessemer; *Cambrian Ridge*, P, 27, Greenville; *Cotton Creek Club*, SP, 27, Gulf Shores; *Goose Pond Colony*, R, 18, Scottsboro; *Grand National Golf Club*, P, 54, Opelika; *Gulf State Park*, P, 18, Gulf Shores; *Hampton Cove*, P, 36, Owens Cross Roads; *Highland Oaks*, P, 27, Dothan; *Kiva Dunes*, P, 18, Gulf Shores; *Lagoon Park*, P, 18, Montgomery; *Lake Guntersville*, P, 18, Guntersville; *Magnolia Grove*, P, 54, Semmes; *Marriott's Lakewood Golf Club*, R, 36, Point Clear; *Oxmoor Valley*, P, 54, Birmingham; *Rock Creek*, SP, 18, Fairhope; *Silver Lakes*, P, 27, Glencoe; *Still Waters Resort*, R, 18, Dadeville; *Timbercreek Golf Club*, P, 27, Daphne.

Alaska

Anchorage Golf Course, P, 18, Anchorage; *Eagleglen Golf Course*, P, 18, Anchorage; *Kenai Golf Club*, P, 18, Kenai; *Settlers Bay*, P, 9, Wasilla.

Arizona

Antelope Hills, P, 36, Prescott; *Arizona Biltmore*, SP, 36, Phoenix; *The Boulders Club*, R, 36, Carefree; *Canoa Hills*, SP, 18, Green Valley; *Club West Golf Club*, P, 18, Phoenix; *Desert Hills*, P, 18, Yuma; *Eagle's Nest Country Club at Pebble Creek*, SP, 18, Goodyear; *Elephant Rocks*, P, 9, Williams; *Emerald Canyon*, P, 18, Parker; *The 500 Club*, P, 18, Glendale; *Foothills Golf Club*, P, 18, Phoenix; *Foothills Club West*, P, 18, Phoenix; *Gainey Ranch Golf Club*, R, 27, Scottsdale; *Gold Canyon*, R, 18, Apache Junction; *Golf Club at Vistoso*, P, 18, Tucson; *Grayhawk Golf Club*, R, 36, Scottsdale; *Golf Club Happy Trails*, SP, 18, Surprise; *Hillcrest Golf Club*, P, 18, Sun City West; *La Paloma Country Club*, R, 27, Tucson; *Lake Powell National*, P, 18, Page; *Legend Golf Resort at Arrowhead*, P, 18, Glendale; *London Bridge Golf Club*, P, 36, Lake Havasu City; *Los Caballeros Golf Club*, R, 18, Wickenburg; *McCormick Ranch*, R, 36, Scottsdale; *Oakcreek*, SP, 18, Sedona; *Ocotillo Golf Club*, P, 27, Chandler; *Palm Valley*, SP, 18, Goodyear; *Papago Golf Course*, P, 18, Phoenix; *The Phoenician Golf Club*, R, 18, Scottsdale; *The Pointe Golf Club on Lookout Mountain*, R, 18, Phoenix; *Pueblo Del Sol*, P, 18, Sierra Vista; *Red Mountain Ranch*, SP, 18, Mesa; *Rio Rico*, R, 18, Rio Rico; *San Ignacio*, P, 18, Green Valley; *Sedona Golf Resort*, P, 18, Sedona; *Silver Creek*, P, 18, White Mountain Lake; *Starr Pass Golf Club*, SP, 18, Tucson; *Sun City Vistoso Golf Club*, SP, 18, Tucson; *Superstition Springs*, R, 18, Mesa; *Tatum Ranch*, P, 18, Cave Creek; *Tonto Verde*, SP, 18, Rio Verde; *Tournament Players Club at Scottsdale*, R, 36, Scottsdale; *Troon North*, SP, 18, Scottsdale; *Tucson National*, R, 27, Tucson; *Ventana Canyon*, R, 36, Tucson; *Westbrook Village*, SP, 18, Peoria; *The Wigwam*, R, 54, Litchfield Park.

Arkansas

Cherokee Village, R, 18, Cherokee Village; *Glenwood Country Club*, P, 18, Glenwood; *Hot Springs Country Club*, R, 36, Hot Springs; *Mountain Ranch*, R, 18, Fairfield Bay; *Prairie Creek*, SP, 18, Rogers; *The Red Apple Inn*, R, 18, Heber Springs.

California

Aviara Golf Club, R, 18, Carlsbad; *Blythe Golf Club*, P, 18, Blythe; *Bodega Harbour Golf Links*, R, 18, Bodega Bay; *Canyon Oaks*, SP, 18, Chico; *Carolton Oaks*, R, 18, Santee; *Castle Oaks*, P, 18, Ione; *Chardonnay Golf Club*, SP, 36, Napa; *Coronado Golf Course*, P, 18, Coronado; *Cypress Golf Club*, P, 18, Los Alamitos; *Desert Dunes*, P, 18, Desert Hot Springs; *Desert Falls*, SP, 18, Palm Desert; *Fall River Valley*,

P, 18, Fall River Mills; *Fort Ord Golf Course*, P, 36, Fort Ord (near Pebble Beach); *Fountaingrove Resort*, SP, 18, Santa Rosa; *Graeagle Meadows*, R, 18, Graeagle; *Griffith Park*, P, 36, Los Angeles; *Half Moon Bay Golf Links*, R, 18, Half Moon Bay; *Harding Park*, P, 18, San Francisco; *Hesperia Golf and Country Club*, SP, 18, Hesperia; *Horse Thief Country Club*, R, 18, Tehachapi; *Hunter Ranch*, P, 18, Paso Robles; *Industry Hills Sheraton Resort*, R, 36, City of Industry; *La Contenta Golf Club*, SP, 18, Valley Springs; *La Costa Resort and Spa*, R, 36, Carlsbad; *La Purisima*, P, 18, Lompoc; *La Quinta Resort*, SP, 36, La Quinta; *Lake Shastina*, R, 18, Weed; *Links at Spanish Bay*, R, 18, Pebble Beach; *Los Serranos Lakes*, P, 36, Chino Hills; *Marriott's Desert Springs Resort*, R, 36, Palm Desert; *Mission Hills North Course*, P, 18, Rancho Mirage; *Moreno Valley Ranch*, P, 27, Moreno Valley; *Mount Woodson*, SP, 18, Ramona; *Oak Valley*, P, 18, Beaumont; *Oakhurst Country Club*, SP, 18, Clayton; *Ojai Valley Inn*, R, 18, Ojai; *Pacific Grove Municipal*, P, 18, Pacific Grove; *Pala Mesa Resort*, R, 18, Fallbrook; *Palos Verdes*, SP, 18, Palos Verdes Estates; *Pasatiempo*, SP, 18, Santa Cruz; *Pebble Beach Golf Links*, R, 18, Pebble Beach; *Pelican Hill*, R, 36, Newport Coast; *PGA West Resort*, R, 36, La Quinta; *Plumas Pines*, P, 18, Blairsden; *Poppy Hills*, P, 18, Pebble Beach; *Rams Hill*, SP, 18, Borrego Springs; *Rancho Murieta Country Club*, SP, 36, Rancho Murieta; *Rancho Park*, P, 18, Los Angeles; *Redhawk Golf Club*, SP, 18, Temecula; *Resort at Squaw Creek*, R, 18, Olympic Valley; *Saddle Creek*, P, 18, Copperopolis; *San Juan Oaks*, P, 18, Hollister; *San Vicente Golf Club*, SP, 18, Ramona; *Sandpiper*, P, 18, Goleta; *Silverado*, R, 36, Napa; *Singing Hills*, R, 36, El Cajon; *Sonoma Golf Club*, P, 18, Sonoma; *Spyglass Hill*, R, 18, Pebble Beach; *Steele Canyon*, P, 18, Jamul; *Stevinson Ranch*, P, 18, Stevinson; *Temecula Creek Inn*, R, 27, Temecula; *Torrey Pines*, P, 36, La Jolla; *Tustin Ranch*, P, 18, Tustin; *Twelve Bridges*, P, 18, Lincoln.

Colorado

Arrowhead Golf Club, P, 18, Littleton; *Battlement Mesa Golf Club*, P, 18, Parachute; *Breckenridge Golf Club*, P, 18, Breckenridge; *Broadmoor Golf Club*, R, 54, Colorado Springs; *Crested Butte Club*, P, 18, Crested Butte; *Dalton Ranch*, SP, 18, Durango; *Fairway Pines*, P, 18, Ridgway; *Fox Hollow at Lakewood Golf Course*, P, 27, Lakewood; *Grandote Golf and Country Club*, R, 18, La Veta; *Indian Peaks*, P, 18, Lafayette; *Inverness Golf Course*, R, 18, Englewood; *Keystone Ranch*, R, 18, Keystone; *Legacy Ridge*, P, 18, Westminster; *Mariana Butte*, P, 18, Loveland; *Plum Creek*, SP, 18, Castle Rock; *Pole Creek*, P, 18, Winter Park; *Ptarmigan Country Club*, SP, 18, Fort Collins;

Riverdale Golf Club, P, 36, Brighton; *Sheraton Steamboat Resort*, R, 18, Steamboat Springs; *Skyland Mountain*, SP, 18, Crested Butte; *Sonnenalp Golf Club*, R, 18, Edwards; *Tamarron Resort*, R, 18, Durango; *The Courses at Hyland Hills*, P, 18, Westminster; *Vail Golf Club*, P, 18, Vail; *Walking Stick*, P, 18, Pueblo.

Connecticut

Crestbrook Park, P, 18, Watertown; *D. Fairchild Wheeler*, P, 36, Fairfield; *H. Smith Richardson*, P, 18, Fairfield; *Hunter Golf Club*, P, 18, Meriden; *Laurel View*, P, 18, Hamden; *Lyman Orchards*, P, 36, Middlefield; *Pequabuck Golf Club*, SP, 18, Pequabuck; *Pine Valley*, P, 18, Southington; *Portland Golf Course*, SP, 18, Portland; *Richter Park*, P, 18, Danbury; *Shennecossett Municipal*, P, 18, Groton; *Simsbury Farms*, P, 18, West Simsbury; *Stanley Golf Club*, P, 27, New Britain; *Sterling Farms*, P, 18, Stamford; *Timberlin*, P, 18, Kensington; *Tunxis Plantation*, P, 36, Farmington; *Willimantic Club*, P, 18, Windham; *Yale Golf Club*, SP, 18, New Haven.

Delaware

Ron Jaworski's Garrisons Lake Golf Club, P, 18, Smyrna; *Three Little Bakers*, SP, 18, Wilmington.

District of Columbia

Langston Golf Course, P, 18, Washington.

Florida

Amelia Island Plantation, R, 45, Amelia Island; *Bay Hill Club and Lodge*, R, 18, Orlando; *Baytree National Golf Links*, SP, 18, Melbourne; *Bloomingdale Golfer's Club*, SP, 18, Valrico; *Bluewater Bay Resort*, R, 36, Niceville; *Breakers West Country Club*, SP, 18, West Palm Beach; *Cimarrone Golf and Country Club*, SP, 18, Jacksonville; *The Club at Hidden Creek*, SP, 18, Navarre; *Colony West Country Club*, P, 18, Tamarac; *Crandon Park*, P, 18, Key Biscayne; *Doral Resort and Spa*, R, 72, Miami; *Doral Park*, SP, 18, Miami; *Eagle Harbor Golf Club*, SP, 18, Orange Park; *Eaglebrook Club*, P, 18, Lakeland; *Eastwood Golf Club*, P, 18, Orlando; *Eastwood Golf Course*, P, 18, Fort Myers; *Emerald Bay*, SP, 18, Destin; *Emerald Dunes*, P, 18, West Palm Beach; *Falcon's Fire*, P, 18, Kissimmee; *Golden Ocala*, P, 18, Ocala; *The Golf Club at Marco*, R, 18, Naples; *The Golf Club of Jacksonville*, P, 18, Jacksonville; *Grand Cypress Resort*, R, 45, Orlando; *Grenelefe Golf and Tennis Resort*, SP, 54, Haines City; *Hombre Golf Club*, SP, 18, Panama City Beach; *Innisbrook*

Resort, R, 63, Palm Harbor; *Killearn Country Club and Inn*, R, 27, Tallahassee; *Links at Key Biscayne*, P, 18, Key Biscayne; *Longboat Key Club*, R, 27, Longboat Key; *LPGA International*, P, 18, Daytona Beach; *Marcus Pointe*, P, 18, Pensacola; *Marriott at Sawgrass Resort*, SP, 36, Ponte Vedra Beach; *Marriott's Bay Point Resort*, SP, 36, Panama City Beach; *The Moors*, P, 18, Milton; *Palm Beach Polo and Country Club*, R, 36, West Palm Beach; *Pelican's Nest Golf Club*, P, 36, Bonita Springs; *PGA Golf Club at the Reserve*, R, 36, Port St. Lucie; *PGA National*, R, 90, Palm Beach Gardens; *Ponte Vedra Inn and Club*, R, 36, Ponte Vedra Beach; *Ravines*, SP, 18, Middleburg; *Riverwood Golf Club*, SP, 18, Port Charlotte; *Saddlebrook Resort*, R, 36, Wesley Chapel; *St. Lucie West Country Club*, SP, 18, Port St. Lucie; *Sandestin Beach Resort*, R, 63, Destin; *Sandridge Golf Club*, P, 36, Vero Beach; *Southern Dunes*, P, 18, Haines City; *Tiger Point*, SP, 36, Gulf Breeze; *Tournament Players Club at Sawgrass*, R, 36, Ponte Vedra Beach; *Turnberry Isle Resort*, R, 36, Aventura; *Walt Disney World Resort*, R, 90, Lake Buena Vista (Orlando); *Windsor Parke*, P, 18, Jacksonville; *World Woods*, R, 36, Brooksville; *Zellwood Station*, P, 18, Zellwood.

Georgia

The Boulders Course at Lake Acworth, P, 18, Acworth; *Callaway Gardens Resort*, R, 54, Pine Mountain; *Chateau Elan*, R, 18, Braselton; *Chicopee Woods*, P, 18, Gainesville; *Eagle Watch*, SP, 18, Woodstock; *Fields Ferry*, P, 18, Calhoun; *Foxfire Golf Club*, SP, 18, Vidalia; *Georgia Veterans State Park*, P, 18, Cordele; *Hampton Club*, SP, 18, St. Simons Island; *Harbor Club*, P, 18, Greensboro; *Jekyll Island Golf Resort*, R, 54, Jekyll Island; *Jones Creek*, P, 18, Evans; *Lake Lanier Islands Resort*, R, 18, Lake Lanier; *Maple Creek*, P, 18, Bremen; *Osprey Cove*, SP, 18, St. Marys; *Port Armour*, R, 18, Greensboro; *Reynold's Plantation*, R, 36, Eatonton; *Royal Lakes Golf and Country Club*, SP, 18, Flowery Branch; *St. Simons Island Club*, P, 18, St. Simons Island; *Sea Island Golf Club*, R, 36, St. Simons Island; *Southbridge Golf Club*, SP, 18, Savannah; *Southerness Golf Club*, SP, 18, Stockbridge; *Stone Mountain Park*, R, 36, Stone Mountain; *Stouffer Pineisle Resort*, R, 18, Lake Lanier Islands; *Wallace Adams*, P, 18, McRae; *White Columns*, P, 18, Alpharetta; *Whitewater Creek*, SP, 18, Fayetteville.

Hawaii

The Challenge at Manele, R, 18, Lanai City, Lanai; *The Experience at Koele*, R, 18, Lanai City, Lanai; *Hapuha Golf Course*, P, 18, Kamuela; *Hualalai Golf Club*, P, 18, Kailua Kona; *Kaanapali Golf Course*, R, 36, Lahaina, Maui; *Kaluakoi Golf Course*,

R, 18, Maunaloa, Molokai; *Kapalua Golf Club*, R, 54, Kapalua, Maui; *Kauai Lagoons Resort*, R, 36, Lihue, Kauai; *Koolau Golf Course*, P, 18, Kaneohe, Oahu; *Makalei Hawaii Country Club*, P, 18, Kailua-Kona; *Makena Resort*, R, 36, Kihei, Maui; *Mauna Kea*, R, 18, Kamuela; *Mauna Lani Resort*, R, 36, Kohala Coast; *Poipu Bay Resort*, R, 18, Koloa, Kauai; *Princeville Resort*, R, 45, Princeville, Kauai; *Sheraton Makaha Resort and Country Club*, R, 18, Waianae, Oahu; *Turtle Bay Hilton Resort*, R, 27, Kahuku, Oahu; *Waikele Golf Club*, SP, 18, Waipahu, Oahu; *Waikoloa Beach Resort*, R, 36, Kamuela; *Waikoloa Village Golf Club*, R, 18, Waikoloa; *Wailea Golf Club*, R, 54, Wailea, Maui; *Wailua Golf Course*, P, 18, Lihue, Kauai; *West Loch Golf Course*, P, 18, Ewa Beach.

Idaho

Avondale Golf Club, SP, 18, Hayden Lake; *Blackfoot Municipal*, P, 18, Blackfoot; *Coeur D'Alene Resort*, R, 18, Coeur d'Alene; *Elkhorn Country Club*, R, 18, Sun Valley; *Hidden Lakes*, R, 18, Sandpoint; *The Highlands Golf Club*, P, 18, Post Falls; *Pinecrest Municipal*, P, 18, Idaho Falls; *Quail Hollow*, SP, 18, Boise; *Ridgecrest Club*, P, 18, Nampa; *Scotch Pines*, P, 18, Payette; *Shadow Valley*, P, 18, Boise; *Sun Valley Resort*, R, 18, Sun Valley; *University of Idaho*, P, 18, Moscow.

Illinois

Aldeen Golf Club, P, 18, Rockford; *Annbriar Golf Course*, P, 18, Waterloo; *Balmoral Woods*, P, 18, Crete; *Big Run*, P, 18, Lockport; *Bon Vivant*, P, 18, Bourbonnais; *Cantigny Golf*, P, 27, Wheaton; *Chalet Hills*, P, 18, Cary; *Cog Hill Golf Club*, P, 72, Lemont; *Eagle Ridge Inn*, R, 54, Galena; *George W. Dunne National*, P, 18, Oak Forest; *Gibson Woods*, P, 18, Monmouth; *Golf Club of Illinois*, P, 18, Algonquin; *Hawthorne Ridge*, P, 18, Aledo; *Heritage Bluffs*, P, 18, Channahon; *Hickory Point*, P, 18, Decatur; *Highland Park Golf Course*, P, 18, Bloomington; *Illinois State University*, P, 18, Normal; *Ironwood Golf Course*, P, 18, Normal; *Kellogg*, P, 18, Peoria; *Kemper Lakes*, P, 18, Long Grove; *Klein Creek*, P, 18, Winfield; *Lake of the Woods*, P, 18, Mahomet; *Lake Shore Golf Club*, SP, 18, Taylorsville; *The Ledges Golf Club*, P, 18, Roscoe; *Lick Creek*, P, 18, Pekin; *Lincoln Greens*, P, 18, Springfield; *The Links*, P, 18, Jacksonville; *Newman Golf Course*, P, 18, Peoria; *Odyssey Golf Course*, P, 18, Tinley Park; *Orchard Valley*, P, 18, Aurora; *The Orchards Golf Club*, P, 18, Belleville; *Park Hills Golf Club*, P, 36, Freeport; *Pine Meadow*, P, 18, Mundelein; *Piper Glen*, P, 18, Springfield; *Plum Tree National*, P, 18, Harvard; *Prairie Landing*,

P, 18, West Chicago; *Prairie Vista*, P, 18, Bloomington; *The Rail*, P, 18, Springfield; *Rend Lake*, P, 27, Benton; *Ruffled Feathers*, SP, 18, Lemont; *Seven Bridges*, P, 18, Woodridge; *Spencer T. Olin*, P, 18, Alton; *Steeple Chase*, P, 18, Mundelein; *Stonewolf*, P, 18, Fairview Heights; *University of Illinois*, P, 36, Savoy; *Village Links of Glen Ellyn*, P, 18, Glen Ellyn.

Indiana

Autumn Ridge, SP, 18, Fort Wayne; *Bear Slide Golf Club*, SP, 18, Cicero; *Blackthorn Golf Club*, P, 18, South Bend; *Brickyard Crossing*, R, 18, Indianapolis; *Brookwood Golf Club*, P, 18, Fort Wayne; *Covered Bridge*, SP, 18, Sellersburg; *Elbel Park*, P, 18, South Bend; *French Lick Springs Resort*, R, 36, French Lick; *Golf Club of Indiana*, P, 18, Lebanon; *Hanging Tree Golf Club*, SP, 18, Westfield; *Hulman Links*, P, 18, Terre Haute; *Indiana University*, P, 18, Bloomington; *Juday Creek*, P, 18, Granger; *The Legends of Indiana*, P, 18, Franklin; *Otter Creek*, P, 18, Columbus; *Pheasant Valley*, SP, 18, Crown Point; *Rock Hollow*, P, 18, Peru; *Sultan's Run*, P, 18, Jasper; *Swan Lake Golf Club*, P, 36, Plymouth; *Timber Ridge*, P, 18, Millersburg; *Turkey Run*, P, 18, Waveland; *Wabash Valley*, P, 18, Geneva.

Iowa

Amana Colonies, P, 18, Amana; *Bos Landen*, P, 18, Pella; *Emerald Hills*, SP, 18, Arnolds Park; *Finkbine Golf Course*, P, 18, Iowa City; *Gates Park*, P, 18, Waterloo; *Glen Oaks*, P, 18, West Des Moines; *Glynns Creek*, P, 18, Long Grove; *Green Valley*, P, 18, Sioux City; *Jester Park*, P, 18, Granger; *Lake Panorama National*, R, 18, Panora; *Landsmeer*, P, 18, Orange City; *The Meadows*, P, 18, Dubuque; *Muscatine Municipal*, P, 18, Muscatine; *Palmer Hills*, P, 18, Bettendorf; *Pheasant Ridge*, P, 18, Cedar Falls; *Pleasant Valley*, P, 18, Iowa City; *Sheaffer Golf Course*, P, 18, Fort Madison; *Spencer Golf and Country Club*, SP, 18, Spencer; *Valley Oaks*, SP, 18, Clinton; *Veenker Memorial*, P, 18, Ames; *Waveland*, P, 18, Des Moines.

Kansas

Alvamar Golf Club, SP, 18, Lawrence; *Buffalo Dunes*, P, 18, Garden City; *Deer Creek*, SP, 18, Overland Park; *Dub's Dread*, P, 18, Kansas City; *Heritage Park*, P, 18, Olathe; *Hesston Municipal*, P, 18, Hesston; *Lake Shawnee*, P, 18, Topeka; *Ironhorse*, P, 18, Leawood; *Macdonald Golf Course*, P, 18, Wichita; *Mariah Hills*, P, 18, Dodge City; *Quail Ridge*, P, 18, Winfield; *Rolling Meadows*, P, 18, Milford; *Salina Munic-*

ipal, P, 18, Salina; *Sunflower Hills*, P, 18, Bonner Springs; *Terradyne Resort*, R, 18, Andover; *Turkey Creek*, P, 18, McPherson; *Willow Bend*, SP, 18, Wichita.

Kentucky

Barren River State Park, P, 18, Lucas; *Crooked Creek*, SP, 18, London; *Doe Valley*, SP, 18, Brandenburg; *Eagle Trace*, P, 18, Morehead; *Frances E. Miller*, P, 18, Murray; *Gibson Bay*, P, 18, Richmond; *The Golf Courses at Kenton County*, P, 54, Independence; *Kearney Hills*, P, 18, Lexington; *Kentucky Dam Village State Resort Park*, R, 18, Gilbertsville; *Lassing Pointe Golf Club*, P, 18, Union; *Lincoln Homestead State Park*, P, 18, Springfield; *Marriott's Griffin Gate Resort*, R, 18, Lexington; *Nevel Meade*, P, 18, Prospect; *Player's Club of Lexington*, SP, 18, Lexington; *Quail Chase Golf Club*, P, 27, Louisville; *Seneca Golf Course*, P, 18, Louisville; *Western Hills Golf Course*, P, 18, Hopkinsville.

Louisiana

Bayou Oaks Golf Courses, P, 54, New Orleans; *Belle Terre*, SP, 18, La Place; *Bluffs on Thompson Creek*, R, 18, St. Francisville; *Eastover Country Club*, R, 18, New Orleans; *Mallard Cove*, P, 18, Lake Charles; *Oak Harbor*, P, 18, Slidell; *Santa Maria*, P, 18, Baton Rouge; *Toro Hills Lodge*, R, 18, Florien.

Maine

Aroostook Valley, SP, 18, Fort Fairfield; *Bangor Municipal*, P, 18, Bangor; *Bethel Inn and Country Club*, R, 18, Bethel; *Biddeford Saco Golf Club*, SP, 18, Saco; *Brunswick Golf Club*, P, 18, Brunswick; *Cape Arundel Golf Club*, SP, 18, Kennebunkport; *Cliff Country Club*, SP, 9, Ogunquit; *Kebo Valley*, P, 18, Bar Harbor; *Penobscot Valley*, SP, 18, Orono; *Poland Spring*, R, 18, Poland Spring; *Riverside Municipal*, P, 18, Portland; *Sable Oaks*, P, 18, South Portland; *Samoset Resort*, R, 18, Rockport; *Sugarloaf Golf Club*, R, 18, Carrabassett Valley; *Va Jo Wa Golf Course*, R, 18, Island Falls; *Val Halla Golf Course*, P, 18, Cumberland; *Waterville Country Club*, SP, 18, Oakland.

Maryland

The Bay Club, R, 18, Berlin; *The Beach Club Golf Links*, SP, 18, Berlin; *Black Rock*, P, 18, Hagerstown; *Breton Bay*, SP, 18, Leonardtown; *Eagle's Landing*, P, 18, Berlin; *Enterprise Golf Course*, P, 18, Mitchellville; *The Golf Club at Wisp*, R, 18, McHenry; *Harbourtowne Golf Resort*, R, 18, St. Michaels; *Hog Neck*, P, 18, Easton; *Mount*

Pleasant Golf Club, P, 18, Baltimore; *Ocean City Golf and Yacht Club*, R, 36, Berlin; *Pine Ridge*, P, 18, Lutherville; *Queenstown Harbor Golf Links*, P, 36, Queenstown; *Redgate Municipal*, P, 18, Rockville; *River Run*, P, 18, Berlin; *Swan Point Golf Club*, SP, 18, Issue; *Turf Valley Hotel*, R, 54, Ellicott City; *University of Maryland*, SP, 18, College Park; *Wakefield Valley*, SP, 27, Westminster.

Massachusetts

Atlantic Country Club, P, 18, Plymouth; *Ballymeade*, SP, 18, North Falmouth; *Bayberry Hills*, P, 18, West Yarmouth; *Cape Cod Country Club*, P, 18, Hatchville; *Captains Golf Course*, P, 18, Brewster; *Chicopee Golf Club*, P, 18, Chicopee; *Cranberry Valley*, P, 18, Harwich; *Crumpin-Fox Club*, SP, 18, Bernardston; *Farm Neck Golf Club*, SP, 18, Oak Bluffs; *Gannon Municipal*, P, 18, Lynn; *Gardner Municipal*, P, 18, Gardner; *George Wright Golf Course*, P, 18, Hyde Park; *Hickory Ridge*, SP, 18, Amherst; *Maplegate*, P, 18, Bellingham; *New England Country Club*, P, 18, Bellingham; *New Seabury Country Club*, R, 36, New Seabury; *Oak Ridge*, P, 18, Feeding Hills; *Ocean Edge*, R, 18, Brewster; *Olde Barnstable*, P, 18, Marstons Mills; *Poquoy Brook Golf Club*, P, 18, Lakeville; *Sankaty Head*, P, 18, Siasconset; *Shaker Hills*, P, 18, Harvard; *South Shore*, SP, 18, Hingham; *Stow Acres*, P, 36, Stow; *Taconic Golf Club*, SP, 18, Williamstown; *Wachusett Country Club*, SP, 18, West Boylston; *Wahconah Country Club*, SP, 18, Dalton.

Michigan

Antrim Dells, P, 18, Ellsworth; *Bay Harbor Club*, P, 18, Bay Harbor; *Bedford Valley*, P, 18, Battle Creek; *Belvedere Golf Club*, SP, 18, Charlevoix; *Binder Park*, P, 18, Battle Creek; *Boyne Highlands Resort*, R, 54, Harbor Springs; *Boyne Mountain Resort*, R, 36, Boyne Falls; *Candlestone Golf Club*, R, 18, Belding; *Cascades Golf Course*, P, 18, Jackson; *Clearbrook Golf Club*, SP, 18, Saugatuck; *Crystal Mountain Resort*, R, 27, Thompsonville; *Dunham Hills*, P, 18, Hartland; *Dunmaglas Golf Club*, SP, 18, Charlevoix; *Eagle Glen*, P, 18, Farwell; *Elk Ridge Golf Club*, P, 18, Atlanta; *Faulkwood Shores*, P, 18, Howell; *The Fortress*, R, 18, Frankenmuth; *Forest Akers Golf Club*, P, 36, East Lansing; *Fox Hills Country Club*, P, 45, Plymouth; *Garland Golf Resort*, R, 54, Lewiston; *Gaylord Country Club*, SP, 18, Gaylord; *Grand Haven Golf Club*, SP, 18, Grand Haven; *Grand Traverse Resort*, R, 36, Acme; *Grand View*, P, 18, New Era; *Gull Lake View*, P, 36, Augusta; *Hampshire Country Club*, SP, 18, Dowagiac; *Hawk Hollow*, P, 18, Bath; *Heather Highlands*, P, 18, Holly; *High-*

land Hills, P, 18, Highland; *Huron Breeze*, P, 18, Au Gres; *Huron Golf Club*, R, 18, Ypsilanti; *L.E. Kaufman Golf Course*, P, 18, Wyoming; *Lake Michigan Hills Golf Club*, P, 18, Benton Harbor; *Lakewood Shores Resort*, R, 36, Oscoda; *The Links of Novi*, P, 27, Novi; *Little Traverse Bay Golf Club*, P, 18, Harbor Springs; *The Majestic at Lake Walden*, P, 27, Hartland; *Marywood Golf Club*, P, 18, Battle Creek; *Matheson Greens*, P, 18, Northport; *The Meadows Golf Club*, P, 18, Allendale; *Milham Park Municipal*, P, 18, Kalamazoo; *Mistwood Golf Course*, P, 18, Lake Ann; *The Orchards Golf Club*, P, 18, Washington; *Pinecroft Golf Club*, P, 18, Beulah; *Pohlcat Golf Course*, R, 18, Mt. Pleasant; *The Rock at Drummond Island*, R, 18, Drummond Island; *St. Ives*, P, 18, Stanwood; *Shanty Creek Resort*, R, 54, Bellaire; *Stonebridge Golf Club*, P, 18, Ann Arbor; *Stonehedge Golf Course*, P, 18, Augusta; *Thoroughbred Golf Club*, R, 18, Rothbury; *Timber Ridge*, P, 18, East Lansing; *Treetops Sylvan Resort*, R, 54, Gaylord; *Twin Lakes*, P, 18, Rochester Hills; *University of Michigan*, SP, 18, Ann Arbor; *Wallinwood Springs*, SP, 18, Jenison; *Wilderness Valley Golf Club*, R, 36, Gaylord.

Minnesota

Alexandria Golf Club, SP, 18, Alexandria; *Baker National*, P, 18, Medina; *Bemidji Town and Country Club*, R, 18, Bemidji; *Braemar Golf Course*, P, 27, Edina; *Bunker Hills*, P, 27, Coon Rapids; *Cuyuna Country Club*, SP, 18, Deerwood; *Edinburgh USA*, P, 18, Brooklyn Park; *Grand View Lodge*, R, 27, Nisswa; *Island View Country Club*, SP, 18, Waconia; *Izatys Golf Club*, R, 18, Onamia; *Keller Golf Course*, P, 18, St. Paul; *The Links at Northfork*, P, 18, Ramsey; *Madden's on Gull Lake*, R, 36, Brainerd; *Mississippi National*, P, 27, Red Wing; *Monticello Country Club*, P, 18, Monticello; *North Links*, P, 18, North Mankato; *Northfield Golf Club*, SP, 18, Northfield; *Pebble Creek*, P, 27, Becker; *Perham Lakeside Country Club*, P, 18, Perham; *Pine Meadows*, P, 18, Brainerd; *Pokegama*, P, 18, Grand Rapids; *Purple Hawk*, SP, 18, Cambridge; *Stonebrooke Golf Club*, SP, 18, Shakopee; *Superior National*, P, 18, Lutsen; *Wedgewood Golf Club*, SP, 18, Woodbury; *Wildflower at Fair Hills*, P, 18, Detroit Lakes; *The Wilds*, P, 18, Prior Lake; *Willinger's Golf Club*, P, 18, Northfield.

Mississippi

Big Oaks, P, 18, Tupelo; *Diamondhead Country Club*, R, 36, Diamondhead; *Kirkwood National*, SP, 18, Holly Springs; *Mississippi National*, P, 18, Gautier; *Mississippi State University*, P, 18, Starkville; *Ole Miss Golf Club*, P, 18, Oxford; *Plan-*

tation Golf Course, SP, 18, Olive Branch; *Timberton Golf Club*, P, 18, Hattiesburg; *Wedgewood Golf Course*, SP, 18, Olive Branch; *Windance Country Club*, SP, 18, Gulfport.

Missouri

Bent Creek, SP, 18, Jackson; *Cherry Hills Golf Club*, P, 18, Grover; *Crystal Highlands*, P, 18, Crystal City; *Eagle Lake Golf Club*, SP, 18, Farmington; *Eagle Knoll*, P, 18, Hartsburg; *Honey Creek*, P, 18, Aurora; *Innisbrook Estates*, R, 18, Wright City; *Lake Valley Golf Club*, P, 18, Camdenton; *Longview Lake*, P, 18, Kansas City; *Marriott's Tan-Tar-A Resort*, R, 27, Osage Beach; *Millwood Golf*, P, 18, Springfield; *Missouri Bluffs*, P, 18, St. Charles; *North Port National*, R, 18, Lake Ozark; *Paradise Point*, P, 36, Smithville; *Quail Creek Golf Club*, P, 18, St. Louis; *Shirkey Golf Club*, SP, 18, Richmond; *Swope Memorial*, P, 18, Kansas City; *Tapawingo National*, P, 18, St. Louis; *The Lodge at Four Seasons*, R, 36, Lake Ozark; *Whitmoor Country Club*, P, 18, St. Charles.

Montana

Big Sky Golf Club, P, 18, Meadow Village, Big Sky; *Bill Roberts Municipal*, P, 18, Helena; *Buffalo Hill Golf Course*, P, 18, Kalispell; *Eagle Bend Golf Club*, P, 18, Bigfork; *Hamilton Golf Club*, P, 18, Hamilton; *Larchmont Golf Course*, P, 18, Missoula; *Meadow Lake Golf Resort*, R, 18, Columbia Falls; *Mission Mountain*, SP, 18, Ronan; *Polson Country Club*, P, 18, Polson; *Whitefish Lake Golf Club*, P, 36, Whitefish.

Nebraska

Benson Park, P, 18, Omaha; *The Champions Club*, P, 18, Omaha; *Grand Island Municipal*, P, 18, Grand Island; *Heritage Hills*, SP, 18, McCook; *Highlands Golf Course*, P, 18, Lincoln; *Himark Golf Course*, P, 18, Lincoln; *Holmes Park*, P, 18, Lincoln; *Indian Creek*, P, 18, Elkhorn; *Meadowlark Hills*, SP, 18, Kearney; *Pioneers Golf Course*, P, 18, Lincoln; *Quail Run*, P, 18, Columbus; *Quarry Oaks*, P, 18, Ashland; *Shadow Ridge*, SP, 18, Omaha; *The Pines Country Club*, SP, 18, Valley; *Tiburon Golf Club*, SP, 18, Omaha; *Valley View*, P, 18, Fremont; *Woodland Hills*, P, 18, Eagle.

Nevada

Angel Park Golf Club, P, 36, Las Vegas; *Calvada Valley*, SP, 18, Pahrump; *Dayton Valley*, SP, 18, Dayton; *Desert Inn*, R, 18, Las Vegas; *Eagle Valley Golf Club*, P, 36,

Carson City; *Edgewood Tahoe*, R, 18, Stateline; *Empire Ranch*, P, 18, Carson City; *The Golf Club at Genoa Lakes*, P, 18, Genoa; *Incline Village Golf Resort*, R, 18, Incline Village; *Lakeridge Golf Course*, P, 18, Reno; *Las Vegas Hilton*, R, 18, Las Vegas; *Las Vegas Paiute Resort*, R, 18, Las Vegas; *The Legacy Golf Club*, P, 18, Henderson; *Northgate Golf Course*, R, 18, Reno; *Oasis Resort Hotel Casino*, R, 36, Mesquite; *Painted Desert Golf Club*, P, 18, Las Vegas; *Rosewood Lakes*, P, 18, Reno; *Ruby View*, P, 18, Elko; *Sun City Las Vegas Golf Club*, SP, 36, Las Vegas; *Tournament Players Club at The Canyons*, R, 18, Las Vegas.

New Hampshire

The Balsams Grand Resort Hotel, R, 18, Dixville Notch; *Beaver Meadow*, P, 18, Concord; *Bretwood Golf Course*, P, 18, Keene; *Campbell's Scottish Highlands*, P, 18, Salem; *Concord Country Club*, SP, 18, Concord; *Country Club of New Hampshire*, P, 18, North Sutton; *Eastman Golf Links*, P, 18, Grantham; *Hanover Country Club*, P, 18, Hanover; *John H. Cain Golf Club*, SP, 18, Newport; *Keene Country Club*, SP, 18, Keene; *Laconia Country Club*, SP, 18, Laconia; *Lake Sunapee*, P, 18, New London; *North Conway Country Club*, SP, 18, North Conway; *Overlook Country Club*, P, 18, Hollis; *Passaconaway Country Club*, P, 18, Litchfield; *Portsmouth Country Club*, SP, 18, Greenland; *Shattuck Golf Course*, P, 18, Jaffrey; *Sky Meadow*, SP, 18, Nashua; *Souhegan Woods*, P, 18, Amherst; *Wentworth-by-the-Sea Country Club*, SP, 18, Portsmouth.

New Jersey

Blue Heron Pines, P, 18, Galloway; *Bowling Green*, SP, 18, Milton; *Buena Vista*, P, 18, Buena; *Cape May National*, SP, 18, Cape May; *Crystal Springs*, SP, 18, Hamburg; *Farmstead Golf*, P, 27, Lafayette; *Flanders Valley*, P, 36, Flanders; *Great Gorge*, P, 27, McAfee; *Greate Bay Resort*, R, 18, Somers Point; *Harbor Pines*, P, 18, Egg Harbor Township; *Hominy Hill*, P, 18, Colts Neck; *Howell Park*, P, 18, Farmingdale; *Marriott's Seaview Resort*, R, 36, Absecon; *Mercer Oaks*, P, 18, Trenton; *Ocean County*, P, 18, Tuckerton; *Sunset Valley*, P, 18, Pompton Plains.

New Mexico

Angel Fire Club, P, 18, Angel Fire; *Cochiti Lake Golf Course*, P, 18, Cochiti Lake; *Inn of the Mountain Gods*, R, 18, Mescalero; *The Links at Sierra Blanca*, P, 18, Ruidoso; *New Mexico State University*, P, 18, Las Cruces; *New Mexico Tech*,

P, 18, Socorro; *Pinon Hills*, P, 18, Farmington; *Santa Ana*, P, 27, Bernalillo; *Taos Coountry Club*, SP, 18, Rancho de Taos; *University of New Mexico*, P, 18, Albuquerque.

New York

Amsterdam Municipal, P, 18, Amsterdam; *Arrowhead Golf Course*, P, 18, East Syracuse; *Ballston Spa Country Club*, SP, 18, Ballston Spa; *Bethpage State Park*, P, 90, Farmingdale; *Blue Hill Golf Club*, SP, 18, Pearl River; *Bluff Point*, SP, 18, Plattsburgh; *Bristol Harbor*, R, 18, Canandaigua; *Centerpointe Country Club*, SP, 18, Canandaigua; *Concord Resort Hotel*, R, 36, Kiamesha Lake; *Conklin Players Club*, P, 18, Conklin; *Craig Wood Golf Course*, P, 18, Lake Placid; *Deerfield Country Club*, SP, 18, Brockport; *En-Joie Golf Club*, P, 18, Endicott; *Foxfire Golf Club*, P, 18, Baldwinsville; *Glen Oak*, R, 18, East Amherst; *Green Lakes State Park*, P, 18, Fayetteville; *Greystone Golf Club*, P, 18, Walworth; *Grossinger Resort*, R, 27, Liberty; *Hanah Country Club*, R, 18, Margaretville; *Hiland Golf Club*, SP, 18, Queensbury; *Kutsher's Country Club*, R, 18, Monticello; *Leatherstocking Golf Course*, R, 18, Cooperstown; *The Links at Hiawatha Landing*, P, 18, Apalachin; *Mark Twain Golf Club*, P, 18, Elmira; *Montauk Downs State Park*, P, 18, Montauk; *Peek 'N Peak Resort*, R, 18, Clymer; *Radisson Greens*, SP, 18, Baldwinsville; *River Oaks Golf Club*, SP, 18, Grand Island; *The Sagamore Golf Club*, R, 18, Bolton Landing; *Saratoga Spa*, P, 18, Saratoga Springs; *Seven Oaks Golf Club*, SP, 18, Hamilton; *Smithtown Landing*, P, 18, Smithtown; *Soaring Eagles*, P, 18, Horseheads; *Spook Rock*, P, 18, Suffern; *Tarry Brae Golf Club*, P, 18, South Fallsburg; *Thendara Golf Club*, SP, 18, Thendara; *Tri County Country Club*, SP, 18, Forestville; *Villa Roma*, SP, 18, Callicoon; *Wayne Hills*, SP, 18, Lyons.

North Carolina

Bald Head Island Club, R, 18, Bald Head Island; *Bryan Park and Golf Club*, P, 36, Brown Summit; *Cypress Landing*, P, 18, Chocowinity; *Deercroft Golf Club*, SP, 18, Wagram; *Devil's Ridge*, SP, 18, Holly Springs; *Duke University*, R, 18, Durham; *The Emerald Club*, SP, 18, New Bern; *Etowah Valley*, R, 27, Etowah; *Gates Four*, SP, 18, Fayetteville; *Grandover Resort*, R, 18, Greensboro; *Highland Creek*, P, 18, Charlotte; *Hound Ears Club*, SP, 18, Blowing Rock; *Jefferson Landing Club*, P, 18, Jefferson; *Keith Hills*, SP, 18, Buies Creek; *Lane Tree*, SP, 18, Goldsboro; *Legacy Links*, P, 18, Aberdeen; *Linville Golf Course*, R, 18, Linville; *Lion's Paw*, R, 18, Sunset Beach;

Marsh Harbour, P, 18, Calabash; *Mid Pines Golf Club*, R, 18, Southern Pines; *Mount Mitchell*, P, 18, Burnsville; *Mountain Glen*, SP, 18, Newland; *The Neuse Golf Club*, SP, 18, Clayton; *North Shore*, SP, 18, Sneads Ferry; *Oak Hollow*, P, 18, High Point; *Oyster Bay Golf Links*, P, 18, Sunset Beach; *The Pearl*, P, 36, Sunset Beach; *Pine Needles*, R, 18, Southern Pines; *Pinehurst Plantation*, SP, 18, Pinehurst; *Pinehurst Resort*, R, 126, Pinehurst; *Porters Neck*, SP, 18, Wilmington; *Reems Creek*, SP, 18, Weaverville; *Sea Trail Plantation*, R, 54, Sunset Beach.; *Seven Lakes*, SP, 18, West End; *Talamore Resort*, P, 18, Southern Pines; *Tanglewood Park*, P, 36, Clemmons; *Woodlake Country Club*, R, 18, Vass.

North Dakota

Bois De Souix Golf Club, P, 18, Wahpeton; *Edgewood*, P, 18, Fargo; *The Links of North Dakota*, P, 18, Ray; *Minot Country Club*, SP, 18, Minot; *Prairie West*, P, 18, Mandan; *Riverwood*, P, 18, Bismarck; *Souris Valley*, P, 18, Minot.

Ohio

Apple Valley, P, 18, Howard; *Avalon Lakes*, R, 18, Warren; *Bent Tree*, P, 18, Sunbury; *Blue Ash*, P, 18, Cincinnati; *Champions Golf Course*, P, 18, Columbus; *Cooks Creek*, P, 18, Ashville; *Eagle Sticks*, P, 18, Zanesville; *Fowler's Mill*, P, 27, Chesterland; *Foxfire Golf Club*, P, 36, Lockbourne; *Granville Golf Club*, P, 18, Granville; *Hawks Nest*, P, 18, Creston; *Hawthorne Hills*, SP, 18, Lima; *Heatherwoode Golf Club*, P, 18, Springboro; *Hemlock Springs*, P, 18, Geneva; *Hueston Woods State Park*, R, 18, Oxford; *Indian Springs*, P, 18, Mechanicsburg; *J.E. Good Park*, P, 18, Akron; *Manakiki Golf Club*, P, 18, Willoughby; *Maumee Bay State Park*, P, 18, Oregon; *Mill Creek Park*, P, 36, Boardman; *Mohican Hills*, P, 18, Jeromesville; *Orchard Hills*, SP, 18, Chesterland; *Pine Hills*, P, 18, Hinckley; *Pipestone Golf Club*, P, 18, Miamisburg; *Punderson State Park*, P, 18, Newbury; *Quail Hollow Resort*, R, 18, Concord; *River Greens*, P, 18, West Lafayette; *Royal American Links*, SP, 18, Galena; *Sawmill Creek*, R, 18, Huron; *Shaker Run*, P, 18, Lebanon; *Sharon Woods*, P, 18, Cincinnati; *Sleepy Hollow*, P, 18, Brecksville; *Sugar Bush*, P, 18, Garretsville; *Tam O'Shanter*, P, 36, Canton; *The Golf Center at Kings Island*, R, 36, Mason; *The Vineyard*, P, 18, Cincinnati; *Valleywood*, SP, 18, Swanton; *Windmill Lakes*, P, 18, Ravenna; *Yankee Run*, P, 18, Brookfield.

Oklahoma

Bailey Golf Ranch, P, 18, Owasso; *Boiling Springs*, P, 18, Woodward; *Cedar Creek*, P, 18, Broken Bow; *Cedar Valley*, P, 36, Guthrie; *Cimarron National*, P, 36, Guthrie; *Coffee Creek*, P, 18, Edmond; *Earlywine Park*, P, 36, Oklahoma City; *Falconhead Ranch*, SP, 18, Burneyville; *Forest Ridge*, P, 18, Broken Arrow; *Heritage Hills*, P, 18, Claremore; *John Conrad Regional*, P, 18, Midwest City; *Karsten Creek*, SP, 18, Stillwater; *Kickingbird*, P, 18, Edmond; *Lake Hefner*, P, 36, Oklahoma City; *Lakeview Golf Course*, P, 18, Ardmore; *Lew Wentz Memorial*, P, 18, Ponca City; *Mohawk Park*, P, 36, Tulsa; *Page Belcher*, P, 36, Tulsa; *Shangri-La Golf Resort*, R, 36, Afton; *Silverhorn Golf Club*, SP, 18, Oklahoma City; *Sunset Hills*, P, 18, Guymon.

Oregon

Black Butte Ranch, R, 36, Black Butte; *Broken Top*, P, 18, Bend; *Eagle Crest Resort*, R, 36, Redmond; *Eagle Point Course*, P, 18, Eagle Point; *Eastmoreland Golf Course*, P, 18, Portland; *Forest Hills*, SP, 18, Cornelius; *Heron Lakes*, P, 36, Portland; *Meadow Lakes*, P, 18, Princeville; *Pumpkin Ridge*, P, 18, Cornelius; *Quail Valley*, P, 18, Banks; *River's Edge*, P, 18, Bend; *Salem Golf Club*, P, 18, Salem; *Salishan Links*, R, 18, Gleneden Beach; *Sandpines Resort*, P, 18, Florence; *Sunriver Lodge/Resort*, R, 36, Sunriver; *Tokatee Club*, P, 18, Blue River; *Trysting Tree*, P, 18, Corvallis; *Widgi Creek*, SP, 18, Bend.

Pennsylvania

Bavarian Hills, P, 18, St. Mary's; *Bucknell Golf Club*, SP, 18, Lewisburg; *Carroll Valley*, P/R, 36, Fairfield; *Center Valley Club*, P, 18, Center Valley; *Champion Lakes*, P, 18, Bolivar; *Chestnut Ridge*, P, 18, Blairsville; *Country Club at Woodloch Springs*, R, 18, Hawley; *Eagle Lodge*, R, 18, Lafayette Hill; *Emporium Country Club*, SP, 18, Emporium; *Foxchase Golf Club*, P, 18, Stevens; *Greencastle Greens*, P, 18, Greencastle; *Hartefeld National*, P, 18, Avondale; *Heritage Hills*, R, 18, York; *Hershey Country Club*, R, 36, Hershey; *Hershey Parkview*, P, 18, Hershey; *Honey Run*, SP, 18, York; *Iron Masters*, SP, 18, Roaring Springs; *Mountain Laurel*, R, 18, White Haven; *Nemacolin Woodlands Resort*, R, 36, Farmington; *Penn National*, SP, 18, Fayetteville; *Penn State University*, P, 36, State College; *Pine Acres*, SP, 18, Bradford; *Quicksilver Club*, P, 18, Midway; *Riverside Golf*, P, 18, Cambridge Springs; *Royal Oaks*, P, 18, Lebanon; *Seven Springs Mountain Resort*, R, 18, Champion; *South Hills*, SP, 18, Pittsburgh; *State College Elks*, SP, 18, Boalsburg; *Stone Hedge*, P, 18,

Tunkhannock; *Sugarloaf Golf Club*, P, 18, Sugarloaf; *Tam O'Shanter*, P, 18, Hermitage; *Toftrees Resort*, R, 18, State College; *Tom's Run*, P, 18, Blairsville; *Treasure Lake*, P, 18, Dubois; *Tyoga*, SP, 18, Wellsboro; *White Tail Golf Club*, P, 18, Bath; *Wilkes-Barre Golf Club*, P, 18, Wilkes-Barre; *Wyncote Golf Club*, SP, 18, Oxford.

Rhode Island

Exeter Club, P, 18, Exeter; *Montaup Country Club*, SP, 18, Portsmouth; *North Kingstown Municipal*, P, 18, North Kingstown; *Richmond Country Club*, P, 18, Richmond; *Triggs Memorial*, P, 18, Providence.

South Carolina

Arrowhead Golf Club, P, 18, Myrtle Beach; *Blackmoor Club*, R, 18, Murrells Inlet; *Caledonia Golf Club*, P, 18, Pawleys Island; *Callawassie Island Club*, SP, 27, Beaufort; *Cedar Creek Club*, SP, 18, Aiken; *Cheraw State Park*, P, 18, Cheraw; *The Club at Seabrook Island*, R, 36, Seabrook Island; *Country Club of Hilton Head*, SP, 18, Hilton Head Island; *Crowfield Golf Club*, SP, 18, Goose Creek; *The Dunes*, P, 18, Myrtle Beach; *The Dunes West*, SP, 18, Mt. Pleasant; *Harbour Town Golf Links*, R, 18, Hilton Head Island; *Heather Glen*, R, 27, Little River; *Heritage Club*, P, 18, Pawleys Island; *Hickory Knob*, R, 18, McCormick; *Hilton Head National*, P, 18, Hilton Head Island; *Indigo Run*, SP, 18, Hilton Head Island; *Kiawah Island Resort*, R, 72, Kiawah Island; *Legends Resorts*, R, 54, Myrtle Beach; *Links O'Tryon*, SP, 18, Campobello; *The Long Bay Club*, R, 18, Longs; *Myrtle Beach National*, R, 54, Myrtle Beach; *Myrtlewood Golf Club*, SP, 36, Myrtle Beach; *Oyster Reef*, SP, 18, Hilton Head Island; *Palmetto Dunes Resort*, R, 54, Hilton Head Island; *Palmetto Hall Plantation*, R, 36, Hilton Head Island; *Pawleys Plantation*, SP, 18, Pawleys Island; *The River Club*, R, 18, Pawleys Island; *River Falls Plantation*, P, 18, Duncan; *Surf Golf Club*, SP, 18, North Myrtle Beach; *Tidewater Golf Club*, P, 18, North Myrtle Beach; *Timberlake Plantation*, SP, 18, Chapin; *Verdae Greens*, R, 18, Greenville; *Wachesaw Plantation*, R, 18, Murrells Inlet; *Wild Dunes Resort*, R, 36, Isle of Palms; *Wild Wing Plantation*, R, 54, Conway; *Willbrook Plantation*, R, 18, Pawleys Island; *The Witch*, R, 18, Conway. Note: The Myrtle Beach area, which had only twenty-seven holes in 1959, now has 100 courses and is one of the most popular golf destinations in the United States. For in-depth details about a golf vacation there, phone Myrtle Beach Golf Holiday, 800-845-4653.

South Dakota

Fox Run, P, 18, Yankton; *Hart Ranch*, P, 18, Rapid City; *Hillcrest Club*, SP, 18, Yankton; *Meadowbrook Course*, P, 18, Rapid City; *Moccasin Creek*, SP, 18, Aberdeen; *Southern Hills*, P, 9, Hot Springs; *Two Rivers*, P, 18, Dakota Dunes; *Willow Run*, P, 18, Sioux Falls.

Tennessee

Big Creek Club, SP, 18, Millington; *Briarwood Course*, P, 18, Crab Orchard; *Egwani Farms*, P, 18, Rockford; *Fall Creek Falls State Park*, P, 18, Pikeville; *Graysburg Hills*, P, 27, Chuckey; *Heatherhurst Club*, R, 27, Fairfield Glade; *Henry Horton State Park*, P, 18, Chapel Hill; *Hermitage Golf Course*, P, 18, Old Hickory; *Legends Club of Tennessee*, SP, 36, Franklin; *Orgill Park*, P, 18, Millington; *River Islands*, P, 18, Kodak; *Roan Valley*, SP, 18, Mountain City; *Stonehenge Club*, R, 18, Fairfield Glade; *Willow Creek Club*, P, 18, Knoxville.

Texas

Barton Creek Resort, R, 54, Austin; *Bay Forest*, P, 18, LaPorte; *Bear Creek Golf World*, P, 54, Houston; *Buffalo Creek*, P, 18, Rockwall; *Cedar Creek*, P, 18, San Antonio; *Circle C Golf Club*, P, 18, Austin; *The Cliffs Golf Club*, R, 18, Graford; *Cypresswood Club*, P, 36, Spring; *Del Lago Resort*, R, 18, Montgomery; *Delaware Springs*, P, 18, Burnet; *Evergreen Point*, P, 18, Baytown; *The Falls*, SP, 18, New Ulm; *Forest Creek*, P, 18, Round Rock; *Four Seasons Resort*, R, 36, Irving; *Garden Valley*, R, 36, Lindale; *Greatwood Golf Club*, P, 18, Sugar Land; *Hill Country Club*, R, 18, San Antonio; *Horseshoe Bay Resort*, R, 54, Horseshoe Bay; *Hyatt Bear Creek*, P, 36, Dallas-Fort Worth Airport; *Indian Creek*, P, 36, Carrollton; *La Cantera*, SP, 18, San Antonio; *Lady Bird Johnson Municipal*, P, 18, Fredericksburg; *Lakeway Resort*, R, 36, Austin; *Marriott's Golf Club at Fossil Creek*, P, 18, Fort Worth; *Mill Creek*, R, 18, Salado; *Old Orchard*, P, 27, Richmond; *Painted Dunes*, P, 18, El Paso; *Peach Tree*, SP, 36, Bullard; *Pecan Valley*, P, 18, San Antonio; *The Quarry Club*, P, 18, San Antonio; *The Ranch Country Club*, SP, 18, McKinney; *Rayburn Resort*, R, 27, Sam Rayburn; *River Place Club*, SP, 18, Austin; *San Saba Municipal*, P, 18, San Saba; *Southwyck Club*, P, 18, Pearland; *Squaw Valley*, P, 18, Glen Rose; *Sugartree Club*, SP, 18, Dennis; *Tapatio Springs Resort*, R, 18, Boerne; *Timarron Golf Club*, P, 18, South Lake; *Tour 18*, P, 18, Humble; *Waterwood National*, R, 18, Huntsville; *The Woodlands Resort*, R, 36, The Woodlands/Houston.

Utah

Birch Creek, P, 18, Smithfield; *Bonneville Golf Course*, P, 18, Salt Lake City; *Bountiful City*, P, 18, Bountiful; *Davis Park*, P, 18, Fruit Heights; *Eagle Mountain*, P, 18, Brigham City; *Eaglewood Golf Course*, P, 18, North Salt Lake City; *Gladstan Golf Club*, P, 18, Payson; *Green Spring*, P, 18, Washington; *Hobble Creek*, P, 18, Springville; *Homestead Golf Club*, R, 18, Midway; *Jeremy Ranch*, P, 18, Park City; *Logan River*, P, 18, Logan; *Moab Golf Club*, P, 18, Moab; *Mountain Dell*, P, 36, Salt Lake City; *Park City Golf Course*, P, 18, Park City; *Park Meadows*, P, 18, Park City; *Spanish Oaks*, P, 18, Spanish Fork; *Sunbrook Golf Club*, P, 18, St. George; *Tri-City*, P, 18, American Fork; *Valley View*, P, 18, Layton; *Wasatch State Park*, P, 27, Midway; *West Ridge*, P, 18, West Valley City; *Wingpointe*, P, 18, Salt Lake City; *Wolf Creek Resort*, R, 18, Eden.

Vermont

Country Club of Barre, P, 18, Barre; *Crown Point*, SP, 18, Springfield; *Gleneagles Golf Course*, R, 18, Manchester Village; *Green Mountain National*, P, 18, Sherburne; *Haystack Golf Club*, SP, 18, Wilmington; *Killington Golf Course*, R, 18, Killington; *Mount Snow*, R, 18, West Dover; *Proctor-Pittsford Country Club*, P, 18, Pittsford; *Rutland Country Club*, SP, 18, Rutland; *St. Johnsbury Club*, P, 18, St. Johnsbury; *Stratton Mountain Resort*, R, 27, Stratton Mountain; *Sugarbush*, R, 18, Warren; *Woodstock Country Club*, R, 18, Woodstock.

Virginia

Augustine Club, P, 18, Stafford; *Bristow Manor*, P, 18, Bristow; *The Crossings*, P, 18, Glen Allen; *Draper Valley*, P, 18, Draper; *Ford's Colony*, R, 36, Williamsburg; *Golden Horseshoe*, R, 36, Williamsburg; *Hell's Point*, P, 18, Virginia Beach; *The Homestead Resort*, R, 54, Hot Springs; *Kiln Creek*, SP, 18, Newport News; *Kingsmill Resort*, R, 54, Williamsburg; *Lakeview Golf Course*, SP, 27, Harrisonburg; *Lansdowne Golf Club*, R, 18, Lansdowne; *Legends at Stonehouse*, P, 18, Toano; *Newport News Golf Club at Deer Run*, P, 36, Newport News; *Olde Mill*, R, 18, Laurel Fork; *Raspberry Falls*, P, 18, Leesburg; *Reston National*, P, 18, Reston; *River's Bend*, SP, 18, Chester; *Royal New Kent*, P, 18, Williamsburg; *Royal Virginia*, P, 18, Hadensville; *Shenandoah Crossing Resort*, R, 18, Gordonsville; *Shenandoah Valley Golf Club*, SP, 27, Front Royal;

Stonehouse, P, 18, Williamsburg; *The Tides Inn*, R, 18, Irvington; *Tides Lodge Resort*, R, 18, Irvington; *Wintergreen Resort*, R, 36, Wintergreen; *Wolf Creek*, SP, 18, Bastian.

Washington

Apple Tree, P, 18, Yakima; *Avalon Golf Club*, P, 27, Burlington; *Canyon Lakes*, P, 18, Kennewick; *Capitol City*, P, 18, Olympia; *Classic Country Club*, P, 18, Spanaway; *Desert Canyon Resort*, R, 18, Orondo; *Downriver Golf Club*, P, 18, Spokane; *Dungeness*, SP, 18, Sequim; *Gold Mountain*, P, 18, Bremerton; *Hangman Valley*, P, 18, Spokane; *Harbour Pointe*, P, 18, Mukilteo; *Indian Canyon*, P, 18, Spokane; *Kayak Point*, P, 18, Stanwood; *Lake Padden*, P, 18, Bellingham; *Lake Spanaway*, P, 18, Tacoma; *McCormick Woods*, P, 18, Port Orchard; *Meadowwood*, P, 18, Liberty Lake; *Port Ludlow Golf Course*, R, 27, Port Ludlow; *Riverside Country Club*, P, 18, Chehalis; *Semiahmoo*, R, 18, Blaine; *Shuksan Golf Club*, P, 18, Bellingham; *Snohomish Golf Course*, P, 18, Snohomish; *Sudden Valley*, SP, 18, Bellingham; *The Creek at Qualchan*, P, 18, Spokane.

West Virginia

Cacapon State Park Resort, R, 18, Berkeley Springs; *Canaan Valley State Park*, R, 18, Davis; *Glade Springs Resort*, R, 18, Daniels; *The Greenbriar*, R, 54, White Sulphur Springs; *Greenhills Country Club*, SP, 18, Ravenswood; *Hawthorne Valley*, R, 18, Snowshoe; *Lakeview Resort*, R, 36, Morgantown; *Locust Hill*, SP, 18, Charles Town; *Oglebay Park*, P, 36, Wheeling; *Pipestem Golf Club*, P, 18, Pipestem; *Woodbridge Plantation*, P, 18, Mineral Wells; *The Woods Resort*, R, 18, Hedgesville.

Wisconsin

Abbey Springs, R, 18, Fontana on Geneva Lake; *Blackwolf Run*, R, 36, Kohler; *Bristlecone Pines*, P, 18, Hartland; *Brown County*, P, 18, Oneida; *Brown Deer*, P, 18, Milwaukee; *Country Club of Wisconsin*, P, 18, Grafton; *Dretzka Park*, P, 18, Milwaukee; *Eagle River Golf Course*, P, 18, Eagle River; *Geneva National*, R, 36, Lake Geneva; *The Golf Courses at Lawsonia*, R, 36, Green Lake; *Grand Geneva Resort*, R, 36, Lake Geneva; *Kettle Hills*, P, 36, Richfield; *Kettle Moraine*, SP, 18, Dousman; *Lake Arrowhead*, P, 18, Nekoosa; *Mascoutin*, P, 18, Berlin; *Naga-Waukee Golf Course*, P, 18, Pewaukee; *Nemadji Golf Course*, P, 36, Superior; *New Richmond Golf Club*, SP, 18, New Richmond; *Northwood*, P, 18, Rhinelander; *Old Hickory*, SP, 18, Beaver Dam; *Petrifying Springs*, P, 18, Kenosha; *Quit-Qui-Oc Golf Club*, P,

18, Eklhart Lake; *Riverside Golf Course*, P, 18, Janesville; *SentryWorld Golf Course*, P, 18, Stevens Point; *Sparta Municipal*, P, 18, Sparta; *The Springs Resort*, R, 18, Spring Green; *Trappers Turn*, P, 18, Wisconsin Dells; *Turtleback Golf Club*, P, 18, Rice Lake; *University Ridge*, P, 18, Verona.

Wyoming

Bell Nob, P, 18, Gillette; *Buffalo Golf Club*, P, 18, Buffalo; *Jackson Hole Golf Club*, R, 18, Jackson; *Olive Glenn*, SP, 18, Cody; *Riverton Country Club*, SP, 18, Riverton; *Teton Pines Resort*, R, 18, Jackson; *White Mountain*, P, 18, Rock Springs.

CANADA

Alberta

Banff Springs, R, 27, Banff; *Barrhead Golf Course*, P, 18, Barrhead; *Coloniale Golf Club*, SP, 18, Beaumont; *Cottonwood Golf Club*, SP, 18, De Winton; *D'Arcy Ranch*, P, 18, Okotoks; *The Dunes Golf and Winter Club*, P, 18, Grande Prairie; *Goose Hummock*, R, 18, Gibbons; *Heritage Pointe*, R, 27, De Winton; *Jasper Park Lodge*, R, 18, Jasper; *Kananaskis Country Club*, R, 36, Kananaskis Village; *Lakeside Greens*, SP, 18, Chestermere; *Land-O-Lakes*, SP, 18, Coaldale; *Links at Spruce Grove*, P, 18, Spruce Grove; *Paradise Canyon*, SP, 18, Lethbridge; *Ponoka Community*, P, 18, Ponoka; *Redwood Meadows*, SP, 18, Calgary; *Wolf Creek Resort*, R, 27, Ponoka.

British Columbia

Big Sky, R, 18, Pemberton; *Castlegar Golf Club*, P, 18, Castlegar; *Chateau Whistler Golf Club*, R, 18, Whistler; *Cordova Bay*, P, 18, Victoria; *Crown Isle*, SP, 18, Courtenay; *Eagle Point*, P, 18, Kamloops; *Fairview Mountain*, SP, 18, Oliver; *Fairwinds*, R, 18, Nanoose Bay; *Gallagher's Canyon*, SP, 18, Kelowna; *Golden Golf Club*, SP, 18, Golden; *Harvest Golf Club*, R, 18, Kelowna; *Kokanee Springs*, R, 18, Crawford Bay; *Morningstar Golf Club*, SP, 18, Parksville; *Northview Golf Club*, P, 36, Surrey; *Olympic View*, P, 18, Victoria; *Peace Portal*, SP, 18, South Surrey; *Predator Ridge*, R, 18, Vernon; *Rivershore Golf Club*, SP, 18, Kamloops; *Riverside Golf Resort*, R, 18, Fairmont Hot Springs; *Rossland Trail*, SP, 18, Trail; *The Springs at Radium Golf Course*, P, 18, Radium Hot Springs; *Storey Creek*, SP, 18, Campbell River; *Swan-E-*

Set Bay Resort, P, 18, Pitt Meadows; *Trickle Creek*, R, 18, Kimberley; *Whistler Golf Club*, R, 18, Whistler.

Manitoba

Clear Lake, P, 18, Onanole; *Falcon Beach*, P, 18, Falcon Lake; *Hecla Golf Course*, R, 18, Riverton; *The Links at Quarry Oaks*, P, 18, Steinbach.
New Brunswick: *The Algonquin Resort*, R, 18, St. Andrews; *Gowan Brae*, SP, 18, Bathurst.

Newfoundland

Twin Rivers, R, 18, Port Blandford.
Nova Scotia: *Abercrombie*, SP, 18, New Glasgow; *Ashburn Golf Club*, SP, 18, Halifax; *Cape Breton Highlands*, P, 18, Ingonish Beach; *Dundee Resort*, R, 18, West Bay; *Ken-Wo*, SP, 18, Wolfville; *Paragon Golf Club*, SP, 18, Kingston; *The Pines Resort*, R, 18, Digby.

Ontario

Angus Glen, P, 18, Markham; *Blue Springs*, SP, 18, Acton; *Brockville Country Club*, SP, 18, Brockville; *Carlisle Golf Club*, P, 18, Carlisle; *Chestnut Hill*, SP, 18, Richmond Hill; *Chippewa Golf Club*, SP, 18, Southampton; *Deerhurst Resort*, R, 36, Huntsville; *Eagle Creek*, SP, 18, Dunrobin; *Forest City National*, P, 18, London; *Glen Abbey*, P, 18, Oakville; *Hockley Valley Resort*, R, 18, Orangeville; *Horseshoe Valley Resort*, R, 18, Barrie; *Kanata Lakes Club*, SP, 18, Kanata; *Kingsville Golf Club*, SP, 27, Kingsville; *Lionhead Golf Club*, P, 36, Brampton; *Loch March*, P, 18, Kanata; *Monterra*, R, 18, Collingwood; *Nobleton Lakes*, P, 18, Nobleton; *Osprey Valley Heathlands*, P, 18, Alton; *Peninsula Lakes*, P, 18, Fenwick; *Pheasant Run*, P, 27, Sharon; *Richmond Hill Golf Club*, P, 18, Richmond Hill; *Royal Woodbine*, SP, 18, Etobicoke; *Silver Lakes*, SP, 18, Newmarket; *St. Andrews Valley*, P, 18, Aurora; *Whirlpool*, P, 18, Niagara Falls.

Prince Edward Island

Brudenell River Provincial, P, 18, Roseneath; *Green Gables*, P, 18, Cavendish; *The Links at Crowbush Cove*, P, 18, Morell; *Mill River*, R, 18, O'Leary.

Quebec

Golf le Mirage, SP, 18, Terrebonne; *Gray Rocks*, SP, 18, Mont Tremblant; *Le Club de Golf Carling Lake*, R, 18, Pine Hill; *Owl's Head*, R, 18, Mansonville.

Saskatchewan

Cooke Municipal, P, 18, Prince Albert; *Waskesiu Golf Course*, P, 18, Waskesiu; *The Willows Golf Club*, P, 36, Saskatoon.

 Chapter 12

FINDING GOLF'S HERITAGE

During the last century, architects have done their best with American golf-course designs to imitate the links style that originated mainly in Scotland and other parts of the United Kingdom. But there's no substitute for the real thing, and there's no way to duplicate the ambience and special flavor of golf in the land of its birth.

If it is possible, a golfer shouldn't pass up the chance to play golf in England, Ireland, Scotland, or Wales. To tee it up there is to walk the same ground that golf's ancestors and forefathers walked, and to see the same courses they saw 100 to 200 years ago.

American golfers, however, may be in for a surprise. They've been spoiled by the plush courses in the United States, and the way in which the riding golf cart has been embraced so mightily in America. In the United Kingdom, courses aren't manicured to perfection and golf's origin as a walking game is still taken seriously. The challenge for the visiting American, then, is to become comfortable with links-type golf and to not be surprised at the plain, unadorned appearance of the course and clubhouse.

But there is a lot to love about British golf. There is the history, for one, and the beauty of the land for another. The people are infectious in their wit and devotion to golf. And the experience of playing in Britain is just another way of

> "Concentration simply means paying attention so closely to what you're doing that outside interruptions don't bother you. Composure is a matter of accepting what comes along and not letting it bother you. One good tip that can help you keep your composure is don't rush. That's even more important when you're under pressure, because you naturally tend to speed up at such times. The best advice then, whenever you start getting excited, or you're angry over a missed shot, is to slow down. I don't mean that you should dally and waste time, but slow yourself down to a normal relaxed pace."
>
> BYRON NELSON

broadening a golfer's abilities and another part of the learning experience. It is a near guarantee that playing in the United Kingdom will be one of the most exciting golf moments in a person's life.

Pessimists may say that the British golf courses they've seen on television don't look that tremendous to them. But that's the nuance of links golf. It looks easy to play until you play it. Some of the finest courses in the world—particularly the ones used for the British Open—are links-type layouts and they befuddle and baffle the world's greatest players. Regarding the back nine at Royal Troon on the western coast of Scotland, three-time British Open winner Gary Player said, "I've always said that the toughest nine holes in golf is the back nine at Troon. There's no doubt in my mind."

Although the caliber of golf may startle and surprise visitors to the United Kingdom, the simplicity of the area is sure to make an impression as well. There seems to have been a concerted effort on the part of golf developers there to make sure golfers in subsequent generations would feel it their duty to carry on the simplicity of the game as it was created. Even many of the golf clubs that visitors play are simply named after the town in which it's located, such as Cork Golf Club in the town of Cork in County Cork in Ireland.

What's not so simple any more about the United Kingdom is getting onto the courses. Because vacation trips are so popular to the homeland of golf, it's more complicated to get tee times. Most courses, particularly the famous ones such as the Old Course at St. Andrews, Scotland, require prior planning weeks and even months ahead of time. Going as part of a tour group is a big help, but if you're going alone or with a small group, write ahead of time to the club secretary and let them know when you plan on being in the area and the day you would like to play. Suggest a part of the day, such as morning or afternoon, that you would prefer, but don't suggest a specific time, and do mention how many in your group.

Most courses require a letter of introduction from your home course, plus evidence that you have a handicap of approximately 24 or less in the form of a handicap card or confirmation from your home pro. Also, expect that you will have to walk the course and either carry your bag, use a pull cart, or have a caddie carry for you.

Caddies can be one of the most enjoyable parts of your British golf experience, but they can be an expensive part, too. A caddie at St. Andrews costs around $45, and you'll want to tip a good one an extra $8 to $16 (5 to 10 British pounds). Caddies in Britain can be witty, philosophic, local tour guides, psychologists, and more, all at the same time. Plus, they can be marvelous at getting you around the course with their local knowledge. Just hope that you never get into the classic exchange that first surfaced in an old cartoon in which the golfer says to the caddie, "You must be the worst caddie in the world," and the caddie replies, "I doubt that. It would be too much of a coincidence."

For most of your tipping on a golf trip, around 10 percent is acceptable, not quite as much as you would in the United States. Besides caddies, you won't have to tip that often at British courses because there isn't as much going on in the way of amenities or extra attendants.

Here is a listing of some noteworthy courses found in the United Kingdom (listed by country, course, and location).

England

The Belfry—Sutton Coldfield, West Midlands; *Bridlington Links*—Flamborough Road, Marton, Bridlington, East Yorks; *East Sussex National*—Uckfield, East Sussex; *Hill Valley*—Terrick Road, Whitchurch, Shropshire; *Hoebridge*—Old Woking Road, Woking; *The Oxfordshire*—Rycote Lane, Milton Common, Oxfordshire; *Panshanger*—Old Herns Lane, Welwyn Garden City; *Pine Ridge*—Old Bisley Road, Frimley, Camberley, Surrey; *Pype Hayes*—Eachel Hurst Road, Walmley, Sutton Coldfield, West Midlands; *Richmond Park*—Roehampton Gate, Priory Lane, Putney, London; *Royal Liverpool*—Meols Drive, Hoylake, Wirral, Merseyside; *St. Mellion (Nicklaus)*—St. Mellion, Cornwall; *Southampton*—Golf Course Road, Bassett, Southampton; *Stressholme*—Snipe Lane, Darlington, County Durham; *Thorpe*

Wood—Nene Parkway, Peterborough; *Walton Hall*—Warrington Road, Higher Walton, Warrington, Cheshire; *Wentworth Club*—Virginia Water, Surrey; *Woburn*—Bow Brickhill, Bucks.

Ireland

Adare Golf Club—Adare Manor, Adare, County Limerick; *Ballybunion (Old)*—Sandhill Road, Ballybunion, County Kerry; *Ballycastle*—Cushendall Road, Ballycastle, County Antrim, Northern Ireland; *Ballyliffin*—Ballyliffin, County Donegal; *Bantry Golf Club*—Bantry, County Cork; *Beaufort*—Churchtown, Beaufort, Killarney, County Kerry; *Bundoran*—Bundoran, County Donegal; *Carlow*—Deerpark, Carlow, County Carlow; *Carne*—Belmullet, County Mayo; *Castlerock*—Circular Road, Castlerock, County Londonderry, Northern Ireland; *Ceann Sibeal*—Ballyferriter, Dingle, County Kerry; *Connemara*—Ballyconneely, County Galway; *Cork*—Little Island, Cork, County Cork; *County Louth Golf Club*—Baltray, Drogheda, County Louth; *County Sligo*—Rosses Point, County Sligo; *Donegal*—Murvagh, Ballintra, County Donegal; *Dooks*—Dooks, Glenbeigh, County Kerry; *Dromoland Castle Golf Club*—Newmarket-on-Fergus, County Clare; *Druid's Glen*—Kilcole, County Wicklow; *Enniscrone*—Enniscrone, County Sligo;

Lahinch, in County Clare, Ireland.

The European Club—Brittas Bay, County Wicklow; *Fota Island*—Carrigtwohill, Cork, County Cork; *Galway Bay*—Renville, Oranmore, County Galway; *Glasson*—Glasson, Athlone, County Westmeath; *Glengarriff*—Glengarriff, County Cork; *Harbour Point*—Little Island, Cork, County Cork; *The Island Golf Club*—Corballis, Donabate, County Dublin; *Kenmare*—Kilgarvan Road, Kenmare, County Kerry; *Kildare Hotel and Club*—Straffan, County Kildare; *Killarney Golf Club*—Mahony's Point, Killarney, County Kerry; *Kinsale*—Belgooly, Kinsale, County Cork; *Lahinch*—Lahinch, County Clare; *Luttrelstown*—Clonsilla, County Dublin; *Mount Juliet*—Thomastown, County Kilkenny; *Mullingar*—Belvedere, Mullingar, County Westmeath; *Narin and Portnoo*—Portnoo, County Donegal; *Parknasilla*—Parknasilla, County Kerry; *Portmarnock*—Portmarnock, County Dublin; *Portsalon*—Portsalon, County Donegal; *Portstewart*—Strand Road, Portstewart, County Londonderry, Northern Ireland; *Rosapenna*—Downings, County Donegal; *Royal County Down*—Newcastle, County Down, Northern Ireland; *Royal Dublin*—Bull Island, Dollymount, Dublin; *Royal Portrush (Dunluce)*—Bushmills Road, Portrush, County Antrim, Northern Ireland; *Seapoint*—Termonfeckin, County Louth; *Shannon*—Shannon Airport, Shannon, County Clare; *Skibbereen*—Skibbereen, County Cork; *Tralee*—West Barrow, Ardfert, County Kerry; *Tramore*—Newtown Hill, Tramore, County Waterford; *Waterford Castle*—The Island, Ballinakill, Waterford, County Waterford; *Waterville Links*—Waterville, County Kerry; *Westport*—Carrowholly, Westport, County Mayo.

Scotland

Aberdour—Seaside Place, Aberdour, Fife; *Alyth*—Alyth, Blairgowrie, Perthshire; *Anstruther*—Marsfield, Shore Road, Anstruther, Fife; *Auchterarder*—Ochil Road, Auchterarder, Perthshire; *Blairgowrie*—Rosemount, Blairgowrie, Perthshire; *Brora*—Golf Road, Brora, Sutherland; *Carnegie Club*—Skibo Castle, Dornoch, Sutherland; *Carnoustie*—Links Parade, Carnoustie, Angus; *Charleton*—Colinsburgh, Fife; *Crail*—Balcomie Clubhouse, Fifeness, Crail, Fife; *Crieff*—Perth Road, Crieff, Perthshire; *Cruden Bay*—Cruden Bay, Aberdeenshire; Dalmahoy Club—Kirknewtown, Lothian; *Downfield*—Turnberry Avenue, Dundee, Angus; *Duddingston*—Duddingston Road West, Edinburgh; *Dunaverty*—Southend, south of Campbeltown, Argyll; *Dunbar*—East Links, Dunbar, East Lothian; *Glen*—East Links, Tantallon Ter, North Berwick, East Lothian; *Gleneagles Hotel*—Auchterarder, Perthshire; *Golf House Club*—west Elie, Fife; *Golspie*—Ferry Road, Golspie, Sutherland; *Greenock*—Forsyth Street, Greenock, Renfrewshire; *Gullane Club*—

Gullane, East Lothian; *Kirriemuir*—Northmuir, Kirriemuir, Angus; *Ladybank Club*—Annsmuir, Ladybank, Fife; *Letham Grange*—Colliston, Arbroath, Angus; *Leven Links*—Promenade, Leven, Fife; *Luffness New Club*—Aberlady, East Lothian; *Lundin*—Golf Road, Lundin Lunks, Fife; *Machrie Hotel*—Machrie, Port Ellen, Isle of Islay, Argyll; *Machrihanish Club*—Machrihanish, by Campbeltown, Argyll; *Monifieth Links*—The Links, Monifieth, Dundee, Angus; Montrose Links Trust, Traill Drive, Montrose, Angus; *Murcar Club*—Bridge of Don, Aberdeenshire; *Musselburgh*—Monktonhall, Musselburgh, Lothian; *Nairn*—Seabank Road, Nairn, Nairnshire; *North Berwick*—Beach Road, west of North Berwick, East Lothian; *Old Course*—St. Andrews, Fife; *Panmure*—Burnside Road, Barry, near Carnoustie, Angus; *Peterhead*—Craigewan Links, Peterhead, Aberdeenshire; *Powfoot*—Cummertrees, Annan, Dumfriesshire; *Prestwick*—2 Links Road, Prestwick, Ayrshire; *Royal Aberdeen*—Links Road, Balgownie, Bridge of Don, Aberdeenshire; *Royal Dornoch*—Golf Road, Dornoch, Sutherland; *Royal Musselburgh*—Prestongrange House, Prestonpans, Lothian; *Royal Troon*—Craigend Road, Troon, Ayrshire; *Scotscraig*—Golf Road, Tayport, Fife; *Southerness*—Southerness, Dumfriesshire; *Stonehaven*—Cowie, Stonehaven, Kincardineshire; *Tain*—Chapel Road, Tain, Ross-shire; *Turnberry Hotel*—Turnberry, Ayrshire; *Western Gailes*—Gailes, Irvine, Ayrshire; *Whitekirk*—Whitekirk, Dunbar, East Lothian.

Wales

Aberdovey—Dovey estuary, No. Wales; *Ashburnham*—Cliffe Ter, west of Llanelli, Burry Port, mid Wales; *Conwy*—Beacons Way, Morfa, No. Wales; *Holyhead*—Lon Garreg Fawr, Trearddur Bay, No. Wales; *Llandudno*—Hospital Road, Llandudno, No. Wales; *Monmouthshire*—Gypsy Lane, Llanfoist, Abergavenny, So. Wales; *Nefyn & District*—Morfa Nefyn, No. Wales; *Newport*—Great Oak, Rogerstone, Newport, So. Wales; *North Wales*—72 Bryniau Road, West Shore, Llandudno, No. Wales; *Rolls of Monmouth*—The Hendre, Monmouth, So. Wales; *Royal Porthcawl*—northwest of Porthcawl, So. Wales; *Royal St. Davids*—west Harlech, No. Wales; *St. Mellons*—St. Mellons, Cardiff, So. Wales; *St. Pierre Club & Hotel*—St. Pierre Park, Chepstow, Monmouthshire, So. Wales; *Southerndown*—Ewenny, Bridgend, So. Wales; *Tenby*—The Burrows, Tenby, mid Wales; *Tredegar Park*—Bassaleg Road, Newport, So. Wales.

GOING WITH A GROUP CAN BE QUITE A TRIP

Depending on how much of an adventure you want to make your golf trip to the United Kingdom, you can do all the planning yourself or you can use the services of golf-trip planners. Going with a golf group can remove a lot of the headaches from your trip and allow you more time to enjoy yourself as you're free of having to worry about scheduling hassles.

Here is a sampling of some notable golf-trip planners. They can talk with you to see if what they offer is best for your plans, or if you're better off doing things yourself.

Golf International
275 Madison Avenue
New York, NY 10016
(212) 986-9176, 1-800-833-1389

Golfpac
P.O. Box 162366
Altamonte Springs, FL 32716-2366
(407) 260-2288, 1-800-523-0007

Intergolf
P.O. Box 500608
Atlanta, GA 31150-0608
(770) 518-1250, 1-800-468-0051

Jerry Quinlan's Celtic Golf
124 Sunset Boulevard
P.O. Box 417
Cape May, NJ 08204-0417
(609) 884-8090, 1-800-535-6148

OwenOak International
40 Richards International
Norwalk, CT 06854
(203) 854-9000, 1-800-426-4498

PerryGolf
8302 Dunwoody Place
Suite 305
Atlanta, GA 30350-3317
(770) 641-9696, 1-800-344-5257

Value Golf Vacations
260 Fifth Avenue
New York, NY 10001
(212) 986-0393, 1-800-786-7634

Wide World of Golf
P.O. Box 5217
Villa Carmel No. 3
Mission Street and Fourth Avenue
Carmel, CA 93921
(408) 624-6667, 1-800-214-4653

Chapter 13

THE WOMAN'S GAME AND PLAYING BUSINESS GOLF

Sexism. Elitism. Machoism. Women golfers have been "ism-ed" from many directions during golf's history. The result has been discrimination against their right to play and to share the same privileges as male players. Women have had the biggest barriers put before them in getting to do just the simplest things in golf, which men take for granted. Women have put up with:

- Inferior equipment that for many years was thought to be adapted men's clubs.
- Limitations in the times they could play.
- Being denied access to certain parts of the clubhouse, which were designated as men-only areas.
- Stereotypical remarks and insults about trying to play a "man's game."

That's just the short list, and the sad statement is that many of these and other roadblocks are still in place. Women still face great resistance, particularly in the private-club sector, of their participation as equal golfers.

To many male golfers, who have had an easy road from the start, the plight of the female player seems a distant nuisance. "Give 'em an inch and they'll take a foot" is the usual mentality of men who are in positions to make decisions on

The fabulous Joyce Wethered was a legendary Engllish amateur and pioneer who helped women earn recognition as good golfers.

questions of equality. But there are slow changes occurring in the world of women's golf and indications are that, in time, all discriminatory elements could be past history.

ALWAYS BEEN A PLAYER

Women have been a part of golf since it first started taking shape in Scotland, and they've been in hot water since the early years as well. In 1567, Mary Queen of Scots was taken to task for playing golf just a few days after her husband, Lord Darnley, had been murdered. She had been a longtime golfer, having learned while attending school in France.

> "You have to accept responsibility for every shot you hit. Don't fall into self-pity about your performance. That's the most valuable golfing advice ever given to me."
>
> MICKEY WRIGHT

In the 1700s and 1800s, at the same time men's clubs were growing in number, women's golf clubs and societies sprouted up in places such as St. Andrews, North Devon, Lytham and St. Annes, Carnoustie, and Musselburgh. The women's groups formed a Ladies' Golf Union by the early 1890s. Prior to women joining together in this organization, slings and arrows were thrown at them, a taste of what has followed ever since. A female golfer was often thought of as a woman of no social graces and someone to shun and avoid. And they were criticized for being unable to settle quarrels and disputes during play. Authors of the time openly ridiculed them in print as unworthy of being called a golf player. Men who played in a mixed group often commented that they couldn't decide whether to flirt or play golf.

As an example of the identity women lacked then, record books containing the results of competition refer to women without mentioning their first name. They're listed as Mrs. John Smith, for instance.

The women's game definitely differed in scope from the men's. Women usually played shorter courses and their outfits consisted of large hats, high and stiff-collared blouses, and ankle-length skirts. The outlandish outfits required women to wear contraptions such as the "Miss Higgins," a garter that was put in place prior to playing a shot because it kept the wind from blowing the skirt bottom over the ball.

Despite all the obstacles, women golfers carried on so that by the early 1900s some of them were playing well enough to earn respect and a favorable reputation. Unlike the men, who were able to play professional golf, women played amateur golf at that time, playing the game as a pastime rather than a main ambition. Cecil Leitch and Joyce Wethered were two of the best British players as the 1900s moved along, while Glenna Collett Vare, Alexa Stirling, Dorothy Campbell, and Virginia Van Wie were some of the leading Americans.

But even though they were starting to be seen as legitimate players, women still suffered from discrimination in club policies. When golf courses sprouted up in America around the turn of the century, women were given the "honor" of playing on certain afternoons. There wasn't a lot of interest, and in the first women's amateur championship in the United States in 1895, just thirteen women competed.

By the 1920s and '30s, however, the play of women improved in relation to increased practice time and better equipment and apparel. Those cumbersome skirts were shortened to mid-calf, giving women more freedom to execute an athletic swing.

The improved play did little to upgrade the status of women, who were second-class citizens at private clubs. Men blamed them for slow play, so men established policies to ensure they would always have the right of way on the course. Men would openly ridicule women to their faces and comment about how nice it would be to have them off the course. It wasn't unusual for women to be banned from a course on Saturdays and Sundays, and only be allowed to play between 11:30 A.M. and 3 P.M. on weekdays.

There were isolated cases where women won some of the battles. At a few clubs, they were allowed their own nine-hole course. And in a few

All-around athlete Babe Zaharias conquered the game during the infancy of women's golf.

cases it was women who encouraged their husbands to go forward with opening a new course or getting out to practice and play.

The better players sought respect by preferring to be called women, rather than ladies, believing the latter term left the impression of delicate golfers unable to handle the complexities of golf. Another morale booster for women was the Curtis Cup, an international amateur competition started by Margaret and Harriot Curtis in 1932. It was important for women to see other women competing handily as competitors.

Nancy Lopez has electrified the women's golf world like no other player.

By 1944, there were enough respected women golfers in America that a women's professional tour seemed possible. The Women's Professional Golf Association was begun, but it didn't take a firm hold until 1948 when Wilson Sporting Goods and marketing director Fred Corcoran got involved. Two years later the Ladies Professional Golf Association was born, headed by such stars as Babe Zaharias, Patty Berg, Louise Suggs, and Betsy Rawls.

The LPGA Tour in the first twenty years did not provide much of a living for the tour pro. Consistent winners like Mickey Wright and Kathy Whitworth did okay, but prize money for the average player was scarce. It wasn't until the 1970s that the LPGA experienced real growth. It brought in a commissioner, Ray Volpe, in 1975 and his expertise combined with the gallery-attracting talent of Joanne Carner and Nancy Lopez tripled prize money by the early 1980s to $6.4 million annually.

Although the substantial shadows of the PGA Tour and the Senior PGA Tour have hampered the LPGA Tour's growth, it had $30.2 million in prize money in

1997 as well as a host of new stars to take the tour forward into the next century.

But let's get back to the real world of women's golf today, to the amateur woman who doesn't have the pleasure of free, open access to some of the country's best courses the way professionals have it. Have course restrictions and insults ceased for them?

The answer: Changes are occurring slowly. For much of the 1900s, eliminating course-access limitations at clubs was a matter of choice by the club management. It either felt moved to do so or it didn't. Some clubs had the matter forced on them by women who joined together to form a unified front for change. But the real impetus for change was the uproar over, of all things, a men's event. In a strange twist of fate, the furor over the 1990 PGA Championship at Shoal Creek, Alabama, was of extreme benefit for women golfers.

Prior to the event, Shoal Creek's admission policies of banning black members created an explosive reaction throughout the golfing world, but mainly focused on the admission policies at American private clubs.

> "There are two ways, really, that you can gain knowledge. The first is to go to a good teaching professional. The second way is from books. My father saw to it that I had the opportunity to take advantage of the great players' knowledge by exposing me to the best books during my early years."
>
> JOHNNY MILLER

As a result, close scrutiny was applied to the admission policies at private clubs in the United States, and major golf organizations came forward to say they would not stand for discriminatory practices and would not hold competitions at courses that don't allow minorities as members.

Reaping a benefit from this was the women's cause. The restrictions applied to them from another era were given fresh perspective and plenty of publicity. Many courses were forced to break down any barriers to women, although some maintained the status quo and became even more private, preferring not to change the way they did business.

Women were emboldened to speak out and complain about conditions at their course and club. They were tired of restrictive practice and play times, not being allowed to vote or run for club offices, and being forced to do things such as avoid walking through the men's grill because no woman was allowed to step foot in it.

If women couldn't get change by speaking privately with club management, they went public to a media ready to hear these stories of unequal treatment and bias, especially how they tied in with the Shoal Creek incident.

Some women have sued to gain equality, others have asked state legislators to pass laws to ensure equal access. Some of these laws ruled that a club could be subject to a lawsuit or have its liquor license revoked if it continued past practices of sexism.

When women went public with their complaints, the result seen at most clubs was exclusion. Other members treated them as unwelcome outsiders. Some women remained firm despite the opposition, others withdrew from the club and sued the club anyway.

As of October 1997, thirteen states, among them Michigan, Connecticut, New York, New Jersey, Maine, Florida, Kansas, Montana, Minnesota, and Maryland, and many cities had passed laws aimed at making access for minorities a requirement. The laws not only target tee-time equality, but specify that women should be able to vote, have memberships, and hold equity in the club.

Besides the enactment of laws, women have been seen more and more in executive positions in club hierarchies as well as within the industry. Most notably, Judy Bell was the first woman elected as the president of the USGA, serving her term in 1996-97. Alice Dye was named the first female president in the fifty-one-year history of the American Society of Golf Course Architects in 1997.

But laws and elected officials can only go so far in

Judy Bell, the first female president of the U.S. Golf Association changing decades of harsh treatment. What may be the hardest to change is the built-in stereotypes that men have about women. Some of it is based on the fear that women will encroach on the ideal setup men have now. Men don't want to see change if it means the privileges they've enjoyed will be taken away or altered.

If attitudes change so that everyone believes every golfer should be on the same level, then that can only mean more involvement by players of all ages, sex, and race. That translates to more business generated for golf companies of all types.

Women may never totally reach the success level men enjoy in professional golf and as players in general, but no one can take away the attitude they bring to the game. Despite many years of turmoil, women have the typical golfing spirit: a desire and determination to play; a liking of the outdoors; the need to share in the camaraderie and companionship so much a part of golf; and a love to challenge the body and mind with the physical demands of golf.

TRAITS OF TODAY'S WOMAN GOLFER

Women are so important to the golf economy that there is no shortage of information on the typical characteristics of a woman player. In many respects, the female player is quite changeable. Things can fluctuate in their playing characteristics and buying habits from year to year. But their buying power is substantial enough that manufacturers pay close attention to their opinions about the market to ensure that they deliver the products that fit their needs.

Star LPGA player Annika Sorenstam is a great example of the new breed of women golfers.

A study by the National Golf Foundation found that the average score for a female golfer is 114 for eighteen holes. Only 7 percent of women regularly score better than 90, and just 1 percent score better than 80. Women are more likely than men to take a lesson, 35 percent versus 14 percent. But men (38 percent) and women (36 percent) are equal when it comes to practicing regularly at a golf range.

Another study, this one from *Golf for Women* magazine, was released in 1997 and showed women are feeling more favorable about their position in the game. Sixty-five percent feel welcome in golf shops (compared with 59 percent of men), and only 14 percent believe sex discrimination is the same or more on the golf course compared with five years before.

Women are also more determined than ever to play golf well. Nearly 75 percent of women feel that if they hit the ball well, how they score doesn't matter that much. The study found that men are more score oriented; 59 percent of men feel playing well is better than scoring well. And only 33 percent of women have stopped playing golf for a year or more, about the same for men.

Further research by The New York Times Magazine Group's Research Resource Center gave a demographic look to the five million women golfers playing in 1996. The figures showed a positive profile of the female golfer. Most of them are 35 or older. The average age is 49. Most women players are married, but their children are no longer at home. Forty percent are managers or professional types, and 25 percent are homemakers. Thirty-three percent have family incomes in six figures; $103,000 is the average family income. Half of them own more than one home.

Five player types

Traditionalists   Twenty-three percent played mainly at private clubs so they could be outdoors and enjoy the game with their family. This golfer is 60 or more in age, and likes to compete in leagues and be traditional in apparel and outfits.

Hobnobbers   Twenty-one percent play because they believe golf will improve their image and self-confidence and build their career.

Golf nuts   Twenty percent play the most of any female golfing type and have the best games and handicaps.

Party putters   Nineteen percent play for the social activity and environment.

Escape artists   And seventeen percent play to get away from the hectic pace of jobs and daily life.

These five categories could easily be narrowed into just three player types: the previously mentioned traditional woman who has played for many years and is promoting the important values of the game to the next generation; women who play for the pure sport of it and to enjoy it as an athletic endeavor; and the newer type of female golfer who plays it for the opportunities it allows them to mingle with business associates.

Manufacturers, primarily the apparel companies, monitor the likes and dislikes of these groups to design products that appeal directly to them.

SPECIFIC SWING FIXES FOR WOMEN

The movements of the golf swing are the same for every golfer, young and old, male and female. However, there are women-specific traits that have developed over the years and are unique to them. They occur primarily because of the difference in physical strength between men and women.

Men have traditionally been involved in sports all their lives. They began developing good hand-eye coordination playing baseball and basketball. Women were more sporadic in their sports participation. Timing the different body parts to work with each other in an athletic motion didn't come as naturally. But that pattern is changing. More and more girls are getting involved in organized sports at younger ages, benefiting greatly from this early exposure to physical conditioning. Dance clubs have also helped in this manner.

With the physical fitness craze of today, these girl athletes continue to stay in great shape as they move from high school and college sports teams to adulthood. As a result, the following unique golf-swing traits for women are being seen as less of a problem these days. However, they're still worthy of consideration by today's women golfers.

Golf-Swing Traits

A comfortable grip   Women sometimes feel stiff in the arms and shoulders using the overlap and interlocking grips. It might make the swing more comfortable by using the ten-finger grip at first. When confidence is gained with this grip and the player feels confident, she should experiment with the overlap and interlocking grips.

The upper and lower bodies   It's not easy to coordinate the top and bottom halves of the body in perfect sync, especially if you don't have an athletic background. An ideal way to see how the two go together is standing in front of a full-length mirror and watching how the upper body moves in relation to the lower. The two should appear to move together at the start of the swing and the lower body should make the first move forward from the top of the swing.

Using a long waggle   For anyone who is not familiar with moving athletically, getting the swing started can feel awfully uncomfortable. Short, quick waggles can be the wrong way to initiate the swing because they make a golfer feel rushed. A better way for this player is to make a single long waggle, with the club going back on the ideal path and the hands stopping just to the outside of the right thigh. This gives the proper sensation of a smooth takeaway.

Relieving tension   Anxiety at the address position about getting the ball airborne is the cause of some women swinging stiff armed, in which the club is pushed back instead of swung back smoothly. The elbows and shoulders have gotten too tight. This anxiety can be relieved by having confidence that the loft of the clubface will get the ball in the air. By striking the ball first, the clubface pinches it against the turf before rolling up the clubface slightly and lifting in the air.

Increase swing arc   Women may have less strength than men, but they have greater flexibility. A woman can't afford to make a compact swing, she needs swing length to hit the ball a decent distance. Her flexibility can be put to use to make the swing arc bigger, which in turn makes the ball go farther. Instead of stopping the swing with the hands above the shoulder, women can continue until the hands are above the head, while keeping the left arm relatively straight. As you turn more with the shoulders, maintain resistance with the lower body. If the hips and legs continue turning, too, the amount of coil will be lessened. Stop the hip turn at 45 degrees as with a normal turn.

Gaining strength   Two ways to increase golf-muscle strength is swinging a weighted golf club—being careful not to strain the back—and gripping and regripping a golf club while sitting at home watching the television.

The full figure dilemma   Here's a "problem" definitely unique to women: the full figure/large chest. There are two ways to approach the situation. Some teachers advocate that women put their right arm to the side and under the right breast, and the left arm on top of the left breast. One problem with this is it could cause the arms to work separately of each other. Another method is to put both arms to the sides of the breasts. When the club is swung back in proper sequence, the chest is not in the way as much. This situation calls for a lot of experimentation to discover the best and most comfortable swing motion.

Avoid flipping out   Heavy equipment and/or the feeling of having to scoop the ball to get it in the air are reasons why some women spin the upper body on the downswing so that the club flips the ball up rather than drives it forward. A mental tip to avoid this is to think of swinging the club with the forearms instead of controlling the club with the hands.

Extend the arms   A key to a powerful hit is extending the arms away from the body so they can swing freely and smoothly. This extension begins with the take-away and thinking about stretching the left arm and left side as the club is swung back. Continue this feeling of stretching the left side until the arms naturally start moving upward with the club.

Don't hold back   Even with increased athleticism in younger women golfers today, there are still some female players who don't give the ball a hard hit. It could be because of a fear of hitting the ground and taking a divot, or not believing they would look graceful. On the women's pro tour, long hitters such as Laura Davies and Michelle McGann, it is said by most observers, hit the ball like a man. The meaning is that they swing aggressively and deliver a hit to the ball, rather than swing timidly. Focus on swinging gracefully but hitting hard at the same time.

Use women's clubs   How odd to urge women to use women's clubs, but for many years, women's golf clubs were adapted men's clubs or were clubs not built with the women's physique, strength, and golf swing in mind. But women should be sure to obtain clubs designed for them. Women's clubs are lighter than men's, about an inch shorter, with thinner grips and a softer-flex shaft. Most women amateurs are better off with women's clubs, but strong women and those with great skill should experiment with men's clubs to see if they match their game. A set of clubs can cost anywhere from $200 and $300 to a couple thousand.

Cock wrists at the top   Women who don't have a lot of upper-body strength sometimes swing the club to the top and point the club skyward. This is the only way they can support the club at the top of the swing. However, this doesn't allow the woman to apply much pop to the ball. The best position is taking the club to the top and cock the wrists so the toe of the club is pointing downward. The arms can then swing down so the wrist-club angle is maintained for a more powerful hit. The wrists uncock at the bottom of the swing and release the club.

PLAYING WHILE PREGNANT

In recent years, pregnant women have been allowed to do more physical activity later into their pregnancy than ever before. There was great concern for the health of the mother and child if too much stress was exerted. But the endurance level of expectant mothers is being seen in a new perspective. When it comes to golf, it's not unusual to see a woman continue playing into her seventh and eighth month. In the summer of 1997, for example, Swedish professional Catrin Nilsmark finished second in a tournament in her homeland while in her eighth month.

The pregnant golfer faces a challenge that, like her growing and changing physical condition, is different from week to week. Conveniently enough, some of these changes actually improve upon a player's performance. As a woman's girth

The ten-finger baseball grip.

changes, she can continue playing by making slight changes in setup and posture.

Golf is actually a pretty good activity during pregnancy. Something like aerobics and running can limit blood supply to the baby. The amount of blood a woman has increases by one third during pregnancy, so it's crucial that anything she does doesn't overly exert the heart.

How the body changes during pregnancy is fairly obvious. As the stomach area expands, stress is put on the back and abdominal muscles. The shoulders become slouched and curved. These changes must have counter changes if golf is to be continued. There must be more bending from the waist, the club has to be swung more to the outside away from the body, and the stance opened up (meaning the left foot is moved away from the target line).

Many pregnant women find the added weight beneficial to playing golf. It lowers their center of gravity and keeps them grounded and steady. And with more weight behind the ball, there's the potential for more yardage.

Golf fits in well as a healthy activity during pregnancy because it activates every part of the body, but it doesn't leave most women out of breath. That's key to any pregnancy: don't do anything that can't be done while maintaining a conversational tone of voice.

Every woman has different tolerances, so she should check with her doctor about continuing a golf schedule. Here are some points about playing while pregnant, which could be discussed between the doctor and patient.

Walking   If you're allowed to walk, use a pull cart. This prevents a lot of bending, which aggravates the back. Another back breaker is bending over to pick the ball out of the cup. See if someone in the group would do that for you, or buy one of those suction cups for the end of the putter to lift the ball out of the hole.

Putting   A larger abdomen will most affect this area of the game because the ball is played closer to the body than for a full swing. There's no room for the grip and hands to swing back and forth. To clear a path for them, widen the stance, lower the body, and play the ball a little farther away. Also angle the elbows outward slightly. An added benefit from this posture is it steadies the body over the shot.

Nutrition   Stay away from fatty foods and eat plenty of fruits and vegetables as part of a good diet routine. Foods with carbohydrates and potassium are excellent for this condition as well as plenty of fluids.

Heat   As is the case for all golfers, care must be taken when pregnant to avoid going out when the temperature is more than 90 and the humidity is high. Shorten the round if you're outside in this weather, and take the usual precautions in the sun such as sunblock and lots of water. Get the feet elevated for awhile after playing in hot weather.

Ninth month   Golf during the final four weeks is still a possibility, but there's really no point in taking a chance at this time because golf is not important enough to risk premature labor or doing anything harmful to the mother or the baby.

After birth   Depending upon the ease of delivery, and upon whether the mother is nursing, playing golf after birth can usually be done in six to eight weeks. Patience is a key word. Be assured that if you've played up to the ninth month, you won't have lost much of your golf touch. And if you perform the usual strengthening exercises recommended after delivery, there's a great chance you can come back to golf in better shape than before. This renewed strength combined with the confidence gained from having done the miracle of delivering a baby can have an other-world effect on a woman golfer. She can feel that if she went through a pregnancy, she can do anything, even play golf well!

TIPS TO PLAY BUSINESS GOLF

The number of women playing golf to take advantage of its tie-in with business opportunities has put a whole new focus on how to entertain a guest at a course. Many women who have benefitted from equal-access changes at private clubs have learned how to bring a client to the course and mix business with pleasure.

Golf and business have been side by side on the golf course since just after clubs started sprouting up in the United States. For decades, men were the main proponents and users of the golf course as a place of business with clients and associates while having some fun, too.

Golf's social atmosphere and outdoor, secluded setting are ideal for conducting business. Golf is a common bond between strangers who come together on the course not having anything else in common but a love to play golf and the need to make a business deal. Somehow, they get things done and continue their relationship as golf pals.

Men members at private clubs were often seen as a combination golfer/deal-maker for many years. The woman was the wife of leisure, playing golf and socializing with friends. Men may still be the same type of club member, but more and more women have become golfers/dealmakers as well. They like golf for the same reasons men do: as exercise, an escape, and a way to meet new business clients and entertain new opportunities. Golf helps people make connections with each other, personally and professionally.

It's said that you can find out more about a person by playing golf with them for four hours than you can by doing anything else for a greater length of time. A person's personality and beliefs are exposed during golf. You can learn how they deal with people, how punctual they are, how honest, and how trustworthy. Golf is very much played by a code of proper conduct and sportsmanship, not exactly the way some people arrange their business affairs, but if a businessperson plays golf honestly, there's a good chance business will be done that way, too.

The fight many women have put up at private clubs for equal access to the club's amenities is often done to ensure they have the same opportunity to do business on the golf course as does the "old boy" network. The restrictions placed on women have fouled up their time schedules in meeting business acquaintances, forcing them to come at odd times, which often don't match with the client's schedule.

Hoping to reverse these schedule restrictions and promote interaction among women golfers has been the goal of the many women's golf leagues that have sprung up in the past five years. The main organization is the Executive Women's Golf League, located at 1401 Forum Way, Suite 100, West Palm Beach, Florida, 33401, phone 1-800-407-1477 and (561) 471-1477.

The EWGL has ninety chapters around the United States with more than 13,000 members. The EWGL bands women executives together to play social golf without the restrictions faced at private clubs. The women share experiences and build a network among themselves for not only business purposes but to have a voice in club policies. The EWGL has tried to promote golf to young girls and bring in adult newcomers to the sport. It keeps tabs on many areas a regular league would, such as handicaps, and holds tournaments, clinics, golf trips, and outings.

Golf is hard enough to break into as a player. But when you add the element of breaking into the business world of golf as a woman, it's probably triple the difficulty. The corporate outing is being used more and more by women; this is an event that brings together important persons from various companies, who play some golf while talking about business. This is an uncomfortable setting for a woman new to the game, but it's not any easier for a man, either. Outings are often the place where infrequent golfers make their couple-of-times-a-year appearances, so whether it's a man or woman, there is an uneasy feeling.

Being among business associates requires a positive frame of mind. Don't try to overstate or undersell your abilities. Be truthful about your state of game and realize that it's unlikely you'll be the worst player there. If you're a woman and are being treated badly by a few men, it's best to let things go and not try to change their attitudes. That can't be done in the time frame of one round of golf. Their attitudes should change as they encounter more women in these situations.

Such is the climate of business golf today that the influx of women is here to stay. There is a vast array of things to learn, such as how to bring a guest to the club, how to tip attendants, and how to schedule the guest to arrive in time to have lunch and practice before the round. It's important the day goes smoothly because it has a definite affect on how a business relationship with a guest pans out.

That's where the following tips should provide some help, not just for the female business golfer, but for men, too.

1. Taking a business client or associate to a public course is a rarity. Unless the course is the caliber of a Pebble Beach, there isn't any special appeal of a public layout. A private course has the prestige setting to properly entertain a guest. The amenities are top-notch, and a private course has great flexibility in the pairings it allows. You can go off as a twosome—the host with the guest—or as a foursome. Public courses usually frown on letting groups of under four off the first tee.
2. Playing as a twosome is usually an awkward arrangement. A guest will probably feel more comfortable if there is a third party in the group. But don't have three people from your side with one from the guest's side. They will feel like they're being ganged-up on. Try to find a balanced group of players.
3. When there's someone you've picked out to have as a guest, have a few dates in mind and call the club to be sure there aren't any special events scheduled that would prevent your playing. Also check whether you need a starting time, and doublecheck the club policy on when men and women can play. There probably aren't any restrictions, but find out if

there are. It would be an embarrassment if you found out women weren't allowed to play at the time you'd picked out.

4. Give your guest good directions to the course, and a time to arrive. Let them know they can drop their clubs off at a specific spot so an attendant can have it ready on a cart or with a caddie when it's time to tee off. Make sure you arrive ahead of the guest. It's not good manners to leave a guest wandering the club property trying to figure out where to go. If you have a target time to tee off at, say, 1:30 P.M., have the guest arrive at noon for a lunch and warm-up session. Ninety minutes is a good amount of time to eat and practice before play; forty-five minutes is a good time if you're only warming up.

5. It wouldn't hurt to tell guests where you'll meet them. It could be in the locker area, the golf shop, or the lobby. You'll also want to let them either share your locker or use one that's vacant. Check with the locker-room attendant on available lockers.

6. Let the guest know ahead of time what the club dress code is and if there's a ban on metal-spiked shoes. If you're having dinner after golf, check on what men and women must wear in the dining room.

7. Ask your guest if they like to walk or ride. Don't assume they'll automatically do one or the other. It's not good form to make a walker take a cart or a rider have to walk.

8. It's up to the host to take care of all fees and tips. The host should check in with the golf shop when they arrive so they know you'll be teeing it up that day. Find out when you should head out to the first hole. Sign for the green fee and/or cart fee in the shop.

9. Make sure you have enough small bills on hand to tip the appropriate persons. It's usually fine to give support staffers, such as the cart person, bag handlers, shoe-shine person, and locker-room attendant, $2 to $5 each, depending on how much they did for each guest. Caddies are tipped an extra $5 to $10, or 20 percent above the carrying rate, unless the club has a policy against tipping them. But you can also make a statement about the poor job a caddie did by not giving a tip at all. Keep in mind that tips are basically meant to tell a worker thanks for a job well done. Don't tip for mediocre service. A caddie, for instance, is supposed to clean the clubs, rake bunkers, watch errant shots so the ball isn't lost, tend the flag, and give advice on shot yardage and club selec-

tion. In addition to tipping, there will be regular fees for shoe shines and using a caddie.

10. Many people in business have to play with a wager on the line, but don't assume your guest has to. Bring some extra money just in case, and ask at some point before play begins if they want to put some money on the match. Don't be upset if they don't, and don't make an out-of-sight wager if they do. Play for something low-key, such as a $5 nassau, so the pressure of the match isn't too intense. Keep in mind you're playing for enjoyment, not to make money off the guest. (A nassau is a match-play style game in which there is a $5 bet—or another agreed-upon sum—for the front nine, $5 for the back and $5 for the entire eighteen. Agree upon handicap strokes ahead of time, and whether a press will be allowed, which is an automatic doubling of the bet if either side is two holes down.)

11. Try your best not to complain or moan about your game if you're playing badly. Most people can recognize a good player, even when they're having an off day. Remain positive and maintain a pleasant attitude. On the other hand, don't boast if you're having an incredibly good day. Just enjoy it and remain on an even emotional level so the guest doesn't feel like they're playing twice as bad.

12. Learn as much as you can about your guest's personality by watching him handle the many different situations there are on the course. See how he behaves toward course

"My first rule is 'distance without direction is worse than no distance at all.' The key to having both distance and direction is making solid contact every time, and that's pretty hard to do if you are swinging out of your shoes trying to murder the ball. Most really good players swing at about 75 percent of full speed. That is a swing they can control but that will still deliver enough clubhead speed to hit a good drive. When they need a bigger drive, they increase their swing speed slightly, but never more than 90 percent, because anything faster than that is a swing headed out of control."

NANCY LOPEZ

workers and others in the playing group. Watch how well he abides by the rules. Get a general feel for what the person would be like to deal with in a business situation.

13. Be on your own best behavior in treating others with respect, avoiding vulgar language, temper tantrums, and attempts to be overly chummy and a smooth talker. Smothering a guest with kindness can make you appear desperate for their future business.

14. There should be hardly any or no business talk on the course while golfing. Use that time to build a rapport with each other. But all situations are different. If the guest starts talking about work, join in the conversation. Make sure you've done your homework ahead of time and studied any pertinent areas about their business and/or how the two of you can work together.

15. At the end of the round, settle any bets you had quickly and accurately. Ask the guest to stay for a drink, snack, or full meal. While relaxing in the "nineteenth hole," remind the guest why you had them to the club, discussing the business aspect in which you hope to engage. Exchange phone numbers, E-mail addresses, and business cards. Make plans to contact the person in the near future to continue the business talk—or to play the next round of golf.

 Chapter 14

JUNIORS—A PARTNERSHIP WITH THEIR PARENTS

Junior golf, the time span from toddler age through high school, is not what it used to be. The junior golfer walking the fairways today has exceeded the junior of thirty years ago: in playing ability, appearance and just plain golf smarts. The junior golfer today has the looks of someone well beyond her youthful years.

To be sure, the typical junior can still be seen at the local muni. You can still find the junior player in high-top sneakers, baggy clothes, and baseball cap, worn-out bag over the shoulder, with hand-me-down clubs of an odd assortment.

But where junior golf has evolved and grown the most is in the development of great talent at a young age, and there are now more great golfers at a young age than ever before. These days, the top level of junior players is stacked with confident kids who emerge from their junior days with much more assurance that their golfing ability is going to take them great places than their predecessors. This bold attitude is the result of stronger junior programs that have kids starting younger, and an often-times intense competitive schedule through high school.

The desire among juniors to be intense competitors at an early age will only increase because of the success Tiger Woods has had since he turned pro as a 21-year-old. He had the finest career ever as a junior and has brought a great flood of youngsters who want to have things turn out for them the way they did for him.

WHEN AND HOW TO GET STARTED

Anyone who has played golf, regardless of when they got started, will agree that the time to learn golf is at a young age. Golfers who learned as an adult moan about how they wish they'd started earlier. And players who started in the junior ranks say a prayer of thanks they had the opportunity to start their learning at a young age.

Because of the difficulty in playing golf well, and the amount of time it takes, the earlier someone learns golf the better they are. There have been exceptions to that rule, however. Larry Nelson, who won the U.S. Open and two PGA Championships, didn't begin playing until he was in his 20s and had returned from military service in Vietnam.

But it's rare to play golf well the later you wait to get started. Most of the great golf champions started at a young age, such as Arnold Palmer at 3 and Jack Nicklaus at 10. One of the key things about starting young is that kids can use their great ability to mimic and imitate what they see other people doing. They are the human equivalent to the phrase "monkey see, monkey do." Children don't have preconceived notions of what the swing should look like. They see it demonstrated and try to duplicate it. Adults, on the other hand, let their own thoughts and expectations get in the way and stifle good learning.

You know it's a good time to start playing golf when a child has a spark of interest in the game, perhaps wanting to hit some shots in the backyard, or go to the local course to putt or just ask questions about the game. That's when you know they would be interested in swinging the club and having a few things introduced to them about playing. It may happen at age three, or five, or eight, and when it happens, take advantage of their interest and work as best you can in giving them the knowledge and answers they want to know.

There's one thing to keep in mind about starting early: It doesn't hurt to have a child

Tiger Woods is a prime example of the benefits of early learning.

swing a golf club as early an age as possible, but don't expect there to be a lot of valuable learning until around 10. A junior may get started at age 4, for instance, but it takes until the age of 8 to 10 to be able to start real learning with quality practice time. That's when the junior is physically strong enough to endure practice sessions, has developed a desire to play, and has the attention span to listen to instructions.

Emotional maturity is another important element that shouldn't be overlooked. If it's lacking in a junior, wait until they seem better able to handle the highs and lows of the sport before having them get too deep into learning.

Davis Love Jr., the late father of professional golfer Davis Love III, felt that golf should be started between ages 4 and 12, and that 10 was the optimum age for starting full-scale learning. He said simplicity and fun were the two things needing emphasis in a junior's golf upbringing.

Expect a junior player to do a lot of things wrong when they first get started, such as gripping the club like a hockey stick instead of a golf club. There will be a great deal of trial-and-error experiments before things start working smoothly. The parent should be there to answer questions or correct things as much as possible so that good traits and habits are ingrained. A junior should not be inundated with too much information, which would garble the message and make it useless.

The goal of parents should be to keep the game fun and light. Emphasize the enjoyable things about golf, such as the outdoor air, the fun of putting, and being with friends. While parents should pass along swing fundamentals and provide help wherever possible, it's usually best if parents, specifically the father, not serve as a junior's coach/instructor, unless the parent is a bonafide swing instructor, as Davis Love Jr. was for Davis Love III. It may be okay at first, but as the junior gets better and more serious about improving, he's better off seeing a third party rather than risk having a parent get too involved in the junior's swing. When a parent tries to be an instructor, it sets up the possibility of a lot of stress and tension between the parent and child. Golf is like a lot of things involving these two sides in that the child usually likes to listen to someone else tell her what to do rather than her own mother or father.

A junior's first club should be a cut-down adult club, unless you can get your hands on clubs that have been made short enough by a manufacturer, but those kinds of clubs usually don't fit a junior until they're around 8 to 10 years old. A 5-wood is often cited as a club that is ideal when cut down and a new grip put on.

Make it a women's club, rather than men's, because the women's will be lighter. Work on getting the club made with a club repairperson, who can make sure the club is the right length and who can put on a junior grip instead of an adult's. The 5-wood is best because it has plenty of loft to get the ball airborne and can be used for a variety of shots. A junior's first set shouldn't be bought until the junior has a basic knowledge of the swing and can consistently hit the ball. A set of clubs right from the start would be too confusing as the junior wouldn't know what to do with each club yet.

Young players usually like to practice with their parents. They may first find it fun to go to the practice putting green at a local course and enjoy putting. It can spread to swinging the club in the backyard, without trying to hit a ball. From there, have a junior go along to the practice range and let them watch an adult hit balls for awhile. Get some interest started and then let the junior take some swings. Don't let the child get bogged down with ball flight at this point. Focus more on swing movements and making the body parts move in correct fashion. A child's first grip should be strong, meaning the left hand should be turned more to the right than normal. After a few years, when they've gotten stronger and are swinging well, have them change to a neutral grip.

During practice, make sure the junior doesn't get bored or passive. Pay attention to their attitude, and try to mix things up a little, perhaps taking a break for a snack or stepping back to watch others for a short time. Avoid anything that creates the feeling that golf is a waste of time. If those thoughts have begun, the junior is likely struggling with something and needs a break. If the interest is strong, they'll be back swinging later.

No junior should ever go to the golf course to play an actual nine or eighteen holes until they have learned how to advance the ball regularly. It's a waste of the junior's time, the parents', and the other players' as well when a junior golfer, or any golfer, for that matter, struggles hole after hole. Make it clear that you're not on the golf course to go on a short walkabout. Each hole has a starting and ending point, and the goal is to get the ball in the hole in as few strokes as possible. Certainly it's important to enjoy the surrounding views of nature, but always remind a junior what the object of the game is, and also remind them to be quick and play without delay. It's always a good idea to ingrain that idea at an early age.

During the first few times on the golf course, there isn't a real need to focus on score, the number of strokes taken on each hole. For the first trips out, only

Learning in a group setting can be an ideal way for a junior to get started with the fundamentals.

play a few holes and make sure the child finishes the hole. You will gradually build up to nine holes and then eighteen.

The age at which a child should get a new set is dependent upon how well they're learning the swing and how many holes they can handle on the golf course. As playing ability increases, so will the need for more and more clubs to fill in for special shots. After the 5-wood, a 6-iron could be next, then a putter. If you can get clubs in the right junior size, that's the best buy, otherwise you'll have to continue to cut down adult clubs. If the junior is up to three or four clubs, get a small bag so he can get used to carrying them as a set.

About the right age for a junior beginner's set is between 10 and 12, or the time when the junior stops worrying about finishing a hole and is more concerned with how many strokes he took. At that point you know she's ready for expanding her arsenal of clubs. A junior set usually has a wooden club with loft, a putter, and the 3-, 5-, 7-, and 9-irons. That set will serve the needs of a junior well during the learning process; more clubs won't be needed until the junior learns to hit toward greens with more precision and accuracy. That's when another wood and the other irons will fill in the gaps.

It's a good idea for parents to investigate at a golf shop to see which club companies offer special sets for junior players. An example is the Karsten Manufacturing youth equipment program. Designed for players up to age 12, the program includes three different youth packages of different combinations of clubs, all available in custom lengths and available for replacement clubs as the junior gets older and improves in talent. Some companies have a special arrangement to replace or supplement a junior set as time goes by.

As for the learning process, a junior's swing coach progresses from the parent to a teacher when the child seems able to handle swing concepts and thoughts. A series of lessons with a teaching pro is quite helpful, costing in the $30 range for each half-hour lesson. Also of great benefit is attending a teaching clinic or camp. Keep in mind that golf camps are for adding to or refining a junior's learning, not to be the primary means for learning. A junior should have some swing smarts before going to a camp. Some parks and recreation department clinics are free or charge very little. Others cost a couple hundred dollars for six classes.

Learning within a group is one of the best ways a junior can learn. He can see that other kids his age are just as interested in golf as he is. And working with the local course professional is also a good plan, as long as the pro has the junior's best interests at heart and has a pleasant attitude toward kids. Lessons with a pro should be spaced apart so instruction is given in steady doses rather than a truckload all at one time. The junior won't feel overburdened and won't feel pressure to be an immediate success.

PARENTS: BE ENCOURAGING, NOT PUSHY

There's a well-known affliction among parents of young athletes called the Pushy Parent Syndrome. This takes place when the parent gets out of control and enforces rules with such strict authority and fervor that the game no longer remains a game for the junior. It becomes a task to be hated, shunned and, eventually, abandoned.

The pushy golf parent picks golf as a sport to keep their child busy and out of trouble, and to learn discipline. But golf becomes an obsession for the parent, who doesn't easily recognize that he has let things get out of control. It takes time for things to develop so that the pushy parent sees the light. Often there are warning signs, such as when the parent pushes practice so hard that over time the junior can't even function anymore and starts swinging like the old way when she had a bunch of swing faults.

Signs of a Pushy Parent

Ignore the rules   Trying to have a legitimate ruling overturned or ignored is a sure sign that something is not right.

Cheating   When the parent pushes too hard for the junior to be a success, both are tempted to cheat to get every advantage. That could include putting down the wrong score, moving the ball around from a bad lie, or doing things to upset or rattle the other players.

Being too forceful   There is a proper amount of practice, and then there is an outrageous amount of practice. Doing the latter more often than the former is a pushy parent trait.

Make comparisons   Each junior out there is a different person from the other. Comparing your child with the other juniors is often useless. Each junior moves forward at a different speed. Recognize that and don't play one youngster off another.

Lacking perspective   Golf is a game, and even if the goal is to be a professional golfer, don't let the knowledge of that ever fade away. The process of playing golf well can be done without making golf seem like drudgery.

Base everything on winning   If a junior plays his best, but loses, is that a reason to blow your top? Help the junior feel good about herself even if she didn't reach the top spot or post the best score. The goal in golf should always be improving and bettering one's self. Let that be the motivation when a junior hasn't come out ahead of everyone else. Encourage the golfer to better their score next time, in essence, having a contest with themself.

There are other subtle symptoms that all point toward giving the junior as much of an advantage as possible to the detriment of everyone else. All of these faults point toward making the junior good enough to be on the pro tour. But parents must ask themselves, am I being pushy because of frustration in my own golfing inability? Is my child going to develop bad manners and dislike golf because of unhappy experiences?

If the answer is yes to those questions, then the end result could be a junior who quits the game rather than makes it a part of their life. Some parents, who

> "Golf can become an addiction and an obsession. You have to guard against loving the game so much that you hate it. It's wise to avoid extreme emotions. If it were an easy game, everyone would be playing it well."
>
> JUDY RANKIN

are good players, can't understand why their child isn't as good as they are. Their impatience doesn't allow them to let the child develop on their own time. Golf definitely isn't a sport that can be mastered by forced practice. Don't ever let a junior feel he has to play golf to please anyone else but himself.

There's a big danger when parents are so involved in the child's performance that the junior withdraws emotionally when things don't go right. It's very damaging to shun or ignore a junior who has done poorly. Parents must not take away their love or the child's feeling of self-worth by withdrawing from them on an emotional level. Juniors play as well as they feel about themselves. A junior that feels good will learn faster, perform better under pressure, and have more fun.

The pushy parent needs to reverse direction to prevent their junior from deserting golf. They can do that by altering their behavior in these areas:

Rewards and punishments   Parents should not go to the extreme in either case, and they should not treat the child vastly different if for having done very poorly or very well. Rewarding too much for a job well done can be just as harmful as taking away privileges for poor play. Avoid making threats or putting guilt trips on a junior, thinking it will motivate them. Often it puts fear and uneasiness in their minds. Try to remain consistent and level.

Scoring   Parents should remember it is the child making the score, not them. Parents should commiserate with juniors who play badly, but they shouldn't bring everyone down to the depths of depression. Try to encourage better play for next time. Work with the junior in knowing how to turn a failure into a positive. Bad play can be a great motivational tool. A setback can precede a great leap forward as long as the child has a positive approach.

Burnout   There's a rule of thumb about whether a junior is being worked too hard and may suffer burnout. It is that the parents who ask about burnout shouldn't be worried; the parents who don't consider it need to be worried. A junior who is ready at the time of practice and is practically out the door is not burned out; a junior who can't be found at practice time without a search party is probably burned out.

Randy Smith, the teacher of 1997 British Open champion Justin Leonard when he was a junior golfer, has said that one in 500 to 1,000 kids has the dedication to be a champion like Leonard had. Smith noted that for young kids it's not so much physical skills, but the desire to play that's important. "Do they pull on their parents' legs and make them go to the golf course? It's the 'want to' in a kid that's much more important than the raw talent. Justin was the first guy at the club in the morning. And he wouldn't spend a lot of time out by the swimming pool. He worked on chipping and putting, then played golf and came back in the afternoon to practice."

On-course behavior   Children play the game for fun. They haven't reached the age where it's any more serious than that. When they miss a putt, getting chewed out later by a parent doesn't make it any easier to take. Golf teaches juniors lessons just by being played. When a junior misses an easy putt, that's a lesson learned by itself.

Golf can be a family game if the parents play their cards right. Continual support with encouragement and positive comments is imperative. Knowing when to use constructive criticism is also a must; most juniors try their best, so it makes no sense to make them feel any worse. Taking the child to the practice range and course as often as possible will, over time, convince the junior that golf is a family activity. But don't rule out having any other outside interests. A tunnel focus on golf won't make a youngster a well-rounded individual.

Being the parent of a junior golfer means having the ability to be a coach, cheerleader, and counselor at the same time, and knowing when to do the right amount of all three. How the parent treats the junior greatly determines the character and attitude the junior develops over the years. Parents need to be the grown-up in every situation, and be a solid cornerstone for the junior to lean upon.

THE ROAD TO A COLLEGE SCHOLARSHIP

The typical junior golfer today has two goals in mind: getting a scholarship to play golf in college, and then, if things work out, being good enough to play on the pro tour. That's how much juniors have narrowed their focus in recent years. Only the specially talented juniors of thirty years ago would have thought golf could be in their future beyond high school.

Getting a college scholarship can't be a forced issue. The trail begins before high school as the junior practices regularly and slowly builds a competitive schedule. If parents see that their child has the desire and an ability to play a lot, the best thing to do is try every way possible to give them a playing opportunity. Unfortunately, many courses have rules that limit who and when junior golfers can play. Usually there's an age requirement for playing, such as age 12 and up, and an adult has to be in the group. Time restrictions are also tricky, such as not allowing juniors to play until after 3 P.M. on weekdays. When a youngster can play, it's best to have them play as often as possible and leave practicing for later. Playing is more fun. Practice time can be fit in to work on specific swing adjustments.

Competition at an early age shouldn't be overdone, particularly if playing is going to turn into an embarrassment. It can be a horrible experience to whiff a lot of balls, four-putt every green, and shoot the highest score. Start a junior off easy in three-, six-, or nine-hole tournaments; some kind of an event that takes just part of a day. Let that be a starting point and grow the schedule from there.

Some of the events available for juniors take place in city events, competitive tournaments within a junior golf association, and tournaments organized by an outside organization. In high school, competition is done in school matches, invitational tournaments, and the state tournament. There may also be local, state, and regional junior golf associations in your area that hold various tournaments and teaching clinics during the year.

There are a handful of junior golf tours that have been of great value to young golfers today. One of them, the PGA Junior Series, is put on by the PGA of America. There were twelve events in 1997 for golfers ages 13–17, held at various courses in the United States.

Another junior tour is run by the American Junior Golf Association. The AJGA is the most well known and high profile of the junior tours in operation. It started in 1977 and in twenty years has grown to approximately 4,210 junior members who file applications to compete in its events, which numbered forty in 1997 and were played all around the United States. Juniors aged 13 to 18 are eligible.

The value of a tour like the AJGA is seen in the statistic that nearly 100 percent of the kids who participate in it go on to college, and about 75 percent receive some kind of scholarship help. The self-stated purpose of the AJGA—"to provide positive life experiences for aspiring junior golfers through competitive golf while setting high standards to preserve the integrity and traditions of the game"—is a mini-statement about the status of junior golf nowadays. The AJGA is located in Roswell, Georgia, phone (770) 998-4653.

What these junior tours do is give the proficient youngster a place to hone his skills in tournament situations, learn how to handle pressure and compete with the best players of his age group. College coaches have used these tours, as well as high-school state tournaments, to scout out the best talent. The tours have been somewhat controversial in that they've been criticized for being exclusive to the wealthy and have shut out juniors who are financially strapped. But the tours have been overwhelmed by the sheer numbers of juniors who want to get into the events and have had to devise eligibility rules to make sure tournament fields don't get out of hand.

Getting a scholarship is dependent, of course, on how well a junior golfer plays, but it also depends on where she plays. Playing events on a national junior tour is important because many college coaches don't care that much if a junior can beat the local city kids or area high-school crowd. They want to see how a young person does against the best of the nation's players in head-to-head competition. Trying to play a national schedule is an expensive proposition, and the cost effectively shuts out a lot of fine players. But the financial sacrifices and strategies some parents have made have been incredible in ensuring their kid a chance to compete. Somehow they've figured a way to give their child an opportunity.

Anyone wanting to get a scholarship to college also has to be part salesperson. A junior's play may have caught the eye of a college coach, but the junior's chances improve greatly if he also uses videos, letters, and other means to promote himself to the coach and the school. One great source that details this process is the *American College Golf Guide,* by Dean W. Frischknecht and available through Frischknecht Publishing in Hillsboro, Oregon, (503) 648-1333. The guide comes out yearly around October and contains the college tournament results of the most-recent season, and the coaches, addresses, and phone numbers for dozens of two- and four-year colleges in the United States that have golf programs. College guidelines from the National Collegiate Athletic Association are included, along with tips on how to get selected by a college coach or "sell yourself" to a college program.

The odds are certainly quite steep to getting a scholarship to one of the nation's golf powerhouses, but junior players should not feel that those schools are their only hope. There are more than 1,000 colleges and universities that have golf programs, meaning there are thousands of openings for golf team members for both boys and girls. But determination and hard work can turn the most urgent situation into a success. A school may pass on you, but you may not pass on it. Some players, such as Tom Lehman with the University of Minnesota, can make things go their way as a walk-on if they believe in themselves.

A junior's chances to grab a college spot are good if she keeps up a strong game, maintains good grades and test scores, is well disciplined, and has shown the ability to beat top-notch competition. In short, colleges want the strong player who fits in on a team and doesn't cause academic or disciplinary problems and thus reflects well on the school.

 Chapter 15

GOLF LIBRARIES—YOUR OWN AND OTHERS

Most of the early written accounts about golf describe local laws controlling the game and procedures of how to play. One of the most treasured, for instance, is Thomas Kincaid's 1687 diary that gives his thoughts on how to play. Like many of the older writings, Kincaid's work is amazingly relevant in a lot of respects. Much of the game's pioneering literature still is.

Golf's most effective and moving writing is as beautiful and artistic as the loveliest golf swing. Only a golf devotee can feel a true passion for the game and understand its charm. If that devotee happens to be a wordsmith, wonderful prose is the result, with words that reflect quite well on the nuances that make golf such a great game.

The amount of literature available on golf is, arguably, the most abundant of any sport. Thousands of pieces have been printed—from books to pamphlets— poems and novels, biographies and instructional books, and combinations of all of them. Golf, by its nature, lends itself so well to beautifully crafted writing. So many great authors and writers have worked in the golf field that there is a lifetime of reading waiting for anyone ready to dive in.

Authors such as F. Scott Fitzgerald, William Faulkner, John Updike, Ogden Nash, and A.A. Milne have included golf vignettes in their writing, or written short stories about golf.

There are a handful of acknowledged golf-writing masters, some of them having written their works fifty to 100 years ago, such as Bernard Darwin and P.G. Wodehouse. Within the last fifty years, some of the leading writers have been Herbert Warren Wind, Henry Longhurst, Peter Dobereiner, Charles Price, and Pat Ward-Thomas. It's no surprise that most of these men either came from Great Britain or spent much time there, thus being able to more fully understand the origins of golf in the land that gave rise to the game.

Bobby Jones was probably the best player who wrote about the game. Much of his own writing made it past the publisher's editors without hardly any editing or work at all.

These writers had the flare for capturing the essence of golf, no matter whether they were describing the world's great golf courses or great golf swings. On a level below them comes the bulk of the remaining golf writing available, some of great quality and others of such inconsequence that one wonders how the author got the book or article published. But in fact, the popularity of golf is such that the market for any kind of golf-related product is wide open. Writing is one case in point, because it takes a long period of reading the quality writers to understand what's good and what's awful.

I can remember at an early age reading as many golf books as possible. It was so valuable to me to learn about the history, terms, and great players. The information became invaluable and has remained embedded in my mind. I can recall a sense of being lost in this printed world of golf, exploring many corners of it, excited to know and understand as much as I could. Reading time becomes more valuable as we get older, and I hope to catch this fever again soon.

I hope the following list of distinguished and worthwhile books can help you, the golf reader, pick the ones that will do you the most good and be most memorable.

Some of these books are rare and are probably available only through a local collector or a friend. They could also, by pure luck, be available at library sales or tag sales, but a truly priceless volume is unlikely to have been passed off so easily. Other books are still on library shelves, and still others can be found at bookstores or through publishing houses or fulfillment companies. (Probably the two most well-known mail- or phone-order companies for golf books and videos are Golf-Smart/The Booklegger, located in Grass Valley, California, phone 1-800-637-3557 and 1-800-262-1556, and Eyelevel Products in Newton, New Jersey, phone 1-800-666-4660. They have brochures that describe the list of products available for purchase.)

For anyone interested in the history of golf writing and publications, there have been a few valuable bibliographies. These books give a history of golf from the earliest known references, using wonderful detail. In particular are two good ones. First is the *Library of Golf* by Joseph S.F. Murdoch, Gale Research Company, Detroit, 1968. This book lists golf literature from 1743 to 1966. A 56-page addendum was printed in 1978. The second is *The Game of Golf and the Printed Word 1566–1985,* a bibliography of golf literature in the English language, by Murdoch and Richard E. Donovan, Castalio Press, Endicott, New York, 1988. This book is being revised for 1998. (Donovan, in fact, is a good source for people in search of rare books. His address is Richard E. Donovan Enterprises, 305 Massachusetts Avenue, P.O. Box 7070, Endicott, New York 13761, phone (607) 785-5874. Another antiquarian golf book source is George Lewis, P.O. Box 291, Mamaroneck, New York 10543, phone (914) 835-5100.)

The following list is divided into rare books, those for which you might have to go to a dealer; general golf books, those that are probably at either a library or available to buy; and instruction books that should be widely available through either a dealer or by purchase. Some books listed under the rare category have been reprinted, so you might find a newer copy at a bookstore. The books are listed alphabetically by author.

RARE BOOKS

Advanced Golf, or Hints and Instruction for Progressive Players, James Braid, Methuen, London, 1908.

A History of Golf: The Royal and Ancient Game, Robert Browning, J.M. Dent, London, 1955, and Dutton, New York, 1955.

Golfing: A Handbook to the Royal and Ancient Game, W. & R. Chambers, Edinburgh, Scotland, 1887.

Golf: A Royal & Ancient Game, edited by Robert Clark, EP Publishing Limited, West Yorkshire, England, 1975 (reprint of the second edition published in 1893 by Macmillan).

Golfers at Law: The Rules of Golf, Geoffrey Cousins, Alfred A. Knopf. New York, 1959.

British Golf, Bernard Darwin, Collins, London, 1946.

Golf Between Two Wars, Bernard Darwin, Chatto & Windus: London, 1944 (reissued by Classics of Golf, New York, 1985).

A History of Golf in Britain, Bernard Darwin, Henry Longhurst, Henry Cotton, and others, Cassell, London, 1952.

Historic Golf Courses of the British Isles, Bernard Darwin, Gerald Duckworth & Co., London, 1987 (originally published by Duckworth in 1910 as *The Golf Courses of the British Isles*).

Tee Shots and Others, Bernard Darwin, Kegan Paul, Trench, Trubner, London, 1911.

My Partner, Ben Hogan, Jimmy Demaret, McGraw-Hill, New York, 1954.

Golf Fundamentals, Seymour Dunn, originally privately printed in 1922 in Lake Placid, New York (reissued as a Golf Digest Classics book, 1984).

Hints on the Game of Golf, Horace G. Hutchinson, William Blackwood and Sons, Edinburgh, Scotland, 1886 (reissued by Classics of Golf, New York, 1987).

Golf, Horace G. Hutchinson, first published in London by Longmans, Green, 1890 (reissued by Flagstick Books, Norwalk, Conn., 1996).

Swinging into Golf, Ernest Jones and Innis Brown, Whittlesey House, New York, 1937.

Swing the Clubhead, Ernest Jones, Dodd, Mead, New York, 1952.

Scotland's Gift—Golf, Charles B. Macdonald, Charles Scribner's Sons, New York-London, 1928 (reissued by Classics of Golf, New York, 1985)

Fifty Years of American Golf, Harry Brownlaw Martin, Argosy-Antiquarian, New York, 1966 (originally published in 1936 by Dodd, Mead in New York).

A New Way to Better Golf, Alex J. Morrison, Simon & Schuster, New York, 1932 (reprinted by Stratford Press, New York).

A Game of Golf: A Book of Reminiscences, Francis Ouimet, Houghton Mifflin, Boston, 1932.

The Duffer's Handbook of Golf, Grantland Rice and Clare Briggs, Macmillan, New York, 1926.

Thirty Years of Championship Golf, Gene Sarazen with Herbert Warren Wind, Prentice Hall, New York, 1950 (reissued by Classics of Golf, New York, 1987).

The Art of Golf, Sir Walter Grindley Simpson, David Douglas, Edinburgh, Scotland, 1887 (reissued by Classics of Golf, New York, 1987).

Vardon on Golf; compiled and edited by Herbert Warren Wind and Robert Macdonald, Classics of Golf, New York, 1989.

The Complete Golfer, Harry Vardon, McClure, Phillips, New York, 1905 (reissued by Arno Press as a Golf Digest Classics Book, New York, 1977).

Golfing Memories and Methods, Joyce Wethered, Hutchinson, London, 1933.

The Clicking of Cuthbert, P.G. Wodehouse, George H. Doran, New York, 1919 (reissued by Classics of Golf, New York, 1986).

Divots, P.G. Wodehouse, George H. Doran, New York, 1927.

Fore: The Best of Wodehouse on Golf, P.G. Wodehouse, Ticknor & Fields, New Haven & New York, 1983.

The Golf Omnibus, P.G. Wodehouse, Barrie & Jenkins, London, 1973.

Wodehouse on Golf, P.G. Wodehouse, Doubleday, New York, 1940.

GENERAL BOOKS

Zinger, Paul Azinger with Ken Abraham, Zondervan Publishing House, Grand Rapids, Mich., 1995.

Seve: The Young Champion, Severiano Ballesteros and Dudley Doust, Golf Digest Books/Simon and Schuster, New York, 1982.

The Birth of a Legend: Arnold Palmer's Golden Year 1960, Furman Bisher, Prentice Hall, Englewood Cliffs, N.J., 1972.

The Hole Truth, Tommy Bolt with Jimmy Mann, J.B. Lippincott, Philadelphia and New York, 1971.

The Architects of Golf, Geoffrey S. Cornish and Ronald E. Whitten, Harper-Collins, New York, 1993 (first published as *The Golf Course* in 1981 by the Rutledge Press).

Mostly Golf: A Bernard Darwin Anthology, edited by Peter Ryde, first published in 1976 by Adam and Charles Black Ltd., London (reissued by Classics of Golf, New York, 1986).

Davies' Dictionary of Golfing Terms, Peter Davies, Simon and Schuster, New York, 1980 (paperback edition published by Michael Kesend Publishing, New York, 1992).

A History of Golf, Henry Cotton, J.B. Lippincott, Philadelphia and New York, 1975.

The Hogan Mystique, Martin Davis, The American Golfer, Greenwich, Conn., 1994.

The Greatest of Them All: The Legend of Bobby Jones, Martin Davis, The American Golfer, Greenwich, Conn., 1996.

Byron Nelson, Martin Davis, The American Golfer, Greenwich, Conn., 1997, and Broadway Books, New York.

100 Greatest Golf Courses—and Then Some, William H. Davis and the editors *of Golf Digest*, Golf Digest Books, Trumbull, Conn., 1986.

The Anatomy of a Golf Course, Tom Doak, Lyons & Burford, New York, 1992.

The Confidential Guide to Golf Courses, Tom Doak, Sleeping Bear Press, Chelsea, Mich., 1996.

The Glorious World of Golf, Peter Dobereiner, Ridge Press Books/McGraw-Hill, New York, 1973.

The World of Golf: The Best of Peter Dobereiner, Peter Dobereiner, Atheneum, New York, 1981.

Down the 19th Fairway: A Golfing Anthology, Peter Dobereiner, Atheneum, New York, 1983.

Golf à la Carte: The Best of Dobereiner, Peter Dobereiner, Lyons & Burford, New York, 1991.

Golf in the Making, Ian T. Henderson and David I. Stirk, Henderson and Stirk Ltd. and Lund Humphries, Yorkshire, England, 1982 (second edition).

The PGA [of America], Herb Graffis, Thomas Y. Crowell Co., New York, 1975.

Golf: Its History, People and Events, Will Grimsley, Prentice Hall, Englewood Cliffs, N.J., 1966.

The Walter Hagen Story, Walter Hagen as told to Margaret Seaton Heck, Simon and Schuster, New York, 1956.

Bob Hope's Confessions of a Hooker: My Lifelong Love Affair with Golf, Bob Hope with Dwayne Netland, Doubleday, Garden City, N.Y., 1985.

Sports Illustrated's The Best 18 Golf Holes in America, Dan Jenkins, Delacorte Press, New York, 1966.

The Dogged Victims of Inexorable Fate, Dan Jenkins, Sports Illustrated Books/Little, Brown, Boston, 1970 (reissued by Classics of Golf, New York, 1985).

Dead Solid Perfect, Dan Jenkins, Price/Stern/Sloan, Los Angeles, 1986 paperback (first released in hardback, 1974).

Whatta-Gal: The Babe Didrikson Story, William Oscar Johnson and Nancy P. Williamson, Sports Illustrated Books/Little, Brown, Boston, 1975.

Golf Is My Game, Bobby Jones, Doubleday, Garden City, N.Y., 1960 (reissued by Flagstick Books, Norwalk, Conn., 1997).

Down the Fairway, Bobby Jones and O.B. Keeler, Minton, Balch, New York, 1927 (reissued by Classics of Golf, New York, 1984).

Golfers' Gold, Tony Lema with Gwilym S. Brown, Little, Brown, Boston, 1964 (reissued by Classics of Golf, New York, 1987).

The Best of Henry Longhurst; compiled and edited by Mark Wilson with Ken Bowden, Golf Digest Books/Simon & Schuster, New York, 1978.

The Darwin Sketchbook: Bernard Darwin's Writings, edited by Robert S. Macdonald, Classics of Golf, New York, 1991.

Golf Club Design, Fitting, Alteration & Repair, Ralph Maltby, Ralph Maltby Enterprises, Newark, Ohio, fourth edition, January 1995.

Arnie: the Evolution of a Legend, Mark H. McCormack, Simon and Schuster, New York, 1967.

Triumphant Journey: Saga of Bobby Jones and the Grand Slam, Dick Miller, Holt, Rinehart & Winston, New York, 1980.

Peter Thomson: The Complete Golfer, Peter Mitchell, Lothian Books, Port Melbourne, Australia, 1991.

Golf in the Kingdom, Michael Murphy, Viking Press, New York, 1972.

The Crosby: Greatest Show in Golf, Dwayne Netland, Doubleday, Garden City, N.Y., 1975.

On & Off the Fairway, Jack Nicklaus with Ken Bowden, Simon and Schuster, New York, 1978.

The Greatest Game of All: My Life in Golf, Jack Nicklaus with Herbert Warren Wind, Simon and Schuster, New York, 1969.

My Most Memorable Shots in the Majors, Jack Nicklaus with Ken Bowden, Golf Digest Books, Trumbull, Conn., 1988.

The Encyclopedia of Golf Collectibles, Morton and John Olman, Books Americana, Florence, Ala., 1985.

Arnold Palmer's Best 54 Golf Holes, Arnold Palmer with Bob Drum, Doubleday, Garden City, N.Y., 1977.

The Bogey Man, George Plimpton, Harper & Row, New York, 1968.

The World of Golf, Charles Price, Random House, New York, 1962.

Golfer-at-Large, Charles Price, Atheneum, New York, 1982.

A Golf Story: Bobby Jones, Augusta National and the Masters Tournament, Charles Price, Atheneum, New York, 1986.

The American Golfer, edited by Charles Price, Random House, New York, 1964 (reissued by Classics of Golf, New York, 1987).

The Story of the Augusta National Golf Club, Clifford Roberts, Doubleday, Garden City, N.Y., 1976.

The Masters: The Winning of a Golf Classic, Dick Schaap, Random House, New York, 1970.

Massacre at Winged Foot: The 1974 U.S. Open, Dick Schaap, Random House, New York, 1974.

Pro: Frank Beard on the Golf Tour; edited by Dick Schaap, World Publishing Company, New York and Cleveland, 1970.

The Golf Immortals, Tom Scott and Geoffrey Cousins, Hart, New York, 1969.

The Education of a Golfer, Sam Snead with Al Stump, Simon and Schuster, New York, 1962.

Slammin' Sam, Sam Snead with George Mendoza, Donald I. Fine, New York, 1986.

Driving the Green: The Making of a Golf Course, John Strawn, HarperCollins, New York, 1991.

This Wonderful World of Golf, Peter Thomson and Desmond Zwar, Pelham Books, London, 1969.

Dead Heat: The '69 Ryder Cup Classic, Paul Trevillion, Stanley Paul, London, 1969.

They Call Me Super Mex, Lee Trevino and Sam Blair, Random House, New York, 1982.

Golf: The Greatest Game, U.S. Golf Association, HarperCollins, New York, 1994.

Golfgames: The Side Games We Play & Wager, Rich Ussak, Contemporary Books, Chicago, 1993.

The Rules of Golf; illustrated and explained by Tom Watson with Frank Hannigan, Golf Digest Books/Pocket Books, New York, 1996 edition.

Following Through: Herbert Warren Wind on Golf, Herbert Warren Wind, Ticknor & Fields, New York, 1985 (second edition in paperback).

The Complete Golfer; edited by Herbert Warren Wind, Simon and Schuster, New York, 1954 (reissued by Classics of Golf, New York, 1991).

The Story of American Golf, Herbert Warren Wind, Simon and Schuster, New York, 1956.

The Modern Guide to Golf Clubmaking, Tom Wishon, Dynacraft Golf Products, Newark, Ohio, 1987.

This Life I've Led, Babe Didrikson Zaharias, as told to Harry Paxton, A.S. Barnes, New York, 1955.

INSTRUCTION BOOKS

Natural Golf, Seve Ballesteros with John Andrisani, Atheneum, New York, 1988.

The Methods of Golf's Masters, Dick Aultman and Ken Bowden, Stanley Paul, London, 1988 (originally published as *The Masters of Golf: Learning from their Methods,* Coward, McCann & Geohegan, New York, 1975).

A Round of Golf with Tommy Armour, Tommy Armour, Simon and Schuster, New York, 1959.

How to Play Your Best Golf All the Time, Tommy Armour, Simon and Schuster, New York, 1953.

A Woman's Way to Better Golf, Peggy Kirk Bell with Jerry Claussen, E.P. Dutton, New York, 1966.

On Learning Golf, Percy Boomer, Alfred A. Knopf, New York, 1946 (reissued in numerous prints).

How to Play Golf with an Effortless Swing, Julius Boros, Prentice Hall, Englewood Cliffs, N.J., 1953.

Swing Easy, Hit Hard, Julius Boros, Harper & Row, New York, 1965 (reissued in paperback by Lyons & Burford, New York, 1993).

Golf Shotmaking, Billy Casper, Golf Digest Books/Doubleday, Garden City, N.Y., 1966.

Left-Handed Golf, Bob Charles with Roger P. Ganem, Prentice Hall, Englewood Cliffs, N.J., 1965.

Five Lessons: The Modern Fundamentals of Golf, Ben Hogan with Herbert Warren Wind, A.S. Barnes, New York, 1957 (reissued in paperback and hardback reprints).

Practical Golf, John Jacobs with Ken Bowden, Quadrangle, New York, 1972.

Lessons from the Golf Greats, David Leadbetter with Richard Simmons, HarperCollins, New York, 1995.

Bobby Locke on Golf, Bobby Locke, Country Life, London, 1953.

Nancy Lopez' The Complete Golfer, Nancy Lopez with Don Wade, Contemporary Books, Chicago, 1987.

The Master of Putting, George Low with Al Barkow, Atheneum, New York, 1983.

Champagne Tony's Golf Tips, Tony Lema with Bud Harvey, McGraw-Hill, New York, 1966.

The Golf Swing, Cary Middlecoff, edited by Tom Michael, Prentice Hall, Englewood Cliffs, N.J., 1974.

Pure Golf, Johnny Miller with Dale Shankland, Doubleday, Garden City, N.Y., 1976.

Shape Your Swing the Modern Way, Byron Nelson with Larry Dennis, Golf Digest Books/Simon and Schuster, New York, 1976.

The Full Swing, Jack Nicklaus with Ken Bowden, Golf Digest Books/Simon and Schuster, New York, 1982.

My 55 Ways to Lower Your Golf Score, Jack Nicklaus, Simon and Schuster, New York, 1962.

Go for Broke, Arnold Palmer, Simon and Schuster, New York, 1973.

My Game and Yours, Arnold Palmer, Simon and Schuster, New York, 1963.

Situation Golf, Arnold Palmer, McCall, New York, 1970.

A Woman's Guide to Better Golf, Judy Rankin with Peter McCleery, Contemporary Books, Chicago, 1995.

Corey Pavin's Shotmaking, Corey Pavin with Guy Yocom, Golf Digest Books/Pocket Books, New York, 1996.

Harvey Penick's Little Red Book, Harvey Penick with Bud Shrake, Simon and Schuster, New York, 1992.

And If You Play Golf, You're My Friend, Harvey Penick with Bud Shrake, Simon and Schuster, New York, 1993.

For All Who Love the Game, Harvey Penick with Bud Shrake, Simon and Schuster, New York, 1995.

Harvey Penick's The Game for a Lifetime, Harvey Penick with Bud Shrake, Simon and Schuster, New York, 1996.

Golf Begins at 50, Gary Player with Desmond Tolhurst, Simon and Schuster, New York, 1988.

The Short Way to Lower Scoring, Paul Runyan with Dick Aultman, Golf Digest Books/Simon and Schuster, New York, 1979.

The Secret of . . . Holing Putts!, Horton Smith with Dawson Taylor, A.S. Barnes, New York, 1961 (re-released in 1982 as *The Master's Secrets of Putting*).

Natural Golf, Sam Snead, A.S. Barnes, New York, 1953.

Golf Begins at Forty, Sam Snead with Dick Aultman, The Dial Press, New York, 1978.

The Education of a Golfer, Sam Snead with Al Stump, Simon and Schuster, New York, 1962.

Dave Stockton's Putt to Win, Dave Stockton with Al Barkow, Simon and Schuster, New York, 1996.

How to Become a Complete Golfer, Bob Toski and Jim Flick with Larry Dennis, Golf Digest Books/Simon and Schuster, New York, 1984.

Mickey Wright: Play Golf the Wright Way, Mickey Wright, Doubleday, Garden City, N.Y., 1962.

Getting Up and Down, Tom Watson with Nick Seitz, Golf Digest Books/Random House, New York, 1983.

Championship Golf, Mildred (Babe) Didrikson Zaharias, A.S. Barnes, New York, 1948.

Some of the better recent releases include *Golf: the Scientific Way,* Alastair Cochran; *Augusta: Home of the Masters Tournament,* J. Stephen Eubanks; *Fairway to Heaven: My Lessons from Harvey Penick on Golf & Life,* Tom Kite; *View from the Rough,* Mike Klemme; *Every Shot I Take,* Davis Love III; *Spirit of St. Andrews,* Alister Mackenzie (posthumously); *Kingdom of Shivas Irons,* Michael Murphy; *Byron Nelson's Little Black Book,* Byron Nelson; *Tiger Woods: The Makings of a Champion,* Tim Rosaforte; *Golf Has Never Failed Me,* Donald Ross (posthumously); *Golf is a Game of Confidence,* and *Golf is Not a Game of Perfect,* both by Dr. Bob Rotella; *Tiger Woods,* a biography by John Strege; and *Training a Tiger,* by Earl Woods.

GOLF IN THE MOVIES

Golf's penetration into high society during its early years in America, along with its later growth in the public sector, made it a natural as the main story line or part of the background in numerous motion pictures.

Unfortunately, golf movies haven't been of Oscar quality. Often, the sport is portrayed as buffoonish, full of self-absorbed people who devote their lives to a silly game. It's probably safe to say there hasn't been one golf film that totally captures the spirit of the game to any great extent.

Some actors, such as Robert Wagner and Sean Connery, swung the club well enough that they looked like legitimate players. Others (you can discover them for yourselves) look like they had just picked up a club for the first time and look uncomfortable having to do the scene.

The best golf movies were the ones that didn't focus totally on playing golf but simply made golf part of the landscape. The golf scene in *Goldfinger,* for instance, works well because it's a small part of a bigger plot. The scene only lasts four or five minutes, was well done, and depicted golf and golfers accurately.

It is hoped that the future of golf movies is headed toward biographies and adaptations of golf novels, rather than the Happy Gilmore-type movie (see below) that is pure nonsense and doesn't show why millions of people love the game with a passion.

Legends such as Bobby Jones are always good movie subjects, as certainly Tiger Woods will be. There has been a barrage of new golf novels in the 1990s, some of them slated for screen treatment. One of them was the Turk Pipkin novel, *Fast Greens.*

An often-mentioned golf novel that's worthy of making into a movie is *Golf in the Kingdom,* the mystical story of a golfer who discovers the spiritual secrets of golf at St. Andrews after meeting guru Shivas Irons. Everyone's main candidates for the characters are Clint Eastwood and Sean Connery.

Here's a list of some of the well-known movies that featured golf, and comments on the specific golf connection. There are many more films than these that mention golf, but these included references or scenes that stayed with the viewer. Watch for these films on television or check them out from the local video store.

Animal House (1978)—Bad frat boys Tim Matheson and Peter Riegart practice their swings by hitting balls toward a mean ROTC drill officer.
Riegart is off the mark, but Matheson drills the officer's horse in the
rear, causing it to dart around the field with the poor guy in tow. Afterward, Matheson gives sound advice to Riegart about keeping his head
down and hitting through the ball.

Babe (1975)—Before there was Babe the pig, Susan Clark portrayed the life
of the legendary Babe Didrikson Zaharias in this well-done tribute made
for television. Alex Karras is in the George Zaharias role.

Banning (1967)—The same Susan Clark in *Babe* is one of the female leads in
this tale of a swanky Los Angeles country club where pro Robert
Wagner must deal with all the usual behind-the-scenes shenanigans.

Bat*21 (1988)—Golf fanatic Gene Hackman, playing an Air Force colonel,
must use his golf wits and terminology in guiding pilot Danny Glover to
rescue him when he's shot down in Vietnam. A good example of a golf
movie that didn't put golf in the spotlight but let it emerge as an important element of the plot. Hackman gets the funny line of telling a
hacker after a missed shot: "You're standing too close to the ball. . .after
you hit it."

Breaking In (1989)—Burt Reynolds is an aging safecracker who tells an
apprentice his thoughts on the profession while on a golf course.

Bruce Lee, We Miss You (1981)—Unbelievably, a martial arts expert whacks
away at the murderer of a kung-fu film star while on a golf course.

The Caddy (1953)—Jerry Lewis plays the slapstick caddy to Dean Martin's aspiring tour pro in a movie more noted for the cameos of Ben Hogan, Sam Snead, Byron Nelson, and Julius Boros, plus the Martin song "That's Amore."

Caddyshack (1980)—The cult classic that traditionalists hate and everyone else loves. Bill Murray plays a caddie/greenkeeper at a stuffy country club, where Ted Knight is the stuffiest member, Chevy Chase the coolest, and Rodney Dangerfield is stepping on everyone's toes. There are enough subplots going to keep your interest. If you just take it as good, plain fun, you can't help but like it.

Caddyshack II (1988)—The disappointing sequel to the original, but how could anything measure up to the first one. Chevy Chase is back, with Dan Aykroyd, and Jackie Mason is in the Dangerfield role from Caddyshack I, trying to loosen up the country club snobs. This film knocked golf pictures for a loop—downward.

Call Me Bwana (1963)—Bob Hope, while on an African safari, encounters Arnold Palmer playing golf among the wild animals. They play a few holes, with Arnie making a putt that circles around to the hole like a whirlpool.

Carefree (1938)—How can you go wrong with Fred Astaire showing his dancing and golfing prowess at the same time. Look for his dance routine done to "Since they turned Loch Lomond into Swing," while hitting five tee balls in succession. The scene took two weeks to shoot and required 300 balls.

Dead Solid Perfect (1988)—Originally a TV movie based on the Dan Jenkins novel. Randy Quaid plays the PGA Tour pro who tries to overcome the temptations of women and alcohol to make it big. You end up not caring if he does.

Down Periscope (1996)—Kelsey Grammer is a submarine commander who hits golf balls off the deck of his sub, while barking, "Get up there, you miserable little puke!" Honest.

Follow the Sun (1951)—Glenn Ford portrays Ben Hogan in this mediocre telling of Hogan's comeback from a near tragic car-bus crash. Because this movie failed to connect with the audience and golf fans, it's sometimes blamed for setting back golf as a motion picture subject. Ford had to practice so hard to develop a good swing that he grew to dislike the game and never played it again. Part of he fun in this movie is trying to tell which scenes are Ford and which ones have the real Hogan as a stand-in.

Goldfinger (1964)—Sean Connery, as British agent James Bond 007, plays Auric Goldfinger (Gert Frobe) in an eighteen-hole match. Goldfinger's caddie, Odd Job (Harold Sakata), does the old ball-down-the-pantsleg routine to cheat on the seventeenth, but Bond and his caddie, Hawker, revel in outwitting Goldfinger on eighteen to win the match. Hawker utters the memorable line, "If that's his original ball, sir, I'm Arnold Palmer."

The Golf Specialist (1930)—Golf pro W.C. Fields tries to teach a woman how to play golf.

Happy Gilmore (1996)—Adam Sandler is Gilmore, a hockey guy who discovers his great slapshot also hits the ball a mile. He turns the tour into his own farcical domain. Lee Trevino makes a cameo, and TV show host Bob Barker has a memorable fight with Gilmore during a pro-am.

How to Commit Marriage (1969)—Jackie Gleason, Bob Hope, and a monkey play golf.

Houseguest (1996)—A conartist (played by Sinbad) impersonates an oral surgeon who stays at the home of a friend (Phil Hartman) for a few days to attend a convention. They spend part of one day playing golf at Sewickly Country Club but end up zooming around the course in carts to escape some bad guys.

M*A*S*H (1970)—The crazy medical unit operating during the Korean War, headed by Donald Sutherland and Elliott Gould, hits balls off the helicopter pad.

The Old Fashioned Way (1934)—W.C. Fields manages a troupe of performers and during their travels he gets into a snit with a member of the exclusive Vandersnoot Golf and Country Club.

Ordinary People (1980)—One of the shortest golf scenes is in this movie, with Mary Tyler Moore and Donald Sutherland filmed at the end of a round heading for the bar.

The Parent Trap (1961)—Brian Keith and Hayley Mills have a father-daughter chat with the eighteenth hole at Pebble Beach and the bay as a backdrop.

Pat and Mike (1952)—Babe Zaharias, Patty Berg, and other top women golfers appeared in this film about Spencer Tracy managing the career of a top female athlete played by Katharine Hepburn.

The Philadelphia Story (1940)—It's a sad opening scene when socialite Katharine Hepburn throws out her husband, Cary Grant, and his golf clubs, too. She even snaps one of the clubs in half.

Sergeant Bilko (1996)—Steve Martin plays the title role in this remake of the TV series. His big golf moment is hitting practice shots onto a field and nailing a soldier marching in formation.

Should Married Men Go Home (1928)—Stan Laurel and Oliver Hardy join two women at a club to play as a foursome, with obvious hilarity.

The Sting (1973)—Robert Shaw as highroller Doyle Lonnegan plots his next move while on the practice putting green.

Sunset Boulevard (1950)—William Holden explains that when he tried to find his agent he found him working on his game at Bel Air Country Club.

Three Little Beers (1935)—The Three Stooges, playing employees of the Panther Brewing Company, enter the company's golf tournament even though they've never played golf before.

Tin Cup (1996)—Mildly successful tale of Kevin Costner as Roy "Tin Cup" McAvoy, a once-promising golfer who hangs out at a west Texas driving range. Rene Russo is the female interest who is around when McAvoy makes a comeback. The movie is fairly accurate in most areas, but the ending stretches the limits of believability. Has several cameos by PGA Tour golfers.

Viva Las Vegas (1964)—Elvis Presley and Ann-Margret have a moment
together at a golf course.

There have been numerous other golf movies or vignettes, beginning with silent pictures such as *Pleasure Before Business* and *The Golf Widows*. The Our Gang group went golfing in the 1936 film *Divot Diggers,* and Hal Roach Studios made the film *All Teed Up* in 1930 based on the studio's annual golf outing.

Bob Hope and Bing Crosby made golf references in their "road" pictures, and others were made in the old Charlie Chan and Nick Carter series of films. There were three British films made in 1924 of P.G. Wodehouse stories: *Rodney Fails to Qualify, Chester Forgets Himself,* and *Ordeal by Golf.* Agatha Christie's golf murder mystery, *Murder on the Links,* was made into a movie. Also in the early '20s, Walter Hagen appeared in *Green Grass Widows,* a film that starred fellow golfer Leo Diegel along with Marge Beebe and Andy Clyde. And Mack Sennett made a golf comedy in 1929 called *The Golfers.*

A great bonus is seeing two of the all-time greatest TV comedy skits on the same tape, and both deal with golf. A "Honeymooners" episode in which Jackie Gleason (as Ralph Kramden) learns to play golf with the help of his friend Art Carney (Norton) has been paired with an "I Love Lucy" episode on the same video. In that show, Lucille Ball (Lucy) and Vivien Vance (Ethel) get the wool pulled over their eyes by husbands Desi Arnaz (Ricky) and William Frawley (Fred) when they try to butt in and learn the game. Guest Jimmy Demaret sees their plight and helps them turn the tables on Ricky and Fred in the end. If you see this tape available, consider it a good buy.

THE POPULAR VIDEO MARKET

The golf video market had a huge boom from the late 1970s to the early 1990s, but then tapered off when computer games became more popular. The new videos today mainly consist of tournament highlight tapes and an occasional instruction tape.

Tapes can be purchased at golf shops and stores, and also through the GolfSmart and Eyelevel phone-ordering companies mentioned before. Most libraries will have a golf video or two in their collection. The tapes below are among the best produced and nearly all of them are still available for purchase.

Art of Putting—A popular video from putting marksman Ben Crenshaw.

Beginning Golf for Women—One of the better women's golf tapes, demonstrated by LPGA tour pro Donna Horton White.

British Open—Tapes dating back many years were made over in Great Britain, but availability in the United States is limited.

Candid Camera's Golf Gags—If you're looking for golf humor on video, this one will do you nicely; much preferred over the *Dorf on Golf* series done by Tim Conway.

The Complete History of Golf—A marvelous four-video set put out by the PGA of America; phone the PGA at (561) 624-8400 for full information.

Conquering Golf with Butch Harmon—A four-video set in which Tiger Woods' swing coach teaches the game.

Nick Faldo's Fixes—The six-time major championship winner gets too technical sometimes, but he knows his stuff.

Golf and All Its Glory—Six-video set; Vol. 1, "From Paupers to Princes"; Vol. 2, "The Magic of the Majors"; Vol. 3, "Links with Tradition"; Vol. 4, "At Play on Golden Mountain"; Vol. 5, "Golf Versus Technology:; Vol. 6, "Why Golf?"; originally done in England, this historical set was available at one time in the United States.

Golf Digest: Getting Started Right and *Hit It Longer and Straighter*—Two tapes using the experts from the Golf Digest Schools.

Golf for Kids—Wally Armstrong's breakthrough video for juniors; he uses a lot of imagery to explain swing thoughts.

Golf from the Other Side—Nicely done tape by lefty Bob Charles.

Golf Made Easy—A women's video for fans of Nancy Lopez.

Golf with Al Geiberger—One of the tapes that got the whole video business going, this Sybervision tape is an original worth watching.

Heroes of the Game—This USGA tape was done by producer David L. Wolper; nicely entertaining tape about the game's legends.

High Performance Golf—Tips from such pro teachers as Butch Harmon, Hank Haney, and Bob Rotella.

The History of the PGA Tour—It's exactly what it says, beginning with the tour origins in the early 1900s.

Bobby Jones: How I Play Golf—This is a series of four tapes, which put together Jones' thoughts on the swing from the films he made in the 1930s. Excellent to watch simply to see Jones in action.

David Leadbetter's from Beginner to Winner—The well-known swing coach for Nick Faldo and Nick Price provides tips on how to learn the swing as a beginner.

David Leadbetter's Faults and Fixes—With Nick Price; of the seven tapes Leadbetter has done, this is probably his best.

David Leadbetter's Practice Makes Perfect—Numerous drills to use on the practice range.

The Masters Tournament—Available to the public from the last ten to twelve Masters.

Johnny Miller's Golf Clinic and *Johnny Miller's Golf Tips*—The tour great turned broadcaster always has a unique look at every part of the swing.

Byron Nelson's Timeless Golf Lessons—A solid swing tape from the man recognized as the Father of the Modern Golf Swing.

Jack Nicklaus: Golf My Way series of two tapes and *Golf My Way* series of three tapes—Control shots, full swing, and short game. Nicklaus's video work is highly regarded and some of the best done by touring pros.

Leslie Nielsen: Bad Golf Made Easier and *Bad Golf My Way*—Definitely not classic golf humor; it takes an acquired taste to enjoy these.

Greg Norman: The Complete Golfer—Set of two tapes; this set is more recommended than the newer *Better Golf* package; in *Complete Golfer,* he does both the long game and short game.

Arnold Palmer Fundamentals—This multivolume set was well done and passed along "The King's" swing tips in an easy to understand manner.

Harvey Penick: Little Green Video and *Little Red Video*—Both match up with his books of similar titles; Tom Kite and Ben Crenshaw appear in both videos.

PGA Championship—Tapes of the event have been made each year beginning in 1993; selected events were done prior to that.

Rules of Golf—A video hosted by Johnny Miller, is excellent for explaining the rules; produced by the USGA.

Ryder Cup—Hour-long tapes have been made of each Ryder Cup starting in 1993.

Shell's Wonderful World of Golf—If you can get your hands on the original series from the '60s, do so. It's wonderful stuff to see the past greats in action. There are thirty tapes available, each with a great golfer playing another great at an international locale.

Sam Snead: A Swing for a Lifetime—An analysis of the legendary swing, done by teacher Jim McLean.

Tiger's Triple—The exciting story of Tiger Woods's three straight U.S. Amateur victories.

Lee Trevino's Putt for Dough—If you can still find this on the market, get it. It's one of the better putting tapes and Trevino is in fine form.

U.S. Open—The USGA has tapes dating back to the early '60s available for purchase of its Open championship (phone 1-800-755-0293).

Ken Venturi—The 1964 U.S. Open champion has two tapes, *Better Golf Now* and *Stroke Savers* that have solid instruction useful for all players.

Tiger Woods: Son, Hero & Champion—A biography of golf's newest young superstar.

REMEMBERING WHEN

Golfers who like to delve into the history of the sport, even as far back as the 1700s, have some allies in their desire to know as much as possible about golf's important events and people.

The Golf Collectors Society was begun in 1970 and now has 2,300 dues-paying members who converse about collectibles through a newsletter and occasional meetings and auctions. The society contact address is P.O. Box 20546, Dayton, Ohio 45420, phone (937) 256-2474 and fax (937) 256-2974.

The Golf Collectors Society is the leading group in the preservation and collection of golf artifacts, which has grown into a major business/hobby in the 1990s. People collect for the fun of it, as a hobby, or to turn their house into a golf decor. The business has grown so much that a major concern is the authenticity of objects and/or their worthiness as a collectible, and there's confusion over what the proper pricing should be for some items.

Because millions of dollars are paid for extremely rare clubs, anyone with old golf pieces sitting around should take care not to destroy or throw away something without having them examined. In addition to asking the Golf Collectors Society, persons with rare items can check with a collector friend, an auction house, or a local golf professional and club repairperson. Two books that are fine references for golf antiques are *Golf Antiques & Other Treasures of the Game,* and *The Encyclopedia of Golf Collectibles,* both put together by John and Morton Olman. They are available through Market Street Press, phone 1-800-433-1000.

Here's a sampling of the hundreds of kinds of objects that experts would call golf collectibles: embroidery, chairs with cloth patterns, clothing, recordings, license plates, club ballot boxes, flasks, buttons, badges, jewelry, toys, figurines, games, scorecards, admission badges, programs, postcards, illustrations, art prints, photographs, posters, vases, tables, glasses, trophies, sculptures, autographs, letters, stamps, sheet music, advertisements, magazines, greeting cards, cigarette cards, books, clothes, tees, bags, ball packaging, and, of course, clubs and balls. Champion golfers are even selling their special mementos, such as Jack Fleck selling his 1955 U.S. Open medal for $36,000.

The other historical source is the extensive number of golf museums or collections around the country. Here are some of the main locations that showcase golf history.

American Golf Hall of Fame—More than 400 years of golf history are part of this library and museum located at Foxburg Country Club's clubhouse on Harvey Road in Foxburg, Pennsylvania. Foxburg is credited by many as the oldest golf course in continuous use in the United States, having opened in 1887. The museum is open seven days a week, 8 A.M. to dark, April 1 to October 31. Phone (412) 659-3196.

The British Golf Museum—Located in the shadow of the Royal and Ancient building in St. Andrews, Scotland, this reserved but informative museum opened in 1990 and has a great deal of memorabilia and exhibits. Being located in the "home of golf," the museum is a must-see site along with the Old Course, the burial site of Old and Young Tom Morris, and the town itself. The museum traces the game from its origins to today's great champion golfers on a self-guided tour. It's open 9:30 A.M. to 5:30 P.M. seven days a week, Easter time to late October. During winter it's closed Tuesday and Wednesday and the hours are 11 A.M. to 3 P.M. Adult admission is 3.75 British pounds. Phone 011-44-133-447-8880 from the United States.

Ben Hogan Trophy Room—Colonial Country Club in Fort Worth, Texas, has set aside one room to display a host of Hogan's awards and trophies. The club, at 3735 Country Club Circle, phone (817) 927-4278, is open daily 8 A.M. to dark, but is closed on Mondays.

James River Country Club Museum and Library—Begun in 1932, this golf museum is probably the oldest in the world. It's located at 1500 Country Club Road, Newport News, Virginia. Its one primary room has dozens of old clubs from the 1700s and 1800s and feathery balls, too. There are many rare books from golf's early years as well. The museum is open 9 A.M. to 9 P.M. daily year-round, but is closed on Mondays. Entry is free to the public, but it's always best to call ahead before coming. Phone (757) 595-3327.

Ralph W. Miller Library and Museum—This West Coast facility houses the forty-year collection of Miller, a Los Angeles attorney. There are more than 6,000 books and periodicals, plus clubs, balls, and golf art. The museum is located at the Industry Hills Recreation and Conference Center, 1 Industry Hills Parkway, City of Industry, California, phone (818) 854-2354. The museum is open daily except for Mondays.

Robert Tyre Jones Jr. Room at Atlanta Athletic Club—Jones admirers will want to see this room that recently went through a renovation. There are 200 pieces of Jones memorabilia, including replicas of his Grand Slam trophies. The public may view the room by phoning ahead at (770) 448-2166. The club is located on Highway 141 in Duluth, Georgia, in north Fulton County. There is no charge.

Jack Nicklaus Museum—Although there is plenty of Nicklaus memorabilia located at his Muirfield Village Golf Club in Dublin, Ohio, northwest of Columbus, it's not convenient for public viewing. The bigger plans call for an 18,000-square-foot Jack Nicklaus Museum to go up on the campus of his alma mater, Ohio State, as part of a university sports complex. Completion will probably take place in 1999.

Ouimet Museum and Golf House—Located in the Massachusetts Golf Association building is this site devoted to Francis Ouimet, the amateur great from the

Boston area who won the historic 1913 U.S. Open playoff with British greats Harry Vardon and Ted Ray, thus kicking off a surge in fine play by American golfers. There are also tributes to other Massachusetts golfing greats. The museum is at 190 Park Road, Weston, Massachusetts, phone (617) 891-6400. There's no admission fee and the museum is open 9 A.M. to 4:30 P.M. Monday through Friday.

PGA of America—The home of the club professionals' association does not have a formal museum, but it's still worth visiting for its displays and seeing the headquarters complex. The PGA of America is located at 100 Avenue of the Champions, Palm Beach Gardens, Florida, phone (561) 624-8400.

Royal Canadian Golf Association—This museum has been put into a new building at the Glen Abbey Golf Club, located in Oakville, Ontario, phone (905) 844-1800. It's open year-round, 10 A.M. to 5 P.M., Thursday through Monday. There is a $4 admission charge. The collection covers the history of the game in its infancy, then switches to predominantly Canadian golf history after that.

Tournament Players Club at Sawgrass—This site of the annual Players Championship, at 110 TPC Boulevard in Ponte Vedra Beach, Florida, has a lobby full of golf artifacts, the most visible being a collection of the golf trophies awarded at a number of PGA Tour events. And if you're at the TPC course, it means you're within a Tiger Woods tee shot of the tour headquarters, which has limited artifacts. You can get more information on the club and the tour office by calling the PGA Tour main number, (904) 285-3700.

Tufts Archives in Pinehurst—Located at the Given Memorial Library in Pinehurst, North Carolina, this exhibit area devotes much of its space to the history of the Pinehurst area and the influence on it by architect Donald Ross. It's open 9:30 A.M. to 5 P.M. Monday through Friday and 9:30 A.M. to 12:30 P.M. on Saturday; it's closed Sundays. The library number is (910) 295-6022. There is no entrance fee.

U.S. Golf Association—The Golf House museum and library at the USGA headquarters is America's most notable museum. Located in a Georgian colonial since 1972, the museum has a vast collection of famous clubs, such as Alan Shepard's moon club, plus all types of balls amid displays that trace the growth of the game from its origins. There are golf art pieces and apparel and rotating special displays or exhibits. Its library has the largest collection of books available to the public, with more than 8,000 volumes. Golf House is located on Liberty Corner Road in Far Hills, New Jersey. It's open 9 A.M. to 5 P.M. Monday through

Friday and 10 A.M. to 4 P.M. on Saturday and Sunday. There is no entry fee. Phone (908) 234-2300.

World Golf Hall of Fame—Pinehurst, North Carolina, used to be the home of this museum and hall of fame beginning in 1974. But poor attendance was one reason it was closed; however, it will move to the World Golf Village planned for opening in 1998 in St. Johns County near Jacksonville, Florida. The special feature of this museum will be that it's the first time all of the major golf organizations will work together to honor the game and its players in one central location. The World Golf Hall of Fame building will be as large as 75,000 square feet in size to house seventy exhibits and a 300-seat IMAX theater. The new museum will continue the work of the first and continue to induct new members into the World Golf Hall of Fame. Phone the PGA Tour, (904) 285-3700.

Babe Didrikson Zaharias Museum—Perhaps the most famous and best female athlete ever has a museum devoted to her in her birthplace of Beaumont, Texas, at 1750 I-10 East, phone (409) 833-4622. There is no entrance fee and the museum is open 9 A.M. to 5 P.M. every day of the year, except Christmas. After excelling in track and field and any other sport she tried, Babe finished her career with a marvelous golf record before her death in the 1950s. This museum has artifacts on her entire sports career.

Small collections devoted to the history of golf are also located at other isolated spots around the world. In the United States, some private clubs have small displays in hallways or separate rooms. For instance, Augusta National Golf Club in Georgia has memorabilia throughout its clubhouse, which is off limits to the public. Old Marsh Golf Club in Palm Beach Gardens, Florida, has an extensive collection of old clubs from the Auchterlonie family, for so long a part of the Royal and Ancient Golf Club in St. Andrews, Scotland. When you learn of these collections, you must always call for permission to view them or see them in the presence of a club member.

GOLF'S "YELLOW PAGES"

An often-overlooked source of information on all aspects of the golf business and golf's impact on its players is the National Golf Foundation in Jupiter, Florida. In recent years it has published what many would call "the yellow pages of golf."

It's called the *National Golf Foundation's 1998 International Directory of Golf,* and it lists more than 7,500 golf companies, events and associations, and more than 14,000 golf executives, with phone numbers and addresses. There are also 2,500 Internet Web sites and addresses. The directory, at 500-plus pages, is priced at $60 and can be ordered by phoning 1-800-733-6006.

 Chapter 16

BECOMING A GOLF WORDSMITH

I t's not like using Morse Code, but the language that experienced golfers use seems just as baffling to new players. Take, for instance, this commentary that a golfer might say to another member of the group after hitting a shot toward the green—"I definitely pured that one. No banana ball for me. I hit it right on the screws, rather than my usual chunk. I'm on the dance floor, although I can't quite hear the music. I'll have a snake for my first putt, but I just hope I don't three-jack it."

What the fellow would be saying is that he hit a great shot—for him—but he has a long putt on the green. He hopes he doesn't three-putt.

Part of feeling comfortable with longtime golfers is knowing how to talk golf-talk well enough that you understand even the oddest-sounding remarks. When you can respond to someone as in the example above without thinking twice about what you're saying, you know you've come a long way in this game.

There's a lot of slang talk in golf, but the following words and terms are the more straightforward ones that are part of the golf lingo you're likely to come across. Golf has the most wide-ranging collection of words, phrases, and terms of any sport. As you read them, you're sure to recognize many that have become a part of everyday language. And as you play, you'll pick up on some of the slang phrases that many golfers freely throw around.

Ace—(1) Holing out with the tee shot (see hole-in-one); (2) an expert player.

Address—The golfer's stance and posture prior to swinging the club.

Advice—See glossary reference in Chapter 8.

Airmail—A shot that flies over and lands beyond the back of the putting green.

Albatross—Another word for double eagle.

All square—When one side is tied with the opposing side.

Amateur—A golfer who doesn't accept prize money or other compensation.

Amateur side—See low side.

Angle of approach—The path the clubhead travels upon striking the ball; also called "angle of attack."

Approach—The full shot played from the fairway or rough to the green on par-4 and par-5 holes.

Apron—Short-cut grass surrounding the green.

Attest—To verify that the score for a round is correct.

Away—The golfer farthest from the hole, either on the fairway or green, who plays first.

Back door—A putt that falls into the cup by entering on the far side.

Back nine—Also known as the "in nine" or "inward half"; the second nine holes of an eighteen-hole round.

Backspin—Reverse spin put on the ball at impact to make it stop quickly on the green.

Backswing—The swing portion from address to the top of the swing.

Backweighting—Adding weight to the back of a clubhead so the center of gravity is moved backward in order to hit higher trajectory shots.

Baffie—Old term for a 4-wood in the wooden-shaft era.

Bailout areas—"Safe" locations where the golfer can play to on a hole, to avoid hitting into trouble.

Ball—Must not measure less than 1.68 inches in diameter and weigh no more than 1.62 ounces. For glossary references to "ball holed," "ball in play," "ball lost," "ball mark," and "ball moved," see definitions in Chapter 8.

Ball mark—Indentation made when the ball lands on the green.

Banana ball—Ball-flight curvature sharply from left to right.

Bent grass—Type of grass that grows best in northern climates and is used on greens and tees.

Bermuda grass—Type of grass that grows best in hotter regions.

Best ball—Playing format in which the best individual score among teams of two or more players counts toward the team's final score; also better ball.

Birdie—Score on a hole that is one stroke less than par.

Bite—See backspin; how well the ball stops upon hitting the green.

Blade—(1) Putter with a thin clubhead; (2) poorly hit shot in which the ball is struck by the club's leading edge.

Blast—A bunker shot played when the ball is partially buried.

Blind hole—A hole in which the fairway, landing area, and/or green is hidden from the player's view.

Blind shot—Stroke played to a landing area that's hidden from view.

Bogey—Score on a hole that is one stroke more than par.

Borrow—The amount of break or curvature to a putt; same as break.

Bounce—When the trailing edge of the sole is below the leading edge of the sole when the ball is struck squarely.

Brassie—Old term for a 2-wood in the wooden-shaft era.

Break—The amount of curvature as the ball rolls toward the hole on a putt, caused by the green's slopes; also known as borrow.

Bulge—The curvature across the face of a wooden club.

Bump-and-run shot—A low, running shot that is best played to a green that is absent sand and water in front and has fairly flat ground.

Bunker—Depression in the fairway, rough, or near the green that is usually filled with sand, but sometimes just grass, also called a trap. See glossary reference in Chapter 8.

Buried lie—Ball nearly or completely covered in a sand bunker.

Butt end—The end of the club held by the golfer.

Bye—Exemption from playing an opening match in a match-play tournament.

Caddie—Someone assigned to carry a golfer's clubs during play and is allowed to give advice on club selection and strategy. Derived from the French word, cadet, which means "son of a gentleman," but which the Scottish people used in a sarcastic sense to describe a loafer.

Carry—(1) Distance a ball travels from its original spot to its point of landing; (2) amount of land a ball needs to clear to reach a targeted area.

Cart path—The gravel or paved road on a golf course intended for driving carts. It usually runs along tees and greens and in the rough.

Casual water—See glossary reference in Chapter 8.

Cavity-back irons—Clubs with weight removed from the back of the clubhead and redistributed around the clubhead perimeter. A forgiving club for poorer players.

Chili-dip—Similar to a fat shot, this is a poor shot in which a short iron digs into the ground too much during the swing. The ball might not be moved at all.

Chip shot—Short shots played around the green, with a low ball-flight trajectory.

Chop—(1) A swing motion that puts extra spin on the ball; (2) a slang term for a poor player.

Chunk—Poorly hit shot in which the club hits the ground before hitting the ball, severely affecting ball flight.

Close lie—Occurs when the ball sits directly on top of the ground with little or no grass underneath it.

Closed face—A clubface aimed left of the intended target line; can occur at any point of the swing.

Closed stance—Address posture with the left foot closer to the target line than the right (for a right-handed player).

Clubbing—Assisting a player in club selection on the course.

Clubface—Grooved portion of the clubhead that makes contact with the ball.

Clubhouse—The main building at a golf course where the pro shop, locker rooms, and eating and social areas are located.

Collar—Short-cut grass surrounding the putting green; also called the fringe.

Comebacker—The short putt that results from running a longer putt past the hole.

Committee—See glossary reference in Chapter 8.

Course—Includes the entire area where play is permitted.

Course rating—The score a 0-handicap player would be expected to shoot from a certain set of tees; the rating differs from course to course. The easier the course, the lower the rating.

Cross bunker—A fairway bunker that intrudes into the fairway in the landing area for most drives.

Crosshanded—Unorthodox grip style of putting with the left hand lower than the right for a right-handed player, and the right under the left for a lefty.

Crosswind—Wind that blows left to right or right to left as the golfer faces the putting green.

Cup—The hole in the putting green and the golfer's goal to get there in the fewest number of strokes.

Cut shot—A pitch shot in which the ball spins clockwise and rises higher and lands softer than the usual pitch.

Dance floor—Term for the putting green.

Dead—Hitting a shot so close to the hole that it's a certain one-putt.

Deuce—Making a score of 2 on a hole.

Dew-sweeper—Poorly struck shot that rolls along the grass.

Dimple—Indentation on the cover of a golf ball.

Divot—Chunk of turf removed from the ground by the clubhead at impact; the remaining hole is not the divot.

Dogleg—Usually a par-4 hole shaped like an L that bends left or right beyond the driving area.

Dormie—A term in match play used when a player leads an opponent by the same number of holes remaining to be played.

Double bogey—Score on a hole that is two strokes more than par.

Double eagle—Score on a hole that is three strokes less than par.

Down—Being on the losing side in a match.

Downswing—The swing portion from the top of the swing to impact.

Draw—Ball flight that curves slightly from right to left.

Drive—First shot played on a hole, most often with a driver.

Driver—The 1-wood.

Driving iron—A club, usually a long iron, used to hit the ball off the tee for accuracy.

Drop—See glossary reference in Chapter 8.

Drop area—Place where golfers may drop a ball in relief or penalty situations.

Dub—(1) A mis-hit shot; (2) slang term for a poor player who hits numerous "dubbed shots."

Duck hook—Ball-flight curvature sharply from right to left; the opposite of a banana ball.

Duffer—Label for a high-handicap player, similar to dub.

Dunk—(1) Hitting a shot in the water; (2) making a shot on the fly, with the ball going straight in the cup.

Eagle—Score on a hole that is two strokes less than par.

Equipment—See glossary reference in Chapter 8.

Explosion shot—Similar to a blast shot; hitting a partially buried ball out of a bunker.

Executive course—Refers to a short nine-hole course or par-3 course.

Fade—Ball flight that curves slightly from left to right.

Fairway—The short-cut grass area that connects the tee to the green.

Fat—A poorly hit shot in which the turf behind the ball is hit first and then the ball.

Feather—A left-to-right, high shot that lands softly on the green.

Feathery—Ball used primarily in the 1800s; the outside was made of leather and the inside was stuffed with a top hat amount of feathers.

Fellow competitor—In a stroke-play tournament, what one player is to another.

Flagstick—The pole and flag placed in the hole to indicate the hole's location on the green; also called the pin.

Flat stick—Phrase for putter.

Flat swing—A golf swing that is more horizontal than normal.

Floater—(1) A high shot that lands softly; (2) a ball that floats in water.

Flyer—Ball hit from the rough that has little backspin and thus rolls more than usual.

Flub—Poorly hit shot similar to fat and dub shots.

Follow-through—The swing portion from impact to finish.

Fore!—Traditional word of warning yelled to alert players that they are in danger of being hit by a wayward shot.

Forecaddie—Someone who stands in the rough near the driving area to mark where errant drives finish.

Forward press—Slight movement of the knee or hands to trigger the start of the backswing.

Forward swing—The swing portion from the top of the swing to follow-through.

Four ball—Competition in which two golfers play their best ball against the best ball of two others.

Foursome—(1) A group of four players; (2) competition in which two-person teams play against each other in an alternate-shot format.

Fried egg—A ball half-covered in a sand bunker.

Fringe—Closely cut grass surrounding the putting green; same as the apron.

Frog hair—See fringe.

Front nine—Also known as the "out nine" or "outward half"; the first nine holes of an eighteen-hole round.

Gallery—Spectators at a golf tournament or match.

Gimme—A putt so short that it is usually conceded by other players in the group; violates the Rules of Golf.

Golf shop—See pro shop.

Grain—Direction the grass on the putting green grows or lies; affects the break of the ball.

Green—The extremely short-cut grass area used for putting.

Green fee—Cost for a round of golf.

Greenies—Betting game on par-3 holes; player who hits the ball closest to the hole, and makes a par or birdie, wins on that par 3.

Greenkeeper—Superintendent of the grounds crew.

Grip—(1) Putting your hands on the club before swinging; (2) rubber or leather wrapping on the club used by the golfer to hold it.

Grooves—Scoring lines on the clubface that spin and control the ball.

Gross score—Golfer's score without the use of handicap strokes.

Ground under repair—See glossary reference in Chapter 8.

Grounding the club—While at address, touching the ground behind the ball with the clubhead.

Guttie—Popular ball after the feathery; made from gutta-percha.

Hacker—Term for a poor golfer; sometimes just "hack." Might be taken as derogatory, unless you direct it toward yourself.

Half/halved—In match play, describes a hole or match that ends in a tie.

Halfswing—An abbreviated swing with a half-backswing and half-forward swing.

Handicap—Number of strokes a golfer receives to equalize competition between poor (high-numbered handicaps) and better (low numbered) players. See glossary reference in Chapter 7.

Hanging lie—Refers to a ball sitting on a severe downslope. The ball is above or below the player's feet.

Hardpan—Hard turf absent of any grass.

Hazard—Water and sand bunkers. See glossary reference in Chapter 8.

Headwind—Wind blowing against the player.

Heel—Portion of the clubface that connects with the hosel.

Heel-and-toe weighting—Type of club construction that distributes weight around the perimeter of the clubhead; the back of the clubhead has a hollow cavity.

Heeled shot—A poorly hit shot that connects with the heel of the club.

High handicapper—A golfer who receives a high number of handicap strokes, such as 30 or more.

High side—Area to the right of the hole on a right-to-left breaking putt; to the left on a left-to-right putt. Also called the pro side.

Hit a house—Phrase spoken by a golfer urging his putt to slow down near the hole.

Hit it sideways—Golfer's description of playing a round in which the ball is hit all over the place and inconsistently.

Hole—Round opening on the putting green that is 4 inches wide and must be 4 inches deep; also called the cup.

Hole high—Ball that finishes level with the hole on the green or to either side.

Hole-in-one—Making the first shot on a hole.

Home—Used to describe the putting green. When selecting a club, a golfer might ask the caddie, "What do I need to get home from here?"

Honor—See glossary reference in Chapter 8.

Hood—Occurs when the toe of the clubface is ahead of the heel, which decreases the loft of the club.

Hook—Ball flight that sharply curves from right to left.

Hosel—The clubhead portion that connects the shaft and head.

Imbedded lie—Ball that imbeds in wet or muddy turf.

Impact—Precise moment when the clubface and the ball meet during the swing.

In regulation—Refers to hitting onto the fairway in one shot off the tee, and in getting onto the green in the correct number of shots.

Inside—The ground on the golfer's side of the target line.

Inside out—Swinging the club inside the intended target line on the backswing and to the right of it after impact.

Intended line—An imaginary line that starts at the ball and extends to where the player wants the ball to go.

Intermediate target—An aiming point used to line up a shot to a target.

In the leather—A putt slightly longer than a gimme. Originally, it meant the length of a leather grip, now thought to be the length of the clubhead to the bottom of the grip.

Irons—Clubs numbered from 1 to 9 and the wedges; the lower the number, the farther the ball travels.

Jigger—Club used for run-up shots.

Knee-knocker—A short putt, usually in the three-foot range.

Knockdown shot—Partial shot that produces a low trajectory; similar to a half-swing.

Lag—Striking a putt of 25 feet or more so that the ball finishes within a few feet of the hole.

Lateral water hazard—See glossary reference in Chapter 8.

Lay-up shot—Strategic shot played to keep the ball short of a trouble area.

Lie—(1) How well the ball sits on the turf; (2) current number of strokes played on a hole, as in "What do you lie?"; (3) angle formed between the clubshaft and the sole of the club.

Line of play—See glossary reference in Chapter 8.

Line of putt—See glossary reference in Chapter 8.

Links—Traditional meaning is a course by the sea; today it is incorrectly used by some in referring to any type of course.

Lip—Edge of the hole or a sand bunker.

Lip out—Putt that rims or rolls along the edge of the hole and spins away.

Lob shot—A pitch shot with high trajectory that lands softly and rolls a short distance.

Local rules—See glossary reference in Chapter 8.

Loft—Amount in degrees of clubface angle.

Long game—A golfer's individual ability with long irons.

Long iron—The least-lofted irons; the 1-, 2-, and 3-irons.

Loose impediments—See glossary reference in Chapter 8.

Lost ball—See glossary reference in Chapter 8.

Low handicapper—A golfer who receives a low number of handicap strokes, such as 10 or less.

Low side—Area to the left of the hole on a right-to-left breaking putt; to the right on a left-to-right putt; also called the amateur side.

Margarita—Similar to the "back door"; refers to a ball that travels around the edge of the hole and falls in.

Marker—Person appointed to tally a player's score in a stroke-play tournament; walks with the player around the course.

Mashie—Term for a 5-iron in the wooden-shaft era.

Mashie niblick—Term for a 7-iron in the wooden-shaft era.

Match play—Format in which one person or team competes against another person or team in a nine- or eighteen-hole match; the side that wins the most holes wins the match.

Medal play—Competition in which the strokes taken for a round determine the standings; professional medal play tournaments consist of three to five rounds; golfer with the lowest score wins; also called stroke play.

Medalist—Lowest individual scorer in a medal play (stroke) tournament.

Middle iron—The 4-, 5-, and 6-irons.

Middle handicapper—A golfer who receives between 10 and 30 handicap strokes.

Mis-clubbed—Making an error in club selection; refers to either overclubbing or underclubbing.

Mis-hit—Striking a ball off-center of the clubface.

Misread—Playing an improper amount of break on a putt due to reading the wrong break.

Mixed foursome—Competition in which women and men compete simultaneously.

Moved ball—A ball that moves out of the position it was in when it came to a stop.

Mulligan—Playing a second ball from the same spot as the first; usually done on the first tee; violates the Rules of Golf. Canadian David Mulligan is credited with popularizing the practice beginning in the mid-1920s.

Nap—Also known as grain; grass lying in a certain direction.

Nassau—Popular betting game usually played for three points; one each for the front and back nines and one for the entire round.

Net score—Final score after a golfer's handicap has been subtracted from the gross score.

Niblick—Term for a 9-iron during the wooden-shaft era.

Observer—An official who accompanies a group and advises on rulings.

Obstructions—See glossary reference in Chapter 8.

Off-center hit—Shot hit on the perimeter of the clubface.

Off line—Shot hit in a direction other than toward the intended target.

Open face—A clubface aimed right of the intended target line; can occur at any point of the swing.

Open stance—Standing at address with the right foot closer to the target line than the left (for a right-handed player).

Open tournament—Event that allows both amateurs and professionals to compete.

Order of play—Similar to honor; the committee establishes the order of play off the first tee in a tournament.

Out-of-bounds—See glossary reference in Chapter 8.

Outside—The ground on the far side of the ball to the outside of the target line.

Outside agency—See glossary reference in Chapter 8.

Outside in—Swinging the club outside the intended target line on the backswing and to the left of it after impact.

Overclub—Making an error in club selection; using a club that makes the ball fly farther than needed.

Overswing—Making too long of a backswing; swinging out of control.

Par—Score a good player would be expected to make on a hole, including two putts (such as taking two shots to reach the green plus two putts on a par-4 hole). See further glossary reference in Chapter 8.

Par-shooter—Golfer who most often makes pars.

Partner—Player teamed with another golfer on the same side.

Penalty stroke(s)—Added to the score as the result of a Rules of Golf violation, such as hitting a ball out-of-bounds. See Chapter 8 for further glossary reference.

Pin—See flagstick.

Pin high—See hole high.

Pitch and putt—A short, nine-hole par-3 course.

Pitch and run—A pitch shot with a low ball flight that lands short of the green and runs to the hole.

Pitch shot—Using a high-lofted club to hit short shots to the green, giving the ball a low, medium, or high trajectory.

Play through—Occurs when a slower group lets a faster one pass them during the round.

Plugged lie—A ball that remains imbedded within the hole it created upon landing; the ground is usually very wet.

Posture—Body position during the course of the swing.

Pot bunker—A small, deep sand bunker.

Preshot routine—A golfer's aiming and address routine done in preparation to swing the club.

Press—(1) Trying to play beyond a golfer's ability; (2) betting game in which a losing team may double the bet.

Pro side—See high side.

Pro shop—Place to buy a green fee and merchandise at a golf course; also known as the golf shop.

Professional—A golfer who plays the game for monetary compensation; usually a 0-handicapper or better.

Provisional ball—See glossary reference in Chapter 8.

Pull—A faulty shot in which the ball travels to the left of the target.

Punch shot—A shot that flies lower than normal; useful for playing into the wind or under trees.

Push—A faulty shot in which the ball travels to the right of the target.

Putt—One stroke taken on the putting green.

Putter—Club used for putting.

Putting clock—A practice drill of setting balls around a hole like a clock face and then hitting each ball in the hole in order.

Putting green—Area of very short-cut grass that serves as the location for the hole and flagstick.

Quadruple bogey—Score on a hole that is four strokes more than par.

Rabbit—A ball that bounces erraticly after being topped.

Reading the green—Determining a putt's amount of break. See break and borrow.

Recovery shot—An often risky shot made to the fairway or green from a trouble area such as trees or thick rough.

Referee—Official who accompanies a group to assist in rulings.

Relief—Moving the ball out of a poor ground condition. See glossary reference in Chapter 8.

Rim—Ball that rolls over the edge of the hole; same as lip out.

Rough—Tall grass that borders the fairway and surrounds the green.

Round—A complete set of holes, either nine or eighteen.

Round robin—A match-play tournament format; each player competes against every other competitor; the winner is the golfer with the best won-loss record.

Rub of the green—Occurs when a ball in flight is accidentally stopped or deflected by an outside agency, such as a forecaddie.

Run—Ball that rolls a greater distance than normal.

Run-up shot—Playing a shot short of the green with the intention of having the ball roll on.

Sand trap—Same as sand bunker.

Sandbag—A golfer who plays poorly on purpose to get an inflated handicap for their advantage in competition.

Scorecard—Card that lists hole pars and local rules and has space for player to write in her score.

Scoring lines—See grooves.

Scotch foursome—Partners in an alternate-shot format.

Scratch play—Playing format in which no handicap strokes are used.

Scratch player—A player with great skill; a 0-handicap or better.

Scuff—(1) A mis-hit shot as like a flub; (2) marking and damaging a ball's cover because of a poor shot.

Setup—A golfer's posture and ball position during address.

Shaft—The club part that links the grip and clubhead together.

Shank—A poorly hit shot that flies to the right; the ball is struck on the club's hosel.

Shooting stick—Similar to a walking stick; an umbrella with a special seat attachment for use in following groups in the gallery.

Short game—A golfer's individual ability with short irons.

Short irons—The 7-, 8-, and 9-irons and wedges.

Shot—Swinging the club with the intent of hitting the ball.

Shotgun start—A method for starting play in which groups are dispersed around the course and all start play at the same time with the signal of a gun blast or siren.

Single—A golfer playing alone.

Skins—Betting game in which a set amount of money is won by the player with the lowest score on a hole. If players tie for the lowest score, the money is added to the next hole's total.

Skull—A poorly hit shot in which only the top half of the ball is hit; also known as blade or hitting thin.

Skyed shot—A mis-hit shot that flies much higher and shorter than normal.

Slice—Ball flight that sharply curves from left to right.

Snake—A long, curving putt.

Snap hook—Ball flight that sharply curves from right to left, much more than a hook.

Sole—(1) Bottom portion of the club; (2) letting the bottom of the club touch the ground at address.

Sole plate—The metal plate on the bottom of a wooden club.

Spoon—Term for a 3-wood during the wooden-shaft era.

Square—Positioning the feet, shoulders, knees, and elbows parallel to the ball-to-target line.

Square face—A clubface aimed directly toward the intended target line; can occur at any point of the swing.

Staked trees—Newly planted trees that are tagged and held up by a stake; a local rule usually allows players to drop away from staked trees without penalty.

Stance—Position of the feet prior to swinging the club.

Stiff—A shot that finishes within a couple of inches from the hole; see dead.

Stimpmeter—A grooved bar used to measure green speed. A ball is rolled off the bar, and the number of feet the ball rolls is the Stimpmeter rating. A rating of 8 to 10 is normal. Major championships are faster at 12.

Stipulated round—Unless otherwise ruled, refers to a round of eighteen holes played in their proper sequential order.

Stony—Ball hit very close to the flagstick; also called hitting the ball stiff or dead.

Stroke—A full swing or putting stroke made with the intent to hit the ball.

Stroke hole—Hole on which a player receives a handicap stroke.

Stroke play—See medal play.

Stub—A poorly hit shot that's similar to a fat shot.

Stymie—(1) Situation where a shot to the target area is blocked by a tree or other object; (2) an obsolete Rule of Golf whereby on the putting green, a golfer was stymied if a playing partner's ball was between his ball and the hole.

Summer golf—Playing the ball as it lies throughout the course; playing by the official Rules of Golf.

Sunday bag—A lightweight bag with just enough room for three to five clubs; ideal for walking a few holes without the strain of a full set of clubs.

Sweet spot—Usually the center of the clubface; the place where the ball comes off most solid.

Swing—See stroke.

Swing length—Distance the golfer swings the club back on the backswing and through-swing.

Swing plane—Imaginary "plane" the club is swung along from start to finish; connects the shoulders and the ball.

Swing speed—How fast the player swings the club at the moment of impact.

Swing thought—A mental image or phrase the golfer keys on during the swing.

Swingweight—A club's weight distribution about a fixed fulcrum point. The higher the swingweight, the more the club feels heavy in the head.

Tailwind—Wind blowing from behind the golfer toward the target.

Takeaway—Swing portion from address until the hands reach hip height.

Tap in—A putt of very short length, six inches to a foot.

Target—Where the golfer intends the ball to finish.

Target line—Imaginary line from the target to the ball and beyond; used to aim the club and body.

Target side—Side of the body or ball that is closest to the hole or target.

Tee—(1) Peg used to hold the ball while teeing off; (2) area of short grass from where a golfer begins play on each hole.

Tee markers—Indicates where golfers should play from on the tee.

Tee off—Playing a shot from the teeing ground.

Tee time—An assigned time for a group to begin play.

Teeing ground—Area of short grass from where play begins on a hole.

Tempo—The pace at which the player swings.

Tending the flag—See glossary reference in Chapter 8.

Texas wedge—Using a putter from off the green.

Thin shot—Poorly hit shot in which the top half of the ball is hit; similar to skulled and bladed shots.

Threesome—(1) Group of three players; (2) match in which one player plays against two partners who are following an alternate-shot pattern.

Through the green—The entire area of the course except the tee, putting green, and all hazards.

Timing—Coordinating the many moving parts of the body to make a functional and effective swing; see tempo.

Toe—(1) Broad part of the clubface opposite where the shaft and clubhead join; (2) poorly hit shot of striking the ball on the toe.

Top—Poorly hit shot in which the club comes down directly on top of the ball.

Tour pro—A player who travels the professional tournament schedule.

Trajectory—The height and arc of the ball after it's hit.

Trap—See bunker.

Triple bogey—Score on a hole that is three strokes more than par.

Trouble shot—See recovery shot.

Turn—(1) The pivot within the golf swing; (2) making the transition from the front nine holes to the back nine.

Twosome—Group of two players.

Underclub—Making an error in club selection; using a club that makes the ball fly shorter than needed.

Unplayable lie—See glossary reference in Chapter 8.

Up—Side or player leading a match.

Up and down—This occurs after a player misses a green in regulation and then uses a chip shot to get on the green and then one-putts to save par.

Upright swing—A swing that is more vertical than normal.

Waggle—Short, back-and-forth movements with the club prior to the takeaway.

Water hazard—See glossary reference in Chapter 8.

Water hole—A hole that has a water hazard.

Wedge—High-lofted club used for short shots.

Weight shift—Body weight transfered from a centered position to the right side, then centered and moved to the left during the swing (for a right-handed player).

Whiff—Missing the ball completely while swinging; counts as a stroke.

Whipped it around—Getting around the golf course in quick speed; playing well.

Whipping—The thin black string that is wrapped around the hosel on a wooden clubhead.

Wind cheater—A well-hit ball that flies low to avoid being affected by the wind.

Winter rules—Moving the ball six inches from its spot in the fairway, no closer to the hole; violates the Rules of Golf; similar to preferred lies.

Woods—Wooden- or metal-headed clubs used for shots off the tee and fairway; woods hit the ball the farthest distances of all clubs.

Worm burner—Very low shot that scoots along the top of the grass; see dew sweeper.

Wrist cock—Hinging the wrists during the swing.

Wrong ball—Any ball besides the one in play, a provisional ball, or one played under Rule 3-3 or Rule 20-7b. See glossary reference in Chapter 8.

X'd-out ball—Ball with an imperfection sold at a lower cost.

Yips—Muscle nervousness that adversely affects the putting stroke.

APPENDIX A

Golf is unquestionably the game of a lifetime, but for many people it can be a lifetime career, too. Golf has grown steadily in the last forty years and has been immune to any dips in popularity and resistant to economic chaos. Its health is as strong as ever as the 1990s come to a close.

There is exuberance and great optimisim for continued strength entering the next century, with new golfers taking up the sport because of the Tiger Woods phenomenon and a desire to be a part of something that's taking off.

Getting a job in golf is as smart a career move as any right now. There's plenty of money to be made in the right situations, but lower-level jobs can have their own level of satisfaction.

What's the right golf job for you? The answer to that question is simple: Find the one that's suitable for your personality and needs. You can be outdoors, indoors, or a combination of both. You can be in administration or, with a lot of hard work and luck, a player yourself.

The following alphabetical list describes numerous job positions in golf, and suggests associations and organizations that can help lead you in the right direction to making golf a career (phone numbers and addresses are listed at the end of the chapter).

JOB POSITIONS IN GOLF
Club Caddie

This worker used to be as plentiful as the buffalo, but golf carts killed them off in a slow death. Now caddie programs are primarily found at prestigious private clubs. Caddies report to the caddiemaster at the start of the day and are assigned a golfer or two in a group. Each bag he carries is worth a $30 fee at most clubs.

Many clubs have caddies carry two bags in one group, carrying for morning and afternoon rounds. If a caddie does that, say, six times a week, that's $360 a week. Caddies need to have a good working knowledge of the game and the ability to get along well with people. Some caddies who work in the North move to the South during winter months to maintain a year-round income from caddieing.

Club Manager

This is a demanding job that, at the lower-end clubs, might not pay enough to compensate for the headaches and long hours. A degree in business administration is helpful, but some club managers get started as a bartender or waiter and work up. (Club Managers Association of America)

Club Professional

The mainstay of the golf shop, the club pro is a jack-of-all-trades who must know how to teach the swing, sell a sweater, and run a tournament. It has been thus since the early 1900s. The ability to know how to merchandise an inventory, make the right purchases, and spot selling trends has become increasingly important. Club pros usually start with training as an apprentice under the PGA of America program.

Women are welcome in this field as well, and would be encouraged to get their PGA certification first and then do the same with the LPGA. There are four universities that participate in the PGA of America's Professional Golf Management program. They are Ferris State in Big Rapids, Michigan; Mississippi State in Starkville; New Mexico State in Las Cruces; and Penn State in University Park. (PGA of America, LPGA)

Clubmaker/Repairman

This is a position that requires a lot of apprentice work to learn the nuances of how clubs are designed, their function, and how to craft and shape them. A good place to start would be as an assembly-line worker, but classes are available to learn the trade more directly. (Golf Clubmakers Association, Professional Clubmakers Society, Ralph Maltby's GolfWorks)

Golf Association Administration

A golf association helps conduct teaching clinics, competitions, and the overall promotion of golf in whatever state or region it covers. There are positions within the association that range from secretarial to overall director. (PGA of America, International Association of Golf Administrators)

Golf Course Architect

If you have the name Nicklaus or Dye, designing golf courses is a multimillion-dollar career. But for everyone else, there's far less to be made. This job is for those people who love to work with the land and who want to have a lasting legacy that golfers can enjoy for years to come. (American Society of Golf Course Architects)

Golf Course Superintendent

Here's another job for land lovers, but with far less prestige than the club pro and course architect, although things are improving. This job requires long hours and can be fouled by Mother Nature. Excellent superintendents at prestige courses earn around $100,000. (Golf Course Superintendents Association of America)

Golf Retail-store Worker

Years ago, before golf equipment was as high-tech as it is now, any regular Joe could work in the shop and get by with general golf knowledge. But now the store worker needs to be conversant in the new golf materials as well as how equipment functions if they don't want to lose. The store worker has to have a salesperson's technique and be good at communicating. But they also must deal honestly with the customer to ensure they walk out with the right products, otherwise they face the prospect of having the items returned.

Golf Writer

The hard-drinking, chain-smoking writers of yesteryear have made a transformation similar to the players they've covered. Today's writers are computer-smart, have cut their off-hour tippling, but still have a long way to go with the proper diet. However, for the person who likes to mingle and talk with the tour stars, this job isn't too bad. The hours are definitely not 9 to 5, and the travel can be a nuisance, but those writers who get into the tournament routine wouldn't trade it for anything. (Golf Writers Association of America)

Player Agent

Like golf writers, this job puts the person in close touch with the game's great players. Unlike writers, an agent can make a hefty salary in getting commissions from players' earnings and endorsement deals. Working for a superstar easily means $1 million a year. An agent has to be part bulldog in making countless phone calls, lots of travel, and presentations to get the best deal for their client. This is a "people-person job" if there ever was one. Many agents are lawyers, but a degree in business administration is helpful, as is working as an assistant at a players agency.

Sales Representative

This job obviously requires a salesperson's acumen and demeanor. There is a great deal of travel involved, as well as people skills. The best sales reps at the big equipment companies earn six-figure salaries. A golf seller can make the jump from another product area as long as he's good at picking up the traits of a new field, but newcomers should apply for positions with golf equipment or apparel companies to get started on the ground floor.

Starter/Ranger

The crowded public golf courses so common today are the reason the starter and ranger jobs are so important. Yet, they are thankless positions that can subject the worker to criticism and abuse no matter how well they do. Everyone who comes to play wants to get on the golf course as quickly as possible, and they want to get the round finished as quickly as possible. The starter's job is to make sure golfers get out in an orderly fashion; the ranger roves around the course in a cart, looking for slow groups that are holding up play. Most starters and rangers don't get paid much more than minimum wage, but they take more than their share of abuse if people aren't happy about their day.

Tour Caddie

Here's an interesting job. You can be the right-hand man for one of the greatest players in the world, spending every moment on the range and golf course with them. But you're also subject to crazy hours, a lot of travel, lots of waiting around, and, when things don't go right, getting stuck with taking the blame for someone else's bad play. Tour caddies have to be on time, dependable, and willing to do what they're told. They get a regular salary from a player, around $600 a week, plus 10 percent of what they make in prize money. This is not a job for a golf novice. If you're a good player with a lot of past playing experience, that's quite helpful. But getting hooked up with a well-known tour player is quite unlikely. You have to be in the right spot at the right time. The good news is that with the way prize money is increasing, making a six-figure salary is not as big a stretch as it once was, even for the caddie of a middle-of-the-pack pro. (Professional Tour Caddies Association)

Tour Player

There probably haven't been too many golfers who haven't imagined, at least for a few seconds, what it must be like to be a professional golfer playing one of the major tours. There's a lot to like about being a tour player: the talent, glamour, money, freebies such as courtesy cars, and the attention from fans and the media. But the many hours of practice, travel, time away from family, and lack of job security are negative factors that can't be taken lightly. The task to being a tour player is learning to be an expert player in the first place. To do so requires a lot of lessons, practice, patience, and competition. Then you've got to get on the tour (tours conduct qualifying schools at the end of each year). Then you've got to earn a certain amount of money to remain on the tour. One missed putt can decide the success or failure of a season. This job may be the hardest of any position in golf to achieve. (PGA Tour, LPGA)

Tournament Director

If you're a good delegator who can manage a staff that could number as many as 1,000, then being in charge of a tournament might be your line of work. The director is in charge of making sure every item involved in putting on the tournament is being carried out. It's a difficult job that involves a lot of meetings and long hours, and no matter how well the director does the job, she is still at the mercy of how well the staff carries out directions. (Get involved with a regional or area golf association to get experience.)

Television

There is a wealth of employment opportunity in doing golf television work. Some of the positions include announcers, spotters, scorers, camera operators, technicians, and, of course, the director. The more important positions, such as announcers and director, require some previous experience and education in the job, such as through college or work in the business. The other positions can often be done through on-the-job training, but for those jobs that put the worker out on the course, it's important to have previous golf experience. A spotter, for instance, has to be good at following the golf ball and knowing the faces of golfers and their caddies. (Contact television networks)

GOLF ASSOCIATIONS AND ORGANIZATIONS

American Junior Golf Association
2415 Steeplechase Lane
Roswell, GA 30076-3579
Phone: (770) 998-4653; fax: (770) 992-9763
E-mail: AJGA@aol.com
Although it's not the oldest junior golf assocation, the AJGA is the preeminent organization for youth in the United States. In 1977, it became the first group to put together a tour of national scope solely for junior players, ages 13 to 18. In 1997, the AJGA had a record forty-tournament schedule. The AJGA is a nonprofit group managed by a board of directors. It names an All-American team and Scholastic team at the end of the season. And quite impressively, the AJGA has the backing of 42 corporate sponsors. Because of its popularity (3,800 members), the AJGA has to run qualifiers to get its tournament fields into a manageable size. The association believes it creates character in young golfers through its competitions.

American Society of Golf Course Architects
221 North LaSalle Street
Chicago, IL 60601
Phone: (312) 372-7090; fax: (312) 372-6160
E-mail: asgca@selz.com
Web site: http://www.golfdesign.org
Begun in 1947, the ASGCA is the fraternal group for 130 regular and associate members whose profession is designing golf courses. Membership is strictly for those architects who have hands-on involvement in designing.

The First Tee
World Golf Foundation
P.O. Box 3085
St. Augustine, FL 32085-3085
Phone: (904) 273-7668
The First Tee was organized in 1997 and has the involvement of every important golf organization. The intent of First Tee is to create new golf courses and playing opportunities for junior golfers. Its first goal is to have at least 100 courses/facilities at least in the planning stages by the year 2000.

Golf Course Superintendents Association of America
1421 Research Park Drive
Lawrence, KS 66049-3859
Phone: (913) 841-2240, 1-800-472-7878; fax: (913) 832-4433
E-mail: execmail@gcsaa.org
Web site: http://www.gcsaa.org/gcsaa
The GCSAA is for the green thumbs among the professional golf force. Its mission statement is to serve its members, advance their profession, and enrich the quality of golf and its environment.

Organized in 1926 with sixty members, the association now has 18,000 members in the United States and more than fifty other countries. The GCSAA provides the forum for its members to learn how to maintain a golf course. It has a continuing education program and a certification program that has approved more than 1,000 members.

Ladies Professional Golf Association
100 International Golf Drive
Daytona Beach, FL 32124-1092
Phone: (904) 274-6200; fax: (904) 274-1099
Web site: http://www.lpga.com
The LPGA had its start as the Women's Professional Golf Association in 1944, but it was reorganized in 1950 as the LPGA. From a schedule of twenty-one events worth a total of $50,000 in prize money in 1952, the LPGA has grown to forty-two events and $31.3 million in money in 1998. More than 300 playing professionals are a part of the LPGA, and 600 women are members of its teaching division. Membership is open to any woman 18 years or older.

National Association of Left-handed Golfers
6448 Shawnee Court
Independence, KY 41051
Phone: 1-800-844-6254.
The goal of the NALG is to make sure that the 10 percent of the golfing population that plays left-handed doesn't become extinct. Left-handed golfers have a difficult existence. They are the subject of jokes, they fight the perception of being offbeat, and they endure the discrimination factors of limited equipment and instruction geared toward right-handed players, although these latter areas are improving. There are more than 1,300 members of the NALG, which runs numerous national and local tournaments.

National Golf Foundation
1150 South U.S. Highway One, Suite 401
Jupiter, FL 33477
Phone: (561) 744-6006, 1-800-733-6006; fax: (561) 744-6107
E-mail: ngf@ngf.org
Web site: http://www.ngf.org
Golf's most important numbers are kept by golfers on their scorecards. The NGF, however, compiles golf's other numbers. The NGF, a nonprofit organization, tracks a wide range of statistical studies on golfers' playing and buying habits, number of golfers, number of courses built and in the works, and product use and preference, and it writes studies to help prospective course owners know the strength of their local markets. This statistical library is part of the NGF's

function as the watchdog for golf's health. Part of the NGF structure is a board of directors and board of governors comprised of representatives from golf manufacturers, associations, and media. The boards help the NGF form a future agenda. In recent years the NGF has conducted a biennial golf summit to discuss the need for more new courses to meet the demand of a growing golf population.

PGA Tour
112 TPC Boulevard
Sawgrass
Ponte Vedra Beach, FL 32082
Phone: (904) 285-3700; fax: (904) 285-2460
Web site: http://www.pgatour.com
At one time, the PGA of America and the PGA Tour were united, but in the late 1960s, the tour became its own entity. The PGA Tour has enjoyed phenomenal growth since professional players first started playing tournament golf on a limited schedule in the 1920s. During the first half of the 1900s, professional golfers mixed in tournament golf with their regular club pro jobs, and some of the best amateur golfers remained amateurs. But when the tour grew in prize money and had a consistent schedule of events, the best-playing pros went to tournament golf full-time and the best amateurs didn't stay amateur for long. In 1960, prize money for the forty-one tour events totaled $1.34 million. By 1997, the amount was $75.2 million for forty-five events, and the figure could double by the year 2000 based largely on a new television contract signed in 1997. A consortium of the PGA Tour and the pro tours of Europe, South Africa, Australasia, and Japan has announced the formation of a World Tour beginning with four events by 2000. By that time, it will be common place to have first-place payouts in the $500,000 range, a figure once approached only by major championships and special events. There has never been a more profitable time to be a touring professional.

Professional Golfers' Association (PGA) of America
100 Avenue of the Champions
Box 109601
Palm Beach Gardens, FL 33410-9601
Phone: (561) 624-8400; fax: (561) 624-8448
Web site: http://www.PGA.com
Since 1916, the PGA of America has united club professionals under one common

voice. The PGA has more than 23,000 club pros and apprentices who have been trained to provide swing instruction, organize tournaments and make sure the golf shop is stocked with merchandise. The PGA educates professionals through seminars, business schools, and its apprentice program under a head professional, but three universities also have accredited curriculums in professional golf management. An executive director oversees a staff of 125 people, working with three professionals elected president, vice president, and secretary. On the competitive level, the PGA operates the PGA Championship along with the biennial Ryder Cup Matches (when in the United States), the PGA Grand Slam of Golf and the PGA Seniors' Championship. The PGA also conducts competitive events for club pros, and it manages two major merchandise shows each year. (See Chapter 9 for a listing of PGA of America section offices.)

United States Golf Association (USGA)
Golf House
P.O. Box 708
Far Hills, NJ 07931-0708
Phone: (908) 234-2300, 1-800-336-4446; fax: (908) 234-2179
E-mail: usga@usga.org
Web site: http://www.usga.org
The USGA is the oldest golf association in the United States (begun in 1894) and has the broad aim of preserving the game's integrity and promoting the true spirit of golf. Headed by an executive committee of nearly sixteen members, the USGA has a base support of thirty committees comprising 1,200 volunteers, all of whom pay their own expenses. The USGA is the country's governing body for the Rules of Golf and keeps the Rules of Amateur status code, the guidelines that maintain golf as one of the few major sports today whose amateurs truly are amateurs. The USGA also has a handicapping system, first organized in 1912, and conducts thirteen national championships. It also is the game's guardian regarding club and ball testing to ensure conformity by manufacturers.

Western Golf Association
1 Briar Road
Golf, IL 60029
Phone: (847) 724-4600; fax: (847) 724-7133
The role of the WGA has changed little since it began nearly 100 years ago in 1899. It still conducts three of the most prestigious events on their respective

circuits: Western Open, Western Amateur, and Western Junior. And the WGA is still involved in assisting and promoting caddies, as it is the administrator of the Evans Scholars Foundation, a scholarship program for caddies. Financial support for the foundation comes from the Western Open, area clubs, thousands of golfers in the WGA's bag tag program, and corporate-matching gifts. The WGA is managed by a volunteer board of approximately 160 directors.

OTHER ASSOCIATIONS

ABC Sports, 1330 Sixth Avenue, New York, NY 10019; phone: (212) 887-7777

American Golf Corporation (golf course management firm), 2951 28th Street, Santa Monica, CA 90405-2961; phone: (310) 664-4000; fax: (310) 664-6160; E-mail: kj1118@aol.com

Association of Disabled American Golfers, 7200 E. Dry Creek Road, Suite G-102, Englewood, C) 80112; phone: (303) 220-0921; fax: (303) 779-4801; E-mail: adag@usga.org

Bad Golfers Association, c/o Universal Press Syndicate, 4520 Main Street, Kansas City, MO 64111; phone: (816) 932-6600, 1-800-642-6480; Web site: http://www.uexpress.com

Canadian Golf Foundation, Golf House, 1333 Dorval Drive, Oakville, Ontario L6J 4Z3, Canada; phone: (905) 849-9700, 1-800-263-0009; fax: (905) 845-7040; E-mail: cgf@rcga.org

Canadian Ladies Golf Association, Golf House, Glen Abbey, 1333 Dorval Drive, Oakville, Ontario L6J 4Z3, Canada; phone: (905) 849-2542; fax: (905) 849-0188

Canadian Professional Golfers' Association, R.R. 1, 13450 Dublin Line, Acton, Ontario L7J 2W7, Canada; Phone: (519) 853-5450; fax: (519) 853-5449

CBS Sports, 51 West 52nd Street, New York, NY 10019; phone: (212) 975-4321; fax: (212) 975-5425

Club Corporation International (golf course management firm), 3030 LBJ Freeway, Suite 700, Dallas, TX 75234; phone: (972) 243-6191; fax: (972) 888-7795

Club Corporation of America (golf course management firm), 3030 LBJ Freeway, Suite 700, Dallas, TX 75234; phone: (972) 888-7321; fax: (972) 888-7583

College Golf Foundation (administers Collegiate Golf Rankings), 33 State Road, Suite B, Princeton, NJ 08540; phone: (609) 252-1561, (609) 252-0876; Web site: http://chili.collegesportsnews.com/cgf/cgf.htm

ESPN, ESPN Plaza, 935 Middle Street, Bristol, CT 06010; phone: (860) 585-2000

Executive Women's Golf Association, 1401 Forum Way, Suite 100, West Palm Beach, FL 33401; phone: (561) 471-1477, 1-800-407-1477; fax: (561) 471-4299

The Golf Channel, 7580 Commerce Center Drive, Orlando, FL 32819; phone: (407) 363-4653; fax: (407) 363-7976

Golf Clubmakers Association, 11000 North IH 35, Austin, TX 78753; phone: (512) 837-8810, 1-800-456-3344; fax: (512) 837-9347; Web site: http://www.golfsmith.com

Golf Coaches Association of America, P.O. Box 215, Raymore, MO 64083; phone: (816) 322-4666; fax: (816) 942-5989

Golf Collectors Society, P.O. Box 20546, Dayton, OH 45420; phone: (937) 256-2474; fax: (937) 256-2974; E-mail: kkuhl67615@aol.com

Golf Course Builders Association of America, 920 Airport Road, Suite 210, Chapel Hill, NC 27514; phone: (919) 942-8922; fax: (919) 942-6955; Web site: http://www.gcbaa.org

Club Corporation of America (golf course management firm), 3030 LBJ Freeway, Suite 700, Dallas, TX 75234; phone: (972) 888-7321; fax: (972) 888-7583

Golf Writers Association of America, Suite L-7, 25882 Orchard Lake Road, Farmington Hills, MI 48336; phone: (810) 442-1481

International Association of Golf Administrators, c/o Southern California Golf Association, 3740 Cahuenga Boulevard, North Hollywood, CA 91604; phone: (818) 980-3630; fax: (818) 980-5019

International Junior Golf Tour, P.O. Box 5580, Hilton Head Island, SC 29938; phone: 1-800-494-4548;
Web site: http://www.ijgt.com;
E-mail: tour@ijgt.com

Minority Golf Association of America, P.O. Box 1081, Westhampton Beach, NY 11978-1081; phone: (516) 288-8255; fax: (516) 288-4458;
E-mail: mgaagolf@aol.com;
Web site: http://www.mgaa.com

National Amputee Golf Association, P.O. Box 5801, Coralville, IA 52241-5801; phone: (319) 351-3538, 1-800-633-6242; fax: (319) 351-5129; E-mail: nagaoffice@aol.com

National Club Association, One Lafayette Centre, 1120 20th Street, N.W., Suite 725, Washington, DC 20036; phone: (202) 822-9822; 1-800-625-6221; fax: (202) 822-9808

National Golf Course Owners Association, 1470 Ben Sawyer Boulevard, Suite 18, Mt. Pleasant, SC 29464-4535; phone: 1-800-933-4262; fax: (803) 881-9958; E-mail: colesj@ngcoa.com; Web site: www.ngcoa.com

National Hole-in-One Association, 8350 N. Central Expressway, No. 730, Dallas, TX 75206-1679; phone: 1-800-527-6944, (214) 691-6911; fax: (214) 373-1619; Web site: http://www.hio.com

Golf Writers Association of America, Suite L-7, 25882 Orchard Lake Road, Farmington Hills, MI 48336; phone: (810) 442-1481

International Association of Golf Administrators, c/o Southern California Golf Association, 3740 Cahuenga Boulevard,

North Hollywood, CA 91604; phone: (818) 980-3630; fax: (818) 980-5019

International Junior Golf Tour, P.O. Box 5580, Hilton Head Island, SC 29938; phone: 1-800-494-4548;
Web site: http://www.ijgt.com;
E-mail: tour@ijgt.com

Minority Golf Association of America, P.O. Box 1081, Westhampton Beach, NY 11978-1081; phone: (516) 288-8255; fax: (516) 288-4458;
E-mail: mgaagolf@aol.com;
Web site: http://www.mgaa.com

National Amputee Golf Association, P.O. Box 5801, Coralville, IA 52241-5801; phone: (319) 351-3538, 1-800-633-6242; fax: (319) 351-5129; E-mail: nagaoffice@aol.com

National Club Association, One Lafayette Centre, 1120 20th Street, N.W., Suite 725, Washington, DC 20036; phone: (202) 822-9822; 1-800-625-6221; fax: (202) 822-9808

National Golf Course Owners Association, 1470 Ben Sawyer Boulevard, Suite 18, Mt. Pleasant, SC 29464-4535; phone: 1-800-933-4262; fax: (803) 881-9958; E-mail: colesj@ngcoa.com; Web site: www.ngcoa.com

National Hole-in-One Association, 8350 N. Central Expressway, No. 730, Dallas, TX 75206-1679; phone: 1-800-527-6944, (214) 691-6911; fax: (214) 373-1619; Web site: http://www.hio.com

National Minority Golf Foundation, 7226 North 16th Street, Suite 210, Phoenix, AZ 85020; phone: (602) 943-8399; fax: (602) 943-8553; E-mail: golf@halcon.com

NBC Sports, 30 Rockefeller Plaza, New York, NY 10112; phone: (212) 664-4444

PGA European Tour, Wentworth Drive, Virginia Water, Surrey, England GU25 4LX; phone: 011-44-134-484-2881

Professional Clubmakers Society, 70 Persimmon Ridge Drive, Louisville, KY 40245; phone: (502) 241-2816, 1-800-548-6094; fax: (502) 241-2817; E-mail: pcs@ntr.net; Web site: http://www.proclubmakers.org

Professional Tour Caddies Association, 14567 Aqua Vista Court, Jacksonville, FL 32224; phone: (904) 223-1624

Ralph Maltby's GolfWorks, 4820 Jacksontown Road, Newark, OH 43056; phone: (614) 328-4193, 1-800-848-8358; fax: (614) 323-0311;
E-mail: golfwork@infinet.com;
Web site: http://www.golfworks.com

Royal Canadian Golf Association, Golf House, 1333 Dorval Drive, R.R. 2, Oakville, Ontario L6J 4Z3, Canada; phone: (905) 849-9700; fax: (905) 845-7040; E-mail: golfhouse@rcga.org; Web site: http://www.rcga.org

Sporting Goods Manufacturers Association, 200 Castlewood Drive, North Palm Beach, FL 33408-5696; phone: (561) 842-4100; fax: (561) 863-8984; E-mail: paasgma@aol.com; Web site: http://www.sportlink.com

United States Blind Golf Association, 3094 Shamrock North, Tallahassee, FL 32308; phone: (850) 893-4511; fax: (850) 893-4511; E-mail: midnightgolf@delphi.com

APPENDIX B

WINNERS OF PROFESSIONAL MAJOR CHAMPIONSHIPS

Masters Tournament

Annual site: Augusta (Ga.) National Golf Club

Year, winner, score

1934—Horton Smith, 284

1935—Gene Sarazen, 282*

1936—Horton Smith, 285

1937—Byron Nelson, 283

1938—Henry Picard, 285

1939—Ralph Guldahl, 279

1940—Jimmy Demaret, 280

1941—Craig Wood, 280

1942—Byron Nelson, 280*

1943–1945—No tournaments held

1946—Herman Keiser, 282

1947—Jimmy Demaret, 281

1948—Claude Harmon, 279

1949—Sam Snead, 282

1950—Jimmy Demaret, 283

1951—Ben Hogan, 280

1952—Sam Snead, 286

1953—Ben Hogan, 274

1954—Sam Snead, 289*

1955—Cary Middlecoff, 279

1956—Jack Burke, 289

1957—Doug Ford, 283

1958—Arnold Palmer, 284

1959—Art Wall, 284

1960—Arnold Palmer, 282

1961—Gary Player, 280

1962—Arnold Palmer, 280*

1963—Jack Nicklaus, 286

1964—Arnold Palmer, 276

1965—Jack Nicklaus, 271

1966—Jack Nicklaus, 288*

1967—Gay Brewer, 280

1968—Bob Goalby, 277

1969—George Archer, 281

1970—Billy Casper, 279*

1971—Charles Coody, 279

1972—Jack Nicklaus, 286

1973—Tommy Aaron, 283

1974—Gary Player, 278

1975—Jack Nicklaus, 276

1976—Ray Floyd, 271

1977—Tom Watson, 276

1978—Gary Player, 277

1979—Fuzzy Zoeller, 280*

1980—Seve Ballesteros, 275

1981—Tom Watson, 280

1982—Craig Stadler, 284*

1983—Seve Ballesteros, 280

1984—Ben Crenshaw, 277

1985—Bernhard Langer, 282

1986—Jack Nicklaus, 279

1987—Larry Mize, 285*

1988—Sandy Lyle, 281

1989—Nick Faldo, 283*

1990—Nick Faldo, 278*

1991—Ian Woosnam, 277

1992—Fred Couples, 275

1993—Bernhard Langer, 277

1994—Jose Maria Olazabal, 279

1995—Ben Crenshaw, 274

1996—Nick Faldo, 276

1997—Tiger Woods, 270+

U.S. Open Championship

Year, site, winner, score
(Played at 36 holes until 1898)

1895—Newport Golf Club, Horace
Rawlins, 173

1896—Shinnecock Hills Golf Club,
James Foulis, 152

1897—Chicago Golf Club, Joe
Lloyd, 162

1898—Myopia Hunt Club, Fred
Herd, 328

1899—Baltimore Country Club,
Willie Smith, 315

1900—Chicago Golf Club, Harry
Vardon, 313

1901—Myopia Hunt Club, Willie Anderson, 331*

1902—Garden City Golf Club, Laurie Auchterlonie, 307

1903—Baltusrol (Original Course), Willie Anderson, 307*

1904—Glen View Club, Willie Anderson, 303

1905—Myopia Hunt Club, Willie Anderson, 314

1906—Onwentsia Club, Alex Smith, 295

1907—Philadelphia Cricket Club, Alex Ross, 302

1908—Myopia Hunt Club, Fred McLeod, 322*

1909—Englewood Golf Club, George Sargent, 290

1910—Philadelphia Cricket Club, Alex Smith, 298*

1911—Chicago Golf Club, John McDermott, 307*

1912—Country Club of Buffalo, John McDermott, 294

1913—The Country Club, a-Francis Ouimet, 304*

1914—Midlothian Country Club, Walter Hagen, 290

1915—Baltusrol (Revised Course), a-J.D. Travers, 297

1916—Minikahda Club, a-Charles Evans Jr., 286

1917–1918—No championships held.

1919—Brae Burn Country Club, Walter Hagen, 301*

1920—Inverness Club, Edward Ray, 295

1921—Columbia Country Club, James M. Barnes, 289

1922—Skokie Country Club, Gene Sarazen, 288

1923—Inwood Country Club, a-Robert Tyre Jones Jr., 296*

1924—Oakland Hills (South), Cyril Walker, 297

1925—Worcester Country Club, William Macfarlane, 291*

1926—Scioto Country Club, a-Robert Tyre Jones Jr., 293

1927—Oakmont Country Club, Tommy Armour, 301*

1928—Olympia Fields Country Club, Johnny Farrell, 294*

1929—Winged Foot (West), a-Robert Tyre Jones Jr., 294*

1930—Interlachen Country Club, a-Robert Tyre Jones Jr., 287

1931—Inverness Club, Billy Burke, 292*

1932—Fresh Meadow Country Club, Gene Sarazen, 286

1933—North Shore Country Club, a-Johnny Goodman, 287

1934—Merion Club (East), Olin Dutra, 293

1935—Oakmont Country Club, Sam Parks Jr., 299

1936—Baltusrol (Upper Course), Tony Manero, 282

1937—Oakland Hills (South), Ralph Guldahl, 281

1938—Cherry Hills Country Club, Ralph Guldahl, 284

1939—Philadelphia Country Club, Byron Nelson, 284*

1940—Canterbury Golf Club, Lawson Little, 287*

1941—Colonial Country Club, Craig Wood, 284

1942–1945—No championships held

1946—Canterbury Golf Club, Lloyd Mangrum, 284*

1947—St. Louis Country Club, Lew Worsham, 282*

1948—Riviera Country Club, Ben Hogan, 276

1949—Medinah (No. 3 Course), Cary Middlecoff, 286

1950—Merion Club (East), Ben Hogan, 287*

1951—Oakland Hills (South), Ben Hogan, 287

1952—Northwood Country Club, Julius Boros, 281

1953—Oakmont Country Club, Ben Hogan, 283

1954—Baltusrol (Lower Course), Ed Furgol, 284

1955—Olympic Club (Lake Course), Jack Fleck, 287*

1956—Oak Hill (East Course), Cary Middlecoff, 281

1957—Inverness Club, Dick Mayer, 282*

1958—Southern Hills Country Club, Tommy Bolt, 283

1959—Winged Foot (West), Billy Casper, 282

1960—Cherry Hills Country Club, Arnold Palmer, 280

1961—Oakland Hills (South), Gene Littler, 281

1962—Oakmont Country Club, Jack Nicklaus, 283*

1963—The Country Club, Julius Boros, 293*

1964—Congressional Country Club, Ken Venturi, 278

1965—Bellerive Country Club, Gary Player, 282*

1966—Olympic Club (Lake Course), Billy Casper, 278*

1967—Baltusrol (Lower Course), Jack Nicklaus, 275

1968—Oak Hill (East Course), Lee Trevino, 275

1969—Champions Golf Club, Orville Moody, 281

1970—Hazeltine National Golf Club, Tony Jacklin, 281

1971—Merion Club (East), Lee Trevino, 280*

1972—Pebble Beach Golf Links, Jack Nicklaus, 290

1973—Oakmont Country Club, Johnny Miller, 279

1974—Winged Foot (West), Hale Irwin, 287

1975—Medinah (No. 3 Course), Lou Graham, 287*

1976—Atlanta Athletic Club, Jerry Pate, 277

1977—Southern Hills Country Club, Hubert Green, 278

1978—Cherry Hills Country Club, Andy North, 285

1979—Inverness Club, Hale Irwin, 284

1980—Baltusrol (Lower Course), Jack Nicklaus, 272+

1981—Merion (East Course), David Graham, 273

1982—Pebble Beach Golf Links, Tom Watson, 282

1983—Oakmont Country Club, Larry Nelson, 280

1984—Winged Foot (West), Fuzzy Zoeller, 276*

1985—Oakland Hills (South), Andy North, 279

1986—Shinnecock Hills Golf Club, Ray Floyd, 279

1987—Olympic Club (Lake Course), Scott Simpson, 277

1988—The Country Club, Curtis Strange, 278*

1989—Oak Hill (East Course), Curtis Strange, 278

1990—Medinah (No. 3 Course), Hale Irwin, 280*

1991—Hazeltine National Golf Club, Payne Stewart, 282*

1992—Pebble Beach Golf Links, Tom Kite, 285

1993—Baltusrol (Lower Course), Lee Janzen, 272+

1994—Oakmont Country Club, Ernie Els, 279*

1995—Shinnecock Hills Golf Club, Corey Pavin, 280

1996—Oakland Hills Country Club, Steve Jones, 278

1997—Congressional Country Club, Ernie Els, 276

British Open Championship

Year, site, winner, score
(Played at 36 holes until 1892)

1860—Prestwick, Willie Park Sr., 174

1861—Prestwick, Tom Morris Sr., 163

1862—Prestwick, Tom Morris Sr., 163

1863—Prestwick, Willie Park Sr., 168

1864—Prestwick, Tom Morris Sr., 160

1865—Prestwick, Andrew Strath, 162

1866—Prestwick, Willie Park Sr., 169

1867—Prestwick, Tom Morris Sr., 170

1868—Prestwick, Tom Morris Jr., 154

1869—Prestwick, Tom Morris Jr., 157

1870—Prestwick, Tom Morris Jr., 149

1871—No championship held.

1872—Prestwick, Tom Morris Jr., 166

1873—Old Course (St. Andrews), Tom Kidd, 179

1874—Musselburgh Links, Mungo Park, 159

1875—Prestwick, Willie Park Sr., 166

1876—Old Course (St. Andrews), Robert Martin, 176

1877—Musselburgh Links, Jamie Anderson, 160

1878—Prestwick, Jamie Anderson, 157

1879—Old Course (St. Andrews), Jamie Anderson, 169

1880—Musselburgh Links, Robert Ferguson, 162

1881—Prestwick, Robert Ferguson, 170

1882—Old Course (St. Andrews), Robert Ferguson, 171

1883—Musselburgh Links, Willie Fernie, 159*

1884—Prestwick, Jack Simpson, 160

1885—Old Course (St. Andrews), Robert Martin, 171

1886—Musselburgh Links, David Brown, 157

1887—Prestwick, Willie Park Jr., 161

1888—Old Course (St. Andrews), Jack Burns, 171

1889—Musselburgh Links, Willie Park Jr., 155*

1890—Prestwick, a-John Ball, 164

1891—Old Course (St. Andrews), Hugh Kirkaldy, 166

1892—Muirfield, a-Harold H. Hilton, 305

1893—Prestwick, William Auchterlonie, 322

1894—Royal St. George's, John H. Taylor, 326

1895—Old Course (St. Andrews), John H. Taylor, 322

1896—Muirfield, Harry Vardon, 316*

1897—Hoylake, a-Harold H. Hilton, 314

1898—Prestwick, Harry Vardon, 307

1899—Royal St. George's, Harry Vardon, 310

1900—Old Course (St. Andrews), John H. Taylor, 309

1901—Muirfield, James Braid, 309

1902—Hoylake, Alexander Herd, 307

1903—Prestwick, Harry Vardon, 300

1904—Royal St. George's, Jack White, 296

1905—Old Course (St. Andrews), James Braid, 318

1906—Muirfield, James Braid, 300

1907—Hoylake, Arnaud Massy, 312

1908—Prestwick, James Braid, 291

1909—Deal, John H. Taylor, 295

1910—Old Course (St. Andrews), James Braid, 299

1911—Royal St. George's, Harry Vardon, 303*

1912—Muirfield, Edward Ray, 295

1913—Hoylake, John H. Taylor, 304

1914—Prestwick, Harry Vardon, 306

1915–1919—No championships held.

1920—Deal, George Duncan, 303

1921—Old Course (St. Andrews), Jock Hutchison, 296*

1922—Royal St. George's, Walter Hagen, 300

1923—Troon, Arthur Havers, 295

1924—Hoylake, Walter Hagen, 301

1925—Prestwick, James Barnes, 300

1926—Royal Lytham, a-Robert Tyre Jones Jr., 291

1927—Old Course (St. Andrews), a-Robert Tyre Jones Jr., 285

1928—Royal St. George's, Walter Hagen, 292

1929—Muirfield, Walter Hagen, 292

1930—Hoylake, a-Robert Tyre Jones Jr., 291

1931—Carnoustie, Tommy Armour, 296

1932—Prince's, Gene Sarazen, 283

1933—Old Course (St. Andrews), Denny Shute, 292*

1934—Royal St. George's, Henry Cotton, 283

1935—Muirfield, Alfred Perry, 283

1936—Hoylake, Alfred Padgham, 287

1937—Carnoustie, Henry Cotton, 290

1938—Royal St. George's, R.A. Whitcombe, 295

1939—Old Course (St. Andrews), Richard Burton, 290

1940–1945—No championships held.

1946—Old Course (St. Andrews), Sam Snead, 290

1947—Hoylake, Fred Daly, 293

1948—Muirfield, Henry Cotton, 294

1949—Royal St. George's, Bobby Locke, 283*

1950—Troon, Bobby Locke, 279

1951—Royal Portrush, Max Faulkner, 285

1952—Royal Lytham, Bobby Locke, 287

1953—Carnoustie, Ben Hogan, 282

1954—Royal Birkdale, Peter Thomson, 283

1955—Old Course (St. Andrews), Peter Thomson, 281

1956—Hoylake, Peter Thomson, 286

1957—Old Course (St. Andrews), Bobby Locke, 279

1958—Royal Lytham, Peter Thomson, 278*

1959—Muirfield, Gary Player, 284

1960—Old Course (St. Andrews), Kel Nagle, 278

1961—Royal Birkdale, Arnold Palmer, 284

1962—Troon, Arnold Palmer, 276

1963—Royal Lytham, Bob Charles, 277*

1964—Old Course (St. Andrews), Tony Lema, 279

1965—Royal Birkdale, Peter Thomson, 285

1966—Muirfield, Jack Nicklaus, 282

1967—Hoylake, Roberto De Vicenzo, 278

1968—Carnoustie, Gary Player, 289

1969—Royal Lytham, Tony Jacklin, 280

1970—Old Course (St. Andrews), Jack Nicklaus, 283*

1971—Royal Birkdale, Lee Trevino, 278

1972—Muirfield, Lee Trevino, 278

1973—Troon, Tom Weiskopf, 276

1974—Royal Lytham, Gary Player, 282

1975—Carnoustie, Tom Watson, 279*

1976—Royal Birkdale, Johnny Miller, 279

1977—Turnberry, Tom Watson, 268

1978—Old Course (St. Andrews), Jack Nicklaus, 281

1979—Royal Lytham, Seve Ballesteros, 283

1980—Muirfield, Tom Watson, 271

1981—Royal St. George's, Bill Rogers, 276

1982—Royal Troon, Tom Watson, 284

1983—Royal Birkdale, Tom Watson, 275

1984—Old Course (St. Andrews), Seve Ballesteros, 276

1985—Royal St. George's, Sandy Lyle, 282

1986—Turnberry, Greg Norman, 280

1987—Muirfield, Nick Faldo, 279

1988—Royal Lytham, Seve Ballesteros, 273

1989—Royal Troon, Mark Calcavecchia, 275*

1990—Old Course (St. Andrews), Nick Faldo, 270

1991—Royal Birkdale, Ian Baker-Finch, 272

1992—Muirfield, Nick Faldo, 272

1993—Royal St. George's, Greg Norman, +267

1994—Turnberry, Nick Price, 268

1995—Old Course (St. Andrews), John Daly, 282*

1996—Royal Lytham, Tom Lehman, 271

1997—Royal Troon, Justin Leonard, 272

PGA Championship

Year, site, winner, score
(The PGA was contested at match play from 1916 through 1957.)

1916—Siwanoy Country Club, Jim Barnes

1917–1918—No championships held.

1919—Engineers Country Club, Jim Barnes

1920—Flossmoor Country Club, Jock Hutchison

1921—Inwood Country Club, Walter Hagen

1922—Oakmont Country Club, Gene Sarazen

1923—Pelham Country Club, Gene Sarazen

1924—French Lick Country Club, Walter Hagen

1925—Olympia Fields Country Club, Walter Hagen

1926—Salisbury Golf Club, Walter Hagen

1927—Cedar Crest Country Club, Walter Hagen

1928—Five Farms Country Club, Leo Diegel

1929—Hillcrest Country Club, Leo Diegel

1930—Fresh Meadow Country Club, Tommy Armour

1931—Wannamoisett Country Club, Tom Creavy

1932—Keller Golf Club, Olin Dutra

1933—Blue Mound Country Club, Gene Sarazen

1934—Park Country Club, Paul Runyan

1935—Twin Hills Country Club, Johnny Revolta

1936—Pinehurst Country Club, Denny Shute

1937—Pittsburgh Field Club, Denny Shute

1938—Shawnee Country Club, Paul Runyan

1939—Pomonok Country Club, Henry Picard

1940—Hershey Country Club, Byron Nelson

1941—Cherry Hills Country Club, Vic Ghezzi

1942—Seaview Country Club, Sam Snead

1943—No championship held.

1944—Manito Golf and Country Club, Bob Hamilton

1945—Morraine Country Club, Byron Nelson

1946—Portland Golf Club, Ben Hogan

1947—Plum Hollow Country Club, Jim Ferrier

1948—Norwood Hills Country Club, Ben Hogan

1949—Hermitage Country Club, Sam Snead

1950—Scioto Country Club, Chandler Harper

1951—Oakmont Country Club, Sam Snead

1952—Big Spring Country Club, Jim Turnesa

1953—Birmingham Country Club, Walter Burkemo

1954—Keller Golf Club, Chick Harbert

1955—Meadowbrook Country Club, Doug Ford

1956—Blue Hill Country Club, Jack Burke

1957—Miami Valley Country Club, Lionel Hebert

1958—Llanerch Country Club, Dow Finsterwald, 276

1959—Minneapolis Golf Club, Bob Rosburg, 277

1960—Firestone Country Club, Jay Hebert, 281

1961—Olympia Fields Country Club, Jerry Barber, 277*

1962—Aronimink Golf Club, Gary Player, 278

1963—Dallas Athletic Club, Jack Nicklaus, 279

1964—Columbus Country Club, Bobby Nichols, 271

1965—Laurel Valley Country Club, Dave Marr, 280

1966—Firestone Country Club, Al Geiberger, 280

1967—Columbine Country Club, Don January, 281*

1968—Pecan Valley Country Club, Julius Boros, 281

1969—NCR (South) Country Club, Ray Floyd, 276

1970—Southern Hills Country Club, Dave Stockton, 279

1971—PGA National Golf Club, Jack Nicklaus, 281

1972—Oakland Hills Country Club, Gary Player, 281

1973—Canterbury Golf Club, Jack Nicklaus, 277

1974—Tanglewood Golf Club, Lee Trevino, 276

1975—Firestone Country Club, Jack Nicklaus, 276

1976—Congressional Country Club, Dave Stockton, 281

1977—Pebble Beach Golf Links, Lanny Wadkins, 282*

1978—Oakmont Country Club, John Mahaffey, 276*

1979—Oakland Hills Country Club, David Graham, 272*

1980—Oak Hill Country Club, Jack Nicklaus, 274

1981—Atlanta Athletic Club, Larry Nelson, 273

1982—Southern Hills Country Club, Ray Floyd, 272

1983—Riviera Country Club, Hal Sutton, 274

1984—Shoal Creek Golf Club, Lee Trevino, 273

1985—Cherry Hills Country Club, Hubert Green, 278

1986—Inverness Club, Bob Tway, 276

1987—PGA National, Larry Nelson, 287*

1988—Oak Tree Golf Club, Jeff Sluman, 272

1989—Kemper Lakes Golf Club, Payne Stewart, 276

1990—Shoal Creek Golf Club, Wayne Grady, 282

1991—Crooked Stick Golf Club, John Daly, 276

1992—Bellerive Country Club, Nick Price, 278

1993—Inverness Club, Paul Azinger, 272*

1994—Southern Hills Country Club, Nick Price, 269

1995—Riviera Country Club, Steve Elkington, 267*+

1996—Valhalla Golf Club, Mark Brooks, 277*

1997—Winged Foot (West), Davis Love III, 269

Nabisco Dinah Shore

Annual site: Mission Hills Country Club, Rancho Mirage, Calif.

Year, winner, score

1972—Jane Blalock, 213

1973—Mickey Wright, 284

1974—Jo Ann Prentice, 289*

1975—Sandra Palmer, 283

1976—Judy Rankin, 285

1977—Kathy Whitworth, 289

1978—Sandra Post, 283*

1979—Sandra Post, 276

1980—Donna Caponi, 275

1981—Nancy Lopez, 277

1982—Sally Little, 278

1983—Amy Alcott, 282

1984—Juli Inkster, 280*

1985—Alice Miller, 275

1986—Pat Bradley, 280

1987—Betsy King, 283*

1988—Amy Alcott, 274

1989—Juli Inkster, 279

1990—Betsy King, 283

1991—Amy Alcott, 273+

1992—Dottie Mochrie, 279*

1993—Helen Alfredsson, 284

1994—Donna Andrews, 276

1995—Nanci Bowen, 285

1996—Patty Sheehan, 281

1997—Betsy King, 276

U.S. Women's Open

Year, site, winner, score

1946—Spokane Country Club, Patty Berg (match play)

1947—Starmount Forest Country Club, Betty Jameson, 295

1948—Atlantic City Country Club, Babe Zaharias, 300

1949—Prince George's Country Club, Louise Suggs, 291

1950—Rolling Hills Country Club, Babe Zaharias, 291

1951—Druid Hills Golf Club, Betsy Rawls, 293

1952—Bala Golf Club, Louise Suggs, 284

1953—Country Club of Rochester, Betsy Rawls, 302*

1954—Salem Country Club, Babe Zaharias, 291

1955—Wichita Country Club, Fay Crocker, 299

1956—Northland Country Club, Kathy Cornelius, 302*

1957—Winged Foot (East), Betsy Rawls, 299

1958—Forest Lake Country Club, Mickey Wright, 290

1959—Churchill Valley Country Club, Mickey Wright, 287

1960—Worcester Country Club, Betsy Rawls, 292

1961—Baltusrol (Lower Course), Mickey Wright, 293

1962—Dunes Golf and Beach Club, Murle Breer, 301

1963—Kenwood Country Club, Mary Mills, 289

1964—San Diego Country Club, Mickey Wright, 290*

1965—Atlantic City Country Club, Carol Mann, 290

1966—Hazeltine National Golf Club, Sandra Spuzich, 297

1967—Hot Springs Golf Club, a-Catherine Lacoste, 294

1968—Moselem Springs Golf Club, Susie Berning, 289

1969—Scenic Hills Country Club, Donna Caponi, 294

1970—Muskogee Country Club, Donna Caponi, 287

1971—Kahkwa Club, JoAnne Carner, 288

1972—Winged Foot (East), Susie Berning, 299

1973—Country Club of Rochester, Susie Berning, 290

1974—La Grange Country Club, Sandra Haynie, 295

1975—Atlantic City Country Club, Sandra Palmer, 295

1976—Rolling Green Country Club, JoAnne Carner, 292*

1977—Hazeltine National Golf Club, Hollis Stacy, 292

1978—Country Club of Indianapolis, Hollis Stacy, 289

1979—Brooklawn Country Club, Jerilyn Britz, 284

1980—Richland Country Club, Amy Alcott, 280

1981—La Grange Country Club, Pat Bradley, 279

1982—Del Paso Country Club, Janet Alex, 283

1983—Cedar Ridge Country Club, Jan Stephenson, 290

1984—Salem Country Club, Hollis Stacy, 290

1985—Baltusrol (Upper Course), Kathy Baker, 280

1986—NCR Golf Club, Jane Geddes, 287*

1987—Plainfield Country Club, Laura Davies, 285*

1988—Baltimore Country Club, Liselotte Neumann, 277

1989—Indianwood Golf and Country Club, Betsy King, 278

1990—Atlanta Athletic Club, Betsy King, 284

1991—Colonial Country Club, Meg Mallon, 283

1992—Oakmont Country Club, Patty Sheehan, 280*

1993—Crooked Stick Golf Club, Lauri Merten, 280

1994—Indianwood Golf Club, Patty Sheehan, 277

1995—The Broadmoor, Annika Sorenstam, 278

1996—Pine Needles Golf Club, Annika Sorenstam, 272+

1997—Pumpkin Ridge Golf Club, Alison Nicholas, 274

LPGA Championship

Year, site, winner, score

1955—Orchard Ridge Country Club, Beverly Hanson (match play)

1956—Forest Lake Country Club, Marlene Hagge, 291*

1957—Churchill Valley Country Club, Louise Suggs, 285

1958—Churchill Valley Country Club, Mickey Wright, 288

1959—Sheraton Hotel Country Club, Betsy Rawls, 288

1960—Sheraton Hotel Country Club, Mickey Wright, 292

1961—Stardust Country Club, Mickey Wright, 287

1962—Stardust Country Club, Judy Kimball, 282

1963—Stardust Country Club, Mickey Wright, 294

1964—Stardust Country Club, Mary Mills, 278

1965—Stardust Country Club, Sandra Haynie, 279

1966—Stardust Country Club, Gloria Ehret, 282

1967—Pleasant Valley Country Club, Kathy Whitworth, 284

1968—Pleasant Valley Country Club, Sandra Post, 294*

1969—Concord Golf Club, Betsy Rawls, 293

1970—Pleasant Valley Country Club, Shirley Englehorn, 285*

1971—Pleasant Valley Country Club, Kathy Whitworth, 288

1972—Pleasant Valley Country Club, Kathy Ahern, 293

1973—Pleasant Valley Country Club, Mary Mills, 288

1974—Pleasant Valley Country Club, Sandra Haynie, 288

1975—Pine Ridge Golf Club, Kathy Whitworth, 288

1976—Pine Ridge Golf Club, Betty Burfeindt, 287

1977—Bay Tree Golf Plantation, Chako Higuchi, 279

1978—Jack Nicklaus Golf Center, Nancy Lopez, 275

1979—Jack Nicklaus Golf Center, Donna C. Young, 279

1980—Jack Nicklaus Golf Center, Sally Little, 285

1981—Jack Nicklaus Golf Center, Donna Caponi, 280

1982—Jack Nicklaus Golf Center, Jan Stephenson, 279

1983—Jack Nicklaus Golf Center, Patty Sheehan, 279

1984—Jack Nicklaus Golf Center, Patty Sheehan, 272

1985—Jack Nicklaus Golf Center, Nancy Lopez, 273

1986—Jack Nicklaus Golf Center, Pat Bradley, 277

1987—Jack Nicklaus Golf Center, Jane Geddes, 275

1988—Jack Nicklaus Golf Center, Sherri Turner, 281

1989—Jack Nicklaus Golf Center, Nancy Lopez, 274

1990—Bethesda Country Club, Beth Daniel, 280

1991—Bethesda Country Club, Meg Mallon, 274

1992—Bethesda Country Club, Betsy King, 267+

1993—Bethesda Country Club, Patty Sheehan, 275

1994—Du Pont Country Club, Laura Davies, 279

1995—Du Pont Country Club, Kelly Robbins, 274

1996—Du Pont Country Club, Laura Davies, 213#

1997—Du Pont Country Club, Chris Johnson, 281*

Du Maurier Classic

Year, site, winner, score

1973—Montreal Golf Club, Jocelyne Bourassa, 214*

1974—Candiac Golf Club, Carole Jo Callison, 208

1975—St. George's Golf Club, JoAnne Carner, 214*

1976—Cedar Brae Country Club, Donna Caponi, 212*

1977—Lachute Golf and Country Club, Judy Rankin, 214

1978—St. George's Golf Club, JoAnne Carner, 278

1979—Richelieu Valley Golf Club, Amy Alcott, 285

1980—St. George's Golf Club, Pat Bradley, 277

1981—Summerlea Country Club, Jan Stephenson, 278

1982—St. George's Golf Club, Sandra Haynie, 280

1983—Beaconsfield Golf Club, Hollis Stacy, 277

1984—St. George's Golf Club, Juli Inkster, 279

1985—Beaconsfield Golf Club, Pat Bradley, 278

1986—Board of Trade Country Club, Pat Bradley, 276*

1987—Islemere Golf Club, Jody Rosenthal, 272+

1988—Vancouver Golf Club, Sally Little, 279

1989—Beaconsfield Golf Club, Tammie Green, 279

1990—Westmount Golf and Country Club, Cathy Johnston, 276

1991—Vancouver Golf Club, Nancy Scranton, 279

1992—St. Charles Country Club, Sherri Steinhauer, 277

1993—London Hunt & Country Club, Brandie Burton, 277*

1994—Ottawa Hunt Club, Martha Nause, 279

1995—Beaconsfield Golf Club, Jenny Lidback, 280

1996—Edmonton Country Club, Laura Davies, 277

1997—Glen Abbey Golf Club, Colleen Walker, 278

PGA Seniors' Championship

Year, site, winner, score

1937—Augusta National Golf Club, Jock Hutchison, 223

1938—Augusta National Golf Club, Fred McLeod, 154*

1939—No championship held.

1940—Bobby Jones Golf Club/North Shore Country Club, Otto Hackbarth, 146*

1941—Bobby Jones Golf Club/Sarasota Bay Country Club, Jack Burke Sr., 142

1942—Fort Myers Country Club, Eddie Williams, 138

1943 and 1944—No championships held.

1945—PGA National (Dunedin, Fla.), Eddie Williams, 150

1946—PGA National (Dunedin, Fla.), Eddie Williams, 146*

1947—PGA National (Dunedin, Fla.), Jock Hutchison, 145

1948—PGA National (Dunedin, Fla.), Charles McKenna, 141

1949—PGA National (Dunedin, Fla.), Marshal Crichton, 145

1950—PGA National (Dunedin, Fla.), Al Watrous, 142

1951—PGA National (Dunedin, Fla.), Al Watrous, 142*

1952—PGA National (Dunedin, Fla.), Ernest Newnham, 146

1953—PGA National (Dunedin, Fla.), Harry Schwab, 142

1954—PGA National (Dunedin, Fla.), Gene Sarazen, 214

1955—PGA National (Dunedin, Fla.), Mortie Dutra, 213

1956—PGA National (Dunedin, Fla.), Pete Burke, 215

1957—PGA National (Dunedin, Fla.), Al Watrous, 210*

1958—PGA National (Dunedin, Fla.), Gene Sarazen, 288

1959—PGA National (Dunedin, Fla.), Willie Goggin, 284

1960—PGA National (Dunedin, Fla.), Dick Metz, 284

1961—PGA National (Dunedin, Fla.), Paul Runyan, 278

1962—PGA National (Dunedin, Fla.), Paul Runyan, 278

1963—Port St. Lucie Country Club, Herman Barron, 272

1964—PGA National (aka BallenIsles), Sam Snead, 279

1965—Fort Lauderdale Country Club, Sam Snead, 278

1966—PGA National (aka BallenIsles), Fred Haas, 286

1967—PGA National (aka BallenIsles), Sam Snead, 279

1968—PGA National (aka BallenIsles), Chandler Harper, 279

1969—PGA National (aka BallenIsles), Tommy Bolt, 278

1970—PGA National (aka BallenIsles), Sam Snead, 290

1971—PGA National (aka BallenIsles), Julius Boros, 285

1972—PGA National (aka BallenIsles), Sam Snead, 286

1973—PGA National (aka BallenIsles), Sam Snead, 268+

1974—Port St. Lucie Country Club, Roberto De Vicenzo, 273

1975—Walt Disney World, Charlie Sifford, 280*

1976—Walt Disney World, Pete Cooper, 283

1977—Walt Disney World, Julius Boros, 283

1978—Walt Disney World, Joe Jimenez, 286*

1979—Walt Disney World, Jack Fleck, 289*

1979—Turnberry Isle Country Club,
Don January, 270

1980—Turnberry Isle Country Club,
Arnold Palmer, 289*

1981—Turnberry Isle Country Club,
Miller Barber, 281

1982—PGA National Golf Club,
Don January, 288

1983—No championship held.

1984—PGA National Golf Club,
Arnold Palmer, 282

1984—PGA National Golf Club,
Peter Thomson, 286

1985—No championship held.

1986—PGA National Golf Club,
Gary Player, 281

1987—PGA National Golf Club,
Chi Chi Rodriguez, 282

1988—PGA National Golf Club,
Gary Player, 284

1989—PGA National Golf Club,
Larry Mowry, 281

1990—PGA National Golf Club,
Gary Player, 281

1991—PGA National Golf Club,
Jack Nicklaus, 271

1992—PGA National Golf Club,
Lee Trevino, 278

1993—PGA National Golf Club,
Tom Wargo, 275*

1994—PGA National Golf Club,
Lee Trevino, 279

1995—PGA National Golf Club,
Ray Floyd, 277

1996—PGA National Golf Club,
Hale Irwin, 280

1997—PGA National Golf Club,
Hale Irwin, 274

Note: Two championships were held in 1979 and 1984.

U.S. Senior Open Championship

Year, site, winner, score

1980—Winged Foot Golf Club,
Roberto De Vicenzo, 285

1981—Oakland Hills Country Club,
Arnold Palmer, 289*

1982—Portland Country Club,
Miller Barber, 282

1983—Hazeltine National Golf
Club, Billy Casper, 288*

1984—Oak Hill Country Club,
Miller Barber, 286

1985—Edgewood Tahoe Golf Club,
Miller Barber, 285

1986—Scioto Country Club, Dale
Douglass, 279

1987—Brooklawn Country Club,
Gary Player, 270+

1988—Medinah Country Club, Gary Player, 288*

1989—Laurel Valley Golf Club, Orville Moody, 279

1990—Ridgewood Country Club, Lee Trevino, 275

1991—Oakland Hills Country Club, Jack Nicklaus, 282*

1992—Saucon Valley Country Club, Larry Laoretti, 275

1993—Cherry Hills Country Club, Jack Nicklaus, 278

1994—Pinehurst Country Club (No. 2 Course), Simon Hobday, 274

1995—Congressional Country Club, Tom Weiskopf, 275

1996—Canterbury Golf Club, Dave Stockton, 277

1997—Olympia Fields Country Club, Graham Marsh, 280

Key: *Won playoff. +Tournament record. aAmateur. #Weather-shortened event.

HISTORICAL AND NOTABLE PERSONALITIES

The following is an alphabetical list of numerous people who have made an impact on the game. They are worth reading more about if you encounter any material on or by them.

Players and Contributors

Willie Anderson   Winner of the 1901, 1903, 1904, and 1905 U.S. Opens.

Tommy Armour   Winner of the 1927 U.S. Open, the 1930 PGA Championship, and the 1931 British Open; renowned golf teacher.

Severiano Ballesteros   Charismatic Spaniard who won the 1979, 1984, and 1988 British Opens and the 1980 and 1983 Masters.

Jim Barnes   Winner of the 1916 and 1919 PGA Championships, the 1921 U.S. Open, and the 1925 British Open.

Patty Berg   Winner of the 1946 U.S. Women's Open and forty-one LPGA events; lauded for her role as a golf ambassador.

Julius Boros   Winner of eighteen PGA Tour events, including the 1952 and 1963

U.S. Opens and the 1968 PGA Championship.

Pat Bradley   Winner of thirty-one LPGA Tour events, including the 1981 U.S. Women's Open, the 1985 and 1986 du Maurier Classics, the 1986 Dinah Shore, and the 1986 LPGA Championship.

James Braid   English player who won the 1901, 1905, 1906, 1908, and 1910 British Opens.

JoAnne Carner   Crowd-pleasing player with forty-two LPGA Tour victories, including the 1971 and 1976 U.S. Women's Opens; won the U.S. Women's Amateur five times.

Billy Casper   Winner of fifty-one PGA Tour events, including the 1959 and 1966 U.S. Opens and the 1970 Masters.

Harry Cooper   Winner of thirty-one PGA Tour events; recognized as the all-time greatest player never to have won a major championship.

Fred Corcoran   Influential figure in the formation of the PGA and LPGA tours as tournament director and promoter.

Henry Cotton   English star who won the 1934, 1937, and 1948 British Opens.

Bing Crosby   Legendary singer and entertainer who had the first well-known pro-am event on the PGA Tour; a 2-handicap, Crosby once qualified for the British amateur.

Roberto De Vicenzo   Winner of nine PGA Tour events, the 1967 British Open, and more than 200 other tournaments around the world.

Jimmy Demaret   Winner of thirty-one PGA Tour events, including the 1940, 1947, and 1950 Masters.

Joseph C. Dey   Former longtime executive director of the U.S. Golf Association and a noted authority on the Rules of Golf.

Chick Evans Outstanding amateur who won the 1916 U.S. Open and U.S. Amateur, and the 1920 U.S. Amateur; established well-known caddie scholarship program.

Nick Faldo Winner of more than thirty events on the European PGA Tour, including the 1987, 1990, and 1992 British Open, plus the 1989, 1990, and 1996 Masters.

Raymond Floyd Winner of twenty-two PGA Tour events, including the 1986 U.S. Open, the 1976 Masters, and the 1969 and 1982 PGA Championships.

Ralph Guldahl Winner of fourteen PGA Tour events, including the 1937 and 1938 U.S. Opens and the 1939 Masters.

Walter Hagen Winner of five PGA Championships in 1921, 1924, 1925, 1926, and 1927, the 1914 and 1919 U.S. Opens and the 1922, 1924, 1928, and 1929 British Opens; legendary showman who captained six U.S. Ryder Cup teams.

Sandra Haynie Winner of forty-two LPGA Tour events, including the 1974 U.S. Women's Open and LPGA Championship.

Ben Hogan Winner of sixty-two PGA Tour events, including the 1948, 1950, 1951, and 1953 U.S. Opens, the 1946 and 1948 PGA Championships, the 1953 British Open, and the 1951 and 1953 Masters; set standards for practice and determination.

Bob Hope Actor and comedian who has been a longtime promoter of golf; began the Bob Hope Desert Classic on the PGA Tour in 1960.

Hale Irwin Winner of twenty PGA Tour events, including the 1974, 1979, and 1990 U.S. Opens.

Betty Jameson Winner of ten LPGA Tour events, including the 1947 U.S. Women's Open.

Robert Trent Jones   Well-known golf course architect who has been involved in hundreds of golf-course projects worldwide.

Robert Tyre (Bobby) Jones   Regarded as the finest amateur and gentleman golfer of all time; winner of thirteen major championships, including the Grand Slam of 1930; won the U.S. Open in 1923, 1926, 1929, and 1930, the British Open in 1926, 1927, and 1930, the U.S. Amateur in 1924, 1925, 1927, 1928, and 1930, and the British Amateur in 1930; began the Masters Tournament at Augusta National Golf Club.

Betsy King   Winner of thirty-one LPGA Tour events, including the 1987, 1990, and 1997 Dinah Shore, the 1989 and 1990 U.S. Women's Opens, and the 1992 LPGA Championship.

Gene Littler   Winner of twenty-nine PGA Tour events, including the 1961 U.S. Open; overcame cancer condition in the early 1970s.

Bobby Locke   South African player who won the 1949, 1950, 1952, and 1957 British Opens.

Nancy Lopez   Winner of forty-eight LPGA Tour events, including the 1978, 1985, and 1989 LPGA Championships.

Lloyd Mangrum   Winner of thirty-four PGA Tour events, including the 1946 U.S. Open.

Carol Mann   Winner of thirty-eight LPGA Tour events, including the 1965 U.S. Women's Open.

Cary Middlecoff   Winner of thirty-seven PGA Tour events, including the 1949 and 1956 U.S. Opens and the 1955 Masters; respected swing expert.

Johnny Miller   Winner of twenty-four PGA Tour events, including the 1973 U.S. Open, plus the 1976 British Open; later a television golf analyst.

Tom Morris Sr.   Winner of the 1861, 1862, 1864, and 1867 British Opens; well-known clubmaker; influential figure of Scottish golf in the late 1800s.

Tom Morris Jr.   Son to Tom Sr.; winner of the British Open in 1868, 1869, 1870, and 1872 before tragic death at a young age.

Byron Nelson   Winner of fifty-three PGA Tour events, including a record nineteen in 1945; won the 1939 U.S. Open, the 1940 and 1945 PGA Championships, and the 1937 and 1942 Masters.

Jack Nicklaus   Person most-often recognized as the greatest golfer of all time; winner of seventy PGA Tour victories, including eighteen professional majors.

Francis Ouimet   Outstanding amateur who won an epic 1913 U.S. Open playoff against Ted Ray and Harry Vardon. Also won the 1914 and 1931 U.S. Amateur. Arnold Palmer: Most popular golfer of all time; winner of sixty PGA Tour victories, includng the 1960 U.S. Open, the 1958, 1960, 1962, and 1964 Masters, plus the 1961 and 1962 British Opens.

Henry Picard   Winner of thirty-two PGA Tour events, including the 1939 PGA Championship and the 1938 Masters.

Gary Player   Highly successful South African player around the world; winner of twenty-one PGA Tour victories, including the 1965 U.S. Open, the 1961, 1974, and 1978 Masters, and the 1972 PGA Championship, plus the 1959, 1968, and 1974 British Opens.

Clifford Roberts   New Yorker who founded, with Bobby Jones, the Augusta National Golf Club and the Masters Tournament.

Donald Ross   Influential Scottish golf-course architect who created dozens of classic courses, including Pinehurst No. 2.

Paul Runyan   Respected swing teacher who won twenty-three PGA Tour events, including the 1933 and 1938 PGA Championships.

Gene Sarazen Winner of the 1922 and 1932 U.S. Opens, the 1922, 1923, and 1933 PGA Championships, the 1932 British Open, and the 1935 Masters, plus 15 other events.

Patty Sheehan Winner of thirty-five LPGA Tour events, including the 1983, 1984, and 1993 LPGA Championships, the 1992 and 1994 U.S. Women's Opens, and the 1996 Dinah Shore.

Dinah Shore Singer and entertainer who was the women's golf equivalent to Crosby and Hope; namesake of Nabisco Dinah Shore event, which is a major on the LPGA Tour schedule.

Denny Shute Winner of the 1936 and 1937 PGA Championships and the 1933 British Open.

Horton Smith Winner of thirty-one PGA Tour events, including the 1934 and 1936 Masters; set records for winning at the youngest age.

Sam Snead Winner of a PGA Tour record eighty-one events, including the 1949, 1952, and 1954 Masters, and the 1942, 1949, and 1951 PGA Championships, plus the 1946 British Open; first player to shoot his age on tour (66 in 1979 Quad Cities Open); oldest tour winner at age 52 (1965 Greensboro Open).

Louise Suggs LPGA pioneer who won fifty tour events, including the 1949 and 1952 U.S. Women's Opens and the 1957 LPGA Championship.

John H. Taylor Great British player at turn of the century who won the 1894, 1895, 1900, 1909, and 1913 British Opens.

Peter Thomson Australian star who won the 1954, 1955, 1956, 1958, and 1965 British Opens.

Lee Trevino Noted for his rapport with galleries, he won fifty-four PGA Tour and Senior PGA Tour events, including the 1968 and 1971 U.S. Opens, the 1974 and 1984 PGA Championships, plus the 1971 and 1972 British Opens.

Harry Vardon   Was part of the Great Triumvirate of British Golf with Braid, Taylor, and Vardon; winner of a record six British Opens in 1896, 1898, 1899, 1903, 1911, and 1914, plus the 1900 U.S. Open.

Glenna Collet Vare   Influential amateur of American golf who won the 1922, 1925, 1928, 1929, 1930, and 1935 U.S. Women's Amateur.

Tom Watson   Winner of thirty-three PGA Tour events, including the 1982 U.S. Open, the 1977 and 1981 Masters, plus the 1975, 1977, 1980, 1982, and 1983 British Opens.

Joyce Wethered   British amateur star who excelled during the time of Bobby Jones and Glenna Vare; won the 1922, 1924, 1925, and 1929 British Women's Amateur.

Kathy Whitworth   All-time leader among men and women with eighty-eight victories on the LPGA Tour, including the 1967, 1971, and 1975 LPGA Championships.

Tiger Woods   Phenomenal star of the 1990s who won an unprecedented total of three U.S. Junior and U.S. Amateur titles each before turning professional in 1996; won the 1997 Masters Tournament with record score of 270.

Mickey Wright   Winner of eighty-two LPGA Tour events, including the 1958, 1960, 1961, and 1963 LPGA Championships, the 1958, 1959, 1961, and 1964 U.S. Women's Opens; often recognized as being one of the all-time greatest women's athletes of all time.

BIBLIOGRAPHY

The joy in researching this book was the chance it provided to look through many golf books, histories, and periodicals. The following list of reference materials comes highly recommended for anyone wanting to broaden their golf knowledge.

PERIODICALS

Golf Digest
PGA Magazine
PGA Tour Partners
Golf Shop Operations
Golf World

BOOKS (LISTED ALPHABETICALLY BY AUTHOR)

A Round of Golf with Tommy Armour, Tommy Armour, Simon and Schuster, New York, 1959.

How to Play Your Best Golf All the Time, Tommy Armour, Simon and Schuster, New York, 1953.

How to Play Golf with an Effortless Swing, Julius Boros, Prentice Hall, Englewood Cliffs, N.J., 1953.

Swing Easy, Hit Hard, Julius Boros, Harper & Row, New York, 1965 (reissued in paperback in 1993 by Lyons & Burford, New York).

British Golf, Bernard Darwin, Collins, London, 1946.

The Game of Golf and the Printed Word 1566–1985, a bibliography of golf literature in the English language, Richard E. Donovan and Joseph S.F. Murdoch, Castalio Press, Endicott, N.Y., 1988.

Golf—The Winning Formula, Nick Faldo with Vivien Saunders, Lyons & Burford, New York, 1989.

Five Lessons: The Modern Fundamentals of Golf, Ben Hogan with Herbert Warren Wind, A.S. Barnes, New York, 1957 (reissued in paperback and hardback reprints).

David Leadbetter's Faults and Fixes, David Leadbetter with John Huggan, HarperPerennial, New York, 1993.

St. Andrews Golf Links: The First 600 Years, Tom Jarrett, Mainstream Publishing, Edinburgh, Scotland, 1995.

Annals of American Sport, John Allen Krout, The Yale Pageant of America, United States Publishers Association, N.Y., 1929.

Golf in America: A Practical Manual, James P. Lee, Dodd, Mead & Company, New York, 1895 (facsimile copy printed in 1986 by U.S. Golf Association).

Nancy Lopez' The Complete Golfer, Nancy Lopez with Don Wade, Contemporary Books, Chicago, 1987.

Golf Club Design, Fitting, Alteration & Repair, Ralph Maltby, Ralph Maltby Enterprises, Newark, Ohio, 4th ed., 1995.

Fifty Years of American Golf, H.B. Martin, Argosy-Antiquarian Ltd., 1966 (originally published in 1936).

The Golfer's Home Companion, Robin McMillan, Simon and Schuster, New York, 1993.

The World of Golf, edited by Gordon Menzies, British Broadcasting Corporation, London, 1982.

Pure Golf, Johnny Miller with Dale Shankland, Doubleday, Garden City, N.Y., 1976.

Shape Your Swing the Modern Way, Byron Nelson with Larry Dennis, Golf Digest Books/Simon and Schuster, 1976 (reissued by Classics of Golf, New York).

My 55 Ways to Lower Your Golf Score, Jack Nicklaus, Simon and Schuster, New York, 1962.

My Game and Yours, Arnold Palmer, Simon and Schuster, New York, 1963.

Play Great Golf, Arnold Palmer, Doubleday, Garden City, N.Y., 1987.

A Woman's Guide to Better Golf, Judy Rankin with Peter McCleery, Contemporary Books, Chicago, 1995.

Corey Pavin's Shotmaking, Corey Pavin with Guy Yocom, Golf Digest Books/Pocket Books, New York, 1996.

Positive Golf, Gary Player, McGraw-Hill, New York, 1967.

The Carolina Lowcountry: Birthplace of American Golf 1786, Charles Price and George C. Rogers, Sea Pines Co., Hilton Head Island, S.C., 1980.

Golf Etiquette, Barbara Puett and Jim Apfelbaum, St. Martin's Press, New York, 1992.

American Sports: From the Age of Golf Games to the Age of Spectators, Benjamin G. Rader, Prentice Hall, Englewood Cliffs, N.J., 1983.

All About Golf, Rand McNally, Chicago, 1975.

Youth Golf: For Parents and Players, Cliff Schrock, Masters Press/Howard W. Sams, Indianapolis, 1994.

Women's Golf Handbook, Cliff Schrock, Masters Press/Howard W. Sams, Indianapolis, 1995.

Rules of Golf Applied, Cliff Schrock, Masters Press/Howard W. Sams, Indianapolis, 1995.

The Whole Golf Catalog, edited by Larry Sheehan, Atheneum, New York, 1979.

The Guinness Book of Golf, Peter Smith and Keith Mackie, Canopy Books/Abbeville Press, New York, 1992.

Sam Snead Teaches You His Simple Key Approach to Golf, Sam Snead with Larry Sheehan, Atheneum, New York, 1975.

Golf Begins at Forty, Sam Snead with Dick Aultman, The Dial Press, New York, 1978.

Sam Snead's How to Play Golf, Sam Snead, Garden City Books, Garden City, N.Y., 1952.

Golf: The History of an Obsession, David Stirk, Phaidon Press Limited, Oxford, England, 1987.

Dave Stockton's Putt to Win, Dave Stockton with Al Barkow, Simon and Schuster, New York, 1996.

Getting Up and Down, Tom Watson with Nick Seitz, Golf Digest Books/Random House, New York, 1983.

Tom Watson's Strategic Golf, Tom Watson with Nick Seitz, Pocket Books, New York, 1993.

Ken Venturi's Stroke Savers, Ken Venturi with Don Wade, Contemporary Books, Chicago, 1995.

"I Can Help Your Game," Lee Trevino with Oscar Fraley, Fawcett Publications, Greenwich, Conn., 1971.

Tips from the Top, Compiled by Herbert Warren Wind, Prentice Hall, New York, 1955.

Go for the Flag: The Fundamentals of Golf, Tom Weiskopf, Meredith Press, New York, 1969.

The Modern Guide to Golf Clubmaking, Tom Wishon, Dynacraft Golf Products, Newark, Ohio, 1987.

Mickey Wright: Play Golf the Wright Way, Mickey Wright, Doubleday, Garden City, N.Y., 1962.

INDEX